Criticism and Compassion

⚛ METAPHILOSOPHY

METAPHILOSOPHY SERIES IN PHILOSOPHY

Series Editors: Armen T. Marsoobian and Eric Cavallero

The Philosophy of Interpretation, edited by Joseph Margolis and Tom Rockmore (2000)

Global Justice, edited by Thomas W. Pogge (2001)

Cyberphilosophy: The Intersection of Computing and Philosophy, edited by James H. Moor and Terrell Ward Bynum (2002)

Moral and Epistemic Virtues, edited by Michael Brady and Duncan Pritchard (2003)

The Range of Pragmatism and the Limits of Philosophy, edited by Richard Shusterman (2004)

The Philosophical Challenge of September 11, edited by Tom Rockmore, Joseph Margolis, and Armen T. Marsoobian (2005)

Global Institutions and Responsibilities: Achieving Global Justice, edited by Christian Barry and Thomas W. Pogge (2005)

Genocide's Aftermath: Responsibility and Repair, edited by Claudia Card and Armen T. Marsoobian (2007)

Stem Cell Research: The Ethical Issues, edited by Lori Gruen, Laura Gravel, and Peter Singer (2008)

Cognitive Disability and Its Challenge to Moral Philosophy, edited by Eva Feder Kittay and Licia Carlson (2010)

Virtue and Vice, Moral and Epistemic, edited by Heather Battaly (2010)

Global Democracy and Exclusion, edited by Ronald Tinnevelt and Helder De Schutter (2010)

Putting Information First: Luciano Floridi and the Philosophy of Information, edited by Patrick Allo (2011)

The Pursuit of Philosophy: Some Cambridge Perspectives, edited by Alexis Papazoglou (2012)

Philosophical Engineering: Toward a Philosophy of the Web, edited by Harry Halpin and Alexandre Monnin (2014)

The Philosophy of Luck, edited by Duncan Pritchard and Lee John Whittington (2015)

Criticism and Compassion: The Ethics and Politics of Claudia Card, edited by Robin S. Dillon and Armen T. Marsoobian (2018)

Criticism and Compassion

The Ethics and Politics of Claudia Card

Edited by

Robin S. Dillon and Armen T. Marsoobian

CONTENTS

NOTES ON CONTRIBUTORS

Marcia Baron is the James H. Rudy Professor of Philosophy at Indiana University. Her main interests are in moral philosophy and philosophy of criminal law. Publications include *Kantian Ethics Almost Without Apology* (Cornell, 1995), "Manipulativeness" (2003), "Gender Issues in the Criminal Law" (2011), "Self-Defense: The Imminence Requirement" (2011), "The Ticking Bomb Hypothetical" (2013), "Rape, Seduction, Shame, and Culpability in *Tess of the d'Urbervilles*" (2013), and "Rethinking 'One Thought Too Many'" (2017).

Mavis Biss is an associate professor of philosophy at Loyola University Maryland. She specializes in Kantian ethics and conceptions of moral creativity. Her current work deals with the complexities of rational agency in the face of contested moral meaning. She was awarded the 2015 Wilfrid Sellars Prize for "Kantian Moral Striving," *Kantian Review* (2015).

Claudia Card was the Emma Goldman (WARF) Professor of Philosophy at the University of Wisconsin–Madison, where she also taught in women's studies, LGBT studies, Jewish studies, and environmental studies. Her books include *Feminist Ethics* (Kansas, 1991), *Lesbian Choices* (Columbia, 1995), *The Unnatural Lottery: Character and Moral Luck* (Temple, 1996), and a trilogy, *The Atrocity Paradigm: A Theory of Evil* (Oxford, 2002), *Confronting Evils: Terrorism, Torture, Genocide* (Cambridge, 2010), and *Surviving Atrocity* (forthcoming).

Victoria Davion was professor and chair of the Department of Philosophy at the University of Georgia and editor of *Ethics & the Environment*. Her primary interests were in ethics, including environmental ethics and feminist ethics, and political philosophy. Her recent work examines how concepts such as "nature" and "the natural order" are used to justify controversial ethical issues. Among her recent publications is "Feminist Perspectives on Global Warming, Genocide, and Card's Theory of Evil" (*Hypatia*, 2009).

Robin S. Dillon is William Wilson Selfridge Professor of Philosophy at Lehigh University. She writes on self-respect—to which Claudia Card introduced her—and related concepts. Her publications include "Self-Respect and Humility in Kant and Hill," in Timmons and Johnson, eds., *Reason, Value, and Respect* (Oxford, 2015), and "Critical Character Theory: Toward a Feminist Theory of 'Vice,'" in Crasnow and Superson, eds., *Out from the Shadows* (Oxford, 2012). She is writing a book on arrogance.

Ellen K. Feder is William Fraser McDowell Professor of Philosophy at American University in Washington, D.C., and the author of *Making Sense of Intersex: Changing Ethical Perspectives in Biomedicine* (Indiana, 2014) and *Family Bonds: Genealogies of Race and Gender* (Oxford, 2007).

Armen T. Marsoobian is professor and chair of philosophy at Southern Connecticut State University and editor in chief of *Metaphilosophy*. He has published on topics in aesthetics, ethics, pragmatism, and genocide studies. He has edited five books, including *The Blackwell Guide to American Philosophy* and *Genocide's Aftermath: Responsibility and Repair with Claudia Card.* His most recent book, *Fragments of a Lost Homeland: Remembering Armenia*, is based upon extensive research about his family during the declining years of the Ottoman Empire.

Diana Tietjens Meyers is professor emerita of philosophy at the University of Connecticut, Storrs. She currently works in four main areas of philosophy: philosophy of action, feminist ethics, aesthetics, and human rights. Her most recent monograph is *Victims' Stories and the Advancement of Human Rights* (Oxford University Press, 2016). Her most recent edited collection is *Poverty, Agency, and Human Rights* (Oxford University Press, 2014). Her website is https://dianatietjensmeyers.wordpress.com/.

Kathryn J. Norlock is the Kenneth Mark Drain Chair in Ethics at Trent University in Peterborough, Ontario. She is the author of *Forgiveness from a Feminist Perspective* and the editor of *The Moral Psychology of Forgiveness.* Her research interests in ethical theory include moral emotions, pessimism, and relational ethics. Her interests in metaphilosophy include issues of diversity in the profession. She is a cofounder and coeditor of *Feminist Philosophy Quarterly.*

Eliana Peck is a doctoral student in philosophy at Vanderbilt University. She works at the intersection of ethics and social philosophy, with a special interest in the effectiveness of apology, moral repair, and punishment as responses to collectively perpetrated wrongs and structural injustices. More recently, she has been conducting research on questions emerging out of social epistemology and philosophy of race, regarding the affective component of resisting active white ignorance.

Robin May Schott is a senior researcher at the Danish Institute for International Studies in the section Peace, Risk and Violence. She is a philosopher working in feminist philosophy, ethics, and political philosophy in an interdisciplinary key, and has written extensively on issues related to gender, conflict, war, and sexual violence. Among her book publications are *Birth, Death, and Femininity: Philosophies of Embodiment* (editor, 2010) and *School Bullying: New Theories in Context* (coeditor, 2014).

James Snow is a lecturer in the Department of Philosophy at Loyola University Maryland, where he teaches courses in philosophy and genocide and the genealogy of race. His recent publications focus on how gender is framed in genocide scholarship as well as in documentary films and docudramas concerned with the Rwandan genocide. He is the blog editor for the International Association of Genocide Scholars and the philosophy editor for the *Journal of Perpetrator Research.*

Lynne Tirrell is a professor of philosophy at the University of Connecticut, where she is also affiliated with the Human Rights Institute. Her research concerns language, power, and social justice, with a special focus on the role of linguistic practices in genocide. Researching the 1994 genocide of Tutsi in Rwanda led her to trips to Rwanda and the U.N.'s criminal tribunal in Tanzania. Her articles address genocide, hate speech, transitional justice, apology, forgiveness, metaphor, storytelling, and feminism.

INTRODUCTION

ARMEN T. MARSOOBIAN AND ROBIN S. DILLON

Claudia Card epitomized the highest virtues of the philosopher-teacher. Her passing in September 2015 was a great loss to the profession and to the innumerably many students she taught and advised in her nearly forty years in the Department of Philosophy at the University of Wisconsin – Madison. She had a long and distinguished career that began at a time when being a woman in the philosophy profession was not an easy matter—not that we can assume that it is easy today. She earned her Ph.D. in 1969 from Harvard with a dissertation on theories of punishment under the direction of John Rawls, despite the fact that women were not admitted to the Harvard Ph.D. program then except under the aegis of Radcliffe College. She was a pioneer in feminist and lesbian philosophy whose trailblazing work has influenced generations of philosophers. Indeed, as her then chairperson said in nominating her in 2011 for the University of Wisconsin's Hilldale Award, "Her books and articles have become as essential to feminist thinking as *Das Kapital* is to labor theory. You simply can't do feminism without reading Card, and even if you don't read Card, today's feminism bears her mark so deeply that you may not even realize that you have in some other way digested her theoretical perspectives."[1] Her influence goes beyond feminism, even beyond philosophy, however, as demonstrated by her concept of social death, which has had continuing impact in the field of genocide studies.

Card's writings in feminist philosophy and other areas in moral, social, and political philosophy take everyday life and ordinary experiences seriously, displaying a realistic sensitivity to all forms of oppression. Card's

---

[1] Russ Shafer Landau, quoted in "Four Professors Honored with Hilldale Award," http://www.supportuw.org/news-post/professors-honored-with-hilldale-award/

Criticism and Compassion: The Ethics and Politics of Claudia Card.
Edited by Robin S. Dillon and Armen T. Marsoobian.
Chapters and book compilation © 2018 Metaphilosophy LLC and John Wiley & Sons Ltd.

work is marked by a careful attention to and analysis of less obvious ways that oppression structures people's characters and life possibilities, and by a commitment to the necessity of fighting oppression, injustice, cruelty, and violence with integrity and without causing further damage to oneself or others, while also remaining alive to involvement with evil and one's capacity to compromise with it.

Card had a very productive career that unfortunately ended too soon. Starting with her first and still widely cited article, "On Mercy,"[2] she published ten monographs and edited several volumes and nearly 150 articles and reviews, and gave more than 250 talks at conferences, colleges, and universities. Her research interests included ethics and social philosophy, including normative ethical theory; feminist ethics; environmental ethics; theories of justice, of punishment, and of evil; and the ethics of Kant, Schopenhauer, and Nietzsche. Card published articles on mainstream topics such as gratitude and obligation, friendship and fidelity, justice, the value of persons, and the basis of moral rights. But she is most widely known for her influential work in analytic feminist philosophy and on evil. Her work in feminist philosophy was especially notable for discussions of difficult topics, such as sadomasochism, adult-child sex, and lesbian battery, and for challenging standard feminist and lesbian positions on separatism, marriage, and motherhood, including arguing against same-sex marriage. Card's feminist work includes ground-breaking essays and a monograph on lesbian ethics;[3] key essays and a monograph on moral agency, character, and moral luck in circumstances of oppression;[4] and pioneering articles on dimensions of oppression, such as domestic violence, rape as a form of terrorism, gay divorce, homophobic military codes, and the evils of closeting, among many others.

In the later stages of her career, Card's attention turned explicitly to a topic whose various dimensions she had been writing and teaching about for years. In addition to more than twenty-five articles on evils, Card was at the time of her death in the midst of finishing a trilogy of monographs on evil, the first two of which appeared in her lifetime.[5] In the first book, *The Atrocity Paradigm: A Theory of Evil,* she developed a secular conception of evil as foreseeable, intolerable harms produced by culpable wrongdoing, and examined the evils of rape in war, domestic violence, and child

---

[2] "On Mercy," *Philosophical Review* 81, no. 2 (April 1972): 182–207.

[3] *Lesbian Choices* (New York: Columbia University Press, 1995).

[4] *The Unnatural Lottery: Character and Moral Luck* (Philadelphia: Temple University Press, 1996).

[5] *The Atrocity Paradigm: A Theory of Evil* (Oxford: Oxford University Press, 2002), and *Confronting Evils: Terrorism, Torture, Genocide* (Cambridge: Cambridge University Press, 2010). The third, *Surviving Atrocity*, was to have expanded upon her 2011 Presidential Address to the Central Division of the American Philosophical Association, "Surviving Long-Term Mass Atrocities: U-Boats, Catchers, and Ravens."

abuse, the moral powers of victims and the moral burdens and obligations of perpetrators, and the predicament of people who are at once victims and perpetrators, which she called "gray zones." In the second book, *Confronting Evils: Terrorism, Torture, Genocide*, she refined her analysis of evil, focusing on the inexcusability of atrocities and expanding her account to consider structural evil and collectively perpetrated and collectively suffered atrocities, such as genocide. But she also argued that not all evils are extraordinary and urged us to pay attention to evils that are so common that we tend to overlook them, such as racism, violence against women, prison violence and executions, and violence against animals. An important dimension of *Confronting Evils* was addressing the problem of how to preserve humanitarian values in responding to atrocities. The third book, *Surviving Atrocity*, on which she was working extensively until her death, focused on surviving long-term mass atrocities, poverty, and global and local misogyny.

The significant contributions Card made to philosophy were acknowledged with numerous honors. The Society for Women in Philosophy, of which she was a longtime member, named her Distinguished Philosopher of the Year in 1996; the Central Division of the American Philosophical Association elected her president for 2010–2011; the APA invited her to give a John Dewey Lecture in 2008; and she was selected by the APA to deliver the prestigious 2016 Carus Lectures. She completed two of the latter lectures, "Surviving Homophobia" and "Gratitude to the Decent Rescuer," which were delivered by two of the contributors to this volume, Victoria Davion and Diana Tietjens Meyers, respectively.

Just before her death, the Society for Analytical Feminism, of which Card was a long-time member, organized two APA sessions that featured talks on various aspects of her work. Those papers, as well as a number of others that also explore and expand on her philosophical legacy, are contained in this volume. We are also fortunate to be able to include eleven of Card's articles, which here are brought together for the first time in one volume.[6] These articles cover a span of twenty years, beginning in 1996, with the last article published the year after Card died, in 2016. This truly unique volume thus combines her own powerful voice with the best in recent scholarship on issues central to her own philosophical concerns.

Although Card's contributions are far-ranging and cut across a range of topics, we have divided this volume into two parts: "War, Genocide, and Evil" and "Feminist Ethical Theory and Its Applications." Of course, this is a somewhat arbitrary division, for Card always brings her feminist ethical insights to bear on the many social and political issues she explores. Her work on rape and sexual violence as a weapon of war, which

---

[6] We have chosen not to update the references in these articles, since, in this electronic age, readers can do so quite easily.

was ground-breaking when it first appeared in the mid-1990s, is a case in point.

We begin part 1 of our volume, "War, Genocide, and Evil," with "Rape as a Weapon of War" (1996), followed by "Addendum to 'Rape as a Weapon of War'" (1997), in which Card expanded her treatment of the martial weapon of rape to include sex crimes against men. Such crimes can be as racist as they are sexist, and may be quite simply racist. The essays propose social strategies to change the meaning of rape in order to undermine its use as a martial weapon.

In "Stoicism, Evil, and the Possibility of Morality" (1998), Card explores the idea that the very possibility of morality, understood as social or interpersonal ethics, presupposes, contra Stoicism, that we do value things that elude our control. She argues that Stoic ethics is unable to recognize the validity of morality (so understood) and can at most acknowledge duties to oneself. A further implication is that moral luck, far from undermining morality, as some have held, is presupposed by the very possibility of morality.

In "Women, Evil, and Gray Zones" (2000), Card, building upon Primo Levi's reflections on "gray zone" in Nazi death camps and ghettos, contends that such zones develop wherever oppression is severe and lasting. They are inhabited by victims of evil who become complicit in perpetrating on others the evils that threaten to engulf themselves. Women, who have inhabited many gray zones, present challenges for feminist theorists, who have long struggled with how resistance is possible under coercive institutions. Card argues that resistance is sometimes possible, although outsiders are rarely, if ever, in a position to judge when. She also raises questions about the adequacy of ordinary moral concepts to mark the distinctions that would be helpful for thinking about how to respond in a gray zone.

"Genocide and Social Death" (2003) played a pivotal role in Card's two-decade-long eplorations into the concept and consequences of evil, beginning with *The Atrocity Paradigm: A Theory of Evil* and culminating in *Confronting Evils: Terrorism, Torture, Genocide.* Social death, central to the evil of genocide (whether the genocide is homicidal or primarily cultural), distinguishes genocide from other mass murders. Loss of social vitality is loss of identity and thereby of meaning for one's existence. Seeing social death at the center of genocide takes our focus off body counts and loss of individual talents, directing us instead to mourn losses of relationships that create community and give meaning to the development of talents.

In "The Paradox of Genocidal Rape Aimed at Enforced Pregnancy" (2008), Card explores the paradox raised in Beverly Allen's book *Rape Warfare: The Hidden Genocide in Bosnia-Herzegovina and Croatia* (Allen 1996), which centers on whether enforced pregnancy is genocidal or simply a form of forced assimilation that produces "little Serbs." Employing her concept of social death and the insight that military rape is a form of biological warfare, Card concludes that rape aimed at enforced pregnancy contributed to an overall plan of ethnic cleansing that was also genocidal in its intent, and not merely a policy of expulsion or assimilation. Producing unwanted progeny and diminishing reproductivity are a direct consequence of the trauma of rape and can lead to the annihilation of the targeted group. Such a plan was in effect in the Bosnian conflict and is thus more in line with Raphael Lemkin's original definition of "genocide" as "a coordinated plan of different actions aiming at the destruction of essential foundations of the life of national groups, with the aim of annihilating the groups themselves" (Lemkin 1944, 79).

Card's essay "Surviving Long-Term Mass Atrocities" (2012) provides us with a glimpse into the projected final volume of her trilogy on the concept of evil. First, she addresses the conceptual issue of the meaning of "survivor" in cases of mass atrocity. Second, she suggests some answers to the question: What is morally at stake in surviving long-term mass atrocities? The moral costs and burdens incurred by many survivors present meta-survival issues that problematize the judgment that one has survived. The most problematic of these are raised by those who are complicit in evildoing for the sake of their own survival.

The last of Card's essays in part 1 of our volume, "Taking Pride in Being Bad" (2016), concerns the possibility of valuing something in virtue of its being bad and, indeed, of taking pride in being bad. Immanuel Kant denied that human beings were capable of such evil, which he referred to as "diabolical evil." In making sense of such evil, Card considers the limitations of Kant's conception of evil in order to bring into focus an alternative theory of evil, the "atrocity paradigm." Employing this paradigm allows one to make sense of diabolical evil by combining Christine Korsgaard's Kantian conception of normativity with psychologist Lorna Smith Benjamin's theory of social attachment.

The concluding five essays in part 1 are by scholars whose work directly reflects many of the themes found in Card's corpus. Lynne Tirrell, in "Perpetrators and Social Death: A Cautionary Tale," takes up Card's balanced approach of addressing both the grave wrongs done to the victims of evil and the perpetrator of those wrongs. Card's concept of social vitality was developed to explain what génocidaires destroy in their victims. This essay brings that concept into conversation with perpetrator testimony, arguing that the génocidaires' desire for their own social vitality, achieved through their destruction of the social world of their targets, in fact boomerangs to corrode the vitality of their own lives. This is true whether they succeed or fail in their genocidal project. Card's recent analysis of "being a badass" is brought to bear on the cultivation of evil, and the essay suggests four strategies for meeting Card's "moral challenge of avoiding evil responses to evil."

The concept of social death is explored, defended, and criticized in James Snow's "Claudia Card's Concept of Social Death: A New Way of Looking at Genocide." Scholarship in the multidisciplinary field of genocide studies often emphasizes body counts and the number of bio-logical deaths as a way of measuring and comparing the severity and scope of individual genocides. The prevalence of this way of framing genocide is problematic insofar it risks marginalizing the voices and experiences of vic-tims who may not succumb to biological death but nevertheless suffer the loss of family members and other loved ones, and suffer the destruction of relationships as well of as the foundational institutions that give rise to and sustain those relationships. The concept of social death, which Card offers as the central evil of genocide, marks a radical shift in conceptualiz-ing genocide and provides space for recovering the marginalized voices of many who suffer the evils of genocide but do not suffer biological death.

In "Surviving Evils and the Problem of Agency: An Essay Inspired by the Work of Claudia Card," Diana Tietjens Meyers surveys Card's views about the nature of evils and the ethical quandaries of surviving them. Meyers then develops an account of survival agency that is based on Card's insights and in keeping with the agentic capacities exercised by Yezidi women and girls who have escaped from ISIS's obscene program of trafficking in women and sexual violence. Card holds that true survival requires not only staying alive and as healthy as possible but also preserv-ing your good moral character. The essay maintains that while exercising agency to elude evil and protect yourself often depends on your own skills and personality traits, exercising agency to restore or develop your moral character often depends on social support.

Apology is arguably the central act of the reparative work required after wrongdoing. In "Institutional Evils, Culpable Complicity, and Duties to Engage in Moral Repair," Eliana Peck and Ellen K. Feder ask whether apology is required of persons culpably complicit in institutional evils. To better appreciate the benefits of and barriers to apologies offered by culpa-bly complicit wrongdoers, this essay examines doctors' complicity in a prac-tice that meets Card's definition of an evil, namely, the nonmedically nec-essary, nonconsensual "normalizing" interventions performed on babies born with intersex anatomies. It argues that in this instance the complicity of doctors is culpable on Card's terms, and that their culpable complicity grounds rightful demands for them to apologize.

"Part 2: Feminist Ethical Theory and Its Applications" brings together four of Card's essays, beginning with the early and controversial "Against Marriage and Motherhood" (1996). Written nearly two decades before the U.S. Supreme Court constitutionally guaranteed same-sex marriage, this essay has gained an unexpected saliency. Card argues that the advocacy of lesbian and gay rights to legal marriage and parenthood insufficiently crit-icizes both marriage and motherhood as they are currently practiced and structured by Northern legal institutions. Instead we would do better not to let the state define our intimate unions. Parenting would be improved if the power currently concentrated in the hands of one or two guardians were diluted and distributed through an appropriately concerned community.

Now that the reality of gay divorce is legally upon us, Card's "Gay Divorce: Thoughts on the Legal Regulation of Marriage" (2007) holds some timely lessons. Card argues that although the exclusion of LGBT individuals from the rites and rights of marriage is arbitrary and unjust, the legal institution of marriage is itself so riddled with injustice that it would be better to create alternative forms of durable intimate partnership that do not invoke the power of the state. Card's essay develops a case for this position, taking up an injustice sufficiently serious to constitute an evil: the sheltering of domestic violence.

Card's "Challenges of Global and Local Misogyny" (2014) is taken from a volume of essays about the work of her Harvard mentor John Rawls. Card challenges Rawls's hypothesis that the worst evils that target women and girls will disappear once the gravest political injustices are gone. Her essay explores this hypothesis in relation to women's self-defense and mutual defense against evils of misogyny. Card extrapolates and adapts Rawls's work, especially his writing on war, for this purpose, arguing that women need principles for forming social units of defense against global and local misogyny.

The five concluding essays in part 2 take up many of Card's themes, beginning with Marcia Baron's "Hate Crime Legislation Reconsidered." Baron examines Card's arguments questioning the value of hate crime legislation. Card had questioned whether hatred makes a crime worse and whether hatred of the sort pertinent to hate crimes is worse than a more personal type of hatred. Card doubts whether the actual message sent by hate crime legislation is the intended message. Baron questions Card's assumption that penalty enhancement for hate crimes is warranted only if the crimes are worse than otherwise similar crimes that do not count as hate crimes. Instead, it may be the case that it is the proper business of the state to take a particular interest in such crimes, in part because they enact not just any hatred but civic hatred. If hate crimes are understood as enacting civic hatred, hate crime legislation can indeed serve to counter a message that very much needs to be countered.

Robin May Schott, in "Misplaced Gratitude and the Ethics of Oppression," examines Card's notion of misplaced gratitude, which Card explored in one of her last papers, "Gratitude to the Decent Rescuer."[7] Whereas typically philosophers have been interested in the problems of the failures to honor obligations of gratitude, Card is more interested in the opposite fault of misplaced gratitude. Her interest reflects her social indignation and her fundamental commitment to opposing oppression, exploitation, and injustice in all its forms. The phenomenon of misplaced gratitude becomes visible from this perspective, where one catches sight of what oppression does

---

[7] Unpublished manuscript of the Paul Carus Lecture, APA Central Division meeting, Chicago, 2016.

to people. The essay looks at the question: What does Card's analysis of misplaced gratitude tell us about her own philosophical methods and contributions? Schott discusses Card's engagement with both care ethics and Beauvoir's phenomenology of oppression to clarify the centrality of misplaced gratitude in Card's ethics of oppression.

Kathryn J. Norlock, in "The Challenges of Extreme Moral Stress: Claudia Card's Contributions to the Formation of Nonideal Ethical Theory," argues that Card is among the important contributors to nonideal ethical theory. Following philosophers including Lisa Tessman and Charles Mills, Norlock contends that it is important for ethical theory, and for feminist purposes, to carry forward the interrelationship that Mills identifies between nonideal theory and feminist ethics. Card's ethical theorizing assists in understanding that interrelationship. In her philosophical work Card includes basic elements of nonideal ethical theory indicated by Tessman, Mills, and others, and further offers two important and neglected elements to other nonideal ethical theorists: (i) her rejection of the "administrative point of view," and (ii) her focus on "intolerable harms" as forms of "extreme moral stress" and obstacles to excellent ethical lives. Norlock concludes that Card's insights are helpful to philosophers in developing nonideal ethical theory as a distinctive contribution to, and as a subset of, nonideal theory.

Mavis Biss, in "Radical Moral Imagination and Moral Luck," argues that, to a greater extent than other theorists, Card's analysis of moral luck considers the impact of attempts to transform moral meanings on the development of the agent's character and responsibilities, over time and in relation to other agents. Biss argues that this wider frame of reference captures more of what is at stake in the efforts of those who resist oppression by attempting to implement radically revised meanings.

Victoria Davion's essay "The American Girl: Playing with the Wrong Dollie?" extends many of the themes central to Card's feminist critique of oppressive sexist environments, particularly as they impact character development. The American Girl Just Like You doll is the lens through which Davion explores the highly problematic messages conveyed to young girls about self-image and identity. The doll is not emaciated or overtly sexy, and is marketed along with outfits that supposedly send girls the message that they can achieve their goals. Davion adds that the doll comes in a variety of skin, eye, and hair colors, and the line is therefore marketed as racially and ethnically sensitive. Yet Davion argues that although the Just Like You line appears to be empowering and racially sensitive on a superficial level, an in-depth feminist analysis indicates that it is not.

As is evidenced in the essays in this volume, Claudia Card's voice continues to resonate in the work of many philosophers today. Some of us were privileged to have been in her classes, while others encountered her in many forums, either in person or in print. All of us have been enriched in doing so.

References

Allen, Beverly. 1996. *Rape Warfare: The Hidden Genocide in Bosnia-Herzegovina and Croatia*. Minneapolis: University of Minnesota Press.

Lemkin, Raphael. 1944. *Axis Rule in Occupied Europe: Laws of Occupation, Analysis of Government, Proposals for Redress*. Washington: Carnegie Endowment for International Peace.

PART ONE

WAR, GENOCIDE, AND EVIL

CHAPTER 1

RAPE AS A WEAPON OF WAR

CLAUDIA CARD

Rape in war—martial rape—has even arrived in the movies. Within the past year, films I have seen featuring or portraying rape in war or in warlike situations include *Death and the Maiden* (featuring a woman who survived rape by a physician who was hired to oversee her political torture), *Rob Roy* (portraying a strategic rape—intended to provoke a husband—by an English "nobleman" charged with putting down a Scottish rebellion), and *Immortal Beloved* (briefly showing the apparently gratuitous rape of a civilian stage-coach passenger by one of Napoleon's soldiers). Closely related is *Braveheart,* which presents imperial rape in the "rite of the first night," which licensed English "nobles" to rape Scottish "commoner" brides on their wedding nights.[1] Although this imperial rape was not officially an act of *war*, it had some of the same goals as martial rape: genetic imperialism and a realignment of loyalties in future generations (which are made explicit in *Braveheart*). Each of these films displays a different aspect of martial rape. No one (to my knowledge) has yet portrayed *mass* rape in war.

Mass martial rape in the real world, however, is receiving media attention, and public consciousness is being raised about it. What is new is not the practice of mass rape but the extent of its relatively recent publicity and some of rape's consequences for public health in an era of HIV. Martial rape is an ancient practice. Patterns of intelligibility to be found in it have important continuities with patterns to be found also in civilian rape.

---

[1] This feudal custom, also known as *marquette*, was discussed from a radical feminist point of view in 1893 by Gage (1980).

Criticism and Compassion: The Ethics and Politics of Claudia Card.
Edited by Robin S. Dillon and Armen T. Marsoobian.
Chapters and book compilation © 2018 Metaphilosophy LLC and John Wiley & Sons Ltd.

Despite differences in the structures of the relevant causes, Judith Herman argues that the "shell shock" in World War 1 combat survivors has important similarities to posttraumatic stress disorders as experienced by female survivors of domestic violence and rape. She finds that "the most common post-traumatic disorders are those not of men in war but of women in civilian life" and that women and children subject to civilian rape and domestic violence *are* in a war:

> The subordinate condition of women is maintained and enforced by the hidden violence of men. There is war between the sexes. Rape victims, battered women, and sexually abused children are its casualties. Hysteria is the combat neurosis of the sex war. (Herman 1992, 28–32)

Although my focus here is on martial rape as a weapon wielded by male soldiers of one country (or national, political, or cultural group) against typically unarmed female civilians of another, much of what I say can be applied also with certain modifications in (so-called) civilian contexts.

A little more than ten years ago I began writing about rapes that are often "domestic" in two senses: they are (generally) rapes of citizens (or residents) by other citizens (or residents) of the same state, and they were often committed by members of a household against other members of the same household (Card 1991). I now find that an important aspect of both civilian and martial rape is that it is an instrument of domestication: breaking for house service. It breaks the spirit, humiliates, tames, produces a docile, deferential, obedient soul. Its immediate message to women and girls is that we will have in our own bodies only the control that we are granted by men and thereby in general only that control in our environments that we are granted by men.

Instruments of taming include terrorism and torture, which rely on the energy-consuming and debilitating effects of fear and, as Nietzsche noted (1967, 61–62), our ability to remember what hurts.[2] Taming is often for service—utilitarian, recreational, or both—which sets limits to terrorism and torture in that "taming" carried too far may leave an animal who is neither useful for much nor even entertaining. In the case of civilian rape, purposes commonly served include both utilitarian and recreational exploitation. Women and girls raped are often primary instruments of the exploitation of other women and girls. As with other kinds of terrorism, rape as a practice often has two targets (O'Neill 1991). One target may be a throwaway or sacrificial victim who is used to send a message to others. The role of women who are raped and then murdered is like that of people

---

[2] Such reliance on terrorism, however, needs to be balanced by an appreciation of our ability, also, to dissociate under stress.

who are murdered in a bombing. They are used to send a message to the second targets, whose compliance with various demands and expectations is sought by the terrorist.

The ubiquitous threat of rape in war, like that of civilian rape, is a form of terrorism. The aim in war, however, may not be service (the aim generally served by civilian rape) but expulsion or dispersion. Expulsion and dispersion do *not* set limits to the extent and degree of terrorism and torture as the hope of future exploitation would do, because it does not matter to the terrorists whether those to be expelled or dispersed survive. Again, there are often two targets, sacrificial victims and others to whom their sacrifice is used to send a message. Martial rape domesticates not only the women survivors who were its immediate victims but also the men socially connected to them, and men who were socially connected to those who did not survive.

If there is one set of fundamental functions of rape, civilian or martial, it is to display, communicate, and produce or maintain *dominance,* which is both enjoyed for its own sake and used for such ulterior ends as exploitation, expulsion, dispersion, murder. Acts of forcible rape, like other instances of torture, communicate dominance by removing our control over what enters or impinges on our bodies. Rape is a cross-cultural language of male domination (that is, domination *by* males; it can also be domination *of* males). This is its symbolic social meaning. Civilian domination characteristically issues in exploitation for service, although some forms of even civilian rape—such as college fraternity party gang rapes—may be best understood as a kind of training for war.[3] An aim of civilian rape is female heterosexual dependency and service. The rapes of some women send a message to others that they need "protection" (Griffin 1979; Card 1991). The ever-present threat of rape from childhood through old age produces a society of females who are generally oriented toward male service—females animated by the hope of securing male protection as a reward for such service—females who often feel bound to those they serve through misplaced gratitude for a "protection" that is mostly only a withholding of abuse (Card 1991). By contrast, martial rape aims to splinter families and alliances and to bind not women to men but warrior rapists to one another. The activity of martial rape, often relatively public, can serve as a bonding agent among perpetrators and at the same time work in a variety of ways to alienate family members, friends, and former neighbors from each other, as in cases where the perpetrators had been friends or neighbors of those they later raped.

---

[3] For an exposé of fraternity gang rape, including testimony by former fraternity members who defected, see anthropologist Sanday (1990).

Accounts from recently surviving rape victims and perpetrators indicate that purposes currently served in Bosnia-Herzegovina include genocide, expulsion, revenge, and obedience (although in many cases, not service) and that its ultimate targets are entire peoples (Stiglmayer 1993). The same patterns are discernible historically in the rapes of Vietnamese women by U.S. GI's (Brownmillet 1975, 86–113) and of Native American women by British soldiers (Storm 1972).[4] As forcible impregnation, martial rape can also be a tool of genetic imperialism. Where the so-conceived child's social identity is determined by that of the biological father, impregnation by martial rape can undermine family solidarity. Even if no pregnancy results, knowledge of the rape has been sufficient for many men in patriarchal societies to reject wives, mothers, and daughters, as was reported to have happened to many Bengali women raped by Pakistani soldiers in 1971 (Brownmiller 1975, 76–86). Ultimately, martial rape can undermine national, political, and cultural solidarity, changing the next generation's identity, confusing the loyalties of all victimized survivors.

There is more than one way to commit genocide. One way is mass murder, killing individual members of a national, political, or cultural group. Another is to destroy a group's identity by decimating cultural and social bonds. Martial rape does both. Many women and girls are killed when rapists are finished with them. If survivors become pregnant or are known to be rape survivors, cultural, political, and national unity may be thrown into chaos. These have been among the apparently intended purposes of the mass rapes of women in Bosnia-Herzegovina, of Rwandan women by Hutu soldiers (Lorch 1995), of Vietnamese women by U.S. GI's, of the systematic rapes of Bengali women by Pakistani soldiers in 1971, and earlier of Native American women by British soldiers.

Where genocide by cultural decimation is the principal aim, universal slaughter of captives is unnecessary. Instead of being slaughtered, captives may be enslaved or dispersed. Historically, women have often been thus enslaved for sexual service. In his history of slavery, Milton Meltzer (1993) notes that one primary source of slaves in the ancient world was the practice of taking war captives who, in a pre-agricultural age, would have been slaughtered. John Rawls observed in *A Theory of Justice:*

> There may be transition cases where enslavement is better than current practice. For example, suppose that city-states that previously have not taken prisoners of war but have always put captives to death agree by treaty to hold prisoners as slaves instead. Although we cannot allow the institution of slavery on the grounds that the greater gains of some outweigh the losses to others, it may be that under these conditions, since all run the risk of capture in war, this form of slavery is less unjust than present custom. … The arrangement seems an advance

---

[4] Storm (1972, 106–9) offers a fictionalized portrayal of the rape of Native American women, drawing on his knowledge of history from a Native American perspective.

on established institutions, if slaves are not treated too severely. In time it will presumably be abandoned altogether, since the exchange of prisoners of war is a still more desirable arrangement, the return of the captured members of the community being preferable to the services of slaves. (Rawls 1971, 248)

This semi-speculative account, however, does not address the situation of women who are enslaved as war captives and treated as booty. Even in a pre-agricultural age, the practice prior to enslavement of enemy soldiers may have been to slaughter the males but enslave females for sexual service. Captured and impregnated females might be "persuaded" to alter their loyalties where nothing comparable could have been done to change the loyalties of their fathers or spouses. Mary Renault's historical novels (e.g., Renault 1972) present captive women and adolescents of both sexes as enslaved for sexual service in the ancient world and sold on an international market, a practice that may have existed long before any such an agreement as Rawls imagined was reached among men. What would such a new agreement do to improve the lot of women?

For men, enslavement rather than slaughter as war captives has two apparent advantages. First, if any man might become a war captive, it could be to his advantage to survive (rather than be killed) even as a slave and hope for a reversal of fortune. Second, slavery instituted a class system, providing exploitable productive labor for conquerors. But to what advantages could a woman look forward who was enslaved rather than slaughtered? Would a captured woman who was impregnated, gave birth, and then survived to be freed when political fortunes changed be better off after the change of political fortune? What would have become of her identity? Of her children and her ties to them? If she were not a lesbian, who would be eager to have her returned in an exchange of prisoners of war? Or, as a woman of the victorious party, what would it do for her were her husband to take female concubines from defeated peoples?

Under universal (bisexual) slavery for productive labor (as opposed to female concubinage), enslaved women have been permitted to live temporarily in families with enslaved men. This was true, for example, under American slavery. That practice, however, coexisted with enslaved women's continual liability to rape by free men and to fear of being sold. Here rape continues to send the message of dominance, to enforce dominance, and has the potentiality to wreak havoc with bonds among those enslaved, especially as survivors may be portrayed as willing rather than raped.

Although some women have been exploited as sexual slaves and others as sacrificial victims, enslavement and service have not been the apparent *primary* aims of the rapes of women in Bosnia-Herzegovina. Rather, the expulsion and dispersion of entire ethnic groups appears to be a primary aim of some perpetrators and, failing that, genocide by a combination of murder and forcible impregnation. The idea has not been to bind captive women to captors, but to destroy family and community bonds, humiliate and terrorize, ultimately to drive out and disperse entire peoples in "ethnic cleansing," the current euphemism for genocide.

When I refer to the purposes of martial rape, I have in mind its strategic purposes, those appreciable at the level of authority and command. Individual rapists, those who carry out the strategy, may not intend those purposes or be moved by them, just as they may be ignorant of larger purposes served by various orders they implement. Thus there is room, as we will see, at the level of particular acts of rape for many motives. Like civilian rape, martial rape has become a political institution. As with other institutions, the purposes that it serves and that lead those with power to maintain it need not move many of its participants. Sometimes the purpose is more likely to move those who do nothing to resist the practice or who support it as relative outsiders. Thus, civilian rape serves a domestic protection racket (Griffin 1979) whereby males secure the services of females in exchange for protection (against other males). But this does not imply that men who rape *intend* to terrorize women into seeking male protection; they may or they may not. It may be more likely relative outsiders, judging that a raped woman was "asking for it," who intend protectionism. Likewise, martial rape is a practice defined by unwritten rules (for example, the rules that only females are "fair game," that age does not matter, that soldiers who rape "enemy women" are not to be reported for it, that anonymous publicity of it may be desirable). Action in accord with these norms serves purposes identifiable independently of the motives or intentions of individual rapists. A soldier may rape because he was ordered, or because he felt like it. Superior officers, on the other hand, may look the other way because of the martial purposes such rapes serve.

Some women survivors in Bosnia-Herzegovina assume, because those who raped them were previously neighbors from whom they could not imagine such brutality, that the soldiers must have been under orders (Stiglmayer 1993, 120). Yet rape violates international rules of war. Soldiers may not always be given direct orders. They may be induced in other ways, for example, they may be given reason to believe that if they do not participate, they will be beaten or raped themselves. Some interviewed rapist captives gave other explanations. Borislav Herek from Sarajevo, who admits to raping and shooting three unarmed women, said that if he did not do it, his superiors would have sent him "to the worst front line" or to jail and that they would have taken away the Muslim's house that they had given him (Stiglmayer 1993, 147–54). One is reminded, by such accounts, how banal evil can be at the level of motive. When pressed on why he was willing to kill people with whom he had no past history of animosity, he indicated that he was told—apparently in an attempt to incite revenge—that Muslims had killed his father and burned his house. Another motive emerged when Herek admitted that his superiors gave him women to rape along with wine and food as a reward for good behavior and to induce camaraderie with fellow soldiers.

At the level of the motivations of individual rapist soldiers, it can be difficult to see patterns. It is at the level of strategy—of order-giving, hate-mongering, rewarding and penalizing, and, equally important, of refusing to investigate and penalize on the part of military authorities—that coherent strategic patterns emerge. Alexandra Stiglmayer reports (1993, 160–61) that in the opinion of some, paramilitary groups are using rapes "to build up a kind of solidarity" among the rapists, to teach "who is 'good' and who is 'contemptible,' " and to destroy bonds of friendship that had existed between former neighbors. Herek's testimony supports that view.

A sense of purposes served by martial rape is a step toward developing strategies of resistance. But we must also ask why *rape* is used to achieve these purposes. Consider the aims to demoralize and disrupt bonds among those victimized and to create bonds among perpetrators. Many forms of terrorism or torture can achieve this. Why rape?

Many forms of terrorism and torture *are* employed in war for such ends: burning and looting of residences, villages, cities, and destruction of domestic industries, for example. Nietzsche described the phenomenon well (1967, 40), under the illusion that he was describing a prehistoric practice, in his characterization of the blond beasts ("lions," according to Walter Kaufmann) who "emerge from a disgusting procession of murder, arson, rape, and torture, exhilarated and undisturbed of soul, as if it were no more than a student's prank, convinced they have provided the poets with a lot more material for song and praise." Of many forms of martial terrorism, rape in a patriarchal culture has a special potential to drive a wedge between family members and to carry the expression of the perpetrator's dominance into future generations.

Yet many survivors today obtain abortions. According to Alexandra Stiglmayer, writing about women and girls raped in Bosnia-Herzegovina, "Women who become pregnant following a rape normally reject both the pregnancy and the children"; she offers a chart with impressive statistics on abortion (1993,135). According to a front page report in the *New York Times*, of more than 15,700 women and girls between the ages of thirteen and sixty-five who were raped in Rwanda between April 1994 and April 10, 1995, more than 1,100 gave birth but 5,200 had abortions, and many more pregnancies were untrackable (Lorch 1995). Many raped Rwandan women were reported to have abandoned newborns or killed themselves. Many reportedly named as their greatest fear, in a region hard hit by AIDS, infection with the HIV virus.

Thus, genetic domination may be defeated more readily today. Why women are targeted today has more to do with above-mentioned cross-cultural *symbolic meaning* among men in patriarchies of rape as dominance—dominance not simply over women but in war even more importantly over other men who are presumed to take pride in being protectors of women—and with the fact that women in patriarchies are such easy *victims*. Rape symbolizes who is dominant by forcibly, dramatically removing the most elementary controls anyone could be presumed to want: controls over one's intimate bodily contacts with others. By way of the rules of patriarchies, such contacts, however forced, can also have consequences for the future identities of survivors.

Women who lack martial training are an easy mark for those who would communicate the message of domination. Women in patriarchies are commonly unarmed and untrained for physical combat. Perpetrators need fear little direct reprisal. Where there is concern about reprisals, the only troublesome witness is easily eliminable. This suggests that strategies of resistance would have women become armed and skilled in the use of weapons and in other methods of defense and self-defense, not only by martial arts and other civilian classes (perhaps funded by the state) but also by infiltration of the military at every level. Not only do females need to be able to call on skills when attacked (for which conventional military weapons may not be helpful) but the social meaning of "female" needs to be changed so that it no longer connotes "victim." Perhaps females would do better to construct independent military organizations. At any rate, the long-range goal would be to terminate both domestic and international protection rackets and thereby change the symbolic meaning of "rape" at the same time as that of "female."

A major long-range aim of resistance to martial rape would be to eliminate patriarchal and protectionist values. One good way to begin is to reject the idea that women should not be armed and skilled in weapons use. The idea here is not simply to equip females for self-defense against rapists but to equip females generally to need no more protection than males. Just as the domestic protection racket must be dismantled for us to be safe in our homes during times of so-called peace, the transnational protection racket, where men on all sides claim as their reason for going to war that they are fighting to protect their women, must be dismantled as well. One way to undermine it is for women to have the same access to weapons and to military training as men have presently. Probably the best all-around training in combat at the present time, certainly the most expensive (supported by general taxes), is in military institutions, although even military institutions might be encouraged to give more attention to rape resistance, incorporating relevant attitudinal training from feminist self-defense practices. Suppose the response to martial rape were not for men to reject wives, mothers, and daughters, nor for women and girls to commit suicide, run away, or hide, but rather for those raped to get abortions, if pregnant, and for women generally to become informed, armed, trained, and fight back, as Alexandra Stiglmayer reports (1993, 91–93, 98–99) that Hatiza and Razija did after they were raped in Bosnia-Herzegovina. Suppose women entered military institutions in large numbers, at every rank, in every department. There would be, first, fewer civilian females to be raped, although there would still be children, the old, the sick, and their caretakers. But what is the likelihood that males would rape in war if they fought side by side with equally trained and armed females and under the command of even more powerful females, in a society in which this phenomenon was not exceptional? Gang rape is an unlikely instrument of heterosexual peer bonding. All-male armies might still treat female soldiers of other armies as Achilles is reputed to have done with the Amazon Penthesilia during the Trojan War, but female soldiers would not be *easy* targets.[5] It seems unlikely that rape could continue to symbolize dominance if women could dominate as well as men.

Many, not only extreme pacifists, will object to this strategy of resistance as a perpetuation of values that we should wish to replace rather than instantiate.[6] Is it possible to participate in military institutions without succumbing to martial values? Without getting so caught up in supporting military practices that we lose sight of the goal of dismantling protection rackets and instead come to enjoy participating in the rites and rights of the masters?

It may be possible to participate to a greater extent than most women in the United States do today in some military institutions without succumbing to indefensible values. What counts as participating in military institutions? Those who pay taxes without withholding a portion that would support military institutions already participate. Yet one may feel ambivalent about that, regarding it as, at best, a questionably tolerable evil rather than something to be expanded. More important from a feminist point of view is the example of the women's self-defense movement. Since the 1970s major cities throughout the U.S. have been sites of martial arts training of women by women for the purpose of both physical skill acquisition for self-defense and attitudinal change with respect to options of resistance involving uses of violence. Such relatively informal individual training for one-on-one encounters by acquaintances or civilians has been important in saving and transforming individual lives.[7] Yet it puts only a small dent in protection rackets in a world in which formally organized violence, such as war, is an ever-present possibility. We may need to be able to rely on each other in a more organized way than the women's self-defense movement has recognized so far, not simply on our individual raised consciousnesses and on our readiness to defend ourselves as lone individuals. If it makes good sense to be prepared to defend ourselves as individuals, why does it not also make sense to be prepared to defend ourselves as communities? When wars of self-defense are fought not primarily by those who *enjoy* war but primarily by those who *hate* it and are inclined to do it only under grave duress, there may be significantly less likelihood that military values will come to

---

[5] Achilles is said to have fallen in love with Penthesilia's corpse after he slew her, which some translators take to be a euphemistic way of saying that he raped her body.

[6] The case against military thinking has been well developed in Ruddick (1989).

[7] For success stories, see Bart and O'Brien (1985) and Caignon and Groves (1987).

dominate the societies of those who participate in the fighting. This is one reason to prefer a universal draft to reliance on mercenaries or exclusively on voluntary enlistment.

What do you suppose the ancient Amazons did in war with their double-axes? (Why do you suppose male historians are so adamant and unanimous in their denial that the Amazons referred to by ancient Greek historians and geographers ever existed?) What would you be tempted to do with male rapist captives in war if you had a double-axe? For improvements in the direction of justice that were envisaged for males by Rawls (1971, 248) to occur also for females, female threat advantage needs to be improved, and, more basically, female image needs to be changed.

If the double-axe in battle fantasy makes you shudder, consider that changing the symbolic meaning of rape might also be achieved by attaching different social consequences and penalties—legal or extralegal—to rape. Rape is presently a crime that is highly tolerated in civilian and military life even by men who do not do it, many of whom regard it as natural. The tendency to regard rape as natural has roots in the symbolic significance of rape as dominance. Wars have often been fought with the explicit goal of domination. In civilian life, those who find rape natural tend to find male dominance natural.

The penalty instituted by men for martial rape has often been death, a penalty almost never carried out where there has been no murder unless there is a racist reason, and then the rape charge may be purely inflammatory. Instituting death for rape is a sure way to guarantee that the penalty will not be inflicted unless there is another reason (such as racism). I doubt that women would be more willing than men to apply the death penalty. Even where the penalty is imprisonment, rapists are seldom convicted. It could be advantageous to have a penalty that communicated that rape is unnatural and that its reward is not power, a penalty that did this so dramatically that it would be effective even if inflicted on a relatively few but well-publicized perpetrators.

I have a *fantasy* of such a penalty made possible by medical technology. Although only a fantasy, it is serious, not frivolous. It is not, however, serious in the sense that I would urge its legal enactment under present circumstances. I would not wish to trust a patriarchal state with power to inflict it (nor would I support setting the kind of precedent in a patriarchal state that my fantasized penalty would set). But that is moot, because a patriarchal state would not inflict this penalty in any case. My fantasy is serious in the sense that *being able to regret the inadvisability* of carrying it out under present circumstances may be an important step forward attitudinally and may serve as a catalyst for the envisaging of more practical fantasies. My fantasy may be best understood either as set in a nonpatriarchal state (assuming that such a state might still have occasion to fight wars and might still have recognizably female citizens), as a response to martial rape by patriarchal (or phallocratic) enemies, or as a fantasy of feminist guerrilla warriors within a still patriarchal (or phallo-cratic) state. It might be expensive, although appropriately funded research could reduce the expense. Expense almost never deters the development of effective military weapons. And imprisonment is an expensive domestic penalty, although that does not keep states from continuing to expand its use.

My fantasy penalty is what for lack of a better term I will call *compulsory transsexual surgery,* that is, removal of the penis and testicles and construction of a vagina-like canal, accompanied by whatever hormone treatments may be advisable for the sake only of bodily health. I do not have in mind *transgender* training, such as sometimes accompanies currently voluntary applications for transsexual surgery. Part of the point is to impact social conceptions of gender. The resulting "she-males"—as Janice Raymond (1979) has called male-to-female transsexuals—would tend to be recognizable as unnatural females, as male bodies tend to differ from female bodies structurally throughout (consider the bone structures of hands, hips, and jaws, for example), and the surgery would leave most body structures intact. Where recognition was not easy, we might devise ways of distinguishing she-males from natural females in certain contexts.[8] There might be reasons to segregate them in prisons, for example, and all-female organizations might have reasons to want to exclude them. No doubt voluntary she-males would also want to distinguish themselves from compulsory she-males, a matter I leave to them.

Castration is an old feminist fantasy penalty for rape. In that fantasy, castration has been thought a more dramatic piece of surgery than it often is (as in Freud's castration complex fantasies and in the case of the Amazons and their double-axes). Castration for sterilization need remove only the testes. That is not enough for present purposes. It would prevent impregnation but not rape nor the spread of sexually transmitted diseases. The message of domination is communicated not only by the ability to impregnate but by the ability to penetrate forcibly. Penis removal would not, of course, prevent rape with other phallic physical instruments. But it would attack the primary *symbol* of male dominance (which is what suggests the use of such other weapons) with which a rapist or potential rapist is most likely to identify intimately. What needs to go is the phallus.

A natural objection to this fantasy is that treating male-to-female transsexual surgery as a *punishment* reinforces misogyny. An analog to this objection has been raised against "outing" prominent lesbians and gay men as punishment for bad behavior: that doing so relies on and thereby reinforces homophobia. The intention of the transsexual surgery would be partly and temporarily to deter potential rapists primarily by appealing to their fear

---

[8] One commentator on an earlier draft of this essay suggested a suitably positioned scarlet "R."

of being perceived as female, but more importantly it would be to combat the current symbolic meaning of rape as dominance, to combat rape as a symbol of power over females (and through females, over other males). If the symbolic meaning of rape were changed, there would be less to fear about being perceived as female. The primary aim would be to combat the symbolic meaning of rape and thereby to eliminate the impulse on the part of those with power to rely on rape as a weapon of war at the level of strategic planning. I envisage this penalty not as a substitute for but as a supplement to such penalties as court martial and imprisonment, which would be needed for deterrence and prevention in certain kinds of cases anyway, a matter to which I will return.

It might also be objected that transsexual surgery is mutilation and thus violates a valuable prohibition against cruel and inhumane punishments. The objection against cruelty and inhumanity deserves to be taken more seriously than it usually is with respect to penalties currently in common use in penal systems. I doubt that transsexual surgery would be worse. In keeping with respect for humanity, however, my fantasized surgery would be carried out under appropriate anesthesia in sanitary conditions by appropriately qualified medical personnel and would transform the offender into a reasonably healthy but unnatural female. This might be viewed as an extension and reversal of a strategy that men use already to *encourage* rape. Apparently, they do not regard it as inhumane.

Interviews such as those published by Alexandra Stiglmayer illustrate how at present male soldiers are goaded into raping females by threats from other males of being treated like, or regarded as, females. It works. The military has used this strategy for centuries without going all the way surgically. Radical theologian and philosopher Mary Daly (1978) quotes David Halberstam (1972) on former U.S. President Lyndon Baines Johnson as saying of a member of his administration who was becoming a dove on Vietnam, "Hell, he has to squat to piss."[9] Why not attach the threat, or promise, of being "regarded as a female" and "treated like a female" not to failing to rape but to doing it (or ordering it done or tolerating its being done)?

I envisage the infliction of this penalty in wartime. But it might be natural to extend it to civilian rapists. Further, I imagine the penalty inflicted not necessarily on the individual soldier rapist, who may have been coerced, but on those directly or indirectly responsible for the choice and on those who tolerate it by choosing not to exercise their power to investigate reports.

Here a problem may arise. What if the officer issuing the orders or refusing to investigate *is* female? We should not dismiss this possibility. Nazis included females who ordered and inflicted sexual tortures. Such a case

---

[9] Squatting may be culturally specific, but the point is communicated in the context in which the remark was made.

indicates limitations of my fantasy penalty with respect to both deterrence and justice (insofar as justice requires inflicting the same penalty on offenders who have committed the same crime). Such cases would be limited to such conventional penalties as court martial and imprisonment. Female-to-male transsexual surgery could not make the same point in a patriarchal society. Recall, however, that the primary point is not deterrence through fear but to change the symbolic meaning of rape in society at large so that it no longer communicates dominance, thereby undermining the most important *point* (pun intended) of rape as a weapon of war. It is an admitted disadvantage from the point of view of justice that the penalty could not be applied to every conceivable perpetrator and, more seriously, that it might be irreversible in cases of wrongful conviction.

I call this a *fantasy* because until women have more political power, including military power (by which I mean martial power, the power to engage in war), such a penalty has no chance of being implemented as official policy and little chance of success even as a guerrilla strategy. Yet it should be an interesting fantasy, as it directs our attention to the symbolic significance of rape. It suggests a different strategy for responding to rape than the strategy of focusing our attention on individual males who are so inclined and trying simply to prevent or deter them from acting on that inclination. Instead of taking such inclinations as givens, my fantasy suggests a process of the social reconstruction of male inclinations regarding females as an indirect consequence of the surgical reconstruction of a few bodies of male perpetrators in the context of societies where females are vulnerable to rape (either by male neighbors or by males from other societies). This fantasy penalty of compulsory transsexual surgery is less important than the general idea that the symbolic significance of rape needs to be changed from domination to something else, to undermine men's spontaneous inclinations to use it as a weapon. Hopefully, those who dislike this fantasy will propose better ones toward that end.

Notes

Thanks to Bat-Ami Bar On, Harry Brighouse, Chris Cuomo, Vicky Davion, Ruth Ginzberg, Nancy Graham, Lori Grant, William McBride, and the audience at the Symposium on War of the International Association of Women Philosophers in Vienna, September 1995, for helpful comments on forerunners of the present essay.

References

Bart, Pauline B., and Patricia H. O'Brien. 1985. *Stopping Rape: Successful Survival Strategies*. New York: Pergamon.

Brownmiller, Susan. 1975. *Against Our Will: Men, Women, and Rape*. New York: Simon and Schuster.

Caignon, Denise, and Gail Groves. 1987. *Her Wits About Her: Self-defense Success Stories by Women*. New York: Harper and Row.

Card, Claudia. 1991. "Rape as a Terrorist Institution." In *Violence, Terrorism, and Justice*, ed. R. G. Frey and Christopher W. Morris. New York: Cambridge University Press.

Daly, Mary. 1978. *Gyn/ecology: The Metaethics of Radical Feminism*. Boston: Beacon.

Gage, Matilda Jocelyn. 1980. *Woman, Church and State*. Watertown, MA: Persephone Press.

Griffin, Susan. 1979. *Rape: The Power of Consciousness*. New York: Harper and Row.

Halberstam, David. 1972. *The Best and the Brightest*. New York: Random House.

Herman, Judith Lewis. 1992. *Trauma and Recovery*. New York: Basic Books.

Lorch, Donatella. 1995. "Wave of Rape Adds New Horror to Rwanda's Trail of Brutality." *New York Times*, 15 May, A-l, A-4.

Meltzer, Milton. 1993. *Slavery: A World History*. New York: Da Capo.

Nietzsche, Friedrich. 1967. *On the Genealogy of Morals*. Trans. Walter Kaufmann and Robert Hollingdale. New York: Vintage.

O'Neill, Onora. 1991. "Which Are the Offers *You* Can't Refuse?" In *Violence, Terrorism, and Justice*, ed. R. G. Frey and Christopher W. Morris. New York: Cambridge University Press.

Rawls, John. 1971. *A Theory of Justice*. Cambridge, MA: Harvard University Press.

Raymond, Janice G. 1979. *The Transsexual Empire: The Making of the She/male*. Boston: Beacon.

Renault, Mary. 1972. *The Persian Boy*. New York: Pantheon.

Ruddick, Sara. 1989. *Maternal Thinking: Toward a Politics of Peace*. Boston: Beacon.

Sanday, Peggy Reeves. 1990. *Fraternity Gang Rape: Sex, Brotherhood, and Privilege on Campus*. New York: New York University Press.

Stiglmayer, Alexandra. 1993. "The Rapes in Bosnia-Herzegovina." In *Mass Rape: The War Against Women in Bosnia-Herzegovina*, ed. Stiglmayer, trans. Marion Faber. Lincoln: University of Nebraska Press.

Storm, Hyemeyohsts. 1972. *Seven Arrows*. New York: Ballantine.

CHAPTER 2

ADDENDUM TO "RAPE AS A WEAPON OF WAR"

CLAUDIA CARD

Since I returned proofs to *Hypatia* for "Rape as a Weapon of War" (Card 1996), further information has come to my attention regarding martial sex crimes. This information has implications for the power of my proposed fantasy response—compulsory transsexual surgery—to address the symbolism of rape as dominance. It also suggests a more comprehensive view of the meanings of martial rape.

Journalist Beverly Allen quotes a United Nations report (Bassiouni 1994) as documenting that the rape and death camps in Bosnia-Herzegovina have also been sites of forced castrations, "through crude means such as forcing other internees to bite off a prisoner's testicles" (Allen 1996, 78). Accordingly, I revised "Rape as a Weapon of War" for presentations in Copenhagen and St. Louis in the fall of 1996. In the discussion following our papers in Copenhagen, Libby Tata Arcel, who has worked with rape survivors in the former Yugoslavia, reported that martial sex crimes by men against men have a long history, but also that they have almost universally been identified by men not as sex crimes, or even as sexual torture, but simply as torture. Asked whether they were victims of sex crimes, Arcel said, the men answered negatively. She noted that they attached a great stigma to the idea of being the victim of a sex crime. Asked whether they had been tortured by instruments applied to their genitalia, however, the same men answered affirmatively.

These reports are evidence, I conclude, that sex crimes in war can be racist as well as misogynist, insofar as they have or are meant to have the consequence of hindering the reproductive continuation of a people. Both castration and forced impregnation can have this consequence. The men may have been right in a sense, in that the reason they were being thus

Criticism and Compassion: The Ethics and Politics of Claudia Card.
Edited by Robin S. Dillon and Armen T. Marsoobian.
Chapters and book compilation © 2018 Metaphilosophy LLC and John Wiley & Sons Ltd.

(sexually) tortured may have been only incidentally because they were men and more essentially because they were of "the wrong people." Some sex crimes against men, such as rape, may also carry misogynistic symbolism. But castration, like rape, appears to have its own history of symbolizing domination. Historically, martial castration has been not only of men but also predominantly by men. In light of such history, however, many people may have perceived the ancient Amazons' double-axes as symbols of imperialism rather than of self-defense or summary punishment. The idea that rape symbolizes domination is, of course, compatible with the idea that castration symbolizes domination. But if castration, like rape, is an intercultural symbol of domination, my fantasy penalty of compulsory transsexual surgery for martial rapists might easily be self-defeating, because it appears capable of being construed as supporting the very symbolism that I wish to combat. For transsexual surgery includes castration and does not, at present, result in a reproductive she-male.

Reports of forced castration also raise questions about the idea that integrating women into the military might effectively eliminate, or substantially reduce, rape as a weapon of war. If Bosnian male soldiers could bring themselves to force others to bite off the testicles of captive men, it appears that racism overcame any tendency they might have had to identify with their victims as men. Racism is, of course, not peculiar to men. What reason have we, then, to think that militarily trained women would not, out of similarly racist attitudes, order or tolerate martial rape, overcoming whatever tendency they might otherwise have to identify with their victims as women? The self-defense advantage of female military training, however, still remains.

In June of 1996 the *New York Times* carried a front-page article titled "For First Time, Court Defines Rape as War Crime" (Simons 1996). It said that the United Nations International Criminal Tribunal of the Hague had just "announced the indictment of eight Bosnian Serb military and police officers in connection with rapes of Muslim women during the Bosnian war, marking the first time sexual assault has been treated separately as a crime of war." Previous postwar courts had treated rape as "secondary, tolerated as part of soldiers' abusive behavior." This indictment described the ordeal of fourteen Muslim women and girls, some only twelve years old, most detained in a camp, where they were subjected to "almost constant rape and sexual assaults, torture and other abuses." European investigators were reported to have calculated that "in 1992, twenty thousand Muslim women and girls were raped by Serbs" (Simons 1996, A-1).

Christian Chartier, speaking for the United Nations tribunal, is reported to have said of this decision, "It is of major legal significance because it illustrates the court's strategy to focus on gender-related crimes and give them their proper place in the prosecution of war crimes" (Simons 1996, A-1). Court officials are also reported to have said, "this indictment gave organized rape and other sexual offenses their due place in international law as crimes against humanity" (Simons 1996, A-1). These characterizations are clearly not inaccurate, and attention to rape as a war crime is long over-due. But they are incomplete characterizations of the kind of crime that it is, insofar as they do not explicitly acknowledge that, in cases such as this, it is also race-related. Perhaps this seemed too obvious to note, because the entire war in question has been so racially motivated. Yet it is worth point-ing out in a treatment of the general topic of martial rape that martial sex crimes, including rape, can be racist as well as sexist, and that the rape of women and girls can be the intersection of martial racism and sexism.

References

Allen, Beverly. 1996. *Rape Warfare: The Hidden Genocide in Bosnia-Herzegovina and Croatia*. Minneapolis: University of Minnesota Press.

Bassiouni, Cherif. 1994. United Nations document S/25274. Cited in Allen 1996, 43–48.

Card, Claudia. 1996. "Rape as a Weapon of War." *Hypatia* 11(4): 5–18.

Simons, Marlise. 1996. "For First Time, Court Defines Rape as War Crime." *New York Times*, 28 June, A-1, 7.

CHAPTER 3

STOICISM, EVIL, AND THE POSSIBILITY OF MORALITY

CLAUDIA CARD

Evil is a topic with which I have struggled for years.* What is it? What attitudes should we take toward it? How can we resist others' evildoings without doing comparable or worse evil ourselves? Martha Nussbaum's work on attitudes toward fortune helps me explore limits of ethical ideals that give prominence to resisting evil or that are motivated by desires to resist, reduce, prevent, and alleviate evils. Utilitarianism is one ethic so motivated. But we need not be utilitarians to have this concern. John Rawls's theory of justice is also at least partly so motivated.

The importance of contingencies for the value of our lives and the quality of our character is a theme in many of Martha Nussbaum's essays. She resists Plato's Stoic view that it is a mistake to attach great significance to contingencies, that we are wrong to place high value on what eludes our control, or that we can assure the goodness of our lives (even our selves) by having the right values. She says, with simple elegance, in *The Fragility of Goodness*:

> That I am an agent, but also a plant; that much that I did not make goes towards making me whatever I shall be praised or blamed for being; that I must constantly choose among competing and apparently incommensurable goods and that circumstances may force me to a position in which I cannot help being false to something or doing some wrong; that an event that simply happens to me may, without my consent, alter my life; that it is equally problematic to entrust

* A version of this paper was originally presented at a conference titled "Honoring the Philosophy of Martha Nussbaum," which was sponsored by the Illinois Philosophical Association and held in October 1997 at Illinois State University in Normal.

Criticism and Compassion: The Ethics and Politics of Claudia Card.
Edited by Robin S. Dillon and Armen T. Marsoobian.
Chapters and book compilation © 2018 Metaphilosophy LLC and John Wiley & Sons Ltd.

one's good to friends, lovers, or country and to try to have a good life without them – all these I take to be not just the material of tragedy, but everyday facts of lived practical reason. (Nussbaum 1986, 5)

Her recent work on emotion suggests that it is *more* problematic to try to have a good life without entrusting one's good to friends, lovers, country, or something else that eludes one's control than to undertake the risks of such trusts (Nussbaum and Glover 1995, 360–95). Without such commitments and risks, without our valuing highly much that eludes our control, she argues, emotions would have no proper place in our lives. Our lives would not be fully human.

I find this position attractive. Yet supporting it turns out to be more difficult than I expected. If a life without emotions is less than human, a life reduced to misery by misfortune may not be fully human, either. Perhaps this is why Martha Nussbaum often does not so much argue against Stoicism as explore its implications, leaving readers to draw their own conclusions. I would like to be able to argue against Stoicism. The closest I've been able to come so far is to argue that morality—at least a commitment to resisting evil—entails moral luck and is incompatible (or fights) with the Stoic attitude. I set out that reasoning here.

I accept Martha Nussbaum's view that our susceptibility to emotions—fear, anger, joy, grief, and the like—presupposes that we value highly things that elude our control. Emotions, as she understands them, embody judgments that acknowledge our neediness and dependence (our plant side). Compassion that lies at the root of mercy is unlikely to be forthcoming, she argues, in anyone who finds it problematic to acknowledge human neediness and dependence (Nussbaum 1993). Those who find such acknowledgments problematic will likely find others making too much of their bad luck, having the wrong values, not being tough enough, being less invulnerable to fortune than one could and should be. They may take offense at being pitied or sympathized with by others, finding it an affront to their pride and dignity in bearing up under trying circumstances.

Martha Nussbaum's view suggests the general thesis that virtues that invoke compassion (including the sense of justice, if John Rawls is right about its connections with love and trust) and virtues that invoke other emotions are unlikely to develop in those who deny the importance of contingencies for who they really are or for what really counts in their lives (Rawls 1963; also 1971, Chap. 8). Or, such traits, if they do develop, are likely to be a source of continuing and profound internal conflict. Those who have such traits may find them weaknesses, not virtues, and may wish to get over them. This is how many men and some women raised on patriarchal ideals of masculinity appear to regard their own tendencies to sympathize with those who suffer from policies that can have hard consequences for some—for example, the policy of up or out in seven years, which can deny a junior faculty person tenure. The Stoic ideal fits also with Immanuel

Kant's reduction of virtues to the sense of duty and with that strain of his thought that regards emotions primarily as stumbling blocks to virtue. It may explain his early paradoxical advice concerning friendship, which he finds consists at its best in mutual trust. He advises us to so conduct ourselves toward friends that no harm is done should they ever become our enemies (do not tell them secrets that they could use against us if they became enemies). This may be what led him to conclude that "Friendship develops the minor virtues of life" (Kant 1963, 208–9).[1]

The idea that it is more problematic to insulate oneself from the impact of contingencies than to acknowledge our neediness and interdependencies is interesting for feminist ethics and for thinking about oppression and its impact on character. In "Emotions and Women's Capabilities" (Nussbaum and Glover 1995) Martha Nussbaum suggests that women's greater emotionality (to the extent that it is a fact) may be grounded both in women's socialization to value relationships more highly (not a universal socialization, she notes, and, we might add, a socialization that becomes problematic in a society structured by oppressive relationships) and in women's greater social and political dependency (more nearly universal and oppressive).[2] From being forced to acknowledge neediness and dependency, women may be less likely to fail in compassion toward others (Schopenhauer 1995, 151; Kant 1960, 81). This could have interesting implications for gender's impact on international politics. How much failure of compassion lay at the root of the failure of the United States and other nations to accept more immigrants who needed asylum during World War II? Of course, victims can also deny the value of compassion. Those struggling to survive may feel little compassion for others forced to compete with them or for others less successful. It may be not so much that acknowledgment of human neediness explains compassion as that the absence of such acknowledgment might explain the lack thereof.

The question to which I keep returning is not exactly Martha Nussbaum's question but is suggested by her reflections on Stoicism. It is the question of which is the greater source of evil: our vulnerability to fortune or our ability to minimize that vulnerability? By minimizing vulnerability I do not mean just any precautions against harm. It makes good sense for any of us, as she acknowledges, to be immunized against communicable disease, install smoke alarms, get brakes checked periodically. By minimizing our vulnerability I mean aiming to reduce it to a minimum by

---

[1] By virtues I have in mind character traits. What Kant recognizes as "duties of virtue" (Kant 1964) are not character traits but ends to be chosen from a sense of duty. The opening paragraph of his *Groundwork of the Metaphysic of Morals* (Kant 1948, 61) reduces character to possession of a good will, which is then elucidated as a sense of duty.

[2] Carol Gilligan's work (1982) on women's greater tendency to identify themselves in terms of their relationships to others and to see relationships as less replaceable than rules has been criticized for failing to note this problem.

monitoring our values closely. That is what I regard as the classically Stoic attitude.

I must confess that I have not made an independent study of ancient Stoicism beyond consulting Philip Hallie's article in Paul Edwards's *Encyclopedia of Philosophy*, which presents Stoicism as historically more moderate than this characterization might suggest (Hallie 1967, 8: 19–22).[3] Martha Nussbaum, however, describes as Stoic the refusal to value highly what eludes our control, citing ancient Stoics (Nussbaum and Glover 1995, 378–79). As I understand it, Stoicism supports not cultivating unnecessary tastes (fine wines) or desires (for the pleasures of skiing), to avoid disappointment at being unable to satisfy them. A Stoic might not have animal companions, to avoid becoming attached and grieving at their deaths, or might resist falling in love to avoid its nonrequital. By cultivating detachment Stoics resist being seduced by life. Martha Nussbaum mentions Cicero's story of the father who said calmly, upon being informed of his son's death, "I was already aware that I had begotten a mortal" (Nussbaum and Glover 1995, 377).

The question of which is the greater source of evil—our vulnerability to fortune or our ability to minimize that vulnerability—is partly empirical, insofar as it asks how we are likely to behave. But it is partly philosophical, insofar as what counts as evil affects the answer. If we regard contingencies as important, we will regard as important much undeserved suffering and consider it often good to alleviate or at least sympathize with such suffering where we can. We may even regard it as evil not to, depending on the seriousness of the suffering. On the other hand, although Stoics might oppose many motives that would lead people to perpetrate suffering actively, we must ask whether Stoicism offers any basis for alleviating suffering or preventing its infliction. Does it offer any basis for actively opposing evil?

Suppose we understand evil as an ethical concept, that is, as presupposing a very negative ethical assessment of what someone does, not just a negative assessment of something that happens. Also, evil is serious; mere undesirability is not evil. Further, evil, the singular, suggests a focus on doing, whereas evils, plural, suggests a focus on undergoing. Yet this is a matter of focus; both doing and suffering are involved. When we speak of evils we commonly mean the infliction of severe suffering or the unnecessary neglect of basic human needs, where the infliction or neglect involves someone's wrongdoing or is aggravated or sustained by such wrongdoing (Card 1998). The wrongdoing need not be motivated by wickedness,

---

[3] Hallie gives an account of Stoic ethics as including a sense of civic duty, although it does not say in what those duties consisted. And Martha Nussbaum notes that no major thinker in this tradition has been willing to conclude that benevolence does not matter (Nussbaum and Glover 1995, 378–79).

viciousness, or sadism. It could result from carelessness, callousness, or deficiency of scruple.

We might say—to work a variation on one of John Rawls's definitions of primary goods—that sufferings or deprivations that are evil are such that anyone could be presumed to want to avoid them, whatever else he or she might want. (Even Stoics might wish to avoid deterioration of mental health, so as to remain in control of their attitudes.) Or, we might describe evils as sufferings and deprivations no one should have to endure, no matter what it would do for anyone else. The wrongful willingness to tolerate, inflict, or refuse to alleviate or prevent the unnecessary infliction of such sufferings or deprivations is cruelty, paradigmatic evildoing.

As Martha Nussbaum suggests in her observations regarding the value of benevolence, it will be hard for even a Stoic to deny that such things matter. It would seem more in the spirit of Stoic resistance to admitting dependency, however, to balk at counting the *suffering* of cruelty as an evil, even were it admitted that *inflicting* cruelty (*being* cruel) is evil. Yet we will soon have to ask on what basis a Stoic could even regard being cruel as evil.

To return to the question of which is the greater source of evil (our vulnerability to fortune or our ability to minimize that vulnerability), consider to what evils fortune exposes us. Our friends and family can be murdered, our money and property stolen, our houses destroyed, our bodies maimed; we can be raped, tortured, starved, deprived of water and sleep, infected with diseases that follow lack of sanitation. These evils are suffered everywhere by civilians in war. They call to mind the trials of Job. We can be humiliated, see our reputations destroyed, even lose our self-respect and dignity if we become monstrous in seeking revenge. Martha Nussbaum takes Euripides' play *Hecuba* to offer an example of someone whose character deteriorates under horrendous reversals of fortune (Nussbaum 1986, 327–421). After she has been enslaved and her daughter Polyxena sacrificed, Hecuba learns of the murder of her youngest son by the man with whom he was left for safekeeping. This knowledge tips her over the edge and sets her on a plan of terrible revenge that leaves her son's murderer blind and his own two children dead (Euripides in Oates and O'Neill 1938, 2: 807–40). Hecuba becomes monstrous, we might say inhuman.

A Stoic might say of Hecuba that had she not been so attached to her children and to the potentiality of continued worldly existence and future restorations of power that especially the boy symbolized, she might have preserved her dignity and integrity, even her humanity. We do not need so dramatic a case, however, to see how any of us might deteriorate. We can find ourselves between that rock and hard place where to save a friend or loved one we must commit a wrong we would not otherwise have dreamt of. As Martha Nussbaum notes, circumstances can force us to choose to what we will be false or whom we will wrong. We wrong a friend or we wrong someone else. If psychologists are right that having once crossed the line of serious wrongdoing makes doing so again and doing worse easier—as we have less to lose the next time in the way of preserving our dignity or integrity—such conflicts can initiate character deterioration (Thomas 1993, 56–65). Cultivating and expanding our relationships with others increases the likelihood of our confronting conflicting obligations and responsibilities, hence the likelihood of confronting some that are not satisfactorily resolvable. (At the same time, we should remember that it may increase the resources with which we can meet them.)

It is clear that to embrace fortune is to take grave risks with our peace of mind and personal integrity. We may be more aware of these risks than of the costs of Stoicism. I think Martha Nussbaum is right, especially in addressing philosophers, to focus on what we lose if we opt for Stoicism. Much philosophy, as she notes, is an exercise in intellectual self-control and discipline. If we put that together with her observations about mercy and compassion, we might explain some of the cruelty of philosophers (which can be otherwise astonishing).

The costs of the Stoic attitude that worry me most are the social consequences of apathy regarding oppression and injustice. Would a Stoic be apathetic toward what I, as an embracer of fortune, would recognize as oppression and injustice? I fear not that Stoics would directly perpetrate such evils. My fear is that Stoics would be unmotivated to resist, prevent, or alleviate evils, as long as they were not directly involved in the perpetration of those evils. As someone famously observed: all that is required for evil to prevail is that good people do nothing.

For the Stoic, the important thing may be simply to resist becoming evil; the important thing may not be to oppose others' evildoing. But what could it mean, for a Stoic, to become evil or to perpetrate evil? What would make anything that one person did to another evil? If a person cannot harm others who place no special value on what eludes their control, Stoics could not *be* wronged by others. If people who choose to value highly what eludes their control are thereby responsible for their own misery when, as a result, they suffer at the hands of another, then Stoics cannot wrong others, either. At least, this seems to follow by the principle that consent nullifies wrong, if we choose our misery with our values. Stoics can still have a conception of wrongdoing, but it cannot include the idea of wronging another person.

I do not know whether this responsibility argument is one that Stoics would employ. Another argument, however, leads to the same conclusion. If we could always choose not to wrong anyone, we might acknowledge the mere possibility of wronging others and yet retain control of our own virtue. But if wronging others is possible, then it is also possible to be caught between that rock and hard place where we do not have the option of doing something that wrongs nobody. In such cases, it would not be within our control to preserve our virtue and avoid wrongdoing. A Stoic conception of wrongdoing, then, must abstract wrongdoing from the idea of wronging other persons, to preserve the principle that "ought" implies "can." Stoic wrongdoing would not result in anyone else's being wronged.

But what is left of evil, if we try to abstract it from wronging other persons? What is at stake is whether the Stoic ultimately is able to recognize and address evil in human relationships and interaction. How could we betray each other if we did not trust to begin with? If trust goes, who is wronged by lying and deception? Would stealing wrong anyone, if no one should be so attached to worldly goods as to suffer greatly from their loss? Why regard even murder as a wrong to anyone, if the soul is invulnerable? What remains of evil, if we cannot wrong one another? Evil, it seems, is reduced to a mere idea, a hypothetical: those gross wrongs that we could do to each other if it were all right for people to value what eludes their control.

Ethics does not totally evaporate with the disappearance of evil, however. It is still wrong, on the Stoic view, to embrace the wrong values. It seems the only wrongs a Stoic can ultimately recognize are wrongs to oneself. I do not wrong others in embracing the wrong values, even if they suffer from it. For my embracing the values I embrace is beyond their control, whereas what they make of their suffering is not. Stoicism carried to such a conclusion leaves no place for ethics in interpersonal relationships and personal interaction. If morality in particular, as distinct from ethics in general, is socially oriented, it appears that Stoics should reject morality. Perhaps it was the Stoic strain in Nietzsche that led him to do just that.

Are Stoicism's costs greater than those of the alternative? One difference between the two options is that the prices of Stoicism are a sure thing. If Martha Nussbaum is right, emotions lose their proper place in human life. If I am right, so does morality (interpersonal ethics). Risks of refusing the Stoic temptation are, on the other hand, just that—risks. But some of those risks are terrible: becoming Hecuba or becoming her instrument or target of revenge. Which is worse: embracing fortune with its risks that one will become an evildoer and/or suffer intolerably from others' evildoings? Or, to minimize our vulnerability to fortune, becoming so indifferent to suffering that we are not moved to resist oppression and are perhaps unable to acknowledge it?

To oversimplify and put it positively, the Stoic gains peace of mind (at least for a while) whereas the other gains life (at least for a while). Neither is necessarily a blessing, however. Perhaps Martha Nussbaum was right, then, in *The Fragility of Goodness* to find both options equally problematic. We seem left with the depressing thought that an impoverished life may be no worse than a life that is rich predominantly in misfortune. A possible way out is to argue that the Stoic rejection of life is nevertheless mistaken on the ground that we truly are needy and dependent beings and that the illusion of becoming invulnerable to fortune is just that, an illusion (Nussbaum and

Glover 1995, 61–104). (But then one might want to ask, in a Nietzschean mood, so what's wrong with illusions?)

This is as close as I have been able to come to showing that moral luck, so far from undermining morality, as Thomas Nagel and Bernard Williams have suggested (Williams 1981, 20–39; Nagel 1979, 24–38), is presupposed in the very possibility of morality. The very possibility of interpersonal morality presupposes our valuing what eludes our control, including much that is important to who we are and to what we do. Morally we are not free (even were we able) to adjust our values for the sake of peace of mind whenever fortune is unkind.

References

Card, Claudia. (1998). "Living with Evils." In *The Realm of the Spirit: Essays in Honor of Virginia Held*, edited by Mark S. Halfon. New York: Rowman & Littlefield.

Gilligan, Carol. (1982). *In a Different Voice: Psychological Theory and Women's Development*. Cambridge, MA: Harvard University Press.

Hallie, Philip P. (1967). "Stoicism." In *The Encyclopedia of Philosophy*, edited by Paul Edwards. 8 vols. New York: Macmillan.

Kant, Immanuel. (1948). *The Moral Law: Kant's Groundwork of the Metaphysic of Morals*. Trans. H. J. Paton. London: Hutchinson.

———. (1960). *Observations on the Feeling of the Beautiful and Sublime*. Trans. John T. Goldthwait. Berkeley: University of California Press.

———. (1963). *Lectures on Ethics*. Trans. Louis Infield. New York: Harper & Row.

———. (1964). *Doctrine of Virtue: Part II of The Metaphysics of Morals*. Trans. Mary Gregor. New York: Harper & Row.

Nagel, Thomas. (1979). "Moral Luck." In *Mortal Questions*. Cambridge: Cambridge University Press.

Nussbaum, Martha C. (1986). *The Fragility of Goodness: Luck and Ethics in Greek Tragedy and Philosophy*. Cambridge: Cambridge University Press.

———. (1993). "Equity and Mercy." *Philosophy and Public Affairs*, 22, no. 2, 83–125.

Nussbaum, Martha C., and Jonathan Glover, eds. (1995). *Women, Culture and Development: A Study of Human Capabilities*. Oxford: Clarendon Press.

Oates, Whitney J., and Eugene O'Neill, eds. (1938). *The Complete Greek Drama*. 2 vols. New York: Random House.

Rawls, John. (1963). "The Sense of Justice." *Philosophical Review*, 72, 281–305.

———. (1971). *A Theory of Justice*. Cambridge, MA: Harvard University Press.

Schopenhauer, Arthur. (1995). *On the Basis of Morality*. Trans. E. F. J. Payne. Oxford: Berghahn.

Thomas, Laurence. (1993). *Vessels of Evil: American Slavery and the Holocaust*. Philadelphia: Temple University Press.

Williams, Bernard. (1981). "Moral Luck." In *Moral Luck: Philosophical Papers, 1973–1980*. Cambridge: Cambridge University Press.

CHAPTER 4

WOMEN, EVIL, AND GRAY ZONES

CLAUDIA CARD

An early task in fighting oppression is to address undeserved negative judgments and unfriendly stereotypes of the oppressed. Thus early feminism
addressed undeserved negative judgments and stereotypes of women. A
more difficult task for survivors is to identify and overcome the real damage
that oppression works in its victims. Oppressive social structures, whether
they favor or disfavor us, offer an inhospitable context for the development of good character. Thus feminist ethics must confront the likelihood
that many (perhaps most) women have sustained some character damage in
acquiring habits of thought, feeling, and action under oppressive practices.
The gray areas of this essay are danger zones, where those who are already
victims may be in jeopardy of moral character deterioration or untoward
developments. I remain, however, basically optimistic, believing that recognizing the danger is a step toward overcoming it.

Extreme cases suggest a kind of damage to which oppressed people
may be susceptible in varying degrees. I have in mind "the hostage phenomenon," "Hostage Identification Syndrome," or the "Stockholm Syndrome," so named after a hostage incident during the 1973 holdup of the
Sveriges Kreditbank in Stockholm, when four employees were held captive
by two robbers for almost six days (Turner 1985; West and Martin 1996;
Kuleshnyk 1984; Strentz 1982). Contrary to what others expected, the victims feared the police more than they feared the robbers. Some hostages
became sympathetic toward their captors. One hostage fell in love with and
became engaged to one of the robbers and publicly berated the Swedish
prime minister for his failure to understand the robber's point of view. One
analyst reports that "in other instances hostages have been known to visit
their captors in jail up to two years after the incident" (Kuleshnyk 1984, 40).

Criticism and Compassion: The Ethics and Politics of Claudia Card.
Edited by Robin S. Dillon and Armen T. Marsoobian.
Chapters and book compilation © 2018 Metaphilosophy LLC and John Wiley & Sons Ltd.

The next year (1974), nineteen-year-old Patricia Hearst, granddaughter of William Randolph Hearst of newspaper fame, was kidnaped in San Francisco by the Symbionese Liberation Army (SLA) and held for a ransom demand of $6 million for a food giveaway program for the poor of California. After fifty-seven days, during which she was kept tied and blindfolded in a closet, where she was also raped, she agreed to join the SLA, taking the name Tania, and later Pearl. Although she was at first convicted and sentenced to prison for her part in the SLA's most infamous bank robbery (videotaped and shown on national television), she was later pardoned by President Carter, after psychiatrists determined that she had developed a pseudo-identity as a survival strategy (Hearst 1988). Her experience is frequently mentioned in discussions of the Stockholm Syndrome.

In 1979 Kathleen Barry wrote about a similar kind of experience in *Female Sexual Slavery*, including a chapter on Patricia Hearst. She found that young girls "seasoned" for prostitution through torture by a pimp come to identify with the pimp's perspectives to the point of being able to predict his wants before he knows them himself. If identifying with a persecutor's perspective is not simply a deliberate and calculated act, the victim may take up that perspective not just as though it were her own but as her own, at least in the sense of its being the only operative perspective that she now has. Her choices may come to seem normal to her, no longer even morally problematic.

These episodes range from a few days to several months or even a few years. Although some survivors, even after they are freed, continue to defend their captors, eventually they cease. The basic idea of the Stockholm Syndrome has since been extended, however, to victims of domestic battery and to children abused by caretakers (Painter and Dutton 1985; Goddard and Stanley 1994; cf. Frye 1983). Domestic abuse often lasts years, and the victim's identification with the abuser may never totally die. Domestic-abuse survivors are plausibly recognized as having been a hostage for at least part of their lives. People who are dominated and abused, however, are not always used specifically as hostages. Still, the victims may identify strongly with the abuser or dominator. As with Patricia Hearst, doing so can enhance their chances of survival, making them useful to abusers and encouraging a reciprocal identification that makes it psychologically more difficult for abusers to depersonalize and destroy their victims.

In the early twentieth century, the African American philosopher and sociologist W. E. B. Du Bois wrote about his own experience of what he called "twoness," having two selves. He was not referring to any incident, long or short, of being held captive or subjected to obvious and readily identifiable abuse. One self he called "American" and one he called "Negro." He also described "this double-consciousness" as a sense of "always looking at oneself through the eyes of others" (Du Bois 1969, 45). Du Bois was well aware of the conflict of ideals between the two perspectives. But it is possible to be less aware and to discover eventually, through reflection, that one's true self has been smothered, rendered inoperative through a combination of fear and the hope of being able to deflect dangers by learning to perceive and think as one's oppressor does.

Gray Zones

The medical model operative in the terms "Hostage Identification Syndrome" and "Stockholm Syndrome" suggests that the victim is overcome by something like an illness, that the identification process is not voluntary and the victim not morally responsible for her choices. Yet when we look at cases, such as Patricia Hearst's, it is not clear that the victim acts involuntarily or is not morally responsible. Some of her choices seem justifiable as the best way to maximize her chances of survival. There are also good reasons not to think that all her choices were simply calculated, either. Genuine sympathy for the captor's point of view—even mutual bonding— can develop. It is not clear that actions following the sympathy or bonding are involuntary or that the medical model clarifies what is occurring. We may have a morally gray area in some cases, where there is real danger of becoming complicit in evildoing and where the captive's responsibility is better described as problematic than as nonexistent.

In her autobiography Patricia Hearst wrote of her decision to join the SLA as a calculated pretense that would maximize her chances of survival. She did not accept SLA values and objectives but pretended, in order to gain her captors' trust and respect, that she did. It worked. Months later, after she had been drilled in weapons use and emergency response, she found herself alone in the getaway car using her weapon to help two SLA comrades escape from a store where they were being apprehended for shoplifting, instead of taking that opportunity to use the weapon to try to escape herself. That is, she sided with her captors, the SLA, instead of with those who might have been able to rescue her from them. When she realized what she had done, she was puzzled. Explanations she offered were that her response was automatic because she was trained to respond automatically in such a situation and also that she felt by then as much of a criminal in the eyes of the law as other members of the SLA, that in joining the SLA she had made a decision from which there was no turning back and no possible redemption. The second explanation is more interesting because in it she takes responsibility for her action.

One of the greatest evils threatening victims of oppression is the danger of becoming evil oneself, at least of becoming somewhat voluntarily complicit in evils perpetrated against others. Not all victims of oppression are as clearly captives as was Patricia Hearst. Nor do all become or remain complicit. Some resist to the end; many of these do not survive. Nor among those who become complicit is everyone equally so. But avoiding or ceasing complicity can require alertness, habits of reflection, loss of innocence, sensitivity to risks, and then moral imagination and creativity. Most women and most people of color in the United States face to some degree the challenges of avoiding or ceasing complicity in evildoing. For some, the challenge is acute, and when it is, we may face morally gray choices.

In the 1970s feminists identified women's complicity in misogyny in the "Athena" syndrome (being born again from Daddy's head) and in "harem politics" (a power hierarchy among female slaves, some charged to discipline others). In both cases, women appear drawn, by hope of favor and privilege, into being men's instruments of oppression. "Favor and privilege" sound like superfluous goods. In reality they tend to be no more than temporary reprieves from abuse. To resist being "divided and conquered," some women who refuse such favors stand in solidarity with those who do not, refraining from judging women who give in. Yet refusing to evaluate the choices made by those who give in exposes us to being manipulated and worse.

Reflecting on women's involvement in perpetrating evils in a social context of misogyny does not presuppose that one finds most women basically lacking in integrity or hostile, even toward other women. Contrary to patriarchal myth, many women's strongest bonds are with other women, despite the double binds of patriarchy that do so much to pit us against one another. Yet people who are bonded to others can also abuse them. The realization of women's—or any victim's—capacity to compromise with evil is disillusioning. Yet the history of such compromises is undeniable. Being a victim does not imply that one has the character of an angel. If appreciation of female involvement in evil initially poses a risk to feminist solidarity, ignoring that involvement produces a superficial feminism. The main reasons for women to take seriously women's capacity for evil are to move beyond myths of female innocence in our relationships with each other, to confront our responsibilities for past and potential damage to other victims, and to overcome the moral traps that oppression sets for us.

My concern is not with mild misconduct, such as hurtful or insensitive remarks, but with involvement in the real evils of oppression. Evils are losses or deprivations of what is basic to a tolerable existence, when those losses are produced, aided, maintained, or ignored by wrongdoing. Many things are disappointing, undesirable, or just bad, without being evil. Evils command our attention. As Nietzsche saw, it is natural to hate what we find evil (Nietzsche 1998, 1–33). There is danger of becoming obsessed with it, whereas we are unlikely to become overinvolved with what we judge merely poor or inferior.

Evildoers need not be sadists. More commonly, evildoing is negligent, callous, or unscrupulous, more banal than popular paradigms of wickedness (cf. Kekes 1990, 66–105). Yet however banal the motive, the result is far from banal, for it deprives others of what is basic to a tolerable existence.

Misogyny is an evil. Although "misogyny" means "woman hating," feminists use it to refer to practices, behaviors, and socially created environments that are hostile to women and girls. Hostility here is not identical (but is compatible) with the emotion of hatred. It refers to the hindrance of female health and development. Misogynist environments are hostile to women as polluted ground and water are hostile to plants. To find misogynist environments evil is to find that they are also the product of wrongdoing and that the hindrance they pose to female health and development deprives females of what is basic to a tolerable existence.

It has long been observed that misogynist environments are routinely maintained by women. There are many degrees of (in)voluntariness in this participation. Many who appear to participate voluntarily would only do so in an oppressive situation already created by others. Women run whorehouses, sometimes with pride. Mothers socialize daughters into aspects of femininity that endanger their health and safety. Sometimes they ostracize lesbian daughters. Women who do patriarchy's dirty work occupy positions of trust and responsibility, some not only accepted but actively sought. Their tasks draw on female initiative, energy, imagination, creativity, brilliance, and virtuosity. In other cases, such as child abuse, the oppressive behavior in which women engage may be not so much advantageous as an outlet for cruelty (a common result of the demoralization produced by oppression).

Consider Hedda Nussbaum, widely held to share blame in the 1987 death of six-year-old Lisa Steinberg. Hedda Nussbaum was nearly as battered by Joel Steinberg, with whom she had lived since 1976, as was Lisa, his illegally adopted daughter, who finally died from his abuse. Hedda Nussbaum's sojourn with Steinberg was a living death. She did not deserve his abuse. But neither did she, apparently, seek help (such as dialing 911) for Lisa, who was even more vulnerable and had no one else to help her. Years of battery by Joel Steinberg and years of her own compromises had thoroughly demoralized Hedda Nussbaum. Andrea Dworkin, herself a survivor of domestic battery, writes, "I don't think Hedda Nussbaum is 'innocent.' I don't know any innocent adult women. Life is harder than that for everyone. But adult women who have been battered are especially not innocent. Battery is a forced descent into hell and you don't get by in hell by moral goodness" (Dworkin 1997, 51–52). But she continues, "I am upset by the phony mourning for Lisa Steinberg—the hypocritical sentimentality of a society that would not really mind her being beaten to death once she was an adult," and she notes, "There was a little boy, too, Mitchell, seventeen months old, tied up and covered in feces. And the only way to have spared him was to rescue Hedda. Now he has been tortured and he did not die. What kind of man will he grow up to be?" (Dworkin 1997, 53–54).

Such issues confront us with what we might recognize, following Holocaust survivor Primo Levi, as a "gray zone, poorly defined, where the two camps of masters and servants both diverge and converge" (Levi 1989, 42). "Gray zone" was his term for the moral area occupied by kapos (captains) and other prisoners of Nazi concentration camps (and ghettos) who held positions of responsibility and administration.

Gray zones "confuse our need to judge" (Levi 1989, 42). They are inhabited by people who become implicated, through their choices, in perpetrating on others the evil that threatens or engulfs themselves. Levi does not
define gray zones specifically. He conveys the idea mainly by examples, noting that such zones are varied and ambiguous and that they have multiple
roots. Among these roots are the oppressors' need for external auxiliaries
and the oppressors' realization that the best way to bind those auxiliaries
is "to burden them with guilt, cover them with blood, compromise them as
much as possible, thus establishing a bond of complicity so that they can
no longer turn back" (Levi 1989, 43). (Recall that Patricia Hearst felt there
was no turning back.)

"Gray zone" is a problematic term, if it presupposes that "dark" or
"black" represents evil. Such use of color terms may unwittingly reinforce
racism, even if the metaphor of dark as evil originated historically in references to the night in a society where nights are dangerous or difficult
(because it is hard for the visually dependent to make their way). For that
reason I would welcome an alternative metaphor.[1] Meanwhile, I use Levi's
term "gray zone," acknowledging, in case it instantiates what it names, that
"gray zone" may be itself a gray term.

There is also risk in appropriating Levi's term "gray zone" of misappro-
priating the experience of Holocaust victims, although Levi is not the only
writer to use "gray" to refer to morally unclear or problematic choices.[2] I
do not wish to trade on the horrors of the camps and ghettos to bring attention to other evils. From respect for the examples motivating his discussion,
I am inclined to speak of "gray areas," rather than "gray zones," in less
desperate cases that are in important ways morally analogous. "Zone" suggests an enclosure, such as a prison, whereas "area" is more open-ended. I
do wish to explore the significance of the concept that Levi has identified
for more contexts than those that led him to articulate it. It complicates
our understandings of choices people make in oppressive circumstances,
our assessments of the moral positions of victims of oppression, and
the responsibilities victims may have to and for one another. Most of the
choices facing victims of misogyny bear no comparison in urgency or
horror with those that confronted camp or ghetto prisoners. Most women
are not Hedda Nussbaum (although more are than is commonly acknowledged). My point, however, is not to compare suffering or even degrees of
evil but to note patterns in the moral complexity of choices and judgments
of responsibility.

In his chapter "The Gray Zone" in *The Drowned and the Saved*, Levi
wrote of prisoners whose labors were used to carry out the Nazi oppression

---

[1] "Twilight zone" has been preempted by science fiction. In any case, if the only reason it
might work is the color of the twilight, it isn't really an alternative.

[2] See Spelman 1997 for thoughtful reflection on the misappropriation of others' pain.

and genocide (Levi 1989, 36–69). Some prisoners were drafted; others offered their services. Some did clerical or domestic work for officers. Some became camp doctors. Prisoners also served on ghetto councils, which were eventually charged with deportation tasks (see also Trunk 1996 and Hilberg 1985). Others became ghetto police and found themselves charged with rounding up prisoners for deportation.[3] In death camps, prisoners were routinely chosen for the Sonderkommando, which was charged with cremation detail. Almost all Sonderkommando prisoners were murdered within months or weeks (see also Nyiszli 1993). Prisoners who became kapos in exchange for food and other privileges held power over other prisoners (Levi 1989, 36–69). Levi noted that although a minimum of harshness was expected of kapos, there was no upper limit to the cruelty they could inflict with impunity.

Prisoners who occupied such positions lost their innocence.[4] Loss of innocence, even when it involves "dirty hands," is not the same as loss of virtue.[5] Yet it carries moral risk. We lose our innocence when we become responsible through our choices for the suffering of others or when we betray their trust, even when we make the best decision open to us under the circumstances. When we fail to live up to the responsibilities we thereby incur, as we inevitably must when we lack the means, our integrity may be compromised. We risk losing self-respect and moral motivation. Once we feel we have crossed the line of participating in the infliction of evil, we may have less to restrain us from more and worse in the future.

Privileged prisoners, Levi observed, were a minority of the camp populations. But he also claimed that "they represent a majority among survivors" (1989, 40). I do not know whether he was right about that. Presumably, many survived only because they were among the last to be deported. Luck was always a major factor. Nevertheless, how the realization that survivors included many privileged prisoners should affect survivors' attitudes toward themselves and toward other survivors was a question that troubled him profoundly and led him to draw distinctions. Regarding members of the Sonderkommando who did not kill with their own hands, he wrote, "I believe that no one is authorized to judge them, not those who lived through the experience of the Lager [camp] and even less those who did not" (1989, 59). Yet he did not refrain from all judgments of gray-zone inhabitants. He noted that "they are the rightful owners of a quota of guilt" (1989, 49), but also that were it up to him, he "would lightheartedly absolve all those

---

[3] Calel Perechodnik, who became a ghetto police officer in a small town near Warsaw, left a memoir recording his inner conflict over that decision and his ultimate remorse (Perechodnik 1996).

[4] On lost innocence, see Morris 1976, 139–61.

[5] On "dirty hands," see Stocker 1990.

whose concurrence in the guilt was minimal and for whom coercion was of the highest degree" (1989, 54).

Levi may seem, to some, generous in his responses to gray-zone agents, even in his concession that "they are the rightful owners of a quota of guilt." Perhaps he was thinking primarily of the Sonderkommando, although they were not typical even of gray-zone agents (if we can speak of what is typical in gray zones). Even less clear are the right choices for agents who act on their own initiatives and have more control over their options. Patricia Hearst became convinced by the SLA that if the police found their hiding place, she would be killed in the ensuing shootout. She was right. She would have been killed in the shootout and fire, had she been in the Los Angeles hideout when the police found it. At first, the police thought they must have killed her there. She was also convinced (from overheard conversations) that if she did not join them, the SLA would kill her, because she knew too much about them. Even so, her death was less certain than that of members of the Sonderkommando.

The ambivalence of the gray zone is mirrored in the ambivalence of other victims' moral responses to gray choices. On the one hand, other victims may identify with the chooser, thinking to themselves, "Had I the opportunity, I'd seize it, too; how could anyone not?" On the other hand, victims may feel even more wronged by other victims than by their morally unambiguous oppressors, thinking to themselves, "If we cannot trust even those who are as oppressed as we, what can we hope for? Oppressors, in a way, don't betray us, because we don't trust them. Real betrayal comes with hard treatment from those we expect to be able to trust and count upon for assistance." Thus, women may feel, paradoxically, more wronged by other women than by men, even though the women who wrong them have less power to do them harm. When complicity is the price of survival, one may think, on the one hand, "It's good that at least some of us will survive." But if backstabbing is the price of complicity, one may think, on the other hand, "What is the good of surviving in a world where no one is trustworthy?"

Gray areas, whose inhabitants are both victims and perpetrators of oppression, develop wherever the evils of oppression are severe, widespread, and lasting. There are gray areas under slavery, for example, and in the policing of and resistance to organized crime. There are gray areas within organized crime, as in the Cosa Nostra or the Mob, where women are sometimes used, with varying degrees of knowledge, as go-betweens or to arrange meetings, or where women are simply caretakers of men who are fully involved (Siebert 1996). There are gray zones wherever women who are victims of misogyny provide essential services to men who are engaged in conquest, exploitation, annihilation, and oppression. The labor of the oppressed in the daily workings of maintaining and operating oppressive power structures frees the energies of those on top for the joyous pursuits of cultural development. The insulation of being on top enables them to avoid confronting dirt on their own hands, thus offering them the illusion of innocence.

What Makes Gray Zones Gray?

Women have suffered the evils of oppression globally and for millennia. And women have been implicated in perpetrating evils not only of misogyny but of slavery, racism, anti-Semitism, classism, hatred of sexual diversity, and hatred and fear of the poor (see, e.g., Koonz 1987; Pearson 1997). Women can inhabit gray areas in relation to children (as Hedda Nussbaum did in relation to Lisa Steinberg) and in paying male protection rackets for protection against violence.[6] We are not always sensitive to the grayness of the choices we confront. But feminists have been aware of the nature of the problem at least since the lesbian/straight battles of the 1970s.

In her struggle to envision a way out, feminist philosopher Joyce Trebilcot came close to using the gray-area metaphor: "My life is like a muddy lake with some clear pools and rivulets—wimmin's spaces—but many areas thick, in one degree or another, with the silt and poisons of patriarchy" (Trebilcot 1990, 17). Although she was describing her life, she did not at that time want to count as a "wimmin's space" those portions of it marked by oppressive practices. Yet to count only ideal spaces as women's suggests that women interacting with women are better at resisting compromise with evil. History neither supports the view that we are nor yet sustains the hope that we might be. Women's spaces, too, need to confront the challenges of grayness.

Levi's gray zones have three striking features. First, their inhabitants are victims of evil. Second, these inhabitants are implicated through their choices in perpetrating some of the same or similar evils on others who are already victims like themselves. And third, gray-zone inhabitants act under extraordinary stress. Many have lost everything and everyone, and they face the threat of imminent and horrible death. It may seem at first that grayness is conveyed by the first two features alone: being both a victim of evil and implicated in the perpetration of that evil on others. These features can be enough to "confuse our need to judge" (Levi 1989, 42). But the third feature—the extraordinary stress—makes judgment even more problematic, given the frailty of human nature. This third feature is also important, as we will see, for distinguishing gray areas from other mixtures of good and evil. I understand the basic idea of a gray area in such a way that the stress factor is satisfied when agents must choose under such conditions as intense or prolonged fear for their own lives or for the lives of loved ones. Aside from war and slavery, perhaps misogyny's gray areas seldom, if ever,

---

[6] On rape as a male protection racket, see Griffin 1977, 313–32, Peterson 1977, 360–71, and Card 1996, 97–117.

reach the extremity of death-camp conditions. Yet often enough, women's lives contain major stress and the motive of survival or fear for basic security.

Grayness has multiple sources. One is the presence of a mixture of evil and innocence. Victims of oppression undergo suffering that they did nothing to deserve. They are in that sense innocent. Yet services they perform with some degree of voluntariness implicate them in perpetrating evil on others who also did not deserve to suffer it and who may not be similarly implicated themselves. The involvements of those who live in gray areas are not of the same order or extensiveness as the involvements of perpetrators who are not victims. Gray agents lack the same discretion and power to walk away. One would probably not readily describe as "murderers" prisoners who did not kill with their own hands. At the same time, it can be difficult to draw the kind of line that "kill with their own hands" suggests. Agents in gray areas are both innocent and not innocent—in other words, "gray."

Grayness here suggests unclarity regarding the degree of an agent's responsibility. We may not know how to assess the power of the threats facing the agent or the agent's powers of endurance. Or the agent may have to make difficult, irreversible decisions quickly and in the absence of relevant information. There may be a combination of such factors. They make it unclear to observers and to the choosers themselves what was avoidable and at what cost.

Another source of grayness is ambiguity in the agent's motivation. Levi calls gray persons ambiguous and "ready to compromise." He describes the moral status of prisoners in the gray zone as somewhere between the status of victims and that of custodians. Readiness to compromise also suggests ambiguity in the positions themselves. To function effectively, auxiliary functionaries must have some power and some discretion regarding its use. This discretion presents the seductive thought that one may be able to use such a position for sabotage. Some did. Of those involved in secret defense organizations, such as Eugen Kogon in Buchenwald and Herman Langbein in Auschwitz, Levi says that they were only apparently collaborators but that in reality they were camouflaged opponents (1989, 45–46). Even as opponents of the Nazis, however, they had to risk the infliction on others of undeserved suffering or death to further their resistance efforts. It can be argued that those risks were in the interests of even the victims (who would almost certainly have been murdered anyway), as some of our interests outlive us. Yet even such activity carries the moral risks of dirty hands.

The ambiguity in gray-zone agents' motivations is sometimes matched by the difficulty of ascertaining what is the right thing (or range of things) to do. Where evil threatens not only oneself but others and there is some chance that one can alleviate dangers for others, whereas if one fails, one may expose them to even greater evils than they already face, it can be far from clear whether to take the risk. Grayness here stems from unclarity about what would be right or wrong to do. This unclarity may lead us to question whether "right" and "wrong" give us an adequate moral vocabulary to describe the choices the agent faces. Gray-zone choices defy ordinary moral judgment.

Thus, "gray" can mean many things. Sometimes it evokes a complex judgment whose elements are mixed, although individually clear enough. It may be impossible to do justice to the case with an overall summary such as "good on the whole" or "bad on the whole." At other times, "gray" evokes a deed whose moral elements are genuinely unclear or ambiguous.

"Gray" may seem basically an epistemological concept in that it refers to what is unclear or ambiguous (to the agent, to an observer, to both)— whether it be motive, rightness or wrongness, or degree of responsibility. Renate Siebert, a sociology professor at the University of Calabria (Italy), writes, in her book on women and the Mafia, that "the thoughts, fears, desires and dreams of women who live in mafia families are still a grey area for the rest of us," apparently because we do not know enough about them (Siebert 1996, 147).

And yet the unclarity of gray zones can give rise to questions about the ontological status of the choices in question. Are there really always right and wrong choices in such situations (where voluntariness is not the issue)? Are there always responsible or excusable choices (where rightness or wrongness is not the issue)? Is there always such a thing as the agent's real motive? Does our moral vocabulary fail to mark distinctions that we should want to make, to capture the ways things really are? Would gray zones cease to be gray if we had more fine-tuned moral concepts? Or are gray zones ineliminable?

One thing is clear. People who have lived in gray zones have often not abandoned the categories of morality in judging themselves and one another, nor ceased responding in moral ways emotionally, nor ceased entering relationships of trust and holding one another responsible.[7] Skeptics may find them confused, perhaps emotionally akratic, in failing to recognize limits within which moral concepts apply. I prefer to respect the perceptions of agents in gray areas and hope to learn from them.

Women and Morally Gray Choices

Women have lived in many gray areas, including those of slavery, death camps, and ghettos. Although many gray areas are not produced by misogyny alone, misogyny is often an element that complicates women's choices, presenting special possibilities and temptations. In situations less extreme

---

[7] See, for example, Wiesenthal 1998 for an example of a prisoner struggling with a series of moral questions.

than Levi's gray zones, women's choices have often shared some of the features that tend to make choices morally gray.

La Malinche, or Malintzin (also known as Doña Martina), an Aztec noblewoman, is an ambiguous figure in the history of the conquest of Mexico (Alarcón 1981). She appears to me to have faced morally gray choices when she was presented to Hernan Cortés upon his landing in Veracruz in 1519 to serve as his lover, translator, and tactical adviser. Refusal might have cost her life and perhaps the lives of others, although records left by Cortes's biographer and by one of his soldiers suggest that she served willingly and with pride (De Gomara 1964, 56–57; del Castillo 1996). (Should we trust them? Critics said the same of Patricia Hearst.) Did Doña Martina prevent Cortés from doing worse damage than he did? Did she significantly facilitate the Spanish conquest? Did she do both? How much did she know? What had she seen?

And what of Sacajawea (also known as Sacagawea), who traveled with and translated for the explorers Meriwether Lewis and William Clark from 1804 to 1806? Lewis and Clark were not Cortés; their mission was exploration, not conquest. But Sacajawea, like Doña Martina, was a slave. She was enrolled as one of his "wives" by a French Canadian, Toussaint Charbonneau, who also traveled as a translator on the expedition. He had won her in a bet with, or purchased her from, the Hidatsa raiding party, who had stolen her from the Shoshone, or Snake, people four years previously when she was ten or eleven years old (Ambrose 1996, 187). We know relatively little about her contributions to the Lewis and Clark expedition. Her role, it appears, was to translate from the Shoshone so Lewis and Clark could purchase horses from them. Historians find it an exaggeration to call her a guide (Clark and Edmonds 1979). But Lewis's journal documents that she rescued important materials from a capsized boat. Considering how the "Lewis and Clark" explorations were subsequently used by white people, how white people had already treated Native peoples, and what the effects were on Native peoples of this "opening of the American West," as historian Stephen Ambrose calls it, Sacajawea's agency is morally unclear.

Sacajawea birthed a son shortly before the expedition and carried him on her back for the journey. Escape would probably have risked his life. She may not have wished to escape, as she wanted to see her people, the Shoshone, which the expedition enabled her to do. On the other hand, she left Charbonneau later in life because he beat her cruelly. What did she know of European-Native interactions when she was fifteen? What could she have foreseen? Could she do anything for Native peoples? Could she engage in sabotage? Had she any interest in doing so? We have primarily in her case not only the testimony of white men but also the researches in 1924 of Charles Eastman, who was a Sioux Indian. Interviewing people who had known her, he researched her life and death at the request of the commissioner of Indian affairs. Yet much about her life remains unclear. White children in the United States, who learn that she was brave and resourceful (but not that she was a slave), idolize Sacajawea. The Girl Scout camp of my Wisconsin childhood was Camp Sacajawea. But she must be an ambiguous figure from the points of view of Native American interests, as she is for feminists.

Less ambiguous, perhaps not enough to count as gray, were choices faced by slaveowners' wives in the United States who held responsibility for managing house slaves, especially wives who did not resist the system of slavery (as some did, covertly).[8] Yet their positions share features with gray areas. Like kapos, they had discretion regarding the use of their authority, and there was, effectively, no upper limit to the cruelty they could inflict with impunity. Wives who used their power to get revenge on attractive female houseslaves could be plainly guilty of evil; such choices are not gray. Yet some wives' functions were analogous to those of overseer slaves. Both might count as what Levi calls external auxiliary functionaries, although slave overseers were more external and under greater and more obvious stress than white women, who were not vulnerable to being sold away. Wives did not generally live under a death threat, although they were vulnerable to marital rape and domestic battery. If marriage was not totally involuntary, the alternatives could be grim. Marriage saved upper- and middle-class white women from the social death of spinsterhood and the outcast status of prostitution or (other) poverty, with their attendant evils of disease and early death. Such a set of options is itself an evil. But that way of escaping their worst alternatives implicated white women in running the institution of slavery, which inflicted more-atrocious evils on the enslaved. If white women refused to marry slaveowners, perhaps slavery would not have become so well established and lasted so long in the Americas, in much the same way, as some have been tempted to argue, that the Nazi killing machine might have operated less efficiently had Sonderkommando and other prisoners generally and immediately refused their assignments. According to Miklos Nyiszli (1993), a Jewish prisoner doctor who survived, one Sonderkommando at Auschwitz did just that (they were shot immediately).

It can legitimately be objected that such a comparison is unfair, even outrageous, and perhaps also, for some similar reasons, is even comparing kapos with Sonderkommando prisoners. These comparisons ignore real and important differences in the level of control that gray-zone agents have over the consequences of their choices. Most Sonderkommando prisoners faced certain death, whatever they chose; they had so little to lose by

---

[8] On Southern white women's collaboration with black women in resistance to slavery, see Adrienne Rich 1979, 275–310. See also Koger 1995, on prosperous mulattoes and African Americans of lighter skin who not only bought family members and other slaves for humanitarian reasons but also acquired slaves for labor, primarily because they had little access to other sources of labor and also to elevate themselves above the masses. Meltzer (1993) also writes of slaves in ancient Rome who were themselves owners of yet other slaves.

resisting that their not doing so seems more an indication of the power of terror and the frailty of human nature than any reflection of their character. Filip Muller (1979), interviewed in Claude Lanzmann's film *Shoah*, gives a detailed account of what it was like to serve on the Sonderkommando in his testimony *Eyewitness Auschwitz: Three Years in the Gas Chambers*. He is the only prisoner to my knowledge to have survived that experience at Auschwitz. But the position of Sonderkommando prisoners generally was not one of responsibility and administration. The vast majority had no significant discretion or decision-making power.

In contrast, kapos had some discretion. And the wives of white slave-owners (like administrators who have served other oppressors) have often had considerable discretionary power. Incrementally and over time, they were sometimes able to raise the stakes so that although they had little to lose at first, later on they had a great deal to lose by ceasing to cooperate (and much to gain by continuing).[9] Such a pattern does raise questions about character deterioration, and it suggests greater complicity.

What are we to make of Gumbu Smart (who lived from 1750 to 1820), an African slave on Bunce Island (a slave trading center off the coast of Africa)? He rebelled against his own masters and then became involved in the slave trade. He had been sent out by white slavers to purchase slaves, "and because he realized what he was doing, he bought a lot of his countrymen ... and he kept them and built up a formidable force.... Instead of enslaving them, [he] settled them in the village of Rokon," where, "leaning on their gratitude," he formed them into his personal following and rebelled against his own white masters. He then cut off trade coming down the Rokel River and began to charge fees to other traders who wanted to pass upriver to buy people. Edward Ball, who recounts this story in his book *Slaves in the Family* (1998, 422–23), goes on to ask Gumbu Smart's African American descendant (whom he is interviewing) whether this doesn't mean that Gumbu Smart was a victim who became a tyrant, a slave trader. Peter, the descendant, admits that Gumbu Smart was a "middleman" but resists judging him negatively, and Edward Ball sums it up by saying that "Peter knew the gray areas of behavior, and although he was no apologist for the slave business, he understood why his family sold people to America." But Peter himself was more affirmative: "Our family feels just a bit lucky. I'm proud when I see his name, and I have no reason not to be proud of it" (Ball 1998, 423).

Confronted with morally gray choices, one may be tempted to reason, "If I can stay alive, there is a chance I can help, but I can't be any good to anyone dead." Similarly, one may reason, "If I can get some power, I may be able to help, but I can't do any good as long as I acquiesce in my own

---

[9] I owe this observation to my colleague Paula Gottlieb, who commented on an early draft of this essay.

impotence." Yet it is sometimes not true, as some of these cases show, that as long as one is alive, there is any real chance that one can help, or that as long as one has more power, one is in a better position to help. For one may have little or no control over how one's life or one's power is used. Being no good to anyone is not the worst thing. Being an instrument of evil is worse.

Women's gray choices do not always implicate us specifically in the evils of misogyny. Sometimes they implicate us in racism, child abuse, or the torture of animals, wronging those who are already wronged and especially vulnerable. Yet ethically, the differences between the oppression gray agents suffer and that in which they become implicated matter less than the similarities. If slaves were seldom in a position to see white women as victims of misogyny and to expect or hope for sympathy or identification, some white women appreciated that they and slaves had common oppressors. Levi did not treat political distinctions in the sources of evil as important in his reflections on the gray zone. He wrote not only about victims of anti-Semitism but about the male camp prisoners of his experience generally.

Yet if gray choices are understood so widely that they comprehend the choices of all agents who are both victims and perpetrators of evil, they will be too wide. They will include the choices of those who survive to take revenge, for example, by doing to former torturers what was done to themselves, even though the retaliators are no longer in danger of suffering torture. This was allegedly the case with former prisoners of Nazi camps who were hired in 1945 by Russians to staff camps for German inmates who were accused or suspected of having been Nazis or of having served Nazis (Sack 1995). It would also include those who wrong others when doing so saves them from no wrong at the hands of still others and when the wrongs they perpetrate bear no particular relation to the wrongs they suffer. And it will include those who wrong others in order to gain benefits or advance their own positions, where what they gain bears no comparison with what those they victimized lost or suffered. Such was the case, for example, with the thousands of white Protestant women in the United States who joined the Ku Klux Klan in the 1920s not only to promote racist, intolerant, and xenophobic policies, but also to have a social setting in which to enjoy friendship and solidarity among like-minded women and even to safeguard white women's suffrage and expand white women's other legal rights. Interviewed in the 1980s by sociologist Kathleen Blee, an elderly white woman from rural northern Indiana "showed little remorse" but "remembered—with pride, not regret ... the social and cultural life of the Klan, the Klan as 'a way to get together and enjoy'" (Blee 1991, 1).

Such behavior is evil, not gray. It is not ambiguous. It is not even morally difficult or complex. That a person's life as a whole evokes in us a mixed emotional response—sympathy insofar as they are wrongly victimized by others but also anger insofar as they wrong others—does not imply that any of their choices possessed the moral complexity or ambiguity of a gray zone. Probably most people's lives taken as a whole would evoke mixed emotional responses. If gray zones are understood that broadly, they threaten to encompass the entire world.

There are also other choices that are in some sense gray, although not in Levi's sense. Choices may be morally unclear or ambiguous, even though their victims were not already targets of oppression. Francine Hughes of the (in)famous "burning bed" killed her batterer while he slept. Her deed may be morally unclear: was it justifiable self-defense, or not? But this unclarity does not give us a gray zone in which the agent victimizes someone who, like herself, is already a victim or already a target of oppression.

Like Levi, I understand gray zones more specifically to result from choices neither gratuitously nor willfully evil that nevertheless implicate choosers who are themselves victims in perpetrating evils against others who are already also victims, paradigmatically victims of the same evils as the choosers. Like Levi, I also resist the idea that we are all murderers or oppressors, even when we benefit from murder and oppression by others. "I do not know," Levi wrote, "and it does not much interest me to know, whether in my depths there lurks a murderer, but I do know that I was a guiltless victim and that I was not a murderer" (1989, 48). To confuse murderers with their victims, he wrote, is "a moral disease or an aesthetic affectation or a sinister sign of complicity," "service rendered (intentionally or not) to the negators of truth" (1989, 48–49). I agree. Yet moral grayness was not confined to death camps even during the Holocaust. Stella Goldschlag, whose family failed to escape Germany before the war, became a "catcher" for the Gestapo, hunting down hidden Jews in wartime Berlin. She survived the war and was interviewed by Peter Weyden, who wrote a book about her (Weyden 1992).

Conditions less extreme can still produce the ambiguities and complexities of grayness. The evils of everyday misogyny, racism, homophobia, and anti-Semitism are not always imminent or looming in the form of well-defined events. They take shape gradually, over a lifetime or even centuries, and are less readily noticed or identified. They may inflict social rather than biological death, or permanent deformation, disability, or unremitting pain. They may produce self-hatred.

Two decades ago radical feminist philosopher Mary Daly wrote in *Gyn/Ecology: The Metaethics of Radical Feminism* about mothers who bound their daughters' feet and about mothers who participate in their daughters' genital mutilation (Daly 1978, 134–77). These mothers were not under death threats. No spectacular events precipitated their action. Rather, their whole lives prepared them for it. Their own mothers had done the same to them, and likewise their mothers before them. These women acted for the sake of their daughters' marriageability, not to advance their own personal standing. Still, those choices implicated them in the evils of marriage systems that deformed and immobilized women, including themselves.

Like Levi in commenting on many prisoners in the camps, Mary Daly refused to judge mothers who did these things. She called them "token torturers," a term that is deeply troubling if applied to all of women's choices to participate in atrocities. Her analysis could have benefited from a concept like that of the gray zone for distinguishing foot-binding mothers from such women as Irma Griese, Ilse Koch, and other Nazi women in the death camps, notorious for their sadism, whose choices appear no grayer than those of the Indiana women of the Klan.

Mary Daly and Primo Levi reflected on others' past choices. One's position as a potential evaluator changes as one thinks more in a forward-looking and first-person mode (rather than in an observer mode), as one who might find oneself confronting morally gray choices. In the forward-looking, first-person mode, refusal to judge is apt to seem too quick an abdication of responsibility. Feminists have long struggled with the question of how ethically responsible agency is possible under oppression, given that oppressive practices tend to be coercive. Perhaps outsiders are seldom in a position to judge the character of gray-zone agents. But victims may be in a position to hold other victims responsible for their choices. If bonding and trust are still possible among the targets of oppression, so, it would seem, are obligation and responsibility. We may need more distinctions to capture what such obligations require and what such responsibility implies.

Acknowledgments

I am grateful to Paula Gottlieb, David Weberman, Wendy Lee-Lampshire, contributors to my edited volume *On Feminist Ethics and Politics* (Lawrence: University Press of Kansas, 1999), and to audiences at the International Association of Women Philosophers Convention in Boston (August 8, 1998), the Feminist Ethics Revisited conference in Tampa (October 1–3, 1999), the Philosophy Institute of the Goethe University in Frankfurt, the University of Wisconsin, Bryn Mawr College, Dalhousie University, Florida Atlantic University, the University of Georgia, and the American Philosophical Association Central Division 2000 for comments on earlier drafts, and to Lorna Smith Benjamin for helpful references regarding the Stockholm Syndrome. I bear responsibility, however, for the views expressed herein.

References

Alarcon, Norma. (1981). "Chicana's Feminist Literature: A Re-Vision Through Malintzin / Or Malintzin: Putting Flesh Back on the Object." In *This Bridge Called My Back: Writings by Radical Women of Color*, edited by Cherríe Moraga and Gloria Anzaldúa, 182–90. Watertown, Mass.: Persephone.

Ambrose, Stephen E. (1996). *Undaunted Courage: Meriwether Lewis, Thomas Jefferson, and the Opening of the American West*. New York: Simon and Schuster.

Ball, Edward. (1998). *Slaves in the Family*. New York: Farrar, Straus and Giroux.

Barry, Kathleen. (1979). *Female Sexual Slavery*. Englewood Cliffs, N.J.: Prentice-Hall.

Blee, Kathleen M. (1991). *Women of the Klan: Racism and Gender in the 1920s*. Berkeley and Los Angeles: University of California Press.

Card, Claudia. (1996). *The Unnatural Lottery: Character and Moral Luck*. Philadelphia: Temple University Press.

Clark, Ella E., and Margot Edmonds. (1979). *Sacagawea of the Lewis and Clark Expedition*. Berkeley and Los Angeles: University of California Press.

Daly, Mary. (1978). *Gyn/Ecology: The Metaethics of Radical Feminism*. Boston: Beacon.

De Gomara, Francisco Lopez. (1964). *Cortés: The Life of the Conqueror by His Secretary*. Trans. Lesley Byrd Simpson. Berkeley and Los Angeles: University of California Press.

del Castillo, Bernal Diaz. (1996). *The Discovery and Conquest of Mexico*. Trans. A. P. Maudslay. New York: Da Capo.

Du Bois, W. E. B. (1969). *The Souls of Black Folk*. New York: New American Library.

Dworkin, Andrea. (1997). *Life and Death*. New York: Free Press.

Frye, Marilyn. (1983). "In and Out of Harm's Way: On Arrogance and Love." In *The Politics of Reality: Essays in Feminist Theory*, 52–83. New York: Crossing.

Goddard, Christopher R., and Janet R. Stanley. (1994). "Viewing the Abusive Parent and the Abused Child as Captor and Hostage." *Journal of Interpersonal Violence*, 9:2, 258–69.

Griffin, Susan. (1977). "Rape: The All-American Crime." In *Feminism and Philosophy*, edited by Mary Vetterling Braggin, Jane English, and Frederick A. Elliston, 313–32. Totowa, N.J.: Littlefield, Adams.

Hearst, Patricia Campbell, with Alvin Moscow. (1988). *Patty Hearst: Her Own Story*. New York: Avon. Originally published as *Every Secret Thing*, 1982.

Hilberg, Raul. (1985). *The Destruction of the European Jews*. Rev. ed. New York: Holmes and Meier.

Kekes, John. (1990). *Facing Evil*. Princeton, N.J.: Princeton University Press.

Koger, Larry. (1995). *Black Slaveowners: Free Black Slave Masters in South Carolina, 1790–1860*. Columbia: University of South Carolina Press.

Koonz, Claudia. (1987). *Mothers in the Fatherland: Women, the Family, and Nazi Politics*. New York: St. Martin's.

Kuleshnyk, Irka. (1984). "The Stockholm Syndrome: Toward an Understanding." *Social Action and the Law*, 10:2, 37–42.

Levi, Primo. (1989). *The Drowned and the Saved*. New York: Vintage.

Meltzer, Milton. (1993). *Slavery: A World History*. New York: Da Capo.

Morris, Herbert. (1976). "Lost Innocence." In *On Guilt and Innocence: Essays in Legal Philosophy and Moral Psychology*, 139–61. Berkeley and Los Angeles: University of California Press.

Muller, Filip. (1979). *Eyewitness Auschwitz: Three Years in the Gas Chambers*. Literary collaboration by Helmut Freitag. Ed. and trans. Susanne Flatauer. New York: Stein and Day.

Nietzsche, Friedrich. (1998). *On the Genealogy of Morality*. Trans. Maudemarie Clark and Alan J. Swensen. Indianapolis, Ind.: Hackett.

Nyiszli, Miklos. (1993). *Auschwitz: A Doctor's Eyewitness Account*. Trans. Tibere Kreme and Richard Seaver. New York: Arcade.

Painter, Susan Lee, and Don Dutton. (1985). "Patterns of Emotional Bonding in Battered Women: Traumatic Bonding." *International Journal of Women's Studies*, 8:4, 363–74.

Pearson, Patricia. (1997). *When She Was Bad: Violent Women and the Myth of Innocence*. New York: Viking.

Perechodnik, Calel. (1996). *Am I a Murderer?* Boulder, Colo.: Westview.

Peterson, Susan Rae. (1977). "Coercion and Rape: The State as a Male Protection Racket." In *Feminism and Philosophy*, edited by Mary Vetterling Braggin, Jane English, and Frederick A. Elliston, 360–71. Totowa, N.J.: Littlefield, Adams.

Rich, Adrienne. (1979). "Disloyal to Civilization: Feminism, Racism, Gynephobia." In *On Lies, Secrets, and Silence*, 275–310. New York: Norton.

Sack, John. (1995). *An Eye for an Eye*. New York: Basic Books.

Siebert, Renate. (1996). *Secrets of Life and Death: Women and the Mafia*. Trans. Liz Heron. New York: Verso.

Spelman, Elizabeth V. (1997). *Fruits of Sorrow: Framing Our Attention to Suffering*. Boston: Beacon.

Stocker, Michael. (1990). *Plural and Conflicting Values*. New York: Oxford University Press.

Strentz, Thomas. (1982). "The Stockholm Syndrome: Law Enforcement Policy and Hostage Behavior." In *Victims of Terrorism*, edited by Frank M. Ochberg and David A. Soskis, 149–61. Boulder, Colo.: Westview.

Trebilcot, Joyce. (1990). "Dyke Methods." In *Lesbian Philosophies and Cultures*, edited by Jeffner Allen. Albany: State University of New York Press.

Trunk, Isaiah. (1996). *Judenrat: The Jewish Councils in Eastern Europe Under Nazi Occupation*. Lincoln: University of Nebraska Press.

Turner, James T. (1996). "Factors Influencing the Development of the Hostage Identification Syndrome." *Political Psychology*, 6:4, 705–11.

West, Louis Jolyon, and Paul R. Martin. (1996). "Pseudo-identity and the Treatment of Personality Change in Victims of Captivity and Cults." *Cultic Studies Journal*, 13:2, 125–52.

Weyden, Peter. (1992). *Stella*. New York: Simon and Schuster.

Wiesenthal, Simon. (1998). "The Sunflower." In *The Sunflower: On the Possibilities and Limits of Forgiveness*, 3–98. With a symposium edited by Harry James Cargas and Bonny V. Fetterman. Rev. and expanded ed. New York: Schocken.

CHAPTER 5

GENOCIDE AND SOCIAL DEATH

CLAUDIA CARD

This essay develops the hypothesis that social death is utterly central to the evil of genocide, not just when a genocide is primarily cultural but even when it is homicidal on a massive scale. It is social death that enables us to distinguish the peculiar evil of genocide from the evils of other mass murders. Even genocidal murders can be viewed as extreme means to the primary end of social death. Social vitality exists through relationships, contemporary and intergenerational, that create an identity that gives meaning to a life. Major loss of social vitality is a loss of identity and consequently a serious loss of meaning for one's existence. Putting social death at the center takes the focus off individual choice, individual goals, individual careers, and body counts, and puts it on relationships that create community and set the context that gives meaning to choices and goals. If my hypothesis is correct, the term "cultural genocide" is probably both redundant and misleading—redundant, if the social death present in all genocide implies cultural death as well, and misleading, if "cultural genocide" suggests that some genocides do not include cultural death.

1. What Is Feminist About Analyzing Genocide?

The question has been asked, What is feminist about this project?[1] Why might one publish it in a book of feminist philosophy? The answer is both

---

[1] This question was raised by anonymous reviewers of an earlier draft of this essay.

Criticism and Compassion: The Ethics and Politics of Claudia Card.
Edited by Robin S. Dillon and Armen T. Marsoobian.
Chapters and book compilation © 2018 Metaphilosophy LLC and John Wiley & Sons Ltd.

simple and complex. Simply, it is the history behind the project and the perspective from which it is carried out, rather than a focus on women or gender, that make the project feminist. Some of the complexities are as follows.

The evil of genocide falls not only on men and boys but also on women and girls, typically unarmed, untrained in defense against violence, and often also responsible for care of the wounded, the sick, the disabled, babies, children, and the elderly. Because genocide targets both sexes, rather than being specific to women's experience, there is some risk of its being neglected in feminist thought. It is also the case that with few exceptions (such as, Schott 1999; Card 1996 and 1997), both feminist and nonfeminist philosophical reflections on war and other public violence have tended to neglect the impact on victims. Philosophers have thought mostly about the positions of perpetrators and decision-makers (most of them men), with some feminist speculation on what might change if more women were among the decision-makers and if women were subject to military conscription. The damage of war and terrorism is commonly assessed in terms of its ruin of individual careers, body counts, statistics on casualties, and material costs of rebuilding. Attention goes to preventing such violence and the importance of doing so, but less to the experience and responses of the majority of victims and survivors, who are civilians, not soldiers. In bringing to the fore the responses of victims of both sexes, holocaust literature stands in sharp contrast to these trends. Central to holocaust literature is reflection on the meaning of genocide.

Women's Studies, in its engagement with differences among women, has moved from its earlier aim to train a feminist eye on the world and all kinds of issues (such as evil) to the more limited aim of studying women and gender. I return here to the earlier conception that recognizes not only the study of women, feminism, or gender, but also feminist approaches to issues of ethics and social theory generally, whether the word "feminist" is used or not. My interests move toward commonalities in our experiences of evil, not only commonalities among women differently situated but commonalities shared with many men as well. Yet my lens is feminist, polished through decades of reflection on women's multifarious experiences of misogyny and oppression. What we notice, through a feminist lens, is influenced by long habits of attending to emotional response, relationships that define who we (not just women and girls) are, and the significance of the concrete particular.

Centering social death accommodates the position, controversial among genocide scholars, that genocidal acts are not always or necessarily homicidal. Forcibly sterilizing women or men of a targeted group, or forcibly separating their children from them for reeducation for assimilation into another group, can also be genocidal in aim or effect.[2] Such policies can be aimed at or achieve the eventual destruction of the social identity of those so treated. It may appear that transported children simply undergo change in social identity, not that they lose all social vitality. That may be the intent. Yet, parents' social vitality is a casualty of children's forced reeducation, and in reality transported children may fail to make a satisfying transition.

The Holocaust was not only a program of mass murder but also an assault on Jewish social vitality. The assault was experienced by hidden children who survived as well as by those who died. Hitler's sterilization program and Nuremberg laws that left German Jews stateless were parts of the genocide, not preludes to it. Jews who had converted to Christianity (or whose parents or grandparents had done so) were hunted down and murdered, even though one might think their social identities had already changed.[3] This pursuit makes a certain perverted sense if the idea was to extinguish in them all possibility of social vitality, simply on grounds of their ancestral roots. Mass murder is the most extreme method of genocide, denying members of targeted groups any degree or form of social vitality whatever. To extinguish all possibility of social vitality, child transportation and re-education are insufficient; it may be necessary to commit mass murder or drive victims mad or rob them of self-respect, all of which were done to Holocaust victims.

Although I approach genocide from a history of feminist habits of research and reflection, I say little here about the impact of genocide on women and girls as opposed to its impact on men and boys. I would not suggest that females suffered more or worse than males. Nor am I especially interested in such questions as whether lifelong habits of caregiving offer survival advantages to segregated women. (Evidence appears to be that no one survives without others' care and help.) My interest here is, rather, in what makes genocide the specific evil that it is, what distinguishes it from other atrocities, and what kinds of atrocities are rightly recognized as genocidal. Feminist habits of noticing are useful for suggesting answers to these questions.

---

[2] Unlike Native American families whose children were forcibly transported for re-education in the United States, many Jewish families during the Holocaust sought to hide their children in gentile households. Loss of Jewish social vitality to the children was hardly the responsibility of their families' decisions to do this but rather of those whose oppressive measures drove families to try to save their children in this way.

[3] An example well known to philosophers is Edith Stein, student of and later assistant to Edmund Husserl. Her doctoral dissertation on the topic of empathy was originally published in 1917 (Stein 1964). She became a Catholic nun but was nevertheless deported to Auschwitz from her convent in the Netherlands.

2. Genocide, War, and Justice

Genocide need not be part of a larger war, although it commonly is. But it can be regarded as itself a kind of one-sided war. Precedents for regarding one-sided attacks as wars are found in the idea of a "war on drugs" and in the title of Lucy Dawidowicz's *The War Against the Jews* (1975). If genocide is war, it is a profoundly unjust kind of war, perniciously unjust, an injustice that is also an evil.

John Rawls opened his first book on justice with the observation that justice is the first virtue of institutions as truth is of systems of thought. No matter how efficient and well arranged, he wrote, laws and institutions must be reformed or abolished if they are unjust (1999, 3). Like critics who found these claims overstated, even Rawls noted that although "these propositions seem to express our intuitive conviction of the primacy of justice," "no doubt they are expressed too strongly" (4). Not all injustices, even in society's basic structure, make lives insupportable, intolerable, or indecent. Reforms are not always worth the expense of their implementation. Had Rawls made his claim about abolishing unjust institutions in regard to *pernicious* injustices, however, it would not have been controversial: laws and institutions must be abolished when they are evils.

Not all injustices are evils, as the harms they produce vary greatly in importance. Some injustices are relatively tolerable. They may not impact people's lives in a deep or lasting way, even though they are wrong and should be eliminated—unjust salary discriminations, for example, when the salaries in question are all high. An injustice becomes an evil when it inflicts harms that make victims' lives unbearable, indecent, or impossible, or that make victims' deaths indecent.[4] Injustices of war are apt to fall into this category. Certainly genocide does.

3. The Concept of Genocide

"Genocide" combines the Greek *genos* for race or tribe with the Latin *cide* for killing. The term was coined by Raphael Lemkin (1944), an attorney and refugee scholar from Poland who served in the United States War Department. He campaigned as early as the 1930s for an international convention to outlaw genocide, and his persistence resulted in the United Nations Genocide Convention of 1948. Although this convention is widely cited, it was not translated into action in international courts until the 1990s, more than forty years later. The first state to bring a case to the World

---

[4] For elaboration, see Card 2002, which includes chapters on war rape and on terrorism in the home. There is not a chapter on genocide, although genocide figures throughout as paradigmatic of atrocities.

Court under the convention was Bosnia-Herzegovina in 1993. It was not until 1998 that the first verdict interpreting that convention was rendered, when the Rwanda tribunal found Jean-Paul Akayesu guilty on nine counts for his participation in the genocide in Rwanda in 1994 (Orentlicher 1999, 153). The United States did not pass legislation implementing ratification of the 1948 genocide convention until 1988 and then only with significant reservations that were somewhat disabling (Lang 1992, 1:400). Such resistance is interesting in view of questions raised during the interim regarding the morality of U.S. conduct in Vietnam. By the time the United States ratified the convention, ninety-seven other U.N. members had already done so.

The *term* "genocide" is thus relatively new, and the Holocaust is widely agreed to be its paradigmatic instance. Yet Lemkin and many others find the *practice* of genocide ancient. In their sociological survey from ancient times to the present, Frank Chalk and Kurt Jonassohn (1990) discuss instances of apparent genocide that range from the Athenians' annihilation of the people of the island of Melos in the fifth century B.C.E. (recorded by Thucydides) and the ravaging of Carthage by Romans in 146 B.C.E. (also listed by Lemkin, as the first of his historical examples of wars of extermination) through mass killings in Bangladesh, Cambodia, and East Timor in the second half of the twentieth century (Chalk and Jonassohn 1990). Controversies are ongoing over whether to count as genocidal the annihilation of indigenous peoples in the Americas and Australia (who succumbed in vast numbers to diseases brought by Europeans), Stalin's induced mass starvation of the 1930s (ostensibly an economically motivated measure), and the war conducted by the United States in Vietnam.

The literature of comparative genocide that historian Peter Novick (1999) calls "comparative atrocitology" so far includes relatively little published work by philosophers. Here is what I have found. Best known is probably Jean-Paul Sartre's 1967 essay, "On Genocide" (Sartre 1968), written for the Sartre-Russell International War Crimes Tribunal, which was convened to consider war crimes by the United States in Vietnam. In 1974 Hugo Adam Bedau published a long and thoughtful essay "Genocide in Vietnam?" (Bedau 1974, 5–46), responding to Sartre and others who have raised the question of whether the United States was guilty of perpetrating genocide in Vietnam. Bedau argues for a negative answer to that question, relying primarily on intent as an essential factor in genocide. His view is that the intent of the United States in Vietnam was not to exterminate a people, even if that was nearly a consequence. Berel Lang's essay "The Concept of Genocide" (1984/85) and the first chapter of Lang's book *Act and Idea in the Nazi Genocide* (1990) are helpful in their explorations of the meanings and roles of intent in defining "genocide."

Other significant philosophical works include Alan S. Rosenbaum's anthology *Is the Holocaust Unique? Perspectives on Comparative Genocide* (1996), which discusses the Nazi assault on Jews and Romani during

World War 11, the Atlantic slave trade, the Turkish slaughter of Armenians in 1915, and Stalin's induced famine. Legal scholar Martha Minow (1998) reflects philosophically on measures lying between vengeance and forgiveness taken by states in response to genocide and mass murder. Jonathan Glover's *Humanity: A Moral History of the Twentieth Century* (2000), in some ways the most ambitious recent philosophical discussion of evils, includes reflections on Rwanda, Stalin, and Nazism. The Institute for Genocide Studies and the Association of Genocide Scholars (which holds conventions) attract an interdisciplinary group of scholars, including a small number of philosophers. And the Society for the Philosophic Study of Genocide and the Holocaust sponsors sessions at conventions of the American Philosophical Association.

On the whole, historians, psychologists, sociologists, and political scientists have contributed more than philosophers to genocide scholarship. Naturally, their contributions as social scientists have been empirically oriented, focused on such matters as origins, contributing causes, effects, monitoring, and prevention. Yet, philosophical issues run throughout the literature. They include foundational matters, such as the meaning of "genocide," which appears to be a highly contested concept, and such issues of ethics and political philosophy as whether perpetrators can be punished in a meaningful way that respects moral standards. If adequate retribution is morally impossible, and if deterrence is unlikely for those who are ideologically motivated, then what is the point in punishing perpetrators? If there is nevertheless some point sufficient to justify doing so, then who should be punished, by whom, and how?

Controversies over the meaning of "genocide" lead naturally to the closely related question of whether genocide is ethically different from nongenocidal mass murder. The practical issue here is whether, and if so why, it is important to add the category of genocide to existing crimes against humanity and war crimes. Crimes against humanity were important additions to war crimes in that, unlike war crimes, they need not be perpetrated during wartime or in connection with a war, and they can be inflicted by a country against its own citizens. But given that murder of civilians by soldiers is already a war crime and a human rights violation, one may wonder whether the crime of genocide captures anything they omit.

If the social death of individual victims is central to genocide, then, arguably, genocide does capture something more. What distinguishes genocide is not that it has a different kind of victim, namely, groups (although it is a convenient shorthand to speak of targeting groups). Rather, the kind of harm suffered by individual victims of genocide, in virtue of their group membership, is not captured by other crimes. To get a sense of what is at stake in the hypothesis that social death is central, let us turn briefly to controversies over the meaning of "genocide."

The definition of "genocide" is currently in such flux that the Association of Genocide Scholars asks members on its information page (printed in a members directory) to specify which definition of "genocide" they use in their work. A widely cited definition (Robinson 1960, 147) is that of the 1948 U.N. Convention on the Prevention and Punishment of the Crime of Genocide:

> Genocide means any of the following acts committed with the intent to destroy, in whole or in part, a nation, ethnical, racial or religious group, as such: (a) killing members of the group; (b) causing serious bodily or mental harm to members of the group; (c) deliberately inflicting on the group conditions of life calculated to bring about its physical destruction in whole or in part; (d) imposing measures intended to prevent births within the group; (e) forcibly transferring children of the group to another group.

Every clause of this definition is controversial.

Israel Charny (1997) and others criticize the U.N. definition for not recognizing political groups, such as the Communist Party, as possible targets of genocide. Political groups had been recognized in an earlier draft of the genocide convention, and Chalk and Jonassohn (1990) do recognize political groups as targets of genocide in their historical survey. Some scholars, however, prefer the term "politicide" for these cases and reserve the term "genocide" for the annihilation of groups into which one is (ordinarily) born—racial, ethnic, national, or religious groups. Yet, one is not necessarily, of course, born into one's current national or religious group, and either one's current or one's former membership can prove fatal. Further, some people's political identity may be as important to their lives as religious identity is to the lives of others. And so, the distinction between "genocide" and "politicide" has seemed arbitrary to many critics. A difficulty is, of course, where to draw the line if political groups are recognized as possible victims. But line drawing is not a difficulty that is peculiar to political groups.

The last three clauses of the U.N. definition—conditions of life intended to destroy the group "in whole or in part," preventing births, and transferring children—count as genocidal many acts that are aimed at cultural destruction, even though they are not homicidal. "Preventing births" is not restricted to sterilization but has been interpreted to include segregation of the sexes and bans on marriage. Social vitality is destroyed when the social relations—organizations, practices, institutions—of the members of a group are irreparably damaged or demolished. Such destruction is a commonly intended consequence of war rape, which has aimed at family breakdown. Although Lemkin regarded such deeds as both ethnocidal and genocidal, some scholars prefer simply to call them ethnocides (or "cultural genocides") and reserve the term "genocide" (unqualified) for events that include mass death. The idea is, apparently, that physical death is more extreme and therefore, presumably, worse than social death. That physical death is worse, or even more extreme, is not obvious, however, but deserves scrutiny, and I will return to it.

Even the clauses of the U.N. definition that specify killing group members or causing them serious bodily or mental harm are vague and can cover a wide range of possible harms. How many people must be killed in order for a deed to be genocidal? What sort of bodily harm counts? (Must there be lasting disablement?) What counts as "mental harm"? (Is post-traumatic stress sufficient?) If the definition is to have practical consequences in the responses of nations to perpetrators, these questions can become important. They become important with respect to questions of intervention and reparations, for example.

Although most scholars agree on including intention in the definition of genocide, there is no consensus regarding the content of the required intention. Must the relevant intention include destruction of all members of a group as an aim or purpose? Would it be enough that the group was knowingly destroyed, as a foreseeable consequence of the pursuit of some other aim? Must the full extent of the destruction even be foreseeable, if the policy of which it is a consequence is already clearly immoral? Bedau (1974) makes much of the content of the relevant intention in his argument that whatever war crimes the United States committed in Vietnam, they were not genocidal, because the intent was not to destroy the people of Vietnam as such, even if that destruction was both likely and foreseeable.

Charny (1997), however, objects to an analogous claim made by some critics who, he reports, held that because Stalin's intent was to obtain enough grain to trade for industrial materials for the Soviet Union, rather than to kill the millions who died from this policy, Stalin's famine was not a genocide. Charny argues that because Stalin foresaw the fatal consequences of his grain policies, those policies should count as genocidal. As in common philosophical criticisms of the "doctrine of the double effect," Charny appears to reject as ethically insignificant a distinction between intending and "merely foreseeing," at least in this kind of case.

The doctrine of double effect has been relied on by the Catholic Church to resolve certain ethical questions regarding issues of life and death (Solomon 1992, 1:268–69). The doctrine maintains that under certain conditions it is not wrong to do something that has a foreseeable effect (not an aim) which is such that an act *aiming* at that effect would have been wrong. The first condition of its not being wrong is that the act one performs is not wrong in itself, and the second condition is that the effect at which it would be wrong to aim is not instrumental toward the end at which the act does aim. Thus, the Church has found it wrong to perform an abortion that would kill a fetus in order to save the mother but, at the same time, not wrong to remove a cancerous uterus when doing so would also result in the death of a fetus. The reasoning is that in the case of the cancerous uterus, the fetus's death is not an aim; nor is it a means to removing the uterus; it is only a consequence of doing so. Many find this distinction troubling and far from obvious. Why is the death of a fetus from abortion not also only a consequence? The aim could be redescribed as "to remove the fetus from the uterus in order to save the mother," rather than "to kill the fetus to save the mother," and at least when the fetus need not be destroyed in the very process of removal, one might argue that death due to extrauterine nonviability is not a means to the fetus's removal, either.

The position of the critics who do not want to count Stalin's starvation of the peasants as genocide would appear to imply that if the peasants' deaths were not instrumental toward Stalin's goal but only an unfortunate consequence, the foreseeability of those deaths does not make Stalin's policy genocidal, any more than the foreseeability of the death of the fetus in the case of a hysterectomy performed to remove a cancerous uterus makes that surgery murderous. Charny's position appears to imply, on the contrary, that the foreseeability of the peasants' mass death is enough to constitute genocidal intent, even if it was not intended instrumentally toward Stalin's aims.

Some controversies focus on whether the intent was "to destroy a group as such." One might argue with Bedau, drawing on Lang's discussion of the intent issues (Lang 1990, 3–29), that the intent is "to destroy a group as such" when it is not just accidental that the group is destroyed in the process of pursuing a further end. Thus, if it was not just accidental that the peasant class was destroyed in the process of Stalin's pursuit of grain to trade for industrial materials, Stalin could be said to have destroyed the peasants "as such," even if peasant starvation played no more causal role in making grain available than killing the fetus plays in removing a cancerous uterus. Alternatively, some argue that the words "as such" do not belong in the definition because, ethically, it does not matter whether a group is deliberately destroyed "as such" or simply deliberately destroyed. Chalk and Jonassohn (1990) appear to take this view.

Further, one might pursue the question of whether it is really necessary even to be able to foresee the full extent of the consequences in order to be accurately described as having a genocidal intent. Historian Steven Katz argues in *The Holocaust in Historical Context* (1994) that the mass deaths of Native Americans and Native Australians were not genocides because they resulted from epidemics, not from murder. The suggestion is that the consequences here were not reasonably foreseeable. David Stannard, American Studies scholar at the University of Hawaii, however finds the case less simple, for it can be argued that the epidemics were not just accidental (Stannard 1992 and 1996). Part of the controversy regards the facts: to what extent were victims deliberately infected, as when the British, and later Americans, distributed blankets infected with the smallpox virus?[5] And to what extent did victims succumb to unintended infection stemming from

[5] See Stiffarm with Lane (1992, 32–33).

ordinary exposure to Europeans with the virus? But, also, part of the controversy is philosophical. If mass deaths from disease result from wrongdoing, and if perpetrators could know that the intolerably destructive consequences had an uncontrollable (and therefore somewhat unpredictable) extent, then does it matter, ethically, whether the wrongdoers could foresee the full extent of the consequences? One might argue that it does not, on the ground that they already knew enough to appreciate that what they were doing was evil.

What is the importance of success in achieving a genocidal aim? Must genocide succeed in eliminating an entire group? An assault, to be homicide, must succeed in killing. Otherwise, it is a mere attempt, and an unlawful attempted homicide generally carries a less severe penalty than a successful one. Bedau and Lang point out, however, that "genocide" does not appear to be analogous to "homicide" in that way. There may still be room for some distinction between genocide and attempted genocide (although Lang appears not to recognize any such distinction) if we distinguish between partially formed and fully formed intentions, or if we distinguish among stages in carrying out a complex intention. But in paradigmatic instances of genocide, such as the Holocaust, there are always some survivors, even when there is clear evidence that the intention was to eliminate everyone in the group. There is general agreement that at least some mass killing with that wrongful intention is genocidal. The existence of survivors is not sufficient to negate fully formed genocidal intent. There may be survivors even after all stages of a complex genocidal intention have been implemented. Bedau observes, however, that there is a certain analogy between "genocide" and "murder" that enables us to contrast both with homicide. Both genocide and murder include wrongfulness in the very concept, whereas a homicide can be justifiable. Homicide is not necessarily unlawful or even immoral. In contrast, genocide and murder are, in principle, incapable of justification.

On my understanding of what constitutes an evil, there are two basic elements: (1) culpable wrongdoing by one or more perpetrators and (2) reasonably foreseeable intolerable harm to victims resulting from that wrongdoing.[6] Most often the second element, intolerable harm, is what distinguishes evils from ordinary wrongs. Intentions may be necessary to defining genocide. But they are not always necessary for culpable wrongdoing, as omissions—negligence, recklessness, or carelessness—can be sufficient. When culpable wrongdoing *is* intentional, however, its aim need not be to cause intolerable harm. A seriously culpable deed is evil when the doer is willing to inflict intolerable harm on others even in the course of aiming at some other goal. If what is at stake in controversies regarding the meaning of "genocide" is whether a mass killing is sufficiently evil to merit the

---

[6] See Card (2002, chap. 2), for development of this conception of an evil.

opprobrium attaching to the term "genocide," a good case can be made for including assaults on many kinds of groups inflicted through many kinds of culpable wrongdoing. Yet that leaves the question of whether the genocidal nature of a killing has special ethical import, and if so, what that import is and how, if at all, it may restrict the scope of "genocide." I turn to these and related questions next.

4. The Specific Evils of Genocide

Genocide is not simply unjust (although it certainly is unjust); it is also evil. It characteristically includes the one-sided killing of defenseless civilians—babies, children, the elderly, the sick, the disabled, and the injured of both genders along with their usually female caretakers—simply on the basis of their national, religious, ethnic, or other political identity. It targets people on the basis of who they are rather than on the basis of what they have done, what they might do, even what they are capable of doing. (One commentator says genocide kills people on the basis of *what* they are, not even *who* they are.)

Genocide is a paradigm of what Israeli philosopher Avishai Margalit calls "indecent" in that it not only destroys victims but also first humiliates them by deliberately inflicting an "utter loss of freedom and control over one's vital interests" (1996, 115). Vital interests can be transgenerational and thus survive one's death. Before death, genocide victims are ordinarily deprived of control over vital transgenerational interests and more immediate vital interests. They may be literally stripped naked, robbed of their last possessions, lied to about the most vital matters, witness to the murder of family, friends, and neighbors, and made to participate in their own murder; if female, they are also likely to be violated sexually.[7] Victims of genocide are commonly killed with no regard for lingering suffering or exposure. They, and their corpses, are routinely treated with utter disrespect. These historical facts, not simply mass murder, account for much of the moral opprobrium attaching to the concept of genocide.

Yet such atrocities, it may be argued, are already war crimes, if conducted during wartime, and they can otherwise or also be prosecuted as crimes against humanity. Why, then, add the specific crime of genocide? What, if anything, is not already captured by laws that prohibit such things as the rape, enslavement, torture, forced deportation, and degradation of individuals? Is any ethically distinct harm done to members of the targeted group that would not have been done had they been targeted simply as individuals rather than because of their group membership? This is the question that I find central in arguing that genocide is not simply reducible to

---

[7] Men are sometimes also violated sexually (usually by other men), although the overwhelming majority of sex crimes in war are perpetrated by men against female victims of all ages and conditions.

mass death, to any of the other war crimes, or to the crimes against humanity just enumerated. I believe the answer is affirmative: the harm is ethically
distinct, although on the question of whether it is worse, I wish only to
question the assumption that it is not.

Specific to genocide is the harm inflicted on its victims' social vitality. It
is not just that one's group membership is the occasion for harms that are
definable independently of one's identity as a member of the group. When a
group with its own cultural identity is destroyed, its survivors lose their cultural heritage and may even lose their intergenerational connections. To use
Orlando Patterson's terminology, in that event, they may become "socially
dead" and their descendants *"natally alienated,"* no longer able to pass
along and build upon the traditions, cultural developments (including languages), and projects of earlier generations (1982, 5–9). The harm of social
death is not necessarily less extreme than that of physical death. Social
death can even aggravate physical death by making it indecent, removing all
respectful and caring ritual, social connections, and social contexts that are
capable of making dying bearable and even of making one's death meaningful. In my view, the special evil of genocide lies in its infliction of not
just physical death (when it does that) but also social death, producing a
consequent meaninglessness of one's life and even of its termination. This
view, however, is controversial.

African American and Jewish philosopher Lawrence Mordekhai
Thomas argues that although American slavery natally alienated slaves—
that slaves were born severed from most normal social and cultural ties that
connect one with both earlier and later generations—the Holocaust did not
natally alienate Jews (1993, 150–57). He does not explicitly generalize about
genocide and natal alienation but makes this judgment in regard to the particular genocide of the Holocaust. Yet, the apparent implication is that a
genocide no more successful than the Holocaust (an accepted paradigm
of genocide) is not natally alienating, because enough victims survive and
enough potential targets escape that they are able to preserve the group's
cultural traditions. Thomas's analyses of patterns of evil in American slavery and the Holocaust are philosophically ground breaking and have been
very helpful to me in thinking about these topics. Yet I want to question
this conclusion that he draws. I want to consider the Nazi genocide in light
of the more fundamental idea of social death, of which natal alienation is
one special case, not the only case.

Thomas's conception of natal alienation is more specific and more
restricted than Patterson's conception of social death. Thomas seems to be
thinking not of lost family connections and lost community connections,
the particular connections of individuals to one another, but rather of the
connections of each individual with a culture in general, with its traditions
and practices. He finds members of an ethnic group natally alienated when
the cultural practices into which they are born "forcibly prevent most of
them from fully participating in, and thus having a secure knowledge of,

their historical-cultural traditions" (1993, 150). He notes that after seven generations of slavery, the memories of one's culture of origin are totally lost, which is certainly plausible. Patterson used the term "natal alienation" for the extreme case of being *born* to *social death*, with individual social connections, past and future, cut off from all but one's oppressors at the very outset of one's life. Hereditary slavery yields a paradigm of natal alienation in this sense. Slaves who are treated as nonpersons have (practically) no socially supported ties, not only to a cultural heritage but even to immediate kin (parents, children, siblings) and peers. As a consequence of being cut off from kin and community, they also lose their cultural heritage. But the first step is to destroy existing social ties with family and community, to "excommunicate them from society," as Patterson puts it (1982, 5). In Rawlsian terms, they are first excluded from the benefits and protections of the basic structure of the society into which they were born and in which they must live out their lives. Loss of cultural heritage follows.

Those who are *natally* alienated are *born* already socially dead. Natal alienation might be a clue to descent from genocide survivors (although not proof, insofar as genocide depends also on intent). Thus, the natal alienation of slaves and their descendants, when slavery is hereditary, is one clue to a possible history of genocide committed against their ancestors.

Thomas recognizes that alienation is not "all or nothing." A lost cultural heritage can be rediscovered, or partially recovered, later or in other places. Those who were alienated from some cultures may become somewhat integrated into others. Still, he denies that the holocaust natally alienated Jews from Judaism, "because the central tenets of Judaism—the defining traditions of Judaism—endured in spite of Hitler's every intention to the contrary" (1993, 153).

The question, however, should be not simply whether the traditions survived but whether individual Jewish victims were able to sustain their connections to those traditions. Sustaining the connections meaningfully requires a family or community setting for observance. Many Jews, of course, escaped being victimized, because of where they lived (in the United States, for example) and because the Axis powers were contained and defeated. They were able to maintain Jewish traditions with which survivors might conceivably connect or reconnect. But many survivors were unable to do so. Some found family members after the war or created new families. Many did not. Many lost entire families, their entire villages, and the way of life embodied in the *shtetl* (eastern European village). Some could not produce more children because of medical experiments performed on them in the camps. Many survivors lost access to social memories embodied in such cultural institutions as libraries and synagogues.

Responding to the observation that entire communities of Jews were destroyed and that the Yiddish language is on the way out, Thomas argues that members of those communities were destroyed not "as such" (as shtetl Jews, for example) but more simply "as Jews," and that the entire community of Jews was not destroyed.[8] He concludes that "the question must be whether the Holocaust was natally alienating of Jews as such, without regard to any specific community of Jews" (1993, 153). In answering negatively, he is apparently thinking of survivors who reestablished a Jewish life after the war, rather than of non-European Jews who were potential victims and whose positions might be regarded as somewhat analogous to those of unhunted and unenslaved Africans at the time of the African slave trade.

Some European Jews survived, however, only by passing as Christians. Some hidden children who were raised by strangers to be Christians only discovered their Jewish heritage later, if at all. If they were full members of the societies in which they survived, Thomas does not consider them natally alienated. Those who pass as members of another religion need not be socially dead, even if they are alienated from their religion of origin. Still, if they were originally connected in a vital way with their inherited religion and if they then experienced no vital connection to the new one, arguably they do suffer a degree of social death. More clearly, those who were made stateless before being murdered were certainly treated, socially, as nonpersons. National Socialist decrees robbed them of social support for ties to family, peers, and community, stripped them of their rights to earn a living, own property, attend public schools, even ride public transportation, and on arrival at the camps they were torn from family members. Although they were not *born* to social death, they were nevertheless intentionally deprived of all social vitality before their physical murder.

For those who survive physically, mere knowledge and memory are insufficient to create social vitality, even if they are necessary. Those who cannot participate in the social forms they remember do not actually have social vitality; they have only the memory of it. Further, from 1933 to 1945 many children were born to a condition that became progressively more *natally* alienating. Contrary to the apparent implication of Thomas's hypothesis regarding the differences between American slavery and the Holocaust, social death seems to me to be a concept central to the harm of genocide, at least as important to what is evil about the Holocaust as the mass physical murder.

Although social vitality is essential to a decent life for both women and men, the sexes have often played different roles in its creation and maintenance. If men are often cast in the role of the creators of (high?) culture, women have played very central roles in preserving and passing on the traditions, language, and (daily) practices from one generation to the next and in maintaining family and community relationships. Where such

---

[8] It is commonly estimated that two-thirds of European Jews died. That leaves not only one-third of European Jews but also Jewish communities in many other parts of the world, such as Israel (to which some European Jews fled), the Far East, Australia, and the Americas.

generalizations hold, the blocking of opportunities for creativity (being excluded from the professions, for example) would fall very heavily on men. But disruptions of family and community, such as being alienated from one's family by rape or being suddenly deported without adequate provisions (or any means of obtaining them) to a strange environment where one does not even know the language, would also fall very heavily, perhaps especially so, on women.

Most immediate victims of genocide are not born socially dead. But genocides that intentionally strip victims, prior to their murders of the ability to participate in social activity do aim at their social death, not just their physical death. In some cases it may appear that social death is not an end in itself but simply a consequence of means taken to make mass murder easier (concentrating victims in ghettos and camps, for example). When assailants are moved by hatred, however, social death may become an end in itself. Humiliation before death appears often to have been an end in itself, not just a means. The very idea of selecting victims by social group identity suggests that it is not just the physical life of victims that is targeted but the social vitality behind that identity as well.

If the aim, or intention, of social death is not accidental to genocide, the survival of Jewish culture does not show that social death was not central to the evil of the Holocaust, any more than the fact of survivors shows that a mass murder was not genocidal. A genocide as successful as the Holocaust achieves the aim of social death both for victims who do not survive and, to a degree and for a time, for many survivors as well. Thomas's point may still hold that descendants of survivors of the African diaspora produced by the slave trade are in general more alienated from their African cultures of origin than Holocaust survivors are from Judaism today. Yet it is true in both cases that survivors make substantial connection with other cultures. If African Americans are totally alienated from their African cultures of origin, it is also true that many Holocaust survivors and their descendants have found it impossible to embrace Judaism or even a Jewish culture after Auschwitz. The survival of a culture does not by itself tell us about the degree of alienation that is experienced by individual survivors. Knowledge of a heritage is not by itself sufficient to produce vital connections to it.

The harm of social death is not, so far as I can see, adequately captured by war crimes and other crimes against humanity. Many of those crimes are defined by what can be done to individuals considered independently of their social connections: rape (when defined simply as a form of physical assault), torture, starvation. Some crimes, such as deportation and enslavement, do begin to get at issues of disrupting social existence. But they lack the comprehensiveness of social death, at least when the enslavement in question is not hereditary and is not necessarily for the rest of a person's life.

Still, it is true that not all victims of the Holocaust underwent social death to the same extent as prisoners in the camps and ghettos. Entire villages on the Eastern front were slaughtered by the *Einsatzgruppen* (mobile killing units) without warning or prior captivity. Yet these villagers were given indecent deaths. They were robbed of control of their vital interests and of opportunities to mourn. Although most did not experience those deprivations for very long, inflicted en masse these murders do appear to have produced sudden social death prior to physical extermination. The murders were also part of a larger plan that included the death of Judaism, not just the deaths of Jews. Implementing that plan included gradually stripping vast numbers of Jews of social vitality, in some places over a period of years, and it entailed that survivors, if there were any, should not survive as Jews. The fact that the plan only partly succeeded does not negate the central role of social death within it or the importance of that concept to genocide.

If social death is central to the harm of genocide, then it really is right not to count as a genocide the annihilation however heinous, of just any political group. Not every political group contributes significantly to its members' cultural identity. Many are fairly specific and short lived, formed to support particular issues. But then, equally, the annihilation of not just any cultural group should count. Cultural groups can also be temporary and specialized, lacking in the continuity and comprehensiveness that are presupposed by the possibility of social death. Some mass murders— perhaps the bombings of September 11, 2001—do not appear to have had as part of their aim, intention, or effect the prior soul murder or social death of those targeted for physical extermination. If so, they are mass murders that are not also genocides. But mass murders and other measures that have as part of their reasonably foreseeable consequence, or as part their aim, the annihilation of a group that contributes significantly to the social identity of its members are genocidal.

References

Bedau, Hugo Adam. 1974. "Genocide in Vietnam?" In *Philosophy, Morality, and International Affairs*, ed. Virginia Held, Sidney Morgenbesser, and Thomas Nagel. New York: Oxford University Press.

Card, Claudia. 1996. "Rape as a Weapon of War." *Hypatia* 11 (4): 5–18.

———. 1997. "Addendum to 'Rape as a Weapon of War.'" *Hypatia* 12 (2): 216–18.

———. 2002. *The Atrocity Paradigm: A Theory of Evil*. New York: Oxford University Press.

Chalk, Frank, and Kurt Jonassohn, eds. 1990. *The History and Sociology of Genocide: Analyses and Case Studies*. New Haven: Yale University Press.

Charny, Israel. 1997. "Toward a Generic Definition of Genocide." In *Genocide: Conceptual and Historical Dimensions*, ed. George Andreopoulos. Philadelphia: University of Pennsylvania Press.

Davidowicz, Lucy W. 1975. *The War Against the Jews, 1933–1945*. New York: Holt, Rinehart, and Winston.

Glover, Jonathan. 2000. *Humanity: A Moral History of the Twentieth Century*. New Haven: Yale University Press.

Katz, Steven. 1994. *The Holocaust in Historical Context*, vol. 1, *Mass Death Before the Modern Age*. New York: Oxford University Press.

Lang, Berel. 1984/85. "The Concept of Genocide." *Philosophical Forum* 16 (1/2): 1–18.

———. 1990. *Act and Idea in the Nazi Genocide*. Chicago: University of Chicago Press.

———. 1992. Genocide. *Encyclopedia of Ethics*, vol. 1, ed. Lawrence C. Becker with Charlotte B. Becker. New York: Garland.

Lemkin, Raphael. 1944. *Axis Rule in Occupied Europe: Laws of Occupation, Analysis of Government, Proposals for Redress*. Washington D. C.: Carnegie Endowment for International Peace, Division of International Law.

Margalit, Avishai. 1996. *The Decent Society*, trans. Naomi Goldblum. Cambridge: Harvard University Press.

Minow, Martha. 1998. *Between Vengeance and Forgiveness: Facing History After Genocide and Mass Violence*. Boston: Beacon.

Novick, Peter. 1999. *The Holocaust in American Life*. Boston: Houghton Mifflin.

Orentlicher, Diane F. 1999. "Genocide." In *Crimes of War: What the Public Should Know*, ed. Roy Gutman and David Rieff. New York: Norton.

Patterson, Orlando. 1982. *Slavery and Social Death*. Cambridge: Harvard University Press.

Rawls, John. 1999. *A Theory of Justice*. Rev. ed. Cambridge: Harvard University Press.

Robinson, Nehemiah. 1960. *The Genocide Convention: A Commentary*. New York: Institute of Jewish Affairs, World Jewish Congress.

Rosenbaum, Alan S., ed. 1996. *Is the Holocaust Unique? Perspectives on Comparative Genocide*. Boulder: Westview.

Sartre, Jean-Paul. 1968. *On Genocide*. Boston: Beacon.

Schott, Robin. 1999. "Philosophical Reflections on War Rape." In *On Feminist Ethics and Politics*, ed. Claudia Card. Lawrence: University Press of Kansas.

Solomon, William David. 1992. "Double Effect." In *Encyclopedia of Ethics*, vol. 1, ed. Lawrence C. Becker with Charlotte B. Becker. New York: Garland.

Stannard, David E. 1992. *American Holocaust: The Conquest of the New World*. New York: Oxford University Press.

———. 1996. "Uniqueness as Denial: The Politics of Genocide Scholarship." In *Is the Holocaust Unique?* ed. Alan S. Rosenbaum. Boulder: Westview.

Stein, Edith. 1964. *On the Problem of Empathy*, trans. Waltraut Stein. The Hague: Nijhoff.

Stiffarm, Lenore, with Phil Lane Jr. 1992. "The Demography of Native North America." In *The State of Native America*, ed. Annette Jaimes. Boston: South End.

Thomas, Lawrence Mordekhai. 1993. *Vessels of Evil: American Slavery and the Holocaust*. Philadelphia: Temple University Press.

CHAPTER 6

THE PARADOX OF GENOCIDAL RAPE AIMED
AT ENFORCED PREGNANCY

CLAUDIA CARD

1. The Problem and Its Background

A little more than a decade ago, a powerful short book appeared with what was then the provocative title: *Rape Warfare: The Hidden Genocide in Bosnia-Herzegovina and Croatia* (Allen 1996). It was written by Beverly Allen, director of the humanities PhD program at Syracuse University. In that book she introduced the term "genocidal rape" to describe rapes that were done as policy for the purpose of genocide by Serb military forces in Bosnia-Herzegovina and Croatia in the early 1990s. One policy, aimed at enforced pregnancy, poses a logical puzzle. "How," asks Allen, "can rape, forced pregnancy, and resultant childbirths, the production of new persons, be genocide, the annihilation of a people?" (Allen 1996, 92). To answer that question, she reconstructs how Serb rapists might have thought they were producing little Serbs. Yet, as reflection soon reveals, the belief that they were producing little Serbs does not make good sense. My project here re-examines the paradox that Allen articulated and places it in the context of the general question of how war rape can be genocidal, whether aimed at pregnancy or not. Drawing on Allen's amazing insight that sperm so used can and should be regarded as a weapon of biological warfare, I then propose a way to show how rape aimed at enforced pregnancy could indeed be genocidal. And I do so without relying on her conjecture that perpetrators may have thought they were producing little Serbs.

Clearly, there were Serb policies of systematic rape that had a military intent. Those policies were in violation of International Humanitarian Law. Allen quotes an Italian journalist Giuseppe Zaccaria, who summarized the

Criticism and Compassion: The Ethics and Politics of Claudia Card.
Edited by Robin S. Dillon and Armen T. Marsoobian.
Chapters and book compilation © 2018 Metaphilosophy LLC and John Wiley & Sons Ltd.

minutes of a meeting of Serb army officers held in a Belgrade suburb in late 1991. He notes that the officers adopted an explicit policy to target women and children as the most vulnerable part of the Muslim religious and social structure. Journalist Zaccaria writes:

> Our analysis of the behavior of the Muslim communities demonstrates that the morale, will, and bellicose nature of their groups can be undermined *only if we aim our action at the point where the religious and social structure is most fragile. We refer to the women, especially adolescents, and to the children.* Decisive intervention on these social figures would spread confusion among the communities, thus causing first of all fear and then panic, leading to a probable [Muslim] retreat from the territories involved in war activity. (Allen 1996, 57; emphasis and brackets are Allen's)

This plan was referred to by the officers at this meeting as the Brana plan. It went into effect immediately.

That this plan was endorsed by military officers is apparently key to distinguishing the Serbian rapes—morally, politically, and militarily—from retaliatory rapes that were committed by Bosnians and others. Not all war rapes are committed with genocidal intent. Not all war rapes aim, as policy, to destroy the groups to which victims belong. Yet it may not be clear that the aim described at the meeting summarized by Zaccaria actually *is* destruction of the target groups.

What did the Serbian officers mean when they identified children and women, especially adolescents, as the most vulnerable spots in social and religious structures of Muslim communities? Two answers occur to me. The simplest and perhaps most obvious answer is that women and children are almost always unarmed, and they are probably not trained to fight. And so they are vulnerable in the sense that they could not put up very much effective resistance. But, then, why would the officers say, "especially adolescents"? One might expect adolescents to be better able to put up resistance than younger children or older women. And why would the Serb officers locate this fragility of Muslim communities in its "religious and social structure"? A more complex answer to the question of why the vulnerability of Muslim communities was identified in this way, which would be responsive to these issues, is that the relevant vulnerable spot was actually the religious and social concerns of Muslim men for the women and children of their families, especially adolescent women, who could be presumed to be virgins, not yet married, sexually innocent. The whole community was then vulnerable to being manipulated through these concerns of its men. Adolescent women were an especially vulnerable part of the community with respect to their sexual innocence: they had something to lose that could be considered precious to the future of the community. They were no doubt vulnerable in the first sense as well (that is, they would most likely be unarmed and untrained in physical defense).

Allen identified three forms that the ensuing mass rapes took in three different kinds of localities. In the first instance, military forces "enter a village, take several women of varying ages from their homes, rape them in public view, and depart." Several days later, soldiers from the army "arrive and offer the now-terrified residents safe passage away from the village on the condition they never return" (Allen 1996, 62). In the second form of military rape, persons held in "concentration camps are chosen at random to be raped, often as part of torture preceding death" (63). These tortures and murders can, of course, also be used to terrorize. But they can serve other functions as well, such as rewards for and bonding among rapist soldiers (Stiglmayer 1993, 160–61). In the third form of military rape, women are imprisoned in rape/death camps and raped "systematically for extended periods of time" either as torture preceding death or as torture leading to forced pregnancy. Pregnant victims are then "raped consistently until such time as their pregnancies have progressed beyond the possibility of a safe abortion," at which time they are released (Allen 1996, 62). This last kind of case, in which the goal appears to be unabortable pregnancies that result from Serb rapes, is the kind of case that becomes Allen's focus. "Genocidal rape aimed at enforced pregnancy," she writes, "would seem to be a peculiarly Serb contribution to the history of atrocity" (92).

Perpetrators understood the Brana plan as ethnic cleansing. I have always found that use of the term "cleansing" to be grating. It seems a diabolical way to describe a very dirty project, a perfect example of Orwellian "doublethink" (Orwell 1949). But the term "ethnic cleansing" has entered reference works and so seems here to stay.

How is ethnic cleansing related to genocide? Ethnic cleansing, according to a 1993 report to the Security Council by the United Nations Commission of Experts, is defined as "rendering an area ethnically homogeneous by using force or intimidation to remove persons of given groups from the area" (Gutman and Rieff 1999, 136). Its characteristic method is terror created through "killing, destruction, threat, and humiliation" (ibid.). The idea that ethnic cleansing can be genocidal requires some argument and clarification. It is not just obvious that ethnic cleansing is a euphemism for genocide, given the possibility that those removed from a territory may survive the removal and become re-established elsewhere.

Historically, ethnic and religious groups have been eliminated from a territory by means of expulsion. Ordinarily, destroying a group goes beyond merely expelling it from a territory. The expulsions by Spain of the Jews in 1492 and later of the Moriscos, a Muslim group, in 1609 are not commonly cited by historians as genocides, although many Spanish Jews and many of the Moriscos were in fact killed during these purges, a great many entire communities were destroyed, and there is a case for regarding these purges as ethnically, not just religiously, motivated (Netanyahu 2001; Lea 1901/2006). The only difference between such expulsions and "ethnic cleansings" would appear to be that the territory remaining was not so much ethnically homogeneous as religiously homogeneous. (That would appear to make it "religious cleansing"—if anything, an even more grating concept.)

And so a further question arises regarding the characterization of any of the Serbian rape policies as genocidal: if the point of the policies was to intimidate the Muslim population into leaving, why should we regard those policies as any more genocidal than the expulsions of the Moriscos, or earlier, of the Jews, through edicts by Spain? Or should we actually regard *all* of these policies as genocidal? Allen does not probe this kind of question. Her focus is on the enforced pregnancy policy. But a clear answer to the question of how a policy of war rape can be genocidal might help to answer the question of how rape aimed at enforced pregnancy can be.

2. What Is Genocide?

Allen characterizes as genocidal all three of the forms of military rape that she has described. Her claim is that they fit the definition of the 1948 international Genocide Convention. Yet it is not really so clear that they do fit under any of the acts enumerated in that convention's definition. The Genocide Convention defined genocide as follows: "any of the following acts committed with the intent to destroy, in whole, or in part, a nation, ethnical, racial or religious group, as such: (a) killing members of the group; (b) causing serious bodily or mental harm to members of the group; (c) deliberately inflicting on the group conditions of life calculated to bring about its physical destruction in whole or in part; (d) imposing measures intended to prevent births within the group; (e) forcibly transferring children of the group to another group" (Robinson 1960).

As this definition is worded, the intent need not succeed. Yet clearly harm is done if any of the enumerated acts is committed. Any of those acts that are committed with the requisite intent is sufficient to ground a charge of genocide. The definition does not say explicitly that these are the only acts that might ground a charge of genocide. But neither does it provide a general way to identify other acts that might ground such a charge.

Allen invokes this definition of the U.N. Genocide Convention. She asserts that "all forms of genocidal rape constitute the crime of genocide as described in Article II of the 1948 United Nations Convention on the Prevention and Punishment of the Crime of Genocide" (Allen 1996, 63). There surely were many killings of Muslims (clause "a"), and the rapes by Serbs of Muslim women and girls caused mental and bodily harm to those women and girls (clause "b"). Were those rapes done, however, with the intent to destroy, in whole or in part, the ethnic or religious group to which the rape victims belonged? The Brana plan may seem closest to clause "c," which is "deliberately inflicting on the group conditions of life calculated to bring about its physical destruction in whole or in part" because the Brana plan was to intentionally inflict conditions of life calculated to "spread confusion among the communities," to demoralize and destroy the will to fight. But was the intent of the Brana plan to *destroy* Bosnian Muslims as a group? Or was it, rather, the more limited project of *disabling and expelling* Bosnian Muslims? If the destruction of a group is a clearly foreseeable consequence of measures taken in order to disable and expel members of that group, then it will not quite do to say that destruction of the group was unintended even if destruction was not an ultimate aim. To use Kantian language, the foreseeable consequence of destruction of the group belongs in the material maxim of the rapists' actions in that it indicates in a morally relevant way what the perpetrators are willing to do.[1] The Genocide Convention's definition could, and I think should, be amended to accommodate that point. Instead of saying simply "with the intent to destroy, in whole, or in part," it could be amended to say "either with the intent to destroy, or with the reasonably foreseeable consequence of destroying, in whole, or in part, a nation, ethnical, racial or religious group."[2] Whether it should be so amended is currently one of the controversies surrounding the Genocide Convention's definition of genocide.

But *is* it reasonably foreseeable that dispersal, demoralization, and confusion will result in "physical destruction" of the group? "Physical destruction" sounds to many readers (for example, to genocide scholar and sociologist Helen Fein) like mass murder or massive interference with biological reproduction or maybe even with the links between reproduction and socialization (Fein 2002, 74–90). There were indeed mass murders. And socialization of the next generation of Bosnian Muslims was massively thrown into chaos. It is also true that there are other ways to physically destroy a community than to kill its members or to hinder their biological reproduction. When a group is expelled rapidly, significant property is inevitably left behind, and it is not clear that those forced to flee will ever be able to recreate the physical bases of their communities or to recreate the institutions definitive of their communal life that require a material basis. That, of course, is also the predicament of many expelled groups, such as the early seventeenth-century Moriscos and the late fifteenth-century Jews of Spain.

Helpful light is thrown on what sorts of conduct can reasonably be counted as genocidal by the work of Raphael Lemkin, who introduced and defined the term "genocide" in his 1944 book *Axis Rule in Occupied Europe*.

---

[1] For Immanuel Kant, the material maxim of an action is a general statement of its intent, what one is willing to do (Kant 1996, 56, 73). My claim here is that one's intent should not be confined to the action and its purpose or aim but should also include reasonably foreseeable consequences, as they indicate in a morally relevant way what one is willing to do.

[2] Such an amendment would be the simplest way to indicate, without getting into controversies regarding what to include in the concept of "intent," that reasonably foreseeable consequences that one is willing to bring about might be genocidal.

He understands the term "genocide" "to signify a coordinated plan of different actions aiming at the destruction of essential foundations of the life of national groups, with the aim of annihilating the groups themselves" (Lemkin 1944, 79). Elsewhere, he understands potential targets of genocide to include racial or ethnic and religious groups as well. Lemkin's approach is not quite the same as that of the Genocide Convention. Unlike the convention, Lemkin does not understand genocide as consisting in any of a set of enumerable acts, *each* of which might have the intent to destroy a group. Rather, Lemkin understands genocide as an overarching *plan*, and it is to the plan, rather than to specific acts carrying it out, that the requisite intent attaches. Lemkin sees genocide as a process with stages that take place over an extended period of time and that utilize many techniques. Particular activities furthering such a plan take their genocidal character from that of the plan to which they contribute. Thus, military rape as a weapon can become genocidal when it contributes to a larger *plan* that has a genocidal aim. The question then becomes how it can make such a contribution.

Lemkin enumerates and discusses several techniques of genocide under the headings of the political, social, economic, biological, physical, religious, and moral. He illustrates each of these kinds of techniques with Hitler's actual policies in various countries of occupied Europe (Lemkin 1944, 79–90). A genocidal plan, as he understands it, might be put into effect more or less fully. Thus, Lemkin recognizes degrees of genocide.

But one may wonder whether Lemkin's approach is too loose. Is it in danger of counting too much as genocidal and thereby diluting the special moral seriousness of genocide? Fein worries about metaphorical uses of the term "genocide" and complains that the concept is in danger of becoming banalized by being applied to such things as race-mixing (Fein 2002, 74). She argues that we should distinguish genocide from nongenocidal assimilation even if that assimilation is imposed. She maintains, for example, that Hitler's plans for peoples who were genetically related to Germans (such as the Dutch, Luxemburgers, and Norwegians) differed from his plans for non-Germanic peoples (such as Poles and Jews) in that the plans for German-related peoples were *not* genocidal (Fein 2002, 76–77). Rather, they involved an assimilationist policy of "Germanizing" through the imposition of techniques that Lemkin calls political, social, and economic, and through such cultural measures as requiring the speaking of German and prohibiting other languages to be taught in the schools. In contrast, Hitler regarded Poles and Jews un-Germanizable. Only their soil, he said, could be Germanized, not the people.

I find, however, that Lemkin's text does not clearly distinguish Germanizing from genocide, as Fein wishes to do. Lemkin's text can be read as suggesting that the Dutch, for example, were simply targeted for *a lesser degree* of genocide. And so the question naturally arises: what is at stake in the wish to distinguish forced cultural assimilation from genocide? Is it really only the extent of the harm that is done by the policy in question? Or is there something about the nature of the harm that is at stake here? I return to these questions below.

The issue of overinclusiveness arises also for the Genocide Convention's definition in regard to the words "in whole, or in part." Since members can be understood as parts of the groups of which they are members, any intentional killing destroys part of all the groups to which the victim belonged. Of course, not all intentional killing is motivated by hostility based on the victim's group identity (or identities). One might argue that killings that are not so grounded should not be interpreted as intended to destroy a group, even in part. But if all killings motivated by hostility based on the victim's group identity are admitted to be instances of destruction of a group in part, then, it appears that, according to the Genocide Convention's definition, all hate crime murders are genocides. But that result surely is overinclusive.

To respond to these concerns regarding the scope of genocide, I want to invoke the thesis of my earlier paper "Genocide and Social Death" that central to the concept of genocide is destruction of social vitality (Card 2003). I borrow the concept of social death from Orlando Patterson (Patterson 1982). Patterson used the term "social death" to describe the condition of slaves, who lacked social standing and were cut off from their cultures of origin (or those of their forebears). Slaves who were not only socially dead but—as he put it—*natally alienated* were actually *born* socially dead—cut off from kinship ties in both directions, to forebears and to progeny.[3] The argument of my 2003 paper was that central to genocide, whether homicidal or not, is the social death of its victims. What I meant was that victims are stripped as members of the target group of the social identities that gave meaning to their lives and that would ordinarily also have given meaning to their deaths. Not all mass murders do this. Nor do all group expulsions have so severe a consequence. The bombings of September 11, 2001, for example, did not. Those who would maintain that the Spanish expulsions of the Moriscos and earlier the Jews were not genocidal would have to hold, on this view of genocide, that these expulsions did not strip those who were expelled of their social identities, that it did not rob their lives of meaning.[4] Conversely, those who might want to argue that these expulsions *were* genocidal could be expected to argue that indeed they did.

---

[3] I here set aside the controversies over whether Patterson exaggerated the extent of social death under American slavery, whether there were significant slave cultures, and the extent to which social death may be reversible.

[4] A life can be robbed of the meaning that social identities contributed to it without being left entirely meaningless, if not all the meanings a life can have are dependent on the maintenance of social vitality. Nevertheless, the loss is profound. Thanks to comments from Eva Kittay in the discussion of this paper at the Spindel Conference for stimulating further thought on this issue.

A continuing philosophical problem for definitions of genocide that do not make homicide essential to that concept is how to clarify the differences between genocide and cultural assimilation, especially forced assimilation. The assimilation of one group into another may result in the destruction of both groups as they were originally. Does that mean they are destroyed "as such"? Even if assimilation is forced by one group on another, if assimilation is successful, members of neither group become socially dead. That may be reason enough to want to distinguish forced assimilation from genocide. The social identities of those who are forced to assimilate are forcibly changed, at least as those identities are perceived by others. If the assimilation is successful, those who are assimilated are not left with socially meaningless lives. And yet, forced assimilation is not always successful. The self-perceptions of many do not track the change in their socially perceived identities. Perhaps in such cases, there is an argument for regarding forced assimilation as genocidal, for those who are not successfully assimilated really do suffer a loss of meaning to their lives that they may be unable to replace with a new kind of meaning that would give to their lives some genuine social vitality.

To address Allen's problem of the paradox of genocidal rape aimed at enforced pregnancy, we may not need to answer such questions further than to note that Lemkin's looser approach to the concept of genocide need not be interpreted as *so* loose that it banalizes the concept. It can be supplemented by making explicit the idea of social death as either a primary goal or a clearly foreseeable result of genocidal processes. As social death, unlike physical death, can have degrees, so genocide, unlike homicide, can have degrees. In any case, as Allen notes, the forced pregnancies in Bosnia-Herzegovina, unlike those inflicted on the ancient Sabine women, were certainly not aiming at assimilation (Allen 1996, 91).

Lemkin's idea of genocide as an overall plan that tends to be carried out in stages and with a variety of techniques remains a useful idea for explaining how military rape can be genocidal. The escalating forms of terrorism—from the humiliation of public rape to torture preceding murder to exerting control over the future of communities by tampering with the production of the next generation—can all be techniques employed in a plan that has the clearly foreseeable consequence, if not the explicit aim, of destroying a people, not by assimilating those who were members of that people and substituting a new coherent social identity for the old one, but by throwing into chaos the social identities of members of the group.

3. The "Logical Glitch"

Beverly Allen finds that genocide by impregnation has, as she puts it, a "logical glitch." To return to our opening question, "how," she asks, "can rape, forced pregnancy, and resultant childbirths, the production of new persons, be genocide, the annihilation of a people?" (Allen 1996, 92). It would appear, on the face of it, to be just the opposite. To explain, she reasons as follows. The intent of the Serbian rapists appears to have been to produce Serb children. Serb perpetrators, she reasons, may have thought that the presence of these children would change the identity of the next generation and that it would thereby alter the identity of the community to something more Serbian and possibly even swell its numbers. Some rapists are alleged to have gloated over the fact that they were forcing Muslim women to bear "little Chetniks" or Serb children.

Yet, as Allen points out, the child born of military rape contains genes of both biological parents, and if raised, that child will most likely be raised by its mother, if she survives, and will consequently take on whatever culture is then hers. In terms of biological parentage, the child will be as much non-Serb as Serb, and the child's culture will almost certainly not be Serbian. The upshot is that this reconstructed rationale for the rapes does not, of course, make good logical sense. Yet she suggests that this line of thought may nevertheless have been the rationale.

What Allen finds paradoxical is that military rape aimed at enforced pregnancy in the rape/death camps was apparently committed with genocidal intent. The 1948 Genocide Convention did not anticipate that acts of rape might be committed with intent to destroy a group. Although the definition explicitly mentions measures intended to *prevent* births within the group, it does not mention measures intended to *produce* births by members of the group. Even if we follow Lemkin in holding that it is the overall plan to which particular techniques contribute that has the genocidal intent, not necessarily each technique itself, the question remains how this particular technique can contribute to the overall plan rather than undermine it. Taken at face value, a plan to produce births seems contrary to genocide, as it appears to increase rather than decrease the target population. What, other than the logically faulty reasoning of producing little Serbs, could make such a policy appear genocidal to its perpetrators?

One answer, which Allen seems to find offensive, is that forcibly impregnated Muslim women would be rejected by their families and communities as ruined. With so many women ruined, communities would collapse. Susan Brownmiller, in her famous chapter on war rape in *Against Our Will*, cites reports that in 1971 "more than 200,000 Bengali women had been raped by Pakistani soldiers" and that "by tradition, no Moslem husband would take back a wife who had been touched by another man, even if she had been subdued by force" (Brownmiller 1975, 78–79). Thus it appears that forced pregnancies could become genocidal because of misogynous cruelties of the culture to which the women belong. I do not know whether Brownmiller was right about Bangladesh in the 1970s. But Allen finds that kind of rationale insensitive to the Muslim cultures that were targeted in Bosnia-Herzegovina in the 1990s. Nor is it clear that such misogynous practices would explain the significance of the enforced pregnancy policy, as opposed simply to policies of rape. Yet, however offensive to contemporary Muslim cultures, Serb rapists may in fact have believed that Muslim culture was just that misogynous, or they may have projected misogyny from their own culture onto Muslim culture.

Allen's own solution to the logical glitch is to reconstruct how the rape-pregnancy policy could appear to its designers and executors to produce little Serbs. The 1948 Convention requires only that the enumerated acts be committed with a certain *intent*. It does not require that the intent succeed. Allen makes sense of the intent by supposing that in the perpetrators' eyes, victims were stripped of all social and cultural identity and perceived by their assailants only as sexual receptacles for the sperm of Serb rapists. Only Serb identity, if any, could then be transmitted to progeny.

Yet, if it is a problem to rely on perpetrators' false beliefs regarding sexist cruelty in Muslim culture, it should be equally a problem (although a different kind of problem) to rely on their false beliefs regarding biological reproduction. A better explanation of the genocidal nature of these policies would not rely on the ignorance or stupidity of their perpetrators. And a better explanation is available if the prolonged torture of repeated rape during the enforcement of pregnancy really did dehumanize its victims, turning survivors' lives into something less than human—in other words, if such torture imposed a social death on its victims, if, to borrow and expand Hannah Arendt's imagery from her account of "total domination," it turned them into living (and gestating) corpses (Arendt 2000, 119–45).[5] Repeatedly raping Muslim women and forcing them to bear unwanted children is a form of torture that might well be expected to dehumanize the women who endured it.

If such abuse foreseeably produces or contributes to social death, we need not rely on faulty logic in authors and executors of the Brana plan to explain its genocidal intent. Whether the perpetrators thought they were producing little Serbs is irrelevant. What counts is the attack on the social meanings of the lives of the women they tortured.

Repeated and brutal rapes can be sufficiently traumatizing that survivors may not welcome future sexual relationships. In that way, even the enforced pregnancy policy could have a long-range consequence of decreasing, rather than increasing, a target population. Allen does not explicitly use that argument. But it is one of the ideas that is suggested to me by her radical and ingenious claim that when military rape is used to produce and enforce pregnancy, *sperm* actually becomes a weapon of *biological warfare*. There need be no logical glitches in this concept.

4. Sperm as a Biological Weapon

That enforced pregnancy uses sperm as a biological weapon is the most interesting and insightful idea I have encountered regarding genocidal rape.

---

[5] Arendt uses the expression "living corpses" (Arendt 2000, 32).

Surprisingly, Allen presents this idea in her chapter on *remedies, not* in her chapter called "Analysis" (Allen 1996, "Remedies," 103–32; "Analysis," 87–101). Her reason to present it in the chapter on remedies appears to be that there exist international conventions against biological weapons that might be invoked in response to genocidal rape. But Allen seems actually to be ambivalent between two views. One is that "the *faulty logic* of Serb policy views sperm in genocidal rape precisely as an agent of biological warfare" (Allen 1996, 129; my emphasis). The other is that, Serb logic aside, she can "begin to show how serious genocidal rape is, and how universal a menace it might be, by determining, as [she encourages] the judges of the United Nations International Criminal Tribunal to do, that it is a crime of *biological warfare*" (123). Let's go with the second view, namely, that genocidal rape can be viewed, and should be viewed, as a crime of biological warfare. If we factor the idea that genocidal rape really is biological warfare into the *analysis* of the crime, that analysis can be used without relying on faulty logic in the authors and executors of the enforced pregnancy policy to support the charge that the policy is genocidal.

The idea of sperm as a biological weapon presents its own puzzles, however. Biological warfare is usually understood as military use of bacteriological or viral organisms that make people sick fairly quickly with diseases that are so contagious that they spread rapidly through a population. The diseases tend to produce death, permanent disability, or disfigurement, making it impossible for the target people to defend itself. As Allen notes, the military appeal of biological weapons is that they can destroy a people, or a people's will to fight, without destroying the inhabited territory. She also notes some of the classic dangers of such weapons, which explain why these weapons are not used oftener. Even if they do not destroy the territory, the irreversible dispersal of organisms of biological warfare may make that territory uninhabitable for a long time, depending on how long it takes the bacteria or viruses to run their course and die out. Further, disease-causing biological organisms are not fine-tunable weapons that can be made to target specific individuals. And they are not easily controlled once they have been unleashed in a population. Finally, there is the danger of blow-back: the wind can literally blow the organisms back into the faces of those who would use them.

Sperm need not literally make rape victims sick and die. It is not contagious. It need not produce death, disability, or disfigurement, although it can (especially in an era of HIV). Still, like disease, death, and disablement, rape and enforced pregnancy can destroy the morale of a people, especially if inflicted on its youth who represent its hopes for the future. If the objective is to undermine the will to fight, mass rape and enforced pregnancy might contribute to that end as effectively as infectious disease. Classically, soldiers are motivated to fight to protect their homes, families, and the futures of their communities. If families become direct targets, what then is left to protect? What can sustain the will to fight? Direct attack on civilian women and children seems designed to motivate the men to cease fighting as the only way to protect what, if anything, would remain of their families and their ability to shape their futures. But the cost of achieving that end was genocide, the destruction of a people, at least in part, in very substantial part. In Hitler's Final Solution, genocide was an end in itself. In Bosnia-Herzegovina, genocide became the price the Serb military was willing to pay for ethnic cleansing.

Allen argues, interestingly, that the use of sperm as a weapon fits the conception of biological warfare that is found in international documents in that a product of a living organism (the rapist) is used to attack a biological system (the reproductive system) in members of the enemy population. Although this attack need not produce illness, it is designed to produce social chaos. It surely succeeded in Bosnia-Herzegovina. Sperm need not carry the HIV virus or other STDs in order to be toxic. It need not harm the reproductive system, considered from a physiological point of view. But it surely does use the reproductive system against the people. Sperm so used becomes a social and psychological toxin, poisoning the futures of victims and their communities by producing children who, if they survive, will remind whoever raises them of their traumatic origins in torture. Mass rape aiming at enforced pregnancy is intended to create an unwelcome new generation that will be the responsibility of rape victims and any future community to which they may belong.

In fact, Allen notes, many of the impregnated women attempted third trimester abortions, suicide, or infanticide, and others simply walked out of the hospital room leaving the newborn behind, or they tried to find someone less traumatized to raise it (Allen 1996, 99). In such ways, they thwarted some of the intent of the enforced pregnancy policy. But the intent nevertheless makes sense. And, in accord with Lemkin's idea that genocide is an overall plan involving many strategies, the Brana plan was not the only strategy implemented by the Serbs in its project of "ethnic cleansing."

Allen notes that sperm is free of the classic disadvantages of bacterial and viral biological weapons. Unlike bacteria and viruses, sperm is easily containable, storable, preservable, and deliverable by means of men's bodies. It needs no (other) special equipment. If rape and enforced pregnancy are effective in terrorizing a people into evacuating a territory, sperm as a weapon does not risk making the territory uninhabitable. It can be delivered with accuracy to a specific target. Finally, there is no danger of "blowback," or so it might seem. A Croatian woman noted, however, that even though the rapists cannot be impregnated, the next generation might grow up to seek revenge. Allen adds: on whom they would be motivated to seek revenge will depend on how they are raised (Allen 1996, 132). There may be "blowback," after all.

Combining Lemkin's idea that genocide is a complex plan that utilizes several techniques with Allen's idea that rape aimed at producing enforced pregnancy is a kind of biological warfare, the Brana plan can be seen to be genocidal without relying on the idea of producing little Serbs (even if some rapists did think they were doing that, or joked about the idea). On the contrary, thinking of the next generation as Serbian would bring the policy closer to assimilation than to genocide, which was clearly contrary to the Serbian intent. It is enough that the moving cause and half the material cause of the existence of that generation was a mortal enemy. It is enough that those progeny are therefore largely unwanted and yet the responsibility of those who do not want them, that they are a permanent reminder of their origins in torture, that their identity is problematic, and that women who gave birth to them are so traumatized that they may never regain the desire to engage in sexual relationships or to procreate further. All that is enough to sustain the claim that military rape aimed at enforced pregnancy contributed to an overall plan of ethnic cleansing that was also genocidal in its intent, not merely a policy of expulsion.

Notes

Thanks to Steven Nadler, John Niles, Robin Schott, Lissa Skitolsky, David Sorkin, and Thomas Safley for helpful comments on earlier drafts; to the Society for the Philosophical Study of Genocide and the Holocaust for the invitation to try out these ideas at the 2006 meeting of the Society for Phenomenological and Existential Philosophy; and to the Institute for Research in the Humanities for helpful discussion at a lunchtime seminar. This version has not been substantially modified since I received Ann Cudd's thought-provoking comments, presented with this paper at the Spindel Conference, October 18–20, 2007, in Memphis. But endnotes 1, 2, and 4 have been added for clarification, and my future work on this topic will benefit greatly from the Spindel Conference discussion and Ann Cudd's comments.

References

Allen, Beverly. 1996. *Rape Warfare: The Hidden Genocide in Bosnia-Herzegovina and Croatia*. Minneapolis: University of Minnesota Press.

Arendt, Hannah. 2000. *The Portable Hannah Arendt*. Ed. Peter Baehr. New York: Penguin.

Brownmiller, Susan. 1975. *Against Our Will: Men, Women, and Rape*. New York: Simon and Schuster.

Card, Claudia. 2003. "Genocide and Social Death." *Hypatia* 18, no. 1: 63–79.

Fein, Helen. 2002. "Genocide: A Sociological Perspective." In *Genocide: An Anthropological Reader*, ed. Alexander Laban Hinton. Maiden, MA: Blackwell.

Gutman, Roy, and David Rieff, eds. 1999. *Crimes of War: What the Public Should Know*. New York: Norton.

Kant, Immanuel. 1996. *Practical Philosophy*. Trans. and ed. Mary J. Gregor. Cambridge: Cambridge University Press.

Lea, Henry Charles. 1901/2006. *The Moriscos of Spain: Their Conversion and Expulsion*. Philadelphia: Lea Brothers and Co.; unabridged facsimile edition Elibron Classics, 2006.

Lemkin, Raphael. 1944. *Axis Rule in Occupied Europe: Laws of Occupation, Analysis of Government, Proposals for Redress*. Washington: Carnegie Endowment for International Peace.

Netanyahu, Benzion. 2001. *Origins of the Inquisition in Fifteenth Century Spain*. 2nd ed. New York: New York Review Books.

Orwell, George. 1949. *Nineteen Eighty-Four*. New York: Harcourt, Brace.

Patterson, Orlando. 1982. *Slavery and Social Death: A Comparative Study*. Cambridge, MA: Harvard University Press.

Robinson, Nehemiah. 1960. *The Genocide Convention: A Commentary*. New York: Institute of Jewish Affairs, World Jewish Congress.

Stiglmayer, Alexandra, ed. 1993. *Mass Rape: The War Against Women in Bosnia-Herzegovina*. Lincoln: University of Nebraska Press.

CHAPTER 7

SURVIVING LONG-TERM MASS ATROCITIES

CLAUDIA CARD

"May you live in interesting times."[1] So goes the proverbial Chinese curse. Since here we are, I offer you a preview of issues to be taken up in volume three of my trilogy on evil. The topic is survival of long-term mass atrocities. First are conceptual issues: What does "survivor" even *mean*? Second are *ethical* issues: What is morally at stake in surviving long-term mass atrocities? I will make some suggestions about both and tell you some stories—of U-boats, catchers, and ravens. The moral costs and burdens incurred by many survivors present meta-survival issues. They problematize the judgment that one *has* survived.

The atrocities I have in mind, mainly nineteenth century to the present, include genocides, slavery, concentration camps, and POW camps run by captors who did not regard themselves as bound by Geneva conventions. I set aside single-event and short-term mass atrocities, such as the bombings of Oklahoma City (1995) and 9/11 (2001) and the (1995) Tokyo subway gas attack (Murakami 2001). Longer terms offer room for more complex responses: strategizing, learning from mistakes, choices of how or whether to try to survive, to hide, resist, flee, or comply with oppressive demands. Grim options become many survivors' moral luck.[2]

The Nazi Holocaust is the most fully witnessed, documented, and studied long-term mass atrocity from the points of view of survivors,

---

[1] I am grateful for extremely helpful discussions and comments on earlier drafts by Rachel Brenner, Leonard Kaplan, Jeffrey Reiman, and Lissa Skitolsky.

[2] As Lisa Tessman points out (Tessman 2005, 26), my treatment of healing from the bad moral luck of oppression (Card 1996, 21–48) was too quick and too optimistic. I take the term "moral luck" from Williams and Nagel (1976).

Criticism and Compassion: The Ethics and Politics of Claudia Card.
Edited by Robin S. Dillon and Armen T. Marsoobian.
Chapters and book compilation © 2018 Metaphilosophy LLC and John Wiley & Sons Ltd.

many of them educated, articulate, keen observers and conscientious recorders.[3] And so, what might otherwise seem a disproportionate number of my examples are from the Holocaust. This imbalance has advantages. Holocaust memoirs are rich in reflections on the ethics of survival. Also, I know more about Holocaust atrocities than about other long-term mass atrocities. My course on moral philosophy and the Holocaust includes a unit on deliberations of the Jewish Councils of Elders (*Judenräte*) and memoirs of individuals who survived long enough to leave a record (Perechodnik 1996; Trunk 1996).

I undertake this project with trepidation and humility. I am neither a mass atrocity survivor nor the child of one. Any advantage my position might have for objectivity may be outweighed by epistemic and emotional disadvantages of lacking a more intimate acquaintance with what I want to think about. But the concept of survival and the ethics of survival deserve more attention than they have received from analytically trained philosophers writing in English.[4] "Survival" in that tradition has meant survival of the grave or survival of the fittest. My interest is in the survival of individual human beings on earth, many of whom cannot reproduce because of what they endured.

I do not much engage questions of which survival choices are morally defensible. My interest is in both defensible and indefensible choices. It is often clear enough which are which, and in other cases, I am relieved not to have to judge. Lawrence Langer refers to the "choiceless choices" of Holocaust victims (Langer 1991, 26), in situations where every option makes one involuntarily complicit in moral horrors. What I find ethically more interesting in relation to choiceless choices is how survivors respond later to the options they took than how they decided which to take.

My first two books on evil (Card 2002, 2010) set a background for addressing survival (although I did not know as I wrote them that I had embarked on a trilogy). *The Atrocity Paradigm* defined evils as "reasonably foreseeable intolerable harms produced by culpable wrongdoing" (Card 2002, 3, 16). So defined, evils have two irreducibly distinct elements: harm and the agency that produces it. This definition combines an Epicurean view of evil as suffering with a Stoic view of evil as residing in the will. It takes as basic the noun "evils" (plural) and treats adjectival uses of "evil" as derivative. Not all wrongs are evils, only those that do intolerable harm. Nor are all harms evil, only those produced by culpable

---

[3] I capitalize "Holocaust" not to emphasize gravity but because "Holocaust" without qualification now functions as a proper name. It is the name most readers recognize, although what it includes is ambiguous and its connotations of a sacrifice or offering are inappropriate.

[4] Exceptions to analytic philosophy's tendency to ignore atrocity survival are Thomas (1988, 1993) and Sherman (2010). Valuable recent work on atrocity survival by American philosophers trained in or writing within Continental traditions includes Bar On (1991, 2002), Oliver (2001), Schott (2010), and Skitolsky (2010).

wrongs. My approach is secular. It avoids ideas of metaphysical forces and demons.[5]

An animating concern for me has been to counterbalance the nearly exclusive focus by philosophers on perpetrator psychology by highlighting the plight of victims. My work on survival picks up on the last chapter in *The Atrocity Paradigm*, on what Primo Levi called "gray zones." In gray zones victims who accept positions of power over others become complicit in the very evils they endure—slave overseers, for example, or Jewish police officers in the Nazi-created ghettos (Levi 1989, 36–69). Some survive. Or, do they? What does survival mean here? And, what is its value to survivors?

My second "evil book," *Confronting Evils* (Card 2010), is inspired by the ideal of preserving humanitarian values in responding to evils, threatened or real. That ideal is violated by interrogational torture of terror suspects. The responders I had chiefly in mind were relatively unencumbered agents concerned to protect and defend, policy-makers, for example, not individuals in immediate danger. Thinking from a policy-maker point of view I revised the agency element of my definition, substituting "inexcusable wrongs" for "culpable wrongdoing."

The resulting definition of evils is "reasonably foreseeable intolerable harms produced by inexcusable wrongs." "*Inexcusable* wrongs" include wrongs for which no one can plead reduced responsibility. More interestingly, they include wrongs that lack any decent moral defense or significant partial justification. Evils are indefensible from a moral point of view, whether or not anyone is culpable. This revised definition applies better than my earlier one to institutions, practices, and structural evils. The idea of lacking moral defense preserves the contrast of evils with natural catastrophes (to which defense does not apply) and refines the contrast of evils with lesser wrongs.

I turn next to the specific conceptual issues regarding the meaning of survival.

Conceptual Issues

"Surviving" refers both to an activity and to what remains.[6] I want to preserve that ambiguity. It allows us to ask, meaningfully, whether a survivor has truly survived. So let's begin with the idea of "*true* survival," as

---

[5] Avoiding ideas of metaphysical forces does not imply that my views lack metaphysical implications. I think of myself as a moral realist. (Thanks to conversations with Gershon Greeenberg on this point and to Shafer-Landau [2003] for deepening my views on moral realism.)

[6] Rachel Brenner, Professor of Hebrew and Semitic Studies, informs me also that of two Hebrew words each translated as "survivor," one of them—"sored"—means "what remains" and the other—"nitzol"—means "saved," referring to an activity, but not that of the one saved.

contrasted with "mere survival," "barely surviving," "just plain survival," or "surviving, but with qualifications." Like Aristotle's and Kant's *true* friendship, true survival is an ideal (Aristotle 2009, 144–47; Kant 1996, 584–88; Kant 1997, 184–90). Under some interpretations, it is an ethical ideal (of sorts). Picking up on the ambiguity of "surviving," there are two ways to understand true survival. One is by the *means* of survival, a survivor's skills, determination, and the like. Think of that as "skilled survival." The other way is by *what* survives, what is preserved, recoverable, or reparable. Think of that as "preservation survival."

Consider first skilled survival. Luck is always a factor. But some are called true survivors because of roles their skills actually played. At issue is what the survivor deserves credit for (not necessarily moral credit). The starkest contrast is with those who lack the skills but survive anyway by sheer luck. There are many possibilities in between. Impressive survival skills can be insufficient. Or survival may be due to luck rather than to skills one actually possesses.

Preservation survival requires one to come through with mental and physical health in basically decent shape (or basically reparable or recoverable). Dying within hours, days, even weeks of liberation is not *true* survival if death was brought on by the atrocity. Nor is losing one's mind irrecoverably. The starkest contrast to preservation survival is being still alive but not for long or with not much of a life. Langer cites a former death camp inmate who observed that one can be alive after Sobibor without having survived Sobibor (Langer 1991, 159). Insofar as moral health is part of mental health, this ideal is partly ethical. Again, there are degrees.

Combining the two models of survival, it is tempting to see some less than true survivors as analogues of Aristotle's friendships of utility and pleasure. Less valuable than "true" friendships, these affiliations can still have value.[7] One way to survive is by making oneself useful to perpetrators (examples come later). Another is to make oneself attractive, offer pleasure. But whereas friendships of utility or pleasure often deepen into true friendships, such bonding with an oppressor endangers one's integrity. True survivors need not be attractive or useful to perpetrators. Some employ neither strategy. Survivors of utility and pleasure are proof that a true survivor in the first sense (skilled) need not be a true survivor in the second (well-preserved). In long-term mass atrocities, true survival in either sense is apt to be rare. Yet these concepts suggest norms for judging oneself a survivor in any sense.

In long-term atrocities, "survivor" often designates those who live through to *the end* (or to some liberatory event) and then function at a decent level. But "survivor" is also applied to victims who are functioning well enough that it is not yet clear that they will succumb. Those whom

---

[7] Thanks to Jeffrey Reiman in personal correspondence for suggestions on developing the analogy with friendships of utility and friendships of pleasure.

Auschwitz prisoners called *Muselmänner*, Muslims (Bettelheim 1960, 151–56), were alive but not surviving (although, it seems, some recovered and did survive).[8] "Muselmänner" is an unfortunate term.[9] But the concept of the walking dead needs to be acknowledged. Alexander Solzhenitzyn's Ivan Denisovich likewise observes of certain prisoners that with their attitudes, they were not going to make it (Solzhenitzyn 1963). Of special ethical interest are victims who are functioning well enough that Denisovich's observation is not warranted.

With illness or accident, survival can mean simply being alive at the end. With atrocities, more is required. Here, survival is like passing a test. This is so even for surviving grad school or probationary employment. Strictly, what survive grad school, a primary election, or probationary employment are one's candidacy and opportunities. They are what remain viable. But "viable" in these contexts is metaphorical. Candidacy is not an organism. "Surviving" here is also hyperbolical. "Death" of one's candidacy is not comparable to the mortality of an organism. Yet "surviving" retains a literal connotation of success or victory (so far) in what might have meant defeat. When losses drain success of satisfaction, "survivor" goes in scare quotes. Or, with Langer, one might refer to "former victims," rather than to "survivors" (Langer 1991, xii).

"Survivor" is judgment-laden in that it discriminates among those who live through an atrocity. Only those who were wronged and might have died from it (or worse) are survivors. As its intended or likely victims, their position is involuntary. They tend to lack the options and history of choices of perpetrators, collaborators, and bystanders, who could also be said to live through it. But survival is a relative concept. Because it is always *of* some event(s) and *by* someone, those who are perpetrators, collaborators, or bystanders in relation to one atrocity can be survivors of other atrocities in which they did not play those roles. Yet the question arises whether victim collaborators should also be regarded as survivors of the atrocities in which they collaborated. They are less free than other collaborators. This is an issue to which I will return.

Surviving suggests living beyond something that is or was *fatal* for many (or was intended to be or might have been). Or something comparably grave (torture, for example). "Surviving grad school" is hyperbolic insofar as it suggests you might have died. Yet there need be no hyperbole in "rape survivor," "domestic violence survivor," or "torture survivor," even if the victim was not actually (or yet) in mortal danger. These predicaments easily *become* fatal, although not always predictably in the individual case.

---

[8] Agamben's study of what he calls "remnants of Auschwitz" concludes with six pages of quotations from self-identified former Muselmänner (Agamben 1999, 166–71).

[9] Agamben proposes that the most likely origin of "Muselmann" as camp jargon is "the literal meaning of the Arabic word muslim: the one who submits unconditionally to the will of God" (Agamben 1999, 45). The operative idea here would be unconditional submission.

Among noncollaborators, what sorts of relationships to an atrocity enable one to count as a survivor? If you escape physical harm by fleeing, hiding, or passing as someone who is not a target, are you surviving? Or, have you escaped the *need* to survive?[10] Consider some cases.

Hannah Arendt fled Germany for Paris (by way of Czechoslovakia and Switzerland) the year Hitler came to power. She had been arrested for her research activities on anti-Semitic propaganda. In 1940 she was interned at Camp Gurs in the south of France, where many died or were deported to Drancy and from there to Auschwitz. She escaped from Gurs, made it to Lisbon, and in 1941 found safe passage to the United States.

The same year Arendt fled Germany for Paris (1933), Albert Einstein fled Germany for the U.S. Two years later Rudolf Carnap (with the help of the late Willard Van Orman Quine) fled to the U.S. from Czechoslovakia, where he had held a university chair.

Of these fugitives, Arendt is most clearly a Holocaust survivor. She survived the Occupation and Gurs at a time when she was in danger of being deported to Auschwitz. Einstein's and Carnap's emigrations were anticipatory. Thanks to the Allied victory, they escaped rather than survived the Holocaust, although they may have survived atrocities leading up to it.

Many flights during the Holocaust were not emigrations. Rudolf Vrba and Alfred Wetzler escaped and fled from Auschwitz in 1944 and tried unsuccessfully to save the Hungarian Jews (Vrba and Bestic 1964). They were survivors, fugitives, resisters, and attempted rescuers. Captives who jumped or were pushed from death trains (as did Ruth Altbeker Cyprys and her toddler) and fled or hid in occupied territory, enduring terror and hardship until the war's end, were survivors as well as fugitives (Cyprys 1997; see also Appleman-Jurman 1989).

What about long-term hiding that endures to the end? Here are three examples.

First, Harriet Jacobs hid in North Carolina in the 1830s from a slave master who had sexual designs on her. He refused to sell her to friends who wanted to purchase her freedom. She hid seven years in a three-foot high attic, barely sheltered from the elements by a layer of shingles, before she received safe passage to the North and escaped from slavery (Jacobs 2001).

Second, the late French philosopher Sarah Kofman was for three years a hidden child in Paris during the Occupation (Kofman 1996). She and her mother avoided deportation, thanks to shelter in the home of a Catholic widow. The widow asked Sarah to call her "Mémé." Mémé christened Sarah "Suzanne." Through much of that time, little "Suzanne" felt happy.

Third, from May 1943 to July 1944, Ignacy and Paulina Chiger and their children endured filth, stench, malnutrition, and cold as they hid with

---

[10] Thanks to Rachel Brenner for helpful conversation on this point.

six companions, all Jewish, in the sewers of Lvov, Poland (Marshall 1990) to avoid the death trains. They nearly drowned (others did).

Jacobs, Kofman, and the Chiger family totally escaped capture by hiding until liberation. Yet, as targets of oppression, all endured major harms and losses. Harriet Jacobs was a slave for two decades before she went into hiding, where her health deteriorated permanently. Kofman lost her parents very prematurely, her father to Auschwitz and, in a different way, her mother through Mémé, who undermined Kofman's attachment to her mother and to Judaism. The Chiger family's health was permanently compromised, also. They endured illness, accidents, and near detection in the sewers and a close brush with death in the ghetto before they went into hiding.

Jacobs became an articulate abolitionist and published her memoir in 1861 under the pseudonym Linda Brent. She survived, although her health did not. Kofman eventually detached from Mémé and recovered her attachment to Judaism but never to her mother. The year Kofman published her memoir (1994), she killed herself. (Did she survive almost forty years, or was she not truly surviving, even then?) The Chiger family and fellow survivors purchased a small business after liberation for their rescuer Leopold Socha, a Catholic Polish sewer worker who had brought them food and supplies daily and kept watch over them at extreme risk to himself.

Socha's story is also interesting. Formerly an undistinguished criminal who had done prison time, he encountered phenomenally good moral luck in opportunities that enabled him to pull himself together and become a hero. He overcame temptations that could have profited him materially. He persisted faithfully in his rescue activities when nothing remained to reimburse him. He died in 1946 in an unrelated road accident, a true survivor of the Third Reich.

"Passing" as someone who is not a target is a way of hiding, hiding in the open. Resisters and rescuers, like Socha and Mémé, passed as compliant citizens. Hidden children, like Kofman, passed as Christian, as did some, like Cyprys, who jumped from death trains. Passing raises questions I have explored in the context of sexual orientation issues (Card 1995, 194–217). The dangers are not only betrayal and exposure but complicity and worse. What must a passer do to prevent exposure? Can passers avoid betraying targets who do not pass?

There are different cases. Is the passing temporary? Are there contexts in which and people with whom one need not pass?[11] If passers remain alert to opportunities for sabotage, noncompliance, and resistance, they preserve some integrity. The need to pass can be humiliating but need not diminish one morally. Long-term total passers, however, risk becoming what they

---

[11] Bernard Boxill's work on self-respect and protest (Boxill 1976) is helpful for thinking about these issues.

were pretending to be, or else splitting into selves with incompatible norms, values, and attachments, all of which they may be loath to betray.[12] And then, who is passing for whom? Who survives?

A well-known story of passing during the Holocaust is that of Solomon Perel. His memoir *Europa, Europa* (Perel 1997) is also a prize-winning film.[13] As a teenaged Jewish refugee in Russia, Perel fell into the hands of invading Germans. He convinced them he was an ethnic German. He then fought in the Wehrmacht. He lived not only in terror of being de-pantsed but in personal ethical turmoil. Writing his memoir years later became an important survival strategy. Perel had to survive not only the Third Reich but his own long-term deceptions as well.

Passing only briefly does not pose comparable issues. In 1848 light-skinned Ellen Craft escaped slavery disguised as an invalid white gentleman traveling north to consult doctors. Her darker-skinned husband posed as her servant (Sterling 1979, 12). Their ordeal was harrowing, and they were certainly survivors. But they did not confront the same survival issues as were faced by mixed-race individuals who strive to maintain a long-term white social identity.

Solomon Perel's story brings to mind military combat veterans. Some survive atrocious POW camps. But should we regard war itself as an atrocity? There are excellent reasons to find it an indefensible institution, even though it can be justifiable or even mandatory for an individual person or nation to engage in it.[14] Civilians in war-torn areas are often mass atrocity survivors. Arguably, so are many combat veterans who were conscripted (even if conscription is the least undesirable practice to build an army). Suicide and domestic violence among veterans are increasingly recognized issues. In the free world, a conscript's term of service has been relatively limited.[15] But it has still been long enough to give rise to moral setbacks and impose major burdens. Jonathan Shay, psychiatrist to Vietnam veterans, finds physical violence insufficient to explain the PTSD he treats. He finds in addition grave violations within the soldier's own unit, such as betrayal by a superior officer—especially if it resulted in or was followed by death of a buddy—and the "fraggings" consequent on such betrayals. "Fragging," portrayed in Oliver Stone's film *Platoon* (1986), was Vietnam combat slang for assassination of a military superior or officer (Shay 1994, 125). It peaked in Vietnam in 1971 with 333 confirmed

---

[12]Spies and moles take similar moral risks. The film *Donnie Brasco* (1997; DVD 2000; dir. Mike Newell) dramatizes them in the true story of an agent who passed as a "wise guy."

[13]The film *Europa, Europa* (1990) is directed by Agnieska Holland, in German and Russian with English subtitles, MGM (DVD 2003).

[14]Schott (2008) finds war justifiable despite being morally illegitimate. I leave open that it can also be justifiable to refuse to take part in such an institution.

[15]Jewish combat veterans conscripted for twenty-five years' service in nineteenth-century Russia were clearly survivors of a long-term atrocity. I wonder how many survived.

incidents and another 158 possible ones (Holmes 1985, 329).[16] Shay believes grave violations of what soldiers take to be legitimate expectations lie at the root of moral character breakdowns from which the soldier's recovery is usually incomplete. He finds confirmation in Homer's *Iliad*. Achilles goes berserk after betrayal by his superior officer and then Patrocles's death in battle.[17] Patrocles's death, Shay notes, is insufficient to explain Achilles's response. Combat death is not unexpected. Achilles survived not only expected horrors from the enemy but betrayal within his own unit as well. Whether or not war itself is an atrocity, many veterans survive atrocities within war.

What about children of survivors? Harm to survivors does not necessarily harm their children born later. It can have opposite effects. But it presents trials for that next generation. What children survive is not the same as what their parents survived. Survival is not transitive. Atrocity survivors must have lived through at least part of it. But children survive domestic violence that has roots in parents' military traumas. Not only children suffer. In a group targeted by genocide, everyone can be impacted and for more than one generation (Bar On 2002, 87–110). Through nightmares and fears based on what they have heard children can experience vicariously what their parents survived. Revisiting his early life as the child of survivors, Art Spiegelman writes in *Maus II*, "I did have nightmares about S.S. men coming into my class and dragging all us Jewish kids away" (Spiegelman 1991, 16). He recalls, "When I was a kid I used to think about which of my parents I'd let the Nazis take to the ovens if I could save only one of them" (Spiegelman 1991, 14). Vladek, Artie's father, moans in his sleep and Artie remembers, "When I was a kid I thought that was the noise *all* grown-ups made when they slept" (Spiegelman 1991, 74).

By now, one may wonder, what turns on survivor status? Does it matter whether children of survivors are survivors? Or those who hide, flee, or pass? It matters to those who embrace survivor status and to those who reject it or are ambivalent. What turn on it are the values at stake in survival and how it was that one escaped being killed. There are several issues.

We can mostly set aside reparations issues. In the case of American relocation camps for residents and citizens of Japanese ancestry during World War II, all and only survivors who could document their internment were lawfully entitled to compensation by Congress's Civil Liberties Act

---

[16] Richard Holmes says "fragging" is "derived from the use of a fragmentation grenade, conveniently rolled into the victim's hooch at night, although small arms fire in the confusion of a fire fight was not unknown" (Holmes 1985, 329). Subsuming fragging under mutiny, he cites an estimate that "20 percent of American officers who died in Vietnam may have died at the hands of their own men" (ibid.).

[17] The violation here was that Achilles's superior officer claimed for himself a woman that Achilles had been "justly" awarded by fellow soldiers as the prize for his valor.

of 1988.[18] For compensation, all that seems to matter is what you endured wrongfully by no fault of your own and that you are alive, not how well-preserved you are.

Yet it matters to reparations for some atrocities whether you became a collaborator. Victims later convicted of criminal collaboration can lose entitlement to material benefits of survivor status. Even though their status as victims was involuntary, their collaboration is in tension with certain honorific connotations of "survivor."

For those who are not defeated by long-term mass atrocities, "survivor" may sound like a status to own with pride. Many are ambivalent about owning that status when they feel shame at what they endured or did or did not do. When pride is at issue, it matters not just that you suffered wrongfully and are still alive but also how much of yourself and what in yourself you preserved, how well you are doing.

Testifying as a witness is potentially an aid to recovery of self-respect by enabling survivors to contribute to truth and justice. It can also encourage mourning of losses. As in the case of Solomon Perel, it can reinforce one's identity and help put one's choices into perspective. Victims tend to be uniquely positioned to witness the harms of a long-term mass atrocity that they experienced directly. Yet, what victims endure can also block or destroy their *ability* to testify. Levi wrote, "We, the survivors, are not the *true* witnesses." The true witnesses, he said, did not return, "or returned mute" (Levi 1989, 83–84).

Yet, if the ability to testify survives, motives to conceal what one did or suffered complicate testimonial reliability. Collaborators not yet tried for their crimes have powerful motives for concealment. Noncollaborating victims may be reluctant to reveal past humiliations. Over time, with appreciation of what others also suffered, motives for revelation can outweigh motives for concealment when the issue is humiliation.[19] Analogous transformations are less likely in collaborators who have not stood trial, and (as we will see) even in some who have.

Survivor status is also embraced for simpler reasons by political activists. "Survivor" can sound like a winner (relatively speaking) and "victim," a loser or a quitter. So heard, "survivor" sounds like praise or congratulation (albeit of an unenviable sort) and "victim" a term of derogation or pity. Thus, feminist critic Naomi Wolf deplores what she calls "victim feminism," contrasting it with "power feminism" (Wolf 1993, 135–214). And a YouTube video available in July 2010 showed a survivor dancing with his grandchild at Auschwitz (Teibel 2010).

---

[18] Arguably, that requirement was too stringent. The government failed to protect internees from loss by theft of their homes and businesses. More than one generation suffered from those thefts. Children could inherit payments their parents lived long enough to collect. Children whose parents had died were not entitled to payments their parents would have received.

[19] See, for example, Langer's chapter on humiliated memory (Langer 1991, 77–120).

"True survivor" in relation to long-term atrocities *is* ordinarily meant as praise. Yet, what survivors "win" needs scrutiny. And "victim" should not be heard as derogatory or pitiable. Many nonsurvivors were not quitters. They were at critical moments unlucky, unsupported, or betrayed. Some chose, for good reasons, not to survive. And so, I turn to the ethics of surviving.

The Ethics of Surviving

Critical choices for survivors arise at three stages: in anticipation of the onset, through the duration, and in the aftermath. Earlier choices can affect the availability or eligibility of later ones.[20] I focus for now on the duration: issues of noncompliance, silence, resistance, escape, loyalty, deception, even complicity. Unlike collaboration, complicity need not be culpable. But it is morally risky in the temptations it creates and the self-deceptions it makes likely.

The ethics of survival is a sensitive topic. Many are ashamed of or ambivalent about what they did to protect themselves or what they did not do to protect others or protest. Some conclude retrospectively that certain of their choices are not ultimately defensible (e.g., Cohen 1973). Many judge themselves more harshly than anyone else would have a right to. I have no interest in blaming. But neither do I strive for ethical neutrality. To gain perspective on the ethical costs of survival, I find no adequate substitute for reflecting on responses of people who actually faced dangers no one should have to and that I have never faced. Memoirs and testimonies are invaluable. Next best are biographies based on in-depth interviews.

Like Spiegelman, we can *imagine* what we might do or suffer were we in such predicaments. But can we *learn* from others' experience? It is tempting to say, as Langer often implies (Langer 1998, 20, 22, 163), that we cannot learn anything ethically significant that we did not already know. Yet, the same might be said of studying rape (Schott 2010). Who does not already know that rape is wrong? But that kind of judgment centers the perpetrator. If we shift attention to the experience and agency of victims, we might gain ethical insight into their moral luck, the nature of the violation, what challenges they face, and what becomes of their character.[21]

---

[20] Bettelheim notes that because Otto Frank did not emigrate with his family, his options narrowed (Bettelheim 1980, 246–57). Frank, he says, might have hidden Anne and Margot in other families to give them greater chances for survival. Apparently, Otto Frank, or perhaps his family, opted for survival of the family, not just members. Bettelheim says his point "is not to criticize what the Franks did, but only the universal admiration of their way of coping, or rather of not coping." (In view of the "not coping," that seems a distinction without a difference.)

[21] See, for example, Schott's work on war rape (2008, 2010). See Allen (1986, 27–59) and Brison (2002) for autobiographical philosophical reflections by philosophers who survived violent rape.

In the space remaining, I reflect on choices four Holocaust survivors tell us they made, or witnesses reliably report them to have made, and then I conclude briefly with an ancient issue regarding who is harmed the most by evils. Two of the survivors are women; two are men. For three, having to choose was disastrous moral luck that generated further survival issues. The survival of at least these three is compromised. One appears not to have survived her moral setbacks, although she lived a long time. Another appears to have survived better than anyone could have expected. About the third, I have many questions.

The ethics of self-defense ordinarily takes for granted a reasonably coherent self with a tolerably coherent welfare to defend. In criminal law, self-defense justifies using force only against another who is (reasonably perceived as) an unjust aggressor and only as much as needed to protect one's self and its bottom-line needs (Garner 2004, 1390).[22] Long-term mass atrocity complicates this picture. Rationality has less to work with in systematically deceived agents. Their control of consequences is severely diminished. And which bystanders are innocent? What force excessive? More troubling, victims' agency and sense of self can come apart into fragments that do not cohere well with each other. I do not mean that the victim's ability to act is destroyed. Although moral paralysis is possible in some selves, other fragmented selves can be capable of sophisticated action. But who is responsible for what a fragment does? It becomes ambiguous what is being defended and by whom. The agent is liable to lose perspective on what is worth defending.

Consider "U-boats" in Berlin who became catchers (*Greifer*) for the Gestapo. U-boats were "submerged" Jewish fugitives who lived on the streets (without a star) or in hiding while Gestapo agents were rounding up "enemies of the Reich" for transport to Theresienstadt or an extermination camp. To become a catcher, one accepted a deal from the Gestapo: your name will be removed from the transport lists for as long as you are useful in bringing in other U-boats for transport. The Gestapo armed catchers with guns. Many U-boats who were captured refused that deal. Some who had been betrayed by catchers might otherwise have survived. Some who were not betrayed did survive. And we know as much about catchers as we do because some who were betrayed survived anyway and testified later.

In 1943 beautiful twenty-year-old Stella Goldschlag became a catcher.[23] Blonde and blue-eyed, passing as "Aryan," she was a U-boat until a catcher betrayed her. More than once she escaped the clutches of Gestapo officers. They recaptured her and tortured her each time (by beatings) for

---

[22] *Black's Law Dictionary* (Garner 2004, 1390) quotes Ashworth (1991): "The law of self-defence, as it is applied by the courts, turns on two requirements: the force must have been necessary, and it must have been reasonable."

[23] My source is Wyden (1992). He was a childhood classmate of Stella Goldschlag. Stella had so many surnames that I follow Wyden and call her simply "Stella," to avoid confusion.

information they erroneously thought she had regarding the hiding place of her acquaintance, the forger Guenther Rogoff. (She did not know he had escaped to Switzerland.) Finally, after her parents were rounded up while she was in prison broken from beatings, she negotiated a deal: take my name *and* my parents' names off the transport lists, and I will catch U-boats for you. In the end, she saved only herself, if she can rightly be said to have saved herself.

At first, Stella pretended. She let old friends escape when she was not being watched. But her biographer Peter Wyden reports that she formed an attachment to another U-boat turned collaborator, Rolf Isaaksohn, and that under his influence her priorities changed. She became a skillful catcher, widely feared. She continued after her parents were transported and she knew they had died. Wyden relies on interviews with survivors who knew her, some betrayed by her, some who testified against her. At her postwar trials, Stella admitted only to searching for Rogoff and denied everything else. She served ten years in Soviet prisons. She was convicted again in a German court. That sentence was suspended for time served.

When Wyden found her in the 1980s, Stella was living on social security and life insurance from the third of four husbands (Wyden 1992, 286). She considered herself a Christian. She seemed to believe the denials she had maintained for so long. With Wyden she maintained an affectionate, almost gay demeanor. Yet he reports that her routine was to leave her apartment only for a solitary daily meal and otherwise live behind drawn curtains. Her only child, a daughter raised by others, would have nothing to do with her.

Stella Goldschlag's moral luck could hardly be more opposed to Leopold Socha's. Both were at a point in their lives where they had not developed good character. *His* options presented a chance to develop integrity and become, over many months, one of the best selves that he had the potential to be. Her options—fairly immediate (virtually certain) death or collaboration—offered no comparable opportunity. Possibilities for resistance depended on whom she knew or met. Pretending bought her some time but not enough for radical character change. Socha had time to reassess values and habits (although, to be fair, some of his skills as a criminal served him well as a rescuer). Becoming a real catcher developed Stella's worst traits. It allowed her a limited self-esteem, as she became good at it. But it developed a self hard for anyone to live with. Even she could do so only by systematic self-deception. The person she became would also be virtually impossible for her to overcome without miraculous luck (which never happened).

Stella had many skills of a true survivor in the first sense. She was creative, courageous, persistent, and a risk-taker. Yet, although she experienced severe anti-Semitism and gender bias, she never learned to evaluate either. With better luck in whom she met and became attached to, she might have. Wyden says her family lacked the resources and connections that enabled his own to emigrate. So Stella exploited her ability to pass.

She might have succeeded had she not been betrayed and had she not discovered, on being tortured, that her looks were not going to save her. Sizing up her opportunities, she made herself useful. Ultimately, she recovered a life of making herself attractive—to men with comparable values. That virtually sealed her development. But her persistent denials suggest that she could not endorse her past. That continuing need for dishonesty may be the best thing that survived in her.[24]

Shortly after the *Anschluss* of 1938, the now world-famous women's historian Gerda Lerner (then Kronstein) was imprisoned in Vienna, hostage for her father, who was arranging from outside the country for the family's escape. She came to terms with death at age eighteen. She writes, "One can survive by either having hope or by settling with the likelihood of one's own death. I did both" (Lerner 2002, 107). "I thought of death and how one must choose. We all must die and we do not know when or how, but we can choose to live unafraid by being ready to die." (Lerner 2002, 109). So fortified and not knowing how long she might be in prison, she created a "school" and a regimen for her cellmates. She campaigned for her release to take an academic exam. Under questioning by an S.S. officer, she revealed that she had researched the German ballad, although she had no idea he was an expert on that. Her release from prison was just in time for the fortuitously postponed exam that would set a course for her future. She was able to emigrate (another story). Luck was with her. But it would probably not have sufficed. She is a true survivor, in both senses. As of this writing (March 2011), she is ninety and still publishing.

Four years later, prisoners faced grimmer options. Filip Müller, Czechoslovakian and Jewish (and born the same year as Stella), told himself on arrival at Auschwitz (1942) some of the same things as Professor Lerner: "We must all die"; "Death ... was after all, part of our lives and we would have to face it sooner or later" (Müller 1999, 24). But he adds, "These considerations were quite futile and failed lamentably either to stifle or to dismiss my fears" (ibid.). His predicament was unimaginable. Death awaits us all, but not torture. Assigned to the *Sonderkommando* ("special squad" for crematorium duty), this twenty-year-old former player of the violin screwed up his courage and became determined to learn everything possible about what was going on. Müller calls those who worked the ovens "crematorium ravens." He became a master raven, the longest enduring raven of them all.

Unlike the Berlin catchers, crematorium ravens were almost never in a position to decide who would live and who would die (except themselves). They were complicit in the deception of the showers. But they did not betray anyone who could have survived. Still, in July 1944, Levi reports, four hundred Jews from Corfu assigned to the Sonderkommando "refused

[24]Thanks to Jeff Reiman for reminding me of La Rochefoucauld's formulation, "Hypocrisy is the homage vice pays to virtue."

to do the work and were immediately gassed" (Levi 1989, 58). Others committed suicide. Some buried testimony in cans unearthed years later. The twelfth Sonderkommando blew up a crematorium in October 1944 in a plot to which Müller contributed (he supplied maps). That group were killed but took some Nazis with them. Müller was routinely alert to covert ways to sabotage and resist.

It is not hard for me to understand why other Sonderkommandos did not take the route of the courageous Jews from Corfu. Grabbed as they stumbled out of the cattle cars—disoriented, dehydrated, dazed—many were deceived into thinking they had been chosen for an elite job (deceptions that might not have worked by 1944). Once undeceived, they could reasonably fear that overt resistance could get them thrown into a furnace alive. Müller records that the S.S. did that to at least one raven who tried to warn prisoners in the undressing room that the shower room was really a gas chamber (Müller 1999, 80).

After the "family camp" from Theresienstadt was gassed, Müller (recall, he was Czechoslovakian) felt his own further "survival" meaningless. He entered the gas chamber determined to share the fate of others. But two young women pushed him out, urging him to survive to bear witness (Müller 1999, 111–14). Which he did—at the 1965 Auschwitz trials (Naumann 1966, 266–68), in his memoir (Müller 1999 [originally 1979]), and in interviews by Claude Lanzmann in the documentary film *Shoah* (Lanzmann 1985).

Did Müller truly survive? His skills were phenomenal. His memoir is a major testimonial. But what did he preserve of himself? Lacking Stella's capacity for self-deception, he carries a past that is a torment. He lost family and the social contexts that had given his life positive meaning. Auschwitz gave him no space even to grieve. Yet he never identified with his oppressors. His capacity for moral assessment deepened through his vigilance and resistance efforts. His memoir preserves a morally sensitive account of the Sonderkommando, as well as of others' heroic deeds and still others' crimes in which he played no role at all. To a greater extent than anyone could have anticipated, Filip Müller survived his own "survival."

The last case is forty-three-year-old Hungarian Jewish physician Miklos Nyiszli. He arrived at Auschwitz in May 1944 (two years after Müller) and was also chosen for the Sonderkommando (Nyiszli 1993).[25] Müller, who was young and physically robust, had been assigned heavy labor. Dr. Nyiszli, who was neither, stepped forward when Josef Mengele asked for physicians. After questioning him, Mengele picked him to be chief physician in the Sonderkommando. Dr. Nyiszli performed autopsies on twins and dwarfs murdered for Mengele's "experiments" in "racial

---

[25]According to translator Richard Seaver, Nyiszli first published his account in Jean-Paul Sartre's journal, *Les Temps Modernes*. The English translation includes a "Declaration" signed by Nyiszli in March 1946, apparently for Sartre's journal (Nyiszli 1993, 11–12).

science." Nyiszli's services, skills, and diligence would not have been easily replaceable. He reported on what he found in autopsies that might interest Mengele. He kept meticulous records for Berlin. He not only made it his goal, as he says, to *persuade* Mengele that he was too valuable an assistant to gas. He *became* that assistant. With greater mobility, privileges, and discretion than the ravens, he got assistance to his wife and daughter, also prisoners, and they all lived to be reunited.

What did Dr. Nyiszli preserve? He kept himself and his family alive. In his book he invokes the goal of exposing Mengele's crimes as his justification for diligent service to Mengele, and he hopes for redemption thereby after the war. Flawed as an account of Auschwitz, Dr. Nyiszli's book is still a unique source on Mengele. But at what cost did Dr. Nyiszli live to write it? How *much* did he need to redeem? What would his redemption even mean?

Bruno Bettelheim in his polemical foreword of 1960 to the English translation of Dr. Nyiszli's book (Nyiszli 1993, v–xviii) deplores Nyiszli's choices but is convinced of his honesty (by then, Nyiszli had died). Yet, insofar as Dr. Nyiszli's goal was to expose Mengele, he needed to confess just enough of his own role to explain how he knew what Mengele did. What does Dr. Nyiszli not tell us? In his admitted eagerness to impress Mengele, how far did he go? What became of the identity of the man who became Mengele's assistant?

Did Dr. Nyiszli develop a double self? Psychiatrist Robert Lifton proposes, based on his interviews with former Nazi doctors, that *those* doctors developed a separate self for camp life, distinct from the self they embodied at home, each with its own values (Lifton 1986, 418–29). Lifton offers this idea only to explain how the doctors could function in both worlds, not as any moral excuse for what they did. Nazi doctors had options that Dr. Nyiszli lacked. Yet, the question arises whether, as Mengele's assistant, part of Dr. Nyiszli *identified* with Mengele, while another part went into limbo. Did he bond with Mengele, as victims are said to do in the Stockholm or Hostage Syndrome? Doubling, as Lifton presents it, appears to be radical dissociation without amnesia. Is "doubling" just another term for long-term comprehensive passing? If so, which self is passing? Do they both pass? Does Dr. Nyiszli pass as Mengele's too-valuable-to-gas assistant in the camp? And then does the valuable assistant that he became pass as Dr. Nyiszli who was in limbo at Auschwitz? Which self wrote Nyiszli's book?

At *Gorgias* 469ff. Plato has Socrates argue that it is worse to *do* wrong than to *suffer* it, not just morally worse but a greater *harm* (Plato 1961, 251ff.). Wrongdoers, he says, are unhappier, more miserable, than the wronged. Let's call the question who is more miserable "the *Gorgias* question." At issue is not who *feels* worse but who is more harmed: the wrongdoer or the wronged? The Kantian in me has long said to Socrates's answer, "Absurd! Wishful thinking. Would that Nazi criminals were as harmed as the Muselmänner they produced!" Even Hannah Arendt, who once thought totalitarianism made victims and perpetrators alike into automata (see Arendt 2000, 119–40), changed her view about that at Eichmann's trial (Arendt 1965). Eichmann remained shamefully (and shamelessly) all too human, in his very inhumanity.

Suppose, however, that we compare not a voluntary wrongdoer with an involuntary victim but instead two victims, one complicit for survival's sake in wrongs to the other. In gray zones, victims who accept power become complicit in the very evils they suffer. They risk losing perspective, scruples, compassion, integrity. Complicit survivors can fragment into selves with incompatible norms and values, as in Lifton's "doubling" or Stella's systematic self-deception. They can internalize norms hostile to what is best in their former selves. Is that a worse harm than the deaths of victims who refuse complicity? An affirmative answer is not absurd.

On the value of survival, I note (although it is not decisive) that long-term atrocity survivors do not speak with one voice. Like many combat veterans, many Holocaust "survivors"—Sarah Kofman, Jean Améry, Tadeusz Borowski, Bruno Bettelheim, and (it is widely believed) Primo Levi—have killed themselves.[26] Suicide might result from the victory of one fragment of a fragmented self, or depression, or pessimism about world politics. Yet some suicides occurred just after publication or reissue of a memoir that reflects a balanced view. *Something reminiscent* of the *Gorgias* idea lingers in the thought that, owing to the moral burdens of survival through complicity, splitting, or moral paralysis, survivors risk saving a life worse for themselves than death would have been. Yet, here the distinction between wrongdoer and wronged at the heart of the *Gorgias* question is no longer sharp: some wrongs put others into situations in which staying alive requires wrongdoing or ceasing to care what is right. And so, I end with a post-Holocaust *Gorgias*-inspired question. Which harm is greater: to become *in*human, like Eichmann, at the same time remaining shamefully (if also shamelessly) human? Or to be utterly *de*humanized, losing hope as well as self-respect, joining the walking dead, the Muselmänner? The *Gorgias* view suggests that one whose humanity is perverted without being extinguished is more harmed than one whose humanity is extinguished without being perverted. The fallout from evils, like the radioactive fallout from nuclear disasters, contains the very real danger of contaminating what it does not kill.

The late Robert Nozick observed that humanity's disappearance from the planet would not be as regrettable as it might have seemed before the Holocaust (Nozick 1989, 236–42). On a more local scale, there may be lessons for nations regarding the value placed on security by victims of terror.[27] In designing policies to further the survival of national groups,

---

[26]No one witnessed the fall that killed Levi in 1987. He left no suicide note. That he jumped rather than fell in a heart attack or stroke is an inference probably impossible to verify.

[27]See, for example, the chapters on security in Jeremy Waldron's *Torture, Terror, and Trade-Offs: Philosophy for the White House* (New York: Oxford University Press, 2010).

we should reflect on what survival would mean (what would remain, for example) and what its value would be to those who remain.

References

Agamben, Giorgio. 1999. *Remnants of Auschwitz: The Witness and the Archive*, trans. Daniel Heller-Roazen. New York: Zone Books.

Allen, Jeffner. 1986. *Lesbian Philosophy: Explorations*. Palo Alto, CA: Institute of Lesbian Studies.

Appleman-Jurman, Alicia. 1989. *Alicia: My Story*. New York: Bantam.

Arendt, Hannah. 1965. *Eichmann in Jerusalem*. Rev. & enlarged. New York: Viking.

———. 2000. *The Portable Hannah Arendt*. New York: Penguin.

Aristotle. 2009. *The Nicomachean Ethics*, trans. W. D. Ross. Rev. Lesley Brown. New York: Oxford.

Ashworth, Andrew. 1991. *Principles of Criminal Law*. New York: Oxford.

Bar On, Bat-Ami. 1991. "Holocaust and Resistance." In Sander H. Lee, ed., *Inquiries into Values: The Inaugural Session of the International Society for Value Inquiry*. Lewiston, NY: Edwin Mellen, 495–508.

———. 2002. *The Subject of Violence: Arendtean Exercises in Understanding*. Lanham, MD: Rowman and Littlefield.

Bettelheim, Bruno. 1960. *The Informed Heart: Autonomy in a Mass Age*. Glencoe, IL: Free Press.

———. 1980. *Surviving and Other Essays*. New York: Vintage.

Boxill, Bernard R. 1976. "Self Respect and Protest." *Philosophy and Public Affairs* (Fall): 58–69.

Brison, Susan. 2002. *Aftermath: Violence and the Remaking of a Self*. Princeton, NJ: Princeton University Press.

Card, Claudia. 1995. *Lesbian Choices*. New York: Columbia University Press.

———. 1996. *The Unnatural Lottery: Character and Moral Luck*. Philadelphia: Temple University Press.

———. 2002. *The Atrocity Paradigm: A Theory of Evil*. New York: Oxford University Press.

———. 2010. *Confronting Evils: Terrorism, Torture, Genocide*. Cambridge: Cambridge University Press.

Cohen, Elie. 1973. *The Abyss: A Confession*, trans. James Brockway. New York: Norton. Originally in Dutch, Amsterdam, 1971.

Cyprys, Ruth Altbeker. 1997. *A Jump for Life: A Survivor's Journal from Nazi-Occupied Poland*, trans. Elaine Potter. New York: Continuum.

Garner, Bryan A., ed. 2004. *Black's Law Dictionary*, 8th ed. St. Paul, MN: Thomson.

Holmes, Richard. 1985. *Acts of War: The Behavior of Men in Battle*. Glencoe, IL: Free Press.

Jacobs, Harriet. 2001. *Incidents in the Life of a Slave Girl: Contexts, Criticism*. Ed. Nellie Y. McKay and Frances Smith Foster. New York: Norton.

Kant, Immanuel. 1996. *Practical Philosophy*, trans. Mary J. Gregor. Cambridge: Cambridge University Press.

———. 1997. *Lectures on Ethics*. Ed. Peter Heath and J. B. Schneewind, trans. Peter Heath. Cambridge: Cambridge University Press.

Kofman, Sarah. 1996. *Rue Ordener, Rue Labat*, trans. Ann Smock. Lincoln: University of Nebraska Press, 1996. Originally Éditions Galilée, 1994.

Langer, Lawrence L. 1991. *Holocaust Testimonies: The Ruins of Memory*. New Haven, CT: Yale University Press.

———. 1998. *Preempting the Holocaust*. New Haven, CT: Yale University Press.

Lanzmann, Claude. 1985. *Shoah: An Oral History of the Holocaust*. Complete text of the film with preface by Simone de Beauvoir. New York: Pantheon.

Lerner, Gerda. 2002. *Fireweed: A Political Autobiography*. Philadelphia: Temple University Press.

Levi, Primo. 1989. *The Drowned and the Saved*, trans. Raymond Rosenthal. New York: Vintage, 1989. Previously, Simon & Schuster, 1988.

Lifton, Robert J. 1986. *The Nazi Doctors: Medical Killing and the Psychology of Genocide*. New York: Basic Books.

Marshall, Robert. 1990. *In the Sewers of Lvov: A Heroic Story of Survival from the Holocaust*. New York: Scribner.

Müller, Filip. 1999. *Eyewitness Auschwitz: Three Years in the Gas Chambers*, trans. Susanne Flatauer. Chicago: Ivan R. Dee. Previously published by Routledge & Kegan Paul Ltd., 1979.

Murakami, Haruki. 2001. *Underground*, trans. Alfred Birnbaum and Philip Gabriel. New York: Vintage.

Naumann, Bernd. 1966. *Auschwitz: A Report on the Proceedings Against Robert Kal Ludwit Mulka and Others Before the Court at Frankfurt*. trans. Jean Steinberg. Introduction by Hannah Arendt. London: Pall Mall Press.

Nozick, Robert. 1989. *The Examined Life: Philosophical Meditations*. New York: Simon & Schuster.

Nyiszli, Miklos. 1993. *Auschwitz: A Doctor's Eyewitness Account*, trans. Tibère Kreme and Richard Seaver. Foreword by Bruno Bettelheim. New York: Arcade.

Oliver, Kelly. 2001. *Witnessing: Beyond Recognition*. Minneapolis: University of Minnesota Press.

Perechodnik, Calel. 1996. *Am I a Murderer? Testament of a Jewish Ghetto Policeman*, ed. and trans. Frank Fox. Boulder, CO: Westview Press.

Perel, Solomon. 1997. *Europa, Europa*, trans. Margot Bettauer Dembo. New York: Wiley. Originally in French, Éditions Ramsay, 1990.

Plato, 1961. *The Collected Dialogues of Plato, Including the Letters*, ed. Edith Hamilton and Huntington Cairns. New York: Bollingen.

Schott, Robin. 2008. "Just War and the Problem of Evil." *Hypatia* 23: 122–40.

———. 2010. "War Rape, Natality and Genocide," *Journal of Genocide Research* 13: 5–21.

Shafer-Landau, Russ. 2003. *Moral Realism: A Defense*. Oxford: Clarendon Press.

Shay, Jonathan. 1994. *Achilles in Vietnam: Combat Trauma and the Undoing of Character*. New York: Atheneum.

Sherman, Nancy. 2010. *The Untold War: Inside the Hearts Minds and Souls of Our Soldiers*. New York: Norton.

Skitolsky, Lissa. 2010. "Finding Man in *Der Muselmann*." In James R. Watson, ed., *Metacide: In the Pursuit of Excellence*, 93–114. Amsterdam: Rodopi.

Solzhenitzyn, Alexander. 1963. *One Day in the Life of Ivan Denisovich*, trans. Ralph Parker. New York: Dutton.

Spiegelman, Art. 1991. *Maus II*. New York: Pantheon.

Sterling, Dorothy. 1979. *Black Foremothers: Three Lives*. Old Westbury, NY: The Feminist Press.

Teibel, Amy. 2010. "Holocaust Survivor's Dance Sparks Debate." *The Wisconsin State Journal*, 7 July, A1, A7.

Tessman, Lisa. 2005. *Burdened Virtues: Virtue Ethics for Liberatory Struggles*. New York: Oxford University Press.

Thomas, Laurence Mordekhai. 1988. "Liberalism and the Holocaust: An Essay on Trust and the Black-Jewish Relationship." In *Echoes from the Holocaust: Philosophical Reflections on a Dark Time*, ed. Alan Rosenberg and Gerald E. Myers. Philadelphia: Temple University Press.

———. 1993. *Vessels of Evil: American Slavery and the Holocaust*. Philadelphia: Temple University Press.

Trunk, Isaiah. 1996. *Judenrat: The Jewish Councils in Eastern Europe Under Nazi Occupation*. Lincoln: University of Nebraska Press. Previously, New York: Macmillan, 1972.

Vrba, Rudolf, and Alan Bestic. 1964. *I Cannot Forgive*. New York: Bantam. Republished as *I Escaped from Auschwitz*. Fort Lee, NJ: Barricade Books, 2002.

Waldron, Jeremy. 2010. *Torture, Terror, and Trade-Offs: Philosophy for the White House*. New York: Oxford University Press.

Williams, B. A. O., and Thomas Nagel. 1976. "Moral Luck." *Aristotelian Society Proceedings*, Supp. 6: 115–51.

Wolf, Naomi. 1993. *Fire with Fire: The New Female Power and How to Use It*. New York: Fawcett Columbine.

Wyden, Peter. 1992. *Stella*. New York: Simon & Schuster.

CHAPTER 8

PERPETRATORS AND SOCIAL DEATH

A CAUTIONARY TALE

LYNNE TIRRELL

Confronting evils pulls our minds and hearts in several directions. We can focus on acute cataclysmic events that shock us into awareness, or chronic corrosive evils that damage our agency and dull our attention. We can focus on those who commit grave wrongs, or those who suffer them. Any account of evil must encompass these dimensions and more, shifting focus while attending to interconnections of parts to whole. Claudia Card's work has offered a steady focus on the experiences and needs of survivors of atrocities and grave wrongs, in contrast to what she calls "administrative" approaches to ethics that tend to focus on punishing perpetrators. Card explains: "An animating concern for me has been to counterbalance the nearly exclusive focus by philosophers on perpetrator psychology by highlighting the plight of victims" (Card 2011, 8). Nevertheless, she has considerable insights on perpetrators and bystanders, and those caught in gray zones of forced complicity.[1] This paper will explore what Card's most recent work suggests about perpetrators, that is, about the moral risks of participating in evil. Wherever we look, and whatever policies we enact, we

---

[1] Card began discussing gray zones in Card 1999, and has discussed them in essays since then, but the most developed account appears in Card 2002, chapter 10, where she describes a gray zone as an intentionally created stressful situation designed to corrupt the will, place victims in a no-win inescapable situation, and force their complicity in harming others who are very much like themselves. The prime example, drawn from Primo Levi's *The Drowned and the Saved* (Levi 1988), is the way Nazis used concentration camp prisoners to police each other. More generally, Card descries gray zones as situations "in which victims of oppression are used to maintain and administer the very machinery of oppression" (Card 2002, 26).

Criticism and Compassion: The Ethics and Politics of Claudia Card.
Edited by Robin S. Dillon and Armen T. Marsoobian.
Chapters and book compilation © 2018 Metaphilosophy LLC and John Wiley & Sons Ltd.

must join Card in facing "the moral challenge of avoiding evil responses to evil" (Card 2010, 9).[2]

Claudia Card's groundbreaking work on atrocities addresses not only the extraordinary cases that shock but also, importantly, the atrocities often overlooked because they are common, ongoing, supported by institutions and practices that shape our social worlds. Obvious atrocities include terrorism, torture, forced starvation, slavery, rape, and genocide; these each involve many grave wrongs. On the other hand, not all grave wrongs are unusual, as Card warns: "Appreciating the low-profile terrorism and torture that are routine under oppressive regimes, in racist environments, and in families devastated by domestic violence has made me cautious about equating 'grave' with 'extraordinary'" (Card 2010, 17). Rightly so, for some grave wrongs are cumulative—so common that people become inured to them. Some of the ongoing "everyday" atrocities she addresses include rape, incest and family violence, unjust incarcerations and violence against prisoners, the death penalty, animal experimentation, and more. One of Card's major contributions has been to connect extraordinary atrocities to everyday ongoing atrocities so commonly overlooked, and to show how these all count as evils.

Card's secular and demythologized account takes evil primarily as a feature not of persons but rather of actions, situations, institutions, and practices. In real-life evil situations, individuals can switch between victim and perpetrator roles. Moral purity is hard to come by. With characteristic directness, Card says that to "demythologize evil, we must also acknowledge that 'perpetrator' and 'victim' are abstractions. Real people are often both" (Card 2010, 15). Survivors reeling from the concrete damage they have suffered might take issue with being told their victimization is an abstraction, but they would likely accept that "victim" and "perpetrator" are deontic statuses, not essences. A victim to one person's evil might be a perpetrator of evil on someone else. These statuses mark relationships arising from actions and events, and so must be accorded in their local habitations, not taken as sweeping identity descriptions.

Like Card's, my focus has been on victims and survivors. After more than a decade studying genocide, my first thoughts turn to those slaughtered and those who survive with terrible afflictions, inside and out. My heart aches for survivors carrying unseen damages, who struggle to suppress the lingering power of the wrongs and harms they have suffered. I care about their safety and look for routes to promoting their resilience. Their persistent hope for a better future is inspiring. Unable to rectify the wrongs of the past, I seek to witness the truth of their experience, while resisting letting it define their reality too completely. I want them to find safe haven.

---

[2] In what follows, I cite published testimonies from Rwanda, choosing passages that cohere with evidence I have gathered on my own research trips there.

Even if survivors are one's first priority, it is crucial to understand how perpetrators came to behave with such depravity. Card's concept of social vitality was developed to explain what *génocidaires* destroy in their victims.[3] Here I bring that into conversation my own analysis of perpetrator testimony, arguing that the génocidaires' desire for their own social vitality, achieved through their destruction of the social world of their targets, in fact boomerangs to corrode the vitality of their own lives. This thesis is a friendly amendment to Card's analysis. There is always the hope that understanding the forces fostering the participation of ordinary people, neither devils nor saints, might help prevent future genocides. I have my doubts. In particular, I doubt that understanding the boomerang effect of inflicting social death will immunize potential génocidaires from the lures of participation. Card hopes that her account will help us think "about how to respond with as much honor as possible to the worst wrongs of which humanity is capable. It is helpful for setting priorities, constraining responses, and encouraging moral imagination" (Card 2010, 8). If prevention fails, we can still try to find ethical responses that do not perpetuate a cycle of grave wrongs.

In what follows, I highlight some issues raised by Card to guide our thinking about perpetrators—the who, what, when, where, and why of them. My focus is on the génocidaires of Rwanda, specifically members of the Hutu gangs who hunted, tortured, and killed Tutsi in Rwanda in 1994. These actions count as evil according to Card's theory. Valuable lessons are learned from bringing their testimonies into dialogue with Card's account of evil, but these lessons do not automatically apply to everyday wrongs and all bad deeds. Dehumanization and the cultivation of cruelty take many forms, so we must be careful to avoid overgeneralization. I choose this group of perpetrators because of the significance of the genocide of the Tutsi in Rwanda, and because my research over the past decade has made this, for me, slightly less like stepping into quicksand than so many other relevant and important cases.

Perpetrators: Persons, Not Monsters

Janet Connors, a trainer for Boston's Louis D. Brown Peace Institute, is an advocate for restorative justice. She often meets with and talks about the three young men who stabbed and killed her nineteen-year-old son, Joel Turner. Connors said of her son's killers: "We can't think of them as monsters, because then we let them off the hook, because then they are just

---

[3] The term *génocidaire* is now more broadly used but has its origins in the 1994 genocide of the Tutsi in Rwanda, which is the focus of my essay. The term is reserved for actual perpetrators, not used as a generalized designation for Hutu. In that way, it is primarily descriptive, but it can carry strong valances of disapproval or approval, depending on who speaks and what is being said.

monsters doing what monsters do. If I hold them in their humanity, then I hold them accountable."[4] Card's ethics holds us all in our humanity. Even the most heinous actions don't push a person off the moral map. Consider Card's claim that "'evil' may seldom mark monsters. But it often enough marks monstrous deeds" (Card 2002, 23). Persons are always accountable.

This stands in contrast to theorists like John Locke, who, in a well-known passage in his *Second Treatise of Government*, argues that a murderer "has renounced reason, the common rule and standard God has given to mankind, and by the unjust violence and slaughter he has committed on one person, he has declared war against all mankind, so that he can be destroyed as though he were a lion or a tiger" (Locke 1690, chap. 2, sec. 11). If murder sets the perpetrator down as subhuman or nonhuman, surely depraved torture, mayhem, rape, and many other crimes would do the same.[5] Anyone who thinks persons can become nonpersons might think these deeds are proof of such descent, and might join Locke in thinking of the killer as merely a dangerous beast. But we know that's false. Persons have special deontic statuses, and *even if* all of these are somehow cancellable (which Card would deny), the *fact* of that cancellation makes the case distinctive.

Card would not accept that persons could ever become nonpersons. Her work considers perpetrators' status as persons, ways in which their humanity may have been compromised, and what is to be done about that. Locke seems all for throwing them away, to protect the rest of us. Card is sensitive to the weight of moral luck, the lingering potential humanity of even the most depraved persons, and worries deeply about what our responses will do to our own characters. She seeks humane and decent responses to evil, without exposing survivors to intolerable risks.

An adequate account of evil must address both the harm done to the victim and the wrong done by the perpetrator. Card's view respects the perpetrators' agency while not allowing them much distance from the harms they inflict. Defining evils as "reasonably foreseeable intolerable harms produced by *inexcusable* wrongs" (Card 2010, 16), Card links moral and epistemic elements.[6] Reasonable foreseeability sets an epistemic standard. *Inexcusable* doesn't mean there weren't *reasons* motivating the deeds: it

---

[4] Delivered at the Slomoff Symposium for Restorative Justice in Our Communities, April 28, 2015, University of Massachusetts, Boston. For articles, see Devlin-Ross 2013; Kraft 2014. See also Smith 2011.

[5] It would be a mistake to talk about the ways that genocide seems to throw people into a state of nature, because genocide nearly always occurs within war, and Locke explicitly distinguishes between the state of nature and the state of war. Further, the genocide I'm focusing on, Rwanda 1994, was highly organized state-sponsored genocide. So let us assume that the killers in Rwanda 1994 did not renounce reason, even though they violated the murder taboo.

[6] This most recent definition addresses criticisms aimed at the definition offered in *The Atrocity Paradigm*, most notably in shifting away from culpable wrongs, which set the moral bar too low.

means that there is no *moral excuse* for the actions. In fact, the kinds of wrongs done in genocide are obviously intolerable, even though survivors live with them ever after. Many killers' testimonies discuss the suffering they inflicted, but many other killers instead brush the harms aside, saying they saw themselves as just doing a job, just wanting to get through each killing as quickly as possible. Or they were just saving their own lives. There are many ex post facto excuses, but none excuses.

Perpetrators often have mixed and mercurial reactions as they reflect upon their own deeds, and some of these responses or evasions can boomerang back as self-inflicted damage. Most suppress the lingering power and moral remainders of the wrongs they have done. In Rwanda 1994, inflicting suffering was part of why perpetrators inflicted the particular harms they did. Facing one's own capacity to inflict suffering is a diffult moral challenge for anyone, but when the scale of suffering inflicted is so extreme, the need for denial becomes even more pressing. And yet some did not deny their crimes but faced them directly. Acknowledging the intentional infliction of suffering, one génocidaire, Alphonse Hitiyare-mye, explained that perpetrators killed babies very quickly "because their suffering was of no use.... The babies could not understand the why of the suffering, it was not worth lingering over them" (Hatzfeld 2005, 131–32). Alphonse accepted the cruelty of the suffering he inflicted on older children and adults, because their suffering was worth the effort. Consider: in the twisted environment of genocide, it was actually considered *friendly* to inflict a quick death with a bullet instead of a slow painful death from machete blows leading to infection or exsanguination. So some perpetrators might say they were kind or merciful, not cruel, in their quicker killing of neighbors, without stopping to face the wrong done by the killing in itself. As hard as it is to read this, it must be harder to face for the killers who remember these actions as their own. Card talks about the need to become invulnerable to compassion if one wants to be a "badass"; Alphonse shows this invulnerability here (Card 2016, 38). Whether they admit it or not, génocidaires have become damaged in a host of ways through the boomerang effects of the very wrongs they inflicted. And we must never forget that they are more like us than we want to admit. Card squarely faces this hard truth. It is a balancing act to hold someone accountable for his crimes, against particular individuals and against humanity, while also remembering that someone who is a perpetrator in one action or scenario can be a victim in another. Neither erases the other.

The harm of genocide lies not only in the specific crimes done to individuals, like murder, rape, and mayhem, but also in damage done to individuals qua members of groups and so also damage to the social standing and social being of the group. In "Genocide and Social Death," Card argues that the specific harm of genocide, over and above all the crimes against individuals done in the process of committing genocide, is "the harm inflicted on the victims' social vitality" (2003, 73). Social vitality "exists through relationships, contemporary and intergenerational, that create an identity that gives meaning to a life" (2003, 63). Robbing individuals of family and social relations is to damage or destroy their place in what Maria Lugones would call *a world*, complete with shared histories, norms, practices, places of significance, and more (Lugones 1987). I take Card's concept of social vitality to get at our inherent intersubjectivity. Many of the ways we live, things we do, and identity traits we embrace require the participation of others for us to envision and realize them. We enter worlds of norms and practices constructed by others, worlds that make possible our lives and our constructions of new worlds. Destroying someone's world, or exiling her from her world, is inflicting social death.

Survival within damaged worlds is often dubious survival. Damaged social vitality is well illustrated in a poignant scene in Anne Aghion's documentary *Gacaca*. Annonciata Mukanyonga, a survivor, whose whole family was brutally killed, explains that the killers actually *said* they refrained from killing her because it was worse to leave her, battered and mutilated and bereft of all those she loved and who loved her, to be haunted by the grievous loss for the rest of her life. They said, "Leave her, she is sadness incarnate. She will die of sorrow" (Aghion 2002, 2:37–4:34). In rural Rwanda, a woman without family is cast adrift, without a social identity, cast into a meaningless existence.[7] Several women in Aghion's documentaries express a sense of being already dead. The perpetrators' cruelty is enhanced by the foreseeability of the intolerableness of the harm they inflicted, by their forward-looking rationality, generating the pain for a lifetime. Card's concepts of social vitality and social death make sense of such cases, enabling us to see a perpetrator's act as a particular destruction of a survivor's world. These acts work to construct a hostile world in perpetuity. Facing this dimension of human cruelty is crucial work, important for survivors, who so often feel invisible as life moves on. Others can do them a service by witnessing their loss, seeing them into renewed community as best we can.

Social vitality is important for each of us, in all phases of our lives. So when we think about the perpetrators of genocide, whose actions were inflicting not only physical death, blow by blow, but also the social death of many survivors, we must examine the role of social vitality in their own choices and their experiences. My research suggests that their efforts often arose from a quest for social vitality, a need to be part of a social project giving them identity and meaning. Group-based identities are not an intrinsic problem, but this project was based on an illusory us/them dichotomy. Hutu and Tutsi have far more in common than anything that divides them, but over generations, and with a boost from colonialism, these categories took on an important social role shaping hierarchies of power.

---

[7] Not always or forever, as we see when orphans made new families, built new worlds, and thus gave new meaning to their lives. But this took work, and the process is far from complete.

The identity génocidaires seek is doomed whether the project of eradicating the Other succeeds or fails. If the project succeeds, and they kill all Tutsi and wipe out all memory of them, then they are bereft of the Other that gives their identity meaning. If the project fails, as it did, then the loss of purpose and meaning becomes a catalyst of their own self-destruction. The meanings of their actions now require reevaluation, and the génocidaires must find their place in the new world being constructed from the shards of the one they sought to destroy. So génocidaires, in seeking to destroy their targets, succeed not only in damaging the world of their targets but in undermining their own long-term social vitality as well.

Card's work offers guidance in keeping perpetrators human, holding them responsible, and recognizing the forces at work in constructing and reinforcing their very existence as perpetrators. Card's writing on rape as terrorism, for example, pushes us to see perpetrators not simply as individual transgressors of a moral order but as simultaneously *upholders* of a social and political order, enforcers of a hegemony of power (Card 1996; Card 2004, 213–15). In urging that we look at the social vitality of becoming a génocidaire, and the social death of being a failed one, I am extending, to a category of agents with which Card was not generally concerned, her view that the key to understanding genocide is social vitality.

In the next section, I address the paradoxes of social vitality in genocide, drawing on some insights from Card's final essay, in which she asks whether gang members who commit horrible crimes to gain the reputation for being a badass are actually acting under the guise of the good (Card 2016). Card offers a careful ethical refutation of this idea, paying particular attention to Kant. Card's new paper draws on attachment theory, which dovetails with her earlier emphasis on social vitality. In the final section, I take up Card's question: How can one respond to evil without doing evil oneself? We must consider how to understand evildoers without reifying them as monsters and thus failing to understand the potential for evil in each of us. Card warns us "to avoid demonizing most perpetrators" (2010, 5), leaving room to recognize the possibility of a few demons among us.[8]

Gangs, Social Vitality, and Moral Luck

The testimonies of members of the killing gangs in the Rwandan Genocide are challenging resources. Some seem straightforward, others are laced with layers of denials, still others blame other people for the deeds the

---

[8] Card always focused more on ethical analysis, but her emphasis on the norms governing institutions and practices pulled her into the political. Also, her sensitivity to moral luck emphasizes the power of situation to shape character and the array of (really) possible actions, the limits on an agent's choices. The politics of power is clearer when we look at patterns of actions, patterns of impunity, and patterns of target selection. My approach emphasizes the political over the ethical, but we should see these as two sides of one normative coin.

perpetrators nevertheless admit to doing. Some killers claim they were overcome with a kind of collective madness, and seem mystified about how that came about. Some say the situation was "kill or be killed," but many say that no one was under such threats. We do know that there were preparations well in advance of the killings, that machetes were stockpiled and distributed to Hutu all across the country, that divisive rhetoric was the norm since at least Leon Mugusera's infamous 1992 speech, and that many convicted génocidaires will say that they learned to think even more strongly in us/them category terms from 1990 to 1994 (Tirrell 2012). In hindsight, some génocidaires lament that such speeches created conditions for their actions. The power of such normative shifts, enacted through public speeches by leaders, which are then taken up by ordinary people, can reshape the boundaries of permissible action.

Card emphasizes that "evil on the atrocity paradigm wears a human face" (2010, 16). The human face of evil might reveal a truly depraved character, but Card suggests that we should expect to sometimes find more ignorance than malice, more need for peer approval than need to express hatred or disgust. She says, "Atrocities are perpetrated by agents who have epistemological limitations and emotional attachments. They are ambivalent, deluded, changeable, fickle. 'No moral excuse' does not mean 'no humanly understandable reasons'" (2010, 16). Social positions shape both epistemic limits and emotional attachments (see, e.g., Scheman 1995 and Alcoff 2007), creating reasons we might understand without morally condoning them. The source of evils is often social, not primarily a matter of individual pathology. After years of fieldwork in Rwanda, Scott Straus argues against attributing genocidal crimes to individual antipathies, saying that the context of "war, state power, group pressure, and ethnic categorization were the most consequential factors" (2013, 245). Within a context of radical insecurity, maintaining group identity becomes important. Card's account of rape in war emphasizes its social functions: "Mass rape in war splinters families and alliances. It binds not women to men but warriors to one another" (Card 2002, 126). Rape outside war is also enabled by the actions and approvals of others: "In a misogynous climate, assailants acquire the power to shatter victims' lives. The misogyny of others," Card writes, "is sufficient to give them that power" (2010, 86). Group norms and practices and emotional attachments are often the source of evil acts, and while that doesn't offer a moral excuse, it can help us in thinking about prevention and responses to wrongdoing.

Seeing the acts of génocidaires in context, without making excuses, raises the issue of moral luck. Many génocidaires make comments about how it was just their bad luck to have been born in the wrong place at the wrong time and been sucked into a horrible vortex of violence. Thus, they seek to evade personal responsibility by blaming bad luck. Card's concern with issues of moral luck emphasizes character development, what Bernard Williams calls "constitutive moral luck" (Card 1996, 23–24). Moral luck is not, in Card's hands, about evading responsibility but about under-standing the ways that agents find themselves in situations that shape their moral lives. Luck and responsibility go hand in hand. To connect, rather than sever, luck and responsibility, Card introduces her 1996 discussion of moral luck with a reminder of the importance of distinguishing between backward-looking and forward-looking responsibility, putting an empha-sis on looking forward by *taking* responsibility, exercising "commitment, care, and concern" (1996, 25). This fits with her move away from the admin-istrative or managerial perspective of judges, which tends to emphasize backward-looking responsibility (Card 1972; Card 1996, 28).

Taking responsibility is about exercising agency by making commit-ments. Card realizes that we are epistemically limited and emotionally fraught, and so she acknowledges that we often lack full awareness of the scope of our commitments. In *The Unnatural Lottery*'s discussion of moral luck, she quotes Margaret Walker, who said: "The agent is not a self-sufficient rational will fully expressed in each episode of choice, but is a history of choices … for whom episodes are meaningful in terms of rather larger stretches.… We ought not be surprised that … pivotal episodes which give sense to large segments are adequately judgeable [*sic*] only in retro-spect" (Coyne 1985, 319). Card then orients her discussion diachronically, emphasizing history and context. This history of choices includes choices of association—Who is your friend? Whose opinions matter to you? Which groups do you long to belong to and why?

Central to my analysis of the génocidaires is their desire for group identity, which changed many of their social, political, and even moral commitments. Considering a person's history, and the power of the social connections it reveals, does not erase the individual's personal responsibil-ity. Such considerations can teach us about where to intervene in efforts to prevent certain kinds of moral evil. Considerations of such social and historical factors may highlight moral luck without allowing it to diminish individual responsibility.

Consider Joseph-Désiré Bitero, who was a leader of the killing gangs in Nyamata and blames his becoming a killer on bad moral luck: "I came to manhood at the worst moment in Rwandan history, educated in abso-lute obedience, in ethnic ferocity" (Hatzfeld 2009, 93). Interviewer Jean Hatzfeld resists this as evasive: "Bitero was not born evil and did not grow up in an atmosphere of hatred. Quite the contrary: Like many great killers of history, at one period in his life he was cultured, friendly, a good father and good colleague. He was a nice kid, became a happy teacher, had no quarrel with his Tutsi neighbors. There is no sign of any traumatic event in his peaceful early existence in Gatare, a quiet neighborhood in Nyamata" (2009, 92). And yet Joseph-Désiré Bitero became a notoriously ruthless killer. He thinks of himself as a victim of history, not his own agency, and looks for reinforcement in revisionist and negationist materials, only wishing the Hutu had succeeded in eliminating all Tutsi. He expresses no remorse. Many of his colleagues in the killings have expressed remorse, struggling to make moral sense of their actions. In a country where most killers were granted early release to get them back to work in the countryside rebuilding the nation, Joseph-Désiré was sentenced to death. Even after years on death row, Hatzfeld says, Joseph-Désiré remains a "shrewd politician" who "still flashes his jolly smile and winks at everyone with the same old good-guy charisma. And that's exactly his problem: his understanding of the genocide seems to have frozen solid forever the day after the last machete blow" (2009, 93). This is a deep source of remorselessness: to be unable to review and assess one's own deeds and to resist taking new information into account. Joseph-Désiré is a classic example of someone who wants to use claims of bad luck to escape responsibility.

More generally, consider the majority of génocidaires in Rwanda, who were groomed by leaders (like Joseph-Désiré) to accept patterns of inclusion and exclusion, fed with fear, battered by economic distress, and primed to kill. It was their situation, perhaps their moral luck, that social vitality for members of their group was found in participating in crimes against humanity. When they committed to follow the orders of their leaders, they thought of the tin they could get for their own roof, the cows they could bring home, the milk that would flow, the land they could take. Often, they thought of the camaraderie of their gang.

In a very disturbing comment, Alphonse Hitiyaremye, a member of the same gang Joseph-Désiré belonged to, explains his take on the challenge of exposing their experience as génocidaires: "The real truth, the atmosphere … cannot be told. Telling how we lived it so zestfully, how hot we were—no. How we cracked jokes while out hunting, how we had a Primus all around on good days, slaughtered the cows, sang in the marshes, how we casually gang-raped unlucky girls and women, how we had contests in the evenings over who had cut the most victims, or made fun of the dying in their agony and all suchlike amusements—that doesn't bear telling. Saying that everyone joined in except for a few old guys, ladies, and their tiny children—that's another truth that must be filtered" (Hatzfeld 2009, 79–80).[9] In the context of Card's concept of social vitality, I see these ugly acts of telling jokes about the desperation and pain of others, counting kills, gang-raping, all done together, side by side and in roving bands, as ways to simultaneously claim individual responsibility as well as social belonging.

---

[9] In his testimony, Adalbert notes that their group's rhythms changed across the hundred days of the genocide, like a team pacing itself: "At the start of the killings, we worked fast and skimmed along because we were eager. In the middle of the killings we killed casually. Time and triumph encouraged us to loaf around. At first, we could feel more patriotic or more deserving when we managed to catch some fugitives. Later on, those kinds of feelings deserted us. We stopped listening to the fine words on the radio and from the authorities. We killed to keep the job going" (Hatzfeld 2005, 51).

Social vitality is crucial for understanding the actions of perpetrators, before, during, and after their crimes. In his book about the Kibungo gang, French journalist Jean Hatzfeld explains that he decided he had to interview the killers in small groups rather than one on one. He says, "Faced with the reality of genocide, a killer's first choice is to be silent, and his second is to lie" (Hatzfeld 2005, 44). So he interviewed this gang in small groups, so that the killers "would feel protected from the dangers of truth by their friendship and joint complicity, a bunch of pals secure in their group identity established before the genocide, when they helped one another out in their fields and downed bottles of *urwagwa* together after work, a group identity strengthened during the chaos of the killings in the marshes and by their present imprisonment" (Hatzfeld 2005, 44). By allowing them to retain some of their social vitality, each member known to the others, with their shared histories, their complicities, their mutual understanding, Hatzfeld felt their statements would be more accurate if their disclosures checked or confirmed by the others who were there before and then sat together for the prison interviews. It is a tricky business, but Hatzfeld was trying to keep their social vitality intact.

Reading Hatzfeld's *Machete Season* next to his book of survivor testimonies, *Life Laid Bare*, it seemed to me that Hatzfeld had somewhat undermined the génocidaires' identities by fragmenting their testimonies. In *Life Laid Bare*, each survivor has a chapter, and the testimonies are presented directly to the reader, so readers feel they get to know the survivors. In *Machete Season*, the killers are not presented as intact individuals; they are always voices in a conversation. Chapters are topical, and although speakers are identified, there is no attempt to unify individual identities. Each approach asks the reader for a distinct kind of engagement. With Card's concept of social vitality in hand, and Hatzfeld's view that one-on-one interviews with killers lead to silence or lies, the conversational presentation of the men's testimonies suggests that each man's ability to take responsibility was compromised by his group identity and collective participation in such heinous crimes. Perpetrators gained social vitality, within the society they came from and the one they hoped to create, and importantly within their gang, but their individual agency was damaged such that they could not talk about their crimes as truly individual deeds.

"The tiny thing that would change me into a killer"

At the time they began their killings, the members of the Kibungo gang Hatzfeld interviewed did not worry that they would transform into heartless killers, addicted to the blood they were shedding. They did not think of the damage of such actions to their own characters. One member of this gang, Léopord Twagirayezu, killed many, confessed, served his time, and when released confessed even more, to anyone who would listen. While in prison, Léopord said: "This gentleman I killed at the marketplace, I can tell you the exact memory of it because he was the first. For others, it's murky—I cannot keep track anymore in my memory. I considered them unimportant; *at the time of those murders, I didn't even notice the tiny thing that would change me into a killer*" (Hatzfeld 2005, 27, emphasis added). The big transformation that worried Léopord was from ordinary guy into killer. He puzzled over how this happened and sought to atone for it in a variety of ways, most especially by confessing and apologizing whenever he could. In 2004, ten years after the genocide, he was murdered; shot twice, one bullet through the temple and one through the heart, very professionally (Hatzfeld 2009, 31). One of his colleagues suggested that Léopord was killed for talking too much, that his confessions kept the memories too alive (Hatzfeld 2009, 32). Léopord's transformation from ordinary guy to bloodthirsty killer to zealous confessor was hard for people to accept.

This dovetails nicely with Laurie Paul's point in *Transformative Experience* (2014) that we not only might but also *often must* commit to a course of action without actually having a robust understanding of what our commitment entails. Paul is concerned with the limits of decision theory, which might seem out of place here, since no moral theorist is likely to argue that a decision-theoretic analysis would convince a farmer to join a gang of génocidaires to hunt and kill their neighbors with machetes. But sometimes a simple calculus does lead the farmer there, thinking of the immediate costs of resistance and benefits of compliance, without thinking ahead, to the transformative power of his actions.

In undertaking commitments, we are often transformed through many small deeds that actually constitute living up to our commitment. Sometimes making a choice, like choosing to become a parent, is making a choice to undergo the changes that the experience will bring about. This would be to commit to a set of perhaps predictable but also radically unknown changes, most of them strongly endorsable only retrospectively. Joining a group has the potential to be just such a transformative commitment.

In her final essay, "Taking Pride in Being Bad," Card's appeal to attachment theory complements social vitality. Combining this with Paul's concept of transformative experience, we can see some dangers of using group membership for identity formation. A quest for social vitality helps explain perpetrator participation, not only in genocide, but in any crimes that involve groups. Such criminal groups require commitments that transform. Card launches the essay by considering the desire to be a badass and gain a reputation for being one. This involves trying to be really good at being bad, so is it aiming to be good or be bad? Importantly, Card says, it is about being deemed worthy of esteem by others who value such "toughness, meanness, cruelty, hard-heartedness," and more. Not all génocidaires will count as badasses in Card's sense, for to achieve that one must come to not actually care what others think. The transformation from an ordinary farmer on the hill who plays soccer and drinks Primus with his buddies to a ruthless killer is a matter of changing one's sources of pride, culti-vating certain capacities—cruelty, manipulation, and so on—while silenc-ing others—Card mentions "vulnerability to compassion" (2016, 38). Can being bad really be good, or are all these badasses simply confused?

Card is concerned in "Taking Pride in Being Bad" to evaluate Kant's view that there is no diabolical evil in persons, and she argues that Kant is partially right and partially wrong. He is right in that we should not pre-suppose an inherent predisposition to evil in human nature. Where he goes wrong, she argues, is in his moral psychology:

> A predisposition to form attachments to others, missing in Kant's moral psy-chology, could explain why some people come to take pride in being bad. The predisposition to form attachments can explain the persistence across genera-tions of such dangerous principles as racism and nationalism. Yet, it is important to recognize also that there is room for choice later on as adults. Attachments can be renegotiated and even rejected, upon reflection. One who becomes aware of an underlying attachment to an immoral internalized model as a source of attractions to wrongdoing can choose whether to *reaffirm the attachment* or dis-engage. Disengaging could require serious reconstruction of one's self-concept. (Card 2016, 54)

On this view, Léopord's constant confessions suggest an attempt to recon-struct his identity and change his social relations. More of a badass, Joseph-Désiré Bitero in his refusal to confess and show remorse can be interpreted as resisting reconstruction of his identity and the sources of his pride.

Card suggests that to understand habituation to violence and crime, with a concomitant development of morally bad character, we must look at the role of attention and affection. Who is it you are trying to impress? Whose attention and approval do you seek? Card's analysis never directly warns us to be careful in such matters, but Card does note the ongoing power of the models set by those we elevate to the status of approval givers: "The desire to be worthy of approvals that are grounded in a certain way can outlive one's relationships with those whose approval one initially sought to deserve. The thought that one *would* deserve their approval takes on a life of its own" (2016, 38). Further, we can become habituated to the behavior, and the sense of worthiness that comes with it, so that the behavior itself is valued even after the initial attachment is lost or even rejected. This makes room for considering the luck involved in early childhood attachments, and the power dynamics of one's peer group and society.

Card is concerned to show that taking pride in being bad isn't a mat-ter of taking the bad for the good but rather a result of prudence, luck, and unfortunate attachments. Circumstance and moral psychology matter to our moral luck. In assessing responsibility for outcomes of such attach-ments, remembering the killing gangs in Rwanda, it seems clear that assess-ing the individual perpetrator *alone* is surely too simple. Each is responsible, but some take leadership roles, and that carried greater weight in legal penalties. Joseph-Désiré's leadership was a factor in his sentencing. Leadership should carry greater moral weight as well, for establishing oneself as the one whose attention and approval are worthy is a form of power.

Earlier I noted that Card's ethics holds us in our humanity; we are each accountable for our actions, even within corrupt and harmful institutions. Couldn't we argue that persons do actually become evil, and that certain kinds of actions reveal this? Card warns us not to be too quick with such claims. Instead, from *The Atrocity Paradigm* through *Confronting Evils* and into her recent paper on being a badass, she often situates individual evil deeds within evil communities, practices, and norms. Individuals can absorb and adopt these evil practices, but to lay it all on the individual level is to miss the social and political forces that foster such deeds and cultivate such characters. "To call someone evil without qualification is to imply that the person's character is evil. We are not all potentially evil simply because we are human beings, although many of us might acquire that potentiality under circumstances we would not choose" (Card 2002, 22). This is a subtle point: we acquire the potential for evil, but that doesn't justify a simplistic character assessment. We see hints of Aristotle in Card's view that gaining the potential for evil requires more than the capacity for temptations and random bad intentions. Card says, "To be potentially evil…is to have something real (a persistent desire, habits of gross inattention) in one's character, in virtue of which one's evildoing would be no accident. To be human is not necessarily to have such desires or habits" (2002, 22). To avoid the potential for evil, we must take care about the cultivation of desires and habits, and this is a social matter as much as an individual one. We must attend to our attention and choose our groups wisely. The génocidaires were *cultivated*. Card warns, "There may be families and communities whose practices really do have the potential to inculcate evil desires and habits among many of their members" (2002, 22). Some groups promise social vitality, but some offer only a corrupted vitality, one that ultimately damages the very life it offers.

I have argued that trying to explain what's going on with some perpetrators—particularly those in killing gangs—shows that their attempted destruction of the social world of their targets can boomerang to corrode the vitality of their own lives. My discussion of the génocidaire's desire for social vitality takes a concept Card used to show what the perpetrator destroys for the victim and applies it back to the perpetrator. Appealing to Laurie Paul's concept of transformative experience helps orient us toward the power of ongoing commitments to shape someone's habits, desires, and dispositions, which they become. Social groups shape these transformative experiences through their expectations, norms, and practices, and the rewards and punishments they impose. None of this is to let the génocidaires off the hook; it is to dispel the mystery of how an ordinary guy could become first part of a gang and then through that a killer.

Responding to Evil Without Doing Evil

Card says, "Evils change moral relationships among those who become perpetrators, bystanders, beneficiaries, or victims" (2002, 167). Mainly, they create moral powers for victims (blame and forgiveness) and burdens and obligations for perpetrators (guilt, repair, gratitude for forgiveness or mercy). We must also recognize the moral powers of bystanders, outsiders, and sometimes even perpetrators. Bystanders have interesting mixtures and often feel guilt for inaction where action was possible (Card 2002, 19–20), but even those truly outside the action can offer third-party moral perspectives that might nevertheless play important roles. Card is clear about the power of victims to forgive, or not, and the obligations of perpetrators to acknowledge, apologize, atone, offer as much restitution as possible. Alice MacLachlan suggests that we see Card's concept of moral powers as something like "morally significant responses to harm" (2009, 136). Which sorts of morally significant responses are available will depend on many factors, but all parties will have *some*.

On Card's analysis, being concerned with "the moral challenge of avoiding evil responses to evil" does not "require foreswearing revenge or retaliation—only evil forms of it" (Card 2010, 9). Punishment, retaliation, even revenge can be morally acceptable responses so long as the harms inflicted are not intolerable. In her own case, Card took the attitude that living well is the best revenge. She says: "My revenge on those who did what they could to impede my professional endeavors is to exploit opportunities they inadvertently opened up for me to achieve what success I can" (2010, 9). Living well is surely the best thing a survivor can do for herself, and her reclaimed good life might well be seen as a form of revenge, for surely it flies in the face of her opponents' destructive project. This indirect approach leaves open the question about direct responses to perpetrators of evil.

Card's concern for survivors highlights the weakness of punishment and leads her to seek alternative means of remediation. Shunning is an option that suits Card's realistic (nonideal) social approach. Shunning has "the advantage of acknowledging the moral powers of victims, their powers to blame and forgive, as well as some obligations of perpetrators, such as the obligation to apologize" (Card 2002, 171–72). Punishment does not do enough to strengthen and restore victims and survivors, for it "offers little room for the exercise of the moral powers of victims and inadequately acknowledges the obligations of perpetrators, such as the obligation to repair damage" (Card 2002, 172). Furthermore, survivors are often left feeling bereft, because the punishment so rarely fits the crime, as we see with smiling Joseph-Désiré Bitero being a leader of men even in prison.

In conclusion, thinking of how to not respond to evil with evil, there are four crucial points in Card. First, we must *hold perpetrators in their humanity*. Don't push them off the moral map, but see them as *persons* with accountability, no matter how terrible their moral luck has been. They own their actions. Considering moral luck must not lead us to treating persons as nonpersons. Here it would be worth thinking more about Card's analysis of the differences between Nagel's and Williams's treatments of moral luck, and the interplay between action and character.

Also, we must *demand that perpetrators retain or restore their own humanity*. This demand asks them to face and understand the harms they have inflicted, thereby restoring other-directed orientations and perhaps (one would hope) leading them to feel genuine remorse, regret, and repentance. Card defines remorse as "deep moral regret coupled with acute awareness of one's own wrongdoing, profoundly wishing we had not done a wrongful deed, not because of the stain on our own character but because of how it wronged others" (2002, 208). Remorse is thus self-aware but inherently other-regarding, "an emotional gnawing at oneself over one's wrongdoing" (Card 2002, 208). Remorse puts perpetrators at risk, for facing their actions and seeing themselves in their own humanity also may lead them to see the boomerang impact of those actions on their own character.

Third, Card urges us to *exercise mercy, where possible and advisable*. Mercy is "the compassionate withholding or mitigation of a hardship or penalty that one has the authority or power to inflict on another or the power to allow another to suffer" (Card 2002, 190). Card calls mercy "a natural manifestation of forgiveness," but she adds that mercy is possible even without forgiveness (2002, 190). Mercy is clearly something wrongdoers want, but what is its moral value? For one thing, it keeps us from undue cruelty. In cases where the wrongdoer has shown remorse and sought to offer restitution, there may be reasons to work toward rehabilitation and reintegration of the wrongdoer into a shared social world. Here we must tread lighty, keeping a firm grip on Card's concern for the well-being of survivors. Mercy is always something of a sacrifice by the victims, so it must not undermine their self-respect. Compassion distinguishes mercy from mere leniency or pardon, but compassion for someone who truly and deeply harmed you is a tall order. The early release of the génocidaires in Rwanda was generally a matter not of mercy but of expediency, so justice lost out to economic need. The country needed more workers to rebuild its infrastructure and work the land. Most who were released were not pardoned, but their sentences were commuted to time served and community service. Survivors in the countryside lived in fear. Sacrificing justice comes at a steep price to a society and its people, especially survivors. Sacrificing the self-respect of survivors by demanding that they find compassion for their assailants is too high a price. Compassion and mercy might be offered, but they cannot be compelled.[10]

---

[10] For more on these issues of transitional justice in Rwanda, see Tirrell 2015.

The other-directedness of mercy is the flip side of the other-directedness of remorse. Considering the experience of the other might lead to compassion, particularly for the victim's suffering, but asking a victim to consider the mind, heart, and social circumstance of the perpetrator may well lead to terror. Card's caveat, where "possible and advisable," is crucial—mercy should not undermine the demands of justice or self-respect. Mercy can also be a way for victims to exercise their moral powers, because mercy demonstrates both power and control.

Finally, we must *bear witness*. A moral response that is open to bystanders and even those from afar is the power to offer moral condemnation of the deeds done and to witness and comfort victims. Witnessing wrongs *as wrongs* is a profoundly moral act. Think of the power of saying, "You don't deserve this," or "You didn't ask for it," or "No one should be treated this way." This kind of witnessing reverberates through Card's work, although she does not talk about it all that often and does not center it the way she might. One factor in damage to social vitality is what I call *recognition harm*. In failing to recognize the humanity of the other, through words and deeds, one is harmed by being cast out of a shared moral and social world. In extreme contexts, recognition harms can bring about what Card calls "social death." Witnessing is a form of recognition that brings the survivor back within a shared normative world. To find ways to respond to evil without becoming evil ourselves, we must to explore the role of witnessing (by survivors, perpetrators, and bystanders) as a way to offer recognition to those whose status as persons has been undermined by the actions of others.

Card addresses witnessing in her discussion of Simon Wiesenthal's *The Sunflower*:

> *The Sunflower* is not just about forgiveness. It is at the same time about silence and witnessing. The sunflowers of the title were planted each on a soldier's grave in a cemetery that Wiesenthal and other prisoners passed on their way to work. They struck him as like silent periscopes, continuing vital connections of the dead to the world of the living. There were no markers for Jews cremated or buried in mass graves. Wiesenthal's memoir itself is like a sunflower for Jews who did not survive, a vital connection between the dead and the living from one who miraculously survived to bear witness, to be a periscope for those who cannot bear witness themselves. But unlike the sunflowers, the memoir speaks. (Card 2002, 186)

On Card's reading, *The Sunflower* is importantly about the "question of whether and when to speak, whether and when to say anything at all" (Card 2002, 186). Card argues that Wiesenthal's memoir not only presents the Nazi Karl's confession and Wiesenthal's own silent resistance but also gives readers a chance to confront the complex issues of how to deal with perpetrators. Card worries about strategies of silence, for she holds that "what is difficult but has the potential to bring change is reaching out, taking risks, making explicit the complexities in one's heart" (2002, 187).

Joseph-Désiré Bitero, a perpetrator who has shown no remorse, nevertheless offers a fascinating message about responsibility and witnessing. Ironically, he congratulates himself on facing his own crimes even as he distances himself from them. Consider:

> Every civilized person must take responsibility for his or her actions. However, sometimes life presents you with actions you cannot claim out loud. Myself, I was the district leader of the *interahamwe* at the time of the killings. I did not comb the villages and the marshes, I did not wield the machete more than others did, but I accepted that responsibility. Accepting such a truth is not something just anyone can do. Admitting to so grave a sin—that requires more than simple courage. And speaking about the details of something so extraordinary, well, it can be hellish: for the person speaking as well as for the one who listens. Because afterward, society can hate you beyond all understanding if you reveal a situation that society does not wish to believe: a truth it calls inconceivable. (Hatzfeld 2009, 94)

Joseph-Désiré is proud of himself for accepting his responsibility: "Admitting to so grave a sin—that requires more than simple courage." The perpetrator must bear his own survey and stand up to witness what happened. And yet, Joseph-Désiré shows uncharacteristic awareness that the admissions can be painful for the survivor to hear. Knowing when to talk, with whom, how much to share at a time, these are all crucial decisions in the logic of witnessing. "What is difficult but has the potential to bring change is reaching out, taking risks, making explicit the complexities in one's heart" (Card 2002, 187).

In genocide, Card tells us that the génocidaires set out to destroy the social vitality of their targets, and I agree that they do this. It is crucial to notice that, at least in Rwanda, they ended up destroying their own. Genocides usually fail, and in that failure the repudiation of the project and punishment of the perpetrators turns them into pariahs rather than the heroes they sought to be. Further, they cannot adequately share or discuss their experience, so reaching out, which Card sees as so important, becomes not only risky but also sometimes deadly, as we saw in Léopord's case.

Bearing witness to injustice is a way for others to help restore the social vitality of the survivor. Exclusion, isolation, imprisonment and punishment can harm the social vitality of perpetrators. I suggest that, in the face of the most heinous crimes against persons, for those of us *not* in positions of judgment and power, perhaps the best we can do is bear witness, stand up for the rights of victims and survivors, and say, "We believe you" and "You never deserved this." When facing perpetrators, we must insist on their agency and their humanity, and insist that they bear witness to the atrocity. If we are in positions to punish, Card urges us to forswear inflicting intolerable suffering, even if the harms they inflicted were indeed intolerable. So the idea that the punishment should fit the crime cannot, in the face of evil, mean the punishment matches the crime. Responding to evil without doing evil will require moral vigilance, emotional creativity, and a hefty dose of other-directed thinking. Intolerable harm is Card's line in the sand, a worthy line to draw, and one that we cross at our own peril.

Acknowledgments

I am grateful to the audience and participants of the Society for Analytic Feminism session at the Central American Philosophical Association, Chicago, 2016, and especially to Robin S. Dillon and Kathryn J. Norlock.

References

Aghion, Anne. 2002. *Gacaca: Living Together Again in Rwanda*. Icarus Films.

Alcoff, Linda Martin. 2007. "Epistemologies of Ignorance: Three Types." In *Race and the Epistemologies of Ignorance*, edited by Shannon Sullivan and Nancy Tuana, 39–57. Albany: State University of New York Press.

Card, Claudia. 1972. "On Mercy." *Philosophical Review* 81, no. 2:182–207.

———. 1996. *The Unnatural Lottery: Character and Moral Luck*. Philadelphia: Temple University Press.

———. 2002. *The Atrocity Paradigm: A Theory of Evil*. Oxford: Oxford University Press.

———. 2003. "Genocide and Social Death." *Hypatia* 18, no. 1:63–79. Chapter 5 in this collection.

———. 2004. "*The Atrocity Paradigm* Revisited." *Hypatia* 19, no. 4:210–20.

———. 2010. *Confronting Evils: Terrorism, Torture, Genocide*. Cambridge: Cambridge University Press.

———. 2011. "Surviving Long-Term Mass Atrocities: U-Boats, Catchers, and Ravens." Presidential Address. *Proceedings and Addresses of the American Philosophical Association* 85, no. 2:7–26. Chapter 7 in this collection.

———. 2016. "Taking Pride in Being Bad." In *Oxford Studies in Normative Ethics*, volume 6, edited by Mark Timmonos, 37–55. Oxford: Oxford University Press.

Coyne [now Walker], Margaret Urban. 1985. "Moral Luck?" *Journal of Value Inquiry* 19:319–25.

Devlin-Ross, Dax. 2013. "Is This the Moment to Change How We Treat People Who Commit Crimes?" *Next City*. https://nextcity.org/features/view/restorative-justice-cities-Howard-Zehr-communities-for-restorative-justice

Hatzfeld, Jean. 2005. *Machete Season: The Killers in Rwanda Speak*. New York: Macmillan.

———. 2009. *The Antelope's Strategy: Living in Rwanda After the Genocide*. New York: Macmillan.

Kraft, Dina. 2014 "By Talking, Inmates and Victims Make Things More 'Right.'" *New York Times* (5 July). http://www.nytimes.com/2014/07/06/us/by-talking-inmates-and-victims-make-things-more-right.html?_r=0

Levi, Primo. 1988. *The Drowned and the Saved*. Translated by Raymond Rosenthal. New York: Vintage.

Locke, John. 1690. *Second Treatise of Government and A Letter Concerning Toleration*. Oxford: Oxford University Press, 2016.

Lugones, Maria. 1987. "Playfulness, 'World'-Traveling, and Loving Perception." *Hypatia* 2, no. 2:3–19.

MacLachlan, Alice. 2009. "Moral Powers and Forgivable Evils." In *Evil, Political Violence, and Forgiveness: Essays in Honor of Claudia Card*, edited by Kathryn Norlock and Andrea Veltman, 135–56. Lanham, Md.: Rowman and Littlefield.

Paul, Laurie Ann. 2014. *Transformative Experience*. Oxford: Oxford University Press.

Scheman, Naomi. 1995. "Feminist Epistemology." *Metaphilosophy* 26, no. 3:177–190.

Smith, David Livingstone. 2011. *Less Than Human: Why We Demean, Enslave, and Exterminate Others*. New York: St. Martin's Press.

Straus, Scott. 2013. *The Order of Genocide: Race, Power, and War in Rwanda*. Ithaca, N.Y.: Cornell University Press.

Tirrell, Lynne. 2012. "Genocidal Language Games." In *Speech and Harm: Controversies over Free Speech*, edited by Ishani Maitra and Mary Kate McGowan, 174–221. Oxford: Oxford University Press.

———. 2015. "Transitional Justice in Post-Genocide Rwanda: An Integrative Approach." In *Theorizing Transitional Justice*, edited by Claudio Corradetti, Nir Eisikovits, and Jack Rotondi, 237–52. London: Ashgate.

CHAPTER 9

CLAUDIA CARD'S CONCEPT OF SOCIAL DEATH

A NEW WAY OF LOOKING AT GENOCIDE

JAMES SNOW

1. Introduction

The work of Claudia Card has received far less attention in the field of genocide studies than it deserves. The atrocity paradigm, first introduced in her book by that title published in 2002, offers rich insights that can serve to enhance our understanding of genocidal violence. While the secular theory of evil she develops in *The Atrocity Paradigm* does not speak to genocide per se, it nevertheless has far-reaching implications for theorizing genocide. Her book *Confronting Evils: Terrorism, Torture, Genocide*, after offering revisions to her secular theory of evil, does speak directly to the evils of genocide, claiming "genocide is social death" (Card 2010, 237). And her claim that social death is the principal evil of genocide speaks directly to conundrums that are at the very center of current genocide scholarship.

One such conundrum that Card's work speaks to, and is the focus of this essay, is the schism that exists between genocide as a field of scholarship and the experiences of genocide as told by survivors and witnesses of genocidal atrocities. That there is a lack of convergence between scholarship and theory, on the one hand, and the testimonies of survivors and witnesses, on the other, is made manifest in an interview with a Holocaust survivor conducted by Joan Ringelheim in 1984. The victim/survivor whom Ringelheim interviews is a Jewish woman pseudonymously called Pauline. She tells Ringelheim of repeatedly being molested by the male relatives of the Polish family who was hiding the then twelve-year-old girl. The woman tells a horrific tale of these molestations and of the all-pervading fear of repeated molestations she felt while in hiding, a fear

Criticism and Compassion: The Ethics and Politics of Claudia Card.
Edited by Robin S. Dillon and Armen T. Marsoobian.
Chapters and book compilation © 2018 Metaphilosophy LLC and John Wiley & Sons Ltd.

equal to her fear of being discovered by the Nazis; it was and is a fear that she says never abated. After telling Ringelheim her story, she asks: "In respect to what happened, [what we] suffered and saw—the humiliation in the ghetto, seeing our relatives dying and taken away [as well as] my friends...then seeing the ghetto...burn and seeing people jumping out and burn—is this [molestation] important?" (Ringelheim 1997, 19). Ringelheim recounts this story to demonstrate that her interviewee, although she "recognized her experiences as different from men's, she did not know how or where to locate them in the history of the Holocaust.... There is a split between genocide and gender in the memories of witnesses and the historical reconstruction of researchers" (20). The story points to a split between memory and official histories in general, and the split is especially pronounced with respect to women's experiences of genocide.

This fissure between the theorizing of genocide and the marginalizing of the voices of witnesses and survivors of genocides needs to be explored in some detail. In doing just that, this essay shows that the gap is considerable and cannot be sustained if the goal of theorizing genocide is, as it must be, to achieve a richer understanding of genocide as a tool to reduce the scope of genocidal violence, if not to prevent future genocides altogether.

The essay proceeds in three phases. First, it shows that genocide scholarship as well as accounts of genocide by journalists often frame genocide in terms of biological death and body counts. The prevalence of this way of framing genocide is problematic insofar as it risks marginalizing the voices and experiences of victims who may not succumb to biological death but nevertheless suffer the loss of family members and other loved ones, and suffer the destruction of relationships, as well as the foundational institutions that give rise to and sustain those relationships. While it is recognized that the voices and experiences of men can be marginalized if the focus is on body counts, this essay focuses on the experiences of women. I also argue that this frame with its emphasis on body counts fails to take account of genocidal violence that occurs long after the killing ends; death is not the end of genocide. In the second section, I argue that the atrocity paradigm and especially Card's conception of social death are better able to capture the complex realities of genocidal violence, particularly the experiences of women. Still, it must be acknowledged that the frame of social death is not without its limits. In her analysis of social death and the things that constitute social relationships, Card does not include memory, but I argue here that memory is central to social relationships and complements her analysis. A second worry I raise is that social death intimates an irrecoverable finality to social relations that would preclude the possibility of forging new relationships; it is not clear that this was her position. Finally, I claim that the idea of social death enriches our understanding of genocide but question whether her term has juridical implications.

2. Body Counts

Card, in defining the central evil of genocide as social death, claims: "Putting social death at the center of genocide takes the focus off body counts, individual careers cut short, and mourners" (Card 2010, 238). This claim demands attention, for it suggests that a focus on body counts somehow misses the central evil of genocide. Two questions arise: How prevalent is the focus on body counts? And why does focus need to be shifted away from body counts? In other words, is something crucial about the reality of genocide jettisoned by focusing on body counts?

That there is tremendous focus on body counts is evident in both the scholarship and the narratives of journalists. The case studies of individual genocides that make up *Centuries of Genocide* (Totten and Parsons 2013) includes fifteen such studies, arranged chronologically. Of the fifteen cases all but two characterize the genocides in terms of numbers killed.[1] And in the media, numbers and body counts dominate the narratives. The media coverage of the recent conviction and sentencing of Radovan Karadzic in The Hague is replete with references to the numbers of Bosnian Muslims killed under the leadership of Karadzic (see, e.g., Simons 2016).

A focus on body counts governs the work of Adam Jones. Jones makes the claim that genocides are in fact what he calls "gendercides," insofar as males as males are disproportionately targeted and killed. Concerning the war in Kosovo, he writes: "The slaughter of 'battle-age' non-combatant men is at least as prominent and enduring a 'weapon of war,' in the Balkans and throughout history, as is the rape of women—and a more brutal and severe one, by any reasonable standard" (Jones 2009, 103). Jones does acknowledge that the Genocide Convention's definition of genocide does not require murder, and might allow for rape as a genocidal weapon (Jones 2009, 214), but his analysis of the disproportionate targeting of noncombatant males in the cases of Srebrenica, Nanjing, and Bangladesh relies on body counts as a basis of gender comparison (Jones 2009, preface).

That there is such a focus on body counts should come as no surprise. It might well be the case that the focus on body counts reflects the fact that many scholars in the field of genocide studies, being social scientists, embrace a quantitative lens. Theodore Porter shows in his discussion of the works of two early twentieth-century biostatisticians, Karl Pearson and R. A. Fisher, who ushered in a quantitative mind-set, that this quantitative mind-set came to dominate not just the natural sciences but the human

---

[1] One exception is Colin Tatz's "Genocide in Australia" (Tatz 2013); the other is Alex de Waal's "The Nuba Mountains, Sudan" (de Waal 2013). In the former case, the genocide was not marked by mass killings or biological extermination. In the latter case the Nuba fled into the mountains during the civil war in Sudan. They received no international attention or humanitarian aid.

sciences as well. As Porter claims, "Quantitative reasoning would reshape public discourse" with its appeal to "impersonal science and consensus" (2006, 252). Body counts, then, are thought to be a reliable measure of the sheer magnitude of the evil of genocide. Moreover, the number killed is sometimes used comparatively, as a way of saying that the Shoah, for example, is the paradigmatic case of modern genocide because the number of victims far exceeds the numbers of Tutsis and moderate Hutus slaughtered in Rwanda in 1994.

Moreover, the emphasis on biological death might reflect the definition of genocide developed by Raphael Lemkin and adopted at the Convention on the Prevention and Punishment of the Crime of Genocide in December 1948 (United Nations 1948), which specifically refers to "any of the following acts committed with intent to destroy, in whole or in part, a national, ethnical, racial or religious group."[2] The Convention's definition emphasizes "killing" and "physical destruction," and it is sometimes adopted in genocide scholarship.[3] It must nevertheless be recognized that this definition was the result of intense political debate and does not reflect the far more nuanced understanding of genocide that is evident in Lemkin's autobiography, *Totally Unofficial*, in his earlier writings such as *Axis Rule*, and in dozens of never published documents available in the Lemkin archives.[4]

Turning to the second question, why might Card want to move away from a focus on body counts and argue for refocusing attention on social death as the central evil of genocide? Judith Butler is helpful in this regard. Undue focus on body counts is problematic in theorizing genocide, for delimiting both what is included in the frame and, correlatively and more importantly, what is excluded from the frame. As Butler is correct to point out, "The frame does not simply exhibit reality, but actively participates in a strategy of containment, selectively producing and enforcing what will count as reality. It tries to do this, and its efforts are a powerful wager. Although framing cannot always contain what it seeks to make visible or

---

[2] The definition adopted on 9 December 1948 reads as follows, in Article II:

In the present Convention, genocide means any of the following acts committed with intent to destroy, in whole or in part, a national, ethnical, racial or religious group, as such:

(a) Killing members of the group;
(b) Causing serious bodily or mental harm to members of the group;
(c) Deliberately inflicting on the group conditions of life calculated to bring about its physical destruction in whole or in part;
(d) Imposing measures intended to prevent births within the group;
(e) Forcibly transferring children of the group to another group. (http://www.ohchr.org/EN/ProfessionalInterest/Pages/CrimeOfGenocide.aspx).

[3] Eric Weitz is but one example. He writes: "The Genocide Convention, despite its weaknesses, provides us with a fruitful working definition that can guide the study of past regimes and events" (Weitz 2013, 10).

[4] For a detailed study of Lemkin's more nuanced conception of genocide see Snow 2016.

readable, it remains structured by the aim of instrumentalizing certain versions of reality. This means that the frame is always throwing something away, always keeping something out, always de-realizing, de-legitimating alternative versions of reality, discarding negatives of the official version" (Butler 2010, xiii). Following Butler's conception of the frame, it is important to ask what comes into focus and what falls outside the frame when biological death becomes the central element in the frame. This question is best explored by looking first at what Card says regarding social death.

3. Card and Genocide as Social Death

Card offers a much different frame when looking at genocide. When it is contrasted with a focus on the number of biological deaths, two analytically distinct but intersecting points become apparent. First, Card's frame is not just a different frame but rather a radically different one that brings into sharp relief what has been marginalized by the dominant frame—for example, the trauma suffered by witnesses and survivors who escaped biological death. It is a reorientation, a new way of seeing. Much of Card's writing, especially since *The Atrocity Paradigm* (2002), is meant to provoke a radical shift in how traditional philosophical problems are cast. The radical nature of her later work should not be underestimated. Second, and as a new way of seeing, Card's focus on social death creates conceptual space for many women's experience of genocide and even provides space for focusing on women's experiences of genocide. Women's experiences and voices have long been marginalized by the dominant narrative.[5]

As mentioned above, Card offers an alternative way of seeing genocide by focusing on what she terms "social death." She claims, "The intentional production of social death in a people or community is the central evil of genocide" (2010, 237). For Card, what gives meaning to our lives is relationships. These relationships can be personal or institutionally mediated, contemporary or intergenerational; and while a life deprived of social vitality is not necessarily meaningless (here Card cites spiritual vitality), still she claims that "loss of social vitality is a profound loss" (2010, 237). Moreover, she claims that "putting social death at the center of genocide takes the focus off body counts, individual careers cut short, and mourners. It puts the focus instead on relationships, connections, and foundational institutions that create community and sets the context that gives meaning to

---

[5] It is difficult to measure the degree of marginalization of women's experiences of genocide, and it must be acknowledged that women's experiences of genocide have garnered considerable attention since the publication of Card's *Atrocity Paradigm* (2002) and *Confronting Evils* (2010) and Selma Leydesdorff's *Surviving the Bosnian Genocide* (2011). Still, there is considerable work to be done. I offer a more thorough discussion of the myriad ways in which women's experiences of genocide are cast in my "Mothers and Monsters: Women, Gender, and Genocide" (Snow 2018).

careers and goals, lives and deaths" (2010, 238). She claims further that while "social death is not necessarily genocide ... genocide is social death"; and it is "social death that distinguishes the evil of genocide, morally, from the evils of other mass murders" (2010, 237). In other words, genocide is defined as "social death."

To better appreciate her idea of social death, it is important to take note of how Card defines "social," and especially of what she means by a "social group." The context is her distinction between genocide and nongenoci-dal mass murders. She references the bombing in Oklahoma City and the attack on the Twin Towers by way of saying that the victims in each of these cases were a group only in the sense that they constituted an aggregate of individuals. By contrast, "the 'genos' behind 'genocide' is widely understood today to refer to *a people*" (Card 2010, 247). A people, then, "is a *social group* ... that is, a collectivity united by internal relationships and traditions, such as common language and practices. Relationships that constitute a people include connections of kinship and citizenship as well as cultural and social relationships created by such things as common lit-erature, cuisine, humor, and by sharing in the creation and maintenance of laws and traditions. These practices and relationships create the social vitality to the lives of members of peoples. The social vitality of the occu-pants of bombed buildings [by contrast] comes largely from their member-ship in other groups" (247). As noted above, relationships can be, but need not be, personal. They can be the ties of a shared language, shared cuisine, shared literature, shared humor, shared laws and traditions; many other kinds of social bonds could be cited that serve to anchor and define social relationships. But it is precisely these ties that bind a people. It is clear that relationality—relationality with the group as well as with members of the group—is a key element of social groups.

Card's analysis of peoples or social groups helps to make clearer her claim that social death is the central evil of genocide. Hence: "To the extent that the relationships that define the group are important sources of mean-ing and identity in the lives of its members, destruction of the group is for them a serious loss. By the same stroke it is a loss of the possibility of such meaning and identity for descendants" (Card 2010, 248). There are innu-merable published accounts by survivors, witnesses, and even perpetrators of genocides. In addition to published accounts, there are archived testi-monies, oral testimonies, and other documented accounts that speak to the horrors of genocide. In addition, and in the case of the Shoah, there are victims who continue to speak publically to audiences at universities and elsewhere about their experiences in the camps and ghettos. These testi-monies cannot help but elicit what Edith Wyschogrod calls in this context a "*frisson* of horror" (2005, 207). These testimonies and accounts show that those who "survive" physical slaughter nevertheless suffer immeasur-able, and sometimes unspeakable, harm as a result of the annihilation of family and friends and other loved ones, the destruction of homelands, the upheavals of the diaspora that often follows such destruction, the destruction of temples, synagogues, churches, and other places of worship. Genocide often causes the destruction of memory; the trauma of witnessing genocide can destroy the memories of individuals. Moreover, denialism, considered by many in the field of genocide studies to be a stage in the genocidal process (Stanton 1998), has the potential to irrevocably fracture and even destroy the memory that is defining of relationships. Card's conception of social death creates a conceptual framework that founds a space not just for survivors and witnesses to share the stories of their experiences but a space where listeners can better understand the scope and depth of genocidal violence.

Genocide is considered by many to be the worst of all possible crimes. That claim often rests on body counts as the measure. Social death, a recurring theme in survivor and witness testimonies, makes the depth and scope of genocidal violence yet more profound. Social death might well extend beyond the biological death of victims. It is curious, perhaps even unsettling, then, that these testimonies do not figure more prominently in the writings of scholars who theorize genocide from the perspective of law, history, philosophy, or the social sciences. That these testimonies are often absent from or fail to inform genocide scholarship may reflect an all-too-narrow way of theorizing genocide. The idea of social death brings into sharp relief problems and limitations with traditional theorizing, and does so in a way that can embrace and at the same time be informed by the plethora of testimonies that are available. The argument here is not to diminish the importance of theorizing genocide in the aforementioned academic disciplines; the argument is rather a call for a rich intersection of theory and testimony. Card's notion of social death is crucial to this intersection and promises a deeper understanding of the scope and depth of genocidal violence. This is accomplished by using Card's focus on social death and bringing into focus the testimonies of survivors as well as literature and film about life in the camps, life in hiding, and life after the killing stops. Jean Améry's intellectual alienation in the camp, his reduction to the purely physical, and his exile from his homeland is a clear example of social death (Améry 1980).

Imre Kertész's narrator in *Kaddish for an Unborn Child*, who refuses to bring a child into the post-Auschwitz world, is another clear illustration of the lived experience of social death (Kertész 2004). Card, speaking specifically about the murder at Auschwitz of Czechoslovakian Jews of Terezin and about the *Hatikva* anthem, points out that they clung to their social identity by singing their national anthem as they were marched into the gas chambers to their deaths; she mentions in the same passage that their murder "robbed them of their descendants" (2010, 238). While Kertész's narrator is not murdered but indeed survives, the experience of genocide for the narrator negates the possibility of having descendants. In Card's example, biological death negates the possibility of descendants; in the case of Kertész's narrator, it is the experience of Auschwitz that results in social death and precludes the possibility of descendants.

Adorno claimed that the Holocaust changed everything, including culture, history, even the possibility of writing poetry: "The criticism of culture finds itself on the last level of the dialectic of culture and barbarism: to write a poem after Auschwitz is barbaric; and that destroys the possibility of writing poems today" (1963, 30, my translation).[6] Just as Auschwitz destroyed the possibility of poetry and art—themselves at the core of social vitality—so the Holocaust destroyed, in the case of Kertész's narrator, the possibility of progeny.

Social death as a frame for understanding genocide is especially pronounced when one listens to voices of women describing first-hand their experiences of genocide. The remainder of this section focuses on two such cases: one case is the stories told to Selma Leydesdorff by the women of Srebrenica (Leydesdorff 2011).

The quantitative approach is certainly important for understanding genocide; numbers and body counts should not be discounted. In the case of the Bosnian genocide, for example, it is essential to look at numbers. War and genocidal violence began in the former Yugoslavia in 1991. Following the war in Croatia, which ended in 1992, war erupted in Bosnia and Herzegovina, killing approximately a hundred thousand people. Factions involved in this war included Bosnian Serbs, Bosnian Muslims, Bosnian Croats, and military and paramilitary forces from Croatia and Serbia, as well as U.N. forces and NATO forces (Mennecke 2013). In 1993 the U.N. Security Council declared Srebrenica one of six safe zones for Bosnian Muslims. In addition to those living in inhumane conditions at Srebrenica, more than twenty thousand women, children, and elderly people were transferred to Muslim-controlled territory; more than seven thousand men were left behind, and they were systematically slaughtered in the course of one week (Mennecke 2013). Card, however, wants to shift the focus away from body counts and instead focus on the death of the women (and men) who die a social death as the result of genocide. The social death of the women of Srebrenica as described by Selma Leydesdorff complements Card's analysis.

Leydesdorff interviewed seventy of the Muslim women who were forced to say farewell to sons, lovers, husbands, brothers, and fathers on July 13, 1995. While the testimonies are deeply personal, they contain a constellation of intersecting themes. Tikka speaks in a way that suggests social death: "I am dying of loneliness. I sit within these four walls, day and night, I have no one to take care of—no brother, no sister, no father, no mother,

---

[6] "Kulturkritik findet sich der letzten Stufe der Dialektik von Kultur und Barbarei gegenüber: nach Auschwitz ein Gedicht zu schreiben, ist barbarisch, und das frißt auch die Erkenntnis an, die ausspricht, warum es unmöglich ward, heute Gedichte zu schreiben."

no spouse, nothing, nothing. But the heaven is high and the earth is low, and I have to live. Wherever I am, here or somewhere else, my soul aches and I am alone. I have no one who can fetch something for me [her sister-in-law is too weak]. If I can't cook, then no one does it for me. I returned here. I can't work. I own a good bit of land farther up in the village, but I have no one to work it for me" (Leydesdorff 2011, 15). Tikka, like many of the women interviewed by Leydesdorff, speaks of her social isolation, her loneliness. It is worth noting that Leydesdorff is from the Netherlands, and many of the women she interviewed, and many more surviving Bosnian Muslims, blame the Dutch for the catastrophe at Srebrenica. Dutch troops were charged with guarding the so-called safe zones located in Serbian-held territories. Yet these women wanted to tell Leydesdorff their stories. Leydesdorff claims that "no one has really listened to their stories. I am there to listen. I know that later, when my interpreter and I are gone, she [Tikka]—like all the women—will be grateful for the individual attention, grateful and somewhat confused" (Leydesdorff 2011, 16). Giving testimony, even to someone perceived as an enemy, is another social context, another way of existing for others, even if those others do not speak the same language. There are still moments of intimacy when stories are told and heard. The women of Srebrenica forge new relationships by sharing their memories of the genocide.

Ramiza, in an interview conducted in 2006, speaks similarly of social isolation. Ramiza lost a husband, brother, father, and mother in 1993. She says to Leydesdorff: "What am I supposed to do? I don't have any hope left.... I feel hollow in my soul. In every respect, I have no one ... no future, no prospects, nothing. I only have my child. She is my only hope and comfort. I fight for her ... [but] I have no plans, no ideas" (Leydesdorff 2011, 13). Leydesdorff observes of Ramiza: "The void for Ramiza is not only personal and psychological, but an objective fact if we look at her life now. The social fabric and the interconnections of her existence are lost. Her life is missing the same thing that is missing from the lives of other survivors in the camps and shelters—context. Their existence lacks cohesion, and they seem to operate in a social vacuum. This is most palpable among those who returned to Srebrenica; they try stubbornly to reweave the social fabric, but cannot" (Leydesdorff 2011, 13).

The Iraqi Anfal operation in 1988 and the testimony of the Anfal women who survived it present at first blush a picture that complements the stories told by Bosnian women and further illustrate the value of Card's notion of social death. At the same time, the case of Anfal women presents certain challenges to Card's notion and deserves analysis.

The Anfal operation occurred in the context of the Iran-Iraq war that lasted from 1980 to 1988. During the war Kurdish rebels, both the Patriotic Union of Kurdistan and the Kurdistan Democratic Party, received aid from Iran and participated in joint military operations with the Iranian military. Iraq launched a counterinsurgency in 1988—a legitimate counterinsurgency according to Human Rights Watch Middle East—but the Iraqi government went well beyond legitimate military action, and between February and September 1988 an estimated fifty thousand to one hundred thousand Kurds were killed; many of the killed were noncombatant women and children (Human Rights Watch 1995).

To appreciate the ways in which Anfal women might be susceptible to social death as Card understands it, it is necessary to know something about the culture and rhythm of life of Anfal women. Karin Mlodoch points out that the Anfal operation in Germyan struck a rural and illiterate population. "Social and gender relations [are] still regulated by a traditional, patriarchal code of morals and ethics, influenced by Islamic beliefs and tribal law ... [that] subordinated women to the men of their families. The family is organized in patrilineal and patrilocal patterns; married women belong to their husbands and children to their father's [sic] families" (Mlodoch 2012, 23). This means that for a married woman a missing or dead husband threatens the very social structure of Germyan. As Mlodoch observes, "Anfal destroyed the social and economic texture of Germyan" (23). And as one of Mlodoch's interviewees stated, "With Anfal our lives have disappeared as well" (76).

This brief description of the patriarchal culture helps to provide context for Suhaila's lament:

> Every day I think, the day will come, the door will open and he [her husband] will come in. How could I not think about it? I think, who knows where he is, have they shot him? I think who knows, maybe he is in prison, in which prison might he be? I think maybe he is alive; how could I not think about it? Especially at night.... There is no night in which I do not think about it. Many times I do not find any sleep because I think what might have happened to him. Maybe he died of hunger. Maybe he died of an illness; maybe they shot him; but maybe he is still alive. And if he is alive, where might he be? How might he live? ... Every night, all these questions come to me. (Mlodoch 2012, 76)

But for Suhaila, her loss is not only the loss of her husband, an unbearable loss, but also the loss the very social fabric that gives her life meaning. She has not been murdered, but she suffers social death.

There are countless other testimonies and accounts of genocidal violence offered by women who speak of social death, fractured relationships, and the destruction of selves that have been constructed relationally. Moreover, Card's notion of social death provides a pertinent frame for making sense of the stories women tell, stories that are seemingly not relevant if the focus is on murder and body counts. There is, however, yet another way in which her notion of social death is indispensable in coming to terms with the horror of genocide. It could well be argued that social death, as opposed to mass homicide, is the very telos—the end or purpose—of genocide.

That social death is the end of genocide is perhaps most clearly illustrated with the case of the Armenian Genocide of 1915, and the continued denial by Turkey that whatever did occur in the waning days of the Ottoman Empire was certainly not genocide.

As with all genocides, it is impossible to explain in a paragraph why the Armenian Genocide occurred at the particular historical moment that it did. Explanations are even more difficult in this particular case given that before the forced deportation and near elimination of Armenians in western Armenia and Anatolia, Armenians had lived there for approximately three thousand years. Yet in the twilight of the Ottoman Empire, the Armenian population was seen as a threat to Turkishness and imperial sovereignty, and tens of thousands of Armenians were deported to Syria and Mesopotamia. Along the way tens of thousands died of starvation and exposure. Others were mutilated, drowned, burned alive (Adalian 2013).

What is clear, however, is that the violence of *denial* continued after 1917 and well into the twenty-first century. Political elites and academics, among others, have denied the genocide. This shows that in important ways the genocide has not necessarily ended, and that denial itself is a weapon of social death as described by Card. Denial can take different forms: in some cases the denial is outright, a kind of denial propagated by political elites, academics, and rule of law (a genocide becomes that of which one dare not speak); sometimes it is claimed that there is a lack of evidence to warrant the label "genocide" given that such a label after the Genocide Convention of 1948 has tremendous repercussions in international law; sometimes political elites and academics will offer alternative accounts for events that some insist warrant being called genocide. An alternative account seeks to revise an account of events that has been adopted by the victim group and others, and in so doing seeks to contest and delegitimize the narrative that is integral to the very identity of members of the victim group. A shared history is part of the social tapestry that often defines a social group; to deny such a history is tantamount to social death.

Mehmet Talât Pasha was one member of the Turkish political elite to insist on an alternative account. Talât, who became Grand Vizier in 1917, in a speech defending the deportations he orchestrated, refers to the Armenians as "belligerent subjects and enemy combatants," and he claims: "We proceeded to carry out deportations from the war zone for the good of the troops." He concludes: "Every government has the right to defend itself against those who stage armed revolts" (Kévorkian 2011, 700–701). In calling the Armenians "armed combatants," Talât builds a narrative in which the Armenians are seen as a threat to national security, thereby deserving of their slaughter. This narrative denies what is well documented: most of those killed were noncombatant women, children, and elderly Armenians, who died of exposure and starvation as they were driven into the Syrian Desert without provisions.

Under Turkish law (Article 301 of the Turkish Penal Code) it is still forbidden to speak of an Armenian genocide.[7] On the one hand it is important to recognize that while the law has not been revised since its adoption and remains part of the penal code, the discretionary latitude of prosecutors has meant a relatively small number of prosecutions under Article 301 in recent years.[8] On the other hand the Turkish government continues to limit freedom of speech among journalists. Turkey, according to Journalists Without Borders, is the "biggest prison for journalists" (Alemdar 2014, 575). One way for a state to continue denying that it is implicated in a genocide is to restrict the freedom of speech of those, be they journalists or academics, who might contest the dominant narrative.

As recently as 2011, the journal *Middle East Critique* contained a series of articles contesting the claim that Turkey committed genocide against the Armenians in 1915. This pervasive denial of the historical record is an instance of social death, in the sense that it denies what Card calls a people or social group a history, a shared history that binds its members as a group and is central to their identity. In her list of those things that anchor social relationships—for example, common literature, cuisine, and traditions—she does not explicitly mention a common or shared history. However, memory could well be included as part of Card's list of examples. Augustine, especially in his *Confessions*, reminds his readers that memory is the very foundation of community. Memory, he claims, is the very bond of community. Garry Wills, commenting on his own translation of book 10 of the *Confessions* (Wills translates "*confessiones*" as "testimony"), claims: "Community is built up on associations treasured in memory" (Wills 2002, 18). If shared memory is a necessary condition for community as both Augustine and Wills argue, the destruction of memory is tantamount to social death.

Denial of the historical record, then, whether it be Turkish denial of the Armenian genocide or the continuing denial of the Holocaust, is a form of social death. The destruction of memory as a kind of social death can be seen in analytically distinct but related ways. One way of destroying memory is through the obliteration of sites of memory, for example architecture. The destruction of mosques, synagogues, churches, libraries, museums, even bridges and urban neighborhoods rarely if ever should be classified as collateral damage; rather, and especially, such destruction is part of genocidal violence: these architectural monuments are targeted as a way of eradicating the culture, the history, and the memory of a group.

---

[7] Article 301 replaced Article 159 of 1926, and after its amendment in 2008 reads as follows: "A person who publicly denigrates the Turkish Nation, the State of the Republic of Turkey, the Grand National Assembly of Turkey, the Government of the Republic of Turkey or the judicial bodies of the State, shall be sentenced to a penalty of imprisonment for a term of six months to two years" (Algan 2008, 2239–40).

[8] Thanks to an anonymous reader for bringing this point to my attention.

As Robert Bevan writes, "Here architecture takes on a totemic quality: a mosque, for example, is not simply a mosque; it represents to its enemies the presence of a community marked for erasure. A library or art gallery is a cache of historical memory, evidence that a given community's presence extends into the past and legitimizing it in the present and on into the future. In these circumstances structures and places with certain meanings are selected for oblivion with deliberate intent" (2016, 18). The destruction is an attempt to erase a group from history, an attempt to make the group un-be, as it were. It is a way of saying to those members of the victim group who escaped murder, you have no past.

Two brief examples illustrate this claim. First is the example of the Armenian Genocide of 1915. Using figures provided by Bevan, Uğur Ümit Üngör writes:

> The Young Turks wanted to erase the physical traces of the Armenian presence in the country, by destroying churches and buildings and their Armenian inscriptions. Although the Armenians were gone, in a sense they were still too present. Besides the less ancient churches and cathedrals, the Young Turk regime destroyed many medieval Armenian monasteries, such as Narekavank, Varakavank, Arakelots Vank, Surp Garabed, and Surp Khach. Today, very few traces remain of these former centres of Armenian cultural and religious life, yet in 1914, the Armenian community still owned 2,600 churches, 450 monasteries, and 2,000 schools—indicating the magnitude of the erasure. (Üngör 2013, 102)

The case of the destruction of monasteries, churches, and other traces of Armenian cultural and religious life is notable for the fact that the Committee of Union and Progress—the Young Turks—and successor Turkish governments perpetrated this violence after the deportation and murder of the Armenian people. The destruction reflected a determination to expunge from memory any trace of Armenian existence. And in so doing a blank space is created for rewriting history. A second example is *Kristallnacht* in the autumn of 1938 in Germany and Vienna, when hundreds of synagogues (along with sacred objects) and thousands of Jewish businesses were destroyed. Bevan claims, "Despite all this destruction it was the built presence of a people, commercially and symbolically, not the people themselves, that was the primary target on Kristallnacht" (Bevan 2016, 46). And *Kristallnacht* was a prelude to most of the killing that was to occur in the camps in the ensuing years.

Does genocide end when the killing stops? If the end or telos of genocide is social death, then genocides continue well beyond the death of bodies. If genocide is properly understood as the intention to erase from the historical record any trace of a targeted group, the destruction of architecture after the dispersal and extermination of members, as was the case for the Armenians, then genocide might well continue indefinitely.

A second way in which memory is central to community is the memory of the victim group qua victim, as its members look back on the killing and other forms of genocidal violence. A profound and defining memory of a social group or community is the memory of the genocidal violence itself. The construction of post-genocide sites of memory become part of the very fabric of social identity. Examples abound. There is the United States Holocaust Memorial Museum in Washington, D.C.; there is the Ntrarama Church in Rwanda. These are not merely sites of historical record; rather, they are sites for the construction of shared memory and the (re)construction of community. Denialism, then, seeks to destroy not only a past but also a present.

4. Conclusion

One of Robert J. Lifton's interviewees, a physician who survived the Holocaust, tells Lifton: "The professor would like to understand what is not understandable. We ourselves who were there, and who have always asked ourselves the question and will ask it until the end of our lives, we will never understand it, because it cannot be understood" (Lifton 2000, 13). This sentiment is echoed time and again, whether it be in Primo Levi's discussion of "useless violence" (Levi 1989), or Charlotte Delbo's opening sentence in *Days and Memory*—"Explaining the inexplicable" (Delbo 1985, 1), or elsewhere in stories told by survivors. Genocides, and the experiences of genocide, are indeed complex, multifaceted, and continuously changing. Despite these problems and complexities, Card's discussion of social death as "the central evil of genocide" (Card 2010, 237) accomplishes a great deal in advancing our understanding of genocide. First, it destabilizes a dominant narrative that seeks to understand genocide that relies too much on quantitative analysis, with its focus on body counts. It instead puts the focus on relationships as well as, and most important of all, on those institutions and structures that sustain relationships. It provides a radically new way of looking at genocide.

Second, it brings in from the margins the voices and stories of those who have been victims, survivors, family members of victims, and witnesses of genocides, and especially the experiences of women who have been led to believe that their experiences are not important. Social death provides a frame for listening to and understanding those stories of women (and men) who as survivors and witnesses tell their stories in the language of destroyed relationships. Three such examples were highlighted earlier: the woman interviewed by Ringelheim, the women interviewed by Leydesdorff, and the Anfal women who shared their experiences with Mlodoch.

Third, social death recognizes how far-reaching genocidal violence can be. Social death is not something easily counted or measured. It vastly expands the number of those affected and serves as a reminder that those affected cannot always be counted, for, among other reasons, they are sometimes part of future generations.

Still, it must be recognized that there exist possible weaknesses in Card's understanding of genocide. Card's frame, like any frame, brings some things into focus and leaves other things outside the frame. In this regard, it is important not to paint those who experience genocide only as victims. That is not to suggest, although it is sometimes the case, that they should be framed as perpetrators. But the very phrase "social death" might be taken to suggest that those who have been subjected to social death thereby are cast as victims who lose their agency. In other words, "death" means, among other things, the end of agency. Does "social death" mean the irredeemable end of agency? The finality of death would seem to suggest that there can be no recovery of agency. Some of the Anfal women interviewed by Mlodoch clearly spoke the language of social death. Mlodoch quotes one interviewee as saying, "With Anfal our lives have disappeared as well" (2012, 76). Yet others among her interviewees were frustrated by the fact that "images of crying and screaming Anfal women, dressed in black, carrying photos of their disappeared beloved ones, frequently appear on television and in newspapers" (Mlodoch 2012, 80–81). They were frustrated because this was only part of their story. This frame failed to recognize the important contributions these women made to the pre-Anfal insurrection. The title of Mlodoch's article quotes one woman who spoke for others: "We want to be remembered as strong women, not shepherds" (Mlodoch 2012, 63).

Moreover, it is important to insist that the frame of social death should not preclude an openness to the possibility of what is a predominant category in the thought of Hannah Arendt, namely, the idea of natality; natality opens up a space for the possibility of new beginnings, a new and unforeseen horizon. Social death should not preclude the possibility of creating new forms of social existence. Many Anfal women were able to create and sustain a new beginning in a way that Arendt envisioned. Following her introduction of the terms "labor," "work," and "action" to describe the *vita activa*, Arendt claims: "Of the three, action has the closest connection with the human condition of natality; the new beginning inherent in birth can make itself felt in the world only because the newcomer possesses the capacity of beginning something anew, that is, of acting. In this sense of initiative, an element of action, and therefore of natality, is inherent in all human activities" (1998, 9). Following Jeffrey Champlin, we should not read Arendt as talking only, or even primarily, about physical birth, but rather about "the *idea* of birth as a way of speaking about one's insertion in social space" (Champlin 2013, 151).

Reading Arendt in this way, it can then be argued that Anfal women entered and demanded recognition in new social spaces that they themselves created and forged in new communities. In the case of Anfal women, their communities centered around how best to memorialize those who perished in 1988. The women mounted protests against the Kurdish government's plans for how to bury and memorialize victims. They began meeting with artists and architects to plan and construct a counter-memorial. As Mlodoch observes: "The initiative helped them [Anfal women] to step out of their passive roles, enter into dialogue with other societal groups, and engage in public debate on memorializing Anfal against the grain of the dominant Anfal discourse with their own images and narratives" (Mlodoch 2012, 83). These women forged new relationships from the contingency of their own shared experiences as Anfal women. Their actions strongly suggest that in the midst and the wake of the trauma of Anfal, it is possible both to maintain relationships and community and to forge new relationships and communities borne of the resiliency of the human spirit. Social death ought not to be interpreted as preventing the possibility of natality.[9]

Finally, although Card's description of genocide expands and enriches our understanding of genocide considerably, it may not have significant juridical implications. When Raphael Lemkin coined the term "genocide" in 1944–1945, he did so with a clear focus. A close reading of his autobiography, *Totally Unofficial*, reveals how narrow that focus in fact was: his focus was juridical and prosecutorial. He writes in *Totally Unofficial*: "Thus my basic mission in life was formulated: to create a law among nations to protect national, racial, and religious groups from destruction. The need for the innocent to be protected set off a chain reaction in my mind. It followed me all my life. Once I conceived of the destruction of groups as a crime, I could not rest quietly. Neither could I stop thinking about it. When I later coined the word 'genocide,' I found too an expression for my own use, but at the same time I was prepared to work more for the actual transformation of this word into the subject of an international treaty" (Lemkin 2013, 2). A few pages later Lemkin writes: "Now was the time to outlaw the destruction of national, racial, and religious groups. I thought that the crime was so big that nothing less than declaring it an international offense would be adequate, and that it should be done by international treaty or convention" (9).

Since the Genocide Convention adopted a modified and negotiated version of Lemkin's definition, scholars have contested this definition, and it is clear that it has limitations within a juridical framework (May 2010), and similarly has serious limitations within a scholarly context (Snow forthcoming). Card's reconceptualization of genocide as social death serves to expand and develop our understanding of genocide from a scholarly perspective. Whether it can contribute to the ongoing conversation concerning the juridical definition of genocide remains to be seen.

---

[9] As I read Card, it is not clear that social death is a permanent condition; however, her choice of the term "death" suggests finality.

References

Adalian, Rouben. 2013. "The Armenian Genocide." In *Centuries of Genocide: Essays and Eyewitness Accounts*, edited by Samuel Totten and William Parsons, 117–56. New York: Routledge.

Adorno, Theodor W. 1963. *Kulturkritik und Gesellschaft*. Vol. 10 of *Gesammelte Schriften*. Munich: Suhrkamp.

Alemdar, Zeynep. 2014. "'Modelling' for Democracy? Turkey's Historical Issues with Freedom of Speech." *Middle Eastern Studies* 50, no. 4:568–88.

Algan, Bülent. 2008. "The Brand New Version of Article 301 of the Turkish Penal Code and the Future of Freedom of Expression Cases in Turkey." *German Law Review* 9, no. 20:2237–57.

Améry, Jean. 1980. *At the Mind's Limits: Contemplations by a Survivor on Auschwitz and Its Realities*. Translated by Sidney Rosenfeld and Stella Rosenfeld. Indianapolis: Indiana University Press.

Arendt, Hannah. 1998. *The Human Condition*. Chicago: Chicago University Press.

Bevan, Robert. 2016. *The Destruction of Memory: Architecture at War*. 2nd edition. London: Reaktion.

Butler, Judith. 2010. *Frames of War: When Is Life Grievable?* London: Verso.

Card, Claudia. 2002. *The Atrocity Paradigm: A Theory of Evil*. Oxford: Oxford University Press.

———. 2010. *Confronting Evils: Terrorism, Torture, Genocide*. Cambridge: Cambridge University Press.

Champlin, Jeffrey. 2013. "Born Again: Arendt's 'Natality' as Figure and Concept." *Germanic Review* 88, no. 2:150–64.

Delbo, Charlotte. 1985. *Days and Memory*. Translated by Rosette Lamont. Evanston, Ill.: Marlboro Press.

de Waal, Alex. 2013. "The Nubia Mountains, Sudan." In *Centuries of Genocide: Essays and Eyewitness Accounts*, edited by Samuel Totten and William Parsons, 421–46. New York: Routledge.

Jones, Adam. 2009. *Gender Inclusive: Essays on Violence, Men, and Feminist International Relations*. New York: Routledge.

Human Rights Watch Middle East. 1995. *Iraq's Crime of Genocide*. New Haven: Yale University Press.

Kertész, Imre. 2004. *Kaddish for an Unborn Child*. Translated by Tim Wilkinson. New York: Vintage.

Kévorkian, Raymond. 2011. *The Armenian Genocide: A Complete History*. London: I. B. Tauris.

Lemkin, Raphael. 2013. *Totally Unofficial: The Autobiography of Raphael Lemkin*. Translated by Donna-Lee Frieze. New Haven: Yale University Press.

Levi, Primo. 1989. *The Drowned and the Saved*. Translated by Raymond Rosenthal. London: Abacus.

Leydesdorff, Selma. 2011. *Surviving the Bosnian Genocide: The Women of Srebrenica Speak*. Translated by Kay Richardson. Indianapolis: Indiana University Press.

Lifton, Robert. 2000. *The Nazi Doctors: Medical Killing and the Psychology of Genocide*. New York: Basic Books.

May, Larry. 2010. *Genocide: A Normative Account*. Cambridge: Cambridge University Press.

Mennecke, Martin. 2013. "Genocidal Violence in the Former Yugoslavia: Bosnia Herzegovina." In *Centuries of Genocide: Essays and Eyewitness Accounts*, edited by Samuel Totten and William Parsons, 477–12. New York: Routledge.

Miller, Steven. 2014. *War After Death: On War and Its Limits*. New York: Fordham University Press.

Mlodoch, Karin. 2012. "'We Want to be Remembered as Strong Women, Not as Shepherds': Women Anfal Survivors in Kurdistan Iraq Struggling for Agency and Acknowledgement." *Journal of Middle East Women's Studies* 8, no. 1:63–91.

Porter, Theodore. 2006. *Karl Pearson: The Scientific Life in a Statistical Age*. Princeton: Princeton University Press.

Ringelheim, Joan. 1997. "Genocide and Gender: A Split Memory." In *Gender and Catastrophe*, edited by Ronit Lentin, 18–33. London: Zed Books.

Simons, Marlise. 2016. "Radovan Karadzic, a Bosnian Serb, Is Convicted of Genocide," *New York Times*, March 24.

Snow, James. 2016. "'Don't Think but Look: Using Wittgenstein's Notion of Family Resemblances to Look at Genocide." *Genocide Studies and Prevention: An International Journal* 9, no. 3:154–57.

———. 2018. "Mothers and Monsters: Women, Gender, and Genocide." In *A Gendered Lens for Genocide Prevention*, edited by Mary Michele Connellan and Christiane Fröhlich, 49–82. New York: Palgrave.

Stanton, Gregory. 1998. "The Eight Stages of Genocide." Available at http://www.genocidewatch.org/aboutgenocide/8stagesofgenocide.html (accessed 17 September 2016).

Tatz, Colin. 2013. "Genocide in Australia." In *Centuries of Genocide: Essays and Eyewitness Accounts*, edited by Samuel Totten and William Parsons, 55–88. New York: Routledge.

Totten, Samuel, and William Parsons, eds. 2013. *Centuries of Genocide: Essays and Eyewitness Accounts*. New York: Routledge.

Toumani, Meline. 2015. "We Armenians Shouldn't Let Genocide Define Us." *New York Times*, April 17.

United Nations. 1948. General Assembly, *Convention on the Prevention and Punishment of the Crime of Genocide*, 9 December, United Nations,

Treaty Series, vol. 78, p. 277, available at: http://www.refworld.org/docid/3ae6b3ac0.html (accessed 17 September 2016).

Üngör, Uğur Ümi. 2013. "The Armenian Genocide: A Multi-dimensional Approach." *Global Dialogue* 15, no. 1:91–100.

Weitz, Eric. 2013. *A Century of Genocide: Utopias of Race and Nation.* Princeton: Princeton University Press.

Wills, Garry. 2002. *Saint Augustine's Memory.* New York: Viking

Wyschogrod, Edith. 2005. "The Warring Logics of Genocide." In *Genocide and Human Rights: A Philosophical Perspective*, edited by John Roth, 207–19. New York: Palgrave.

CHAPTER 10

SURVIVING EVILS AND THE PROBLEM OF AGENCY

AN ESSAY INSPIRED BY THE WORK OF CLAUDIA CARD

DIANA TIETJENS MEYERS

Before her death Claudia Card had published two volumes of an intended trilogy on evils—*The Atrocity Paradigm* and *Confronting Evils*. The last volume of the trilogy was tentatively entitled *Surviving Atrocities*. I share Card's abiding interest in questions about horrific, humanly inflicted abuse—especially questions about victims, questions about contending with and recovering from abuse, and questions about preventing or, more realistically, reducing the magnitude and frequency of future abuse. So when Robin Dillon first invited me to contribute to this collection, I immediately knew what topic I wanted to work on: Card's most recent, alas unfinished, work on surviving.

As I now take up the task of thinking through her work and trying to build on it, my choice of this topic makes sense to me in a more allusive way. Perhaps one of the attractions of the topic for me was and is its association with the value I place on the survival of Card's remarkable and deeply personal philosophical legacy. One of the hallmarks of Card's approach to philosophical problems was to bring her personal experience to bear on them. Although she took the Holocaust as a paradigmatic case of evil, she knew other evils that she analyzes first-hand—namely, poverty, homophobia, and misogyny. As this list shows, Card didn't think evils were necessarily exceptional or temporally finite episodes in human history. On the contrary, she taught us that some evils are commonplace and persist in liberal democratic societies. This shocking ubiquity magnifies the urgency of the topic.

In this essay, I turn first to Card's views about victims and victimizers, then to her account of surviving evils, and in the final three sections to some

Criticism and Compassion: The Ethics and Politics of Claudia Card.
Edited by Robin S. Dillon and Armen T. Marsoobian.

thoughts about autonomy and agency that extend her thinking. My hope is that these reflections will prompt others to explore and benefit from Card's philosophical methods and insights.

1. A Grim Triad—Victims, Evils, and Survival

Card has always rejected the view that victims are helpless or passive, and she has maintained that philosophical discussions of evil must pivot on the perspective of victims, not that of the perpetrators (2002, 10–11; 2012, 37, 44). A victim, she says, is a "target or recipient of harm," not an identity, not a state of abjection, not a pitiful response to aggression (2014, 27). This is so clearly true, yet so often overlooked when victims are derogated or shamed. In perverting the concept of a victim into an ignominious condition that any self-respecting person ought to shun, we compound the harms that others inflict on them by depriving them of their standing to demand justice. Moreover, we suppress a major source of knowledge regarding the many and varied meanings of the suffering they have endured by sidelining them and silencing their testimony.[1]

Of course, there are many kinds of victims, even if we limit our purview to those who suffer wrongful, humanly inflicted harms. But Card's work is concerned specifically with victims of evils. In her most recent formulation, Card defines evils as "reasonably foreseeable intolerable harms produced (maintained, aggravated, supported, and so on) by inexcusable wrongs" (2014, 23). Not every evil is an atrocity. Atrocities are evils marked by exceptional cruelty or degradation (2014, 24). Not every injustice is an evil. Some injustices inflict harms that are tolerable (2014, 25). Natural disasters can become evils when people inexcusably refuse to alleviate the intolerable harms they cause (2014, 24). So Card's interest in surviving evils concerns the problems posed by coping with harms that it is outrageous anyone should have to endure (the intolerable harm component of evils) and that humans have caused in reasonably foreseeable and inexcusable ways (the human-agency component of evils).

Because there are many kinds of evils, surviving evils isn't a single phenomenon. Evils can be deeds, practices, social structures, or environments. Thus, duration is one way in which evils differ, and duration affects the possibilities for survival. In one sense, a victim survives an evil if she outlives it (Card 2016a). In another sense, a victim is surviving an evil if it hasn't defeated her so far (2016a). Because some evils end, some victims outlive them. Because others perdure, most survivors of these evils only withstand them, seldom, if ever, leaving them behind.

The differences among evils notwithstanding, Card identifies two dimensions of surviving that pertain to all of them. On the one hand, we speak of

---

[1] For detailed discussion of the value of attending to victims' stories, see Meyers 2016.

surviving—a verbal form that references a diachronic active process. Card calls this "skilled survival." Skilled surviving requires a victim to be clever in discerning evasive stratagems and self-protective options, resolute in acting on those that prove beneficial, and quick to notice and abandon those that don't (2014, 25). On the other hand, we speak of survival—a nominal form that suggests a state of being. She calls this "remainder survival" (2012, 38).[2] Remainder survival concerns valuable attributes, such as health and good character, which endure despite the victim's ordeal.

It is possible for skilled and remainder survival to coincide. In the course of shrewdly saving yourself, you may have also saved others and thus preserved your integrity and sense of decency. But it is also possible for skilled and remainder survival to come apart. In the course of shrewdly saving yourself, you may heap misery on other victims and suffer tormenting, unremitting guilt and self-hatred as a result. There are countless permutations—as many as there are evil forms of victimization, victimized individuals, and survival strategies.

Card catalogues a selection of these permutations to be found in the post-Holocaust literature (2012, 45–49). A few heroes come through with clear consciences and intact bodies and minds (2012, 40, 46). Most survivors are left morally or personally scarred in some way or other. Thus, surviving is a matter of degree (2014, 25). Moreover, there are numerous scales on which victims may survive to one degree or another. Some survive their complicity with perpetrators by plunging into denial and self-deception, by losing themselves while retaining their bodily health (2012, 45–46). Others survive such complicity by bearing witness to what happened, by exposing their own deeds and the harms other victims suffered (2012, 47–48). Some survivors do not live out natural lifespans—they commit suicide (2012, 49). Surviving, Card observes, may not be the ultimate good for every victim. True survivors and completely successful survival are rare.

Throughout her discussions of survival, Card takes care to juxtapose the duality of skill and luck. Although skill often plays a role in whether or not a victim survives, good or bad luck is always a factor (2012, 37; 2014, 27). Unless chinks in the administrative and material mechanisms of evil open, victims cannot mobilize know-how and courage to diminish or elude the harms being visited upon them. No doubt luck also plays a role in the allocation of inner resources—talents and traits of character—that enable some to profit from propitious opportunities and that prevent others from doing so. But sheer luck is sometimes all that separates survivors from victims who don't make it. Some Holocaust victims who were lucky enough to be hidden until Hitler's military was near defeat were also lucky enough to be rescued as the Allied armies advanced through Eastern Europe and into Germany.

[2] In an earlier paper, Card calls this type "preservation survival" (2012, 37).

Because some evils are ongoing, seemingly permanent features of social relations, some survivors are never out of danger. For many people born into what Card calls "aggravated subsistence poverty," there is little or no chance of escaping from poverty morally unscathed. Although good fortune occasionally presents an escape route—for example, a subsidized education or a career in the military—it's necessary to bear in mind that nothing guarantees that any particular victim of aggravated subsistence poverty will be able to take advantage of such socially condoned opportunities to escape (2014, 29, 35; also see 2016c). Many victims are doomed to ceaselessly "tread water" (2014, 27). Beset by severe deprivation, their lives and health are never secure, and their moral character is frequently at risk. Misogyny and homophobia are also persistent evils, but, unlike poverty, they currently offer no exit options, only coping options.

2. Survival Tactics

Taking a cue from Primo Levi, Card calls the contexts in which many, perhaps most, victims of evils are compelled to live "gray zones" (2002, 2012; 2014). Three characteristics demarcate gray zones:

(1) Their inhabitants are victims of evil.
(2) These inhabitants are implicated through their choices in perpetrating some of the same or similar evils on others who are already victims like themselves.
(3) These inhabitants act under extraordinary stress. (2000, 517; 2002, 224)

In a gray zone, perpetrators offer some victims privileges—power and surcease—in exchange for their complicity in inflicting intolerable harms on others. The targets of these offers must decide whether to accept them in the midst of "intense or prolonged fear for basic security or their very lives or for the lives or basic security of loved ones" (2002, 224).

The infamous dilemmas that Nazi death camp officials imposed on certain inmates are well known. March fellow victims to the "showers" or die right now (2012, 47). Assist with Josef Mengele's "experiments" and send extra food to your wife and daughter or die with everyone else (2012, 48). Each case of complicity in the camps, each amalgam of evil and innocence, differs from every other—in the agent's motives and willingness, in the nature of the harms perpetrated by the agent, in the agent's ability to sabotage camp operations, and so forth (2000, 518–19; 2002, 226–27).

For Card, the ambiguity saturation of gray zones raises ontological questions about the intelligibility of agents' choices within our standard framework of deliberation and decision making and also about the adequacy of our moral vocabularies to assessing these choices. It seems, as she puts it, that victims of evil can only "grope" through gray zones, and that moral philosophers seeking to grasp the moral significance of their predicaments and actions must grope as well (1999, 16). Surviving evil is never a sure thing, and the ethics of surviving is seldom clear-cut. Yet, Card emphasizes that many of the inhabitants and survivors of gray zones hold fast to moral categories, even as they are forced to navigate opaque, terrifying situations and to look back in anguish on their actions in them (2000, 519).

As I said earlier, Card devotes a great deal of attention to the victims of homicidal Nazi bigotry, for the Holocaust surely epitomizes evil. But she probes a number of other forms of evil and analyzes the action spaces into which they insert victims, including slavery, misogyny, homophobia, and poverty.[3]

Misogyny is an evil that has everyday forms, such as spousal abuse and sex trafficking, and spasmodic forms, such as outbreaks of mass rape during armed conflict (2000, 513). Sieges of misogynist battery and sexual assault trap women in gray zones. A woman who has been humiliated and beaten by her partner month after month may stand by while her assailant beats, molests, perhaps kills her child. In desperation, some battered women resort to killing their abusers when they are defenseless—for instance, while they are asleep. Women who have been trafficked into sex work and mercilessly forced to perform sexual services for clients sometimes "rise through the ranks," becoming madams and trafficking in women themselves. Women repeatedly raped by enemy combatants sometimes abandon or kill the babies they conceive and bear in hopes of resuming their lives as "respectable" women in their communities of origin. Brutal expressions of misogyny beget survival strategies that may require wit or courage but that often doom survivors to lifelong shame and self-reproach, if not to prosecution and prison.

Inspired by Jeremy Waldron's work on hate speech, Card argues that homophobia constitutes an evil environment in which hate crimes normalize the hate of haters and recruit new haters, all the while depriving LGBTQ victims of the good of "a sense of security in the space we all inhabit" (2016a). As a result of this "toxic environment," LGBTQ individuals are highly vulnerable to violence, including sexual assault, torture, and murder, and disproportionately vulnerable to suicide. To protect themselves, therefore, victims may hide in the closet, pass for straight, or form separatist communities (2016a). But none of these strategies is foolproof, for exposure is always a possibility. All carry substantial moral costs, for habits of deception in hazardous spaces undermine spontaneity and candor in safe spaces, too. Moreover, pursuing these strategies may lead victims to betray

---

[3] Card's discussion of surviving slavery is slight compared to her discussions of surviving the Holocaust, misogyny, homophobia, and subsistence poverty. Thus, in this essay I focus on her remarks about surviving the latter four evils.

one another, as laughing at homophobic jokes, voicing homophobic sentiments, or outing other LGBTQ individuals may reinforce the credibility of a victim's masquerade. Still, coming out can incur major costs, including loss of livelihood and loss of friendships or family ties, not to mention being targeted for hate crimes.[4] Like the evil of misogyny, homophobic environments create double binds that turn survival into a core project for victims and prevent them from surviving without sacrificing their integrity or their well-being.

To many, poverty seems like a consequence of irresponsibility or laziness, but Card maintains that subsistence poverty is often an evil: "Poverty that results from injustice is an evil when its inexcusable deprivations are not survivable without jeopardizing its victims' humanity or when it makes survivors deeply ashamed of their lives" (2014, 30). Here, too, the elements of a gray zone converge. An evil renders its victims radically insecure, thereby putting them under extraordinary stress that in turn may lead victims to act in morally compromising ways in order to survive. Some of those strategies take advantage of people who are well off, but many of them prey on other victims of severe poverty.

Writing from the standpoint of her childhood experience of poverty in rural Wisconsin, Card sketches a range of "survival challenges" associated with subsistence poverty, including poor nutrition, poor health, poor housing, and long hours of work (2014, 33–34). Mired in these compound hardships, the needs of people living in subsistence poverty often exceed their ability to pay for them. Thus, they "learn to manipulate others" (2014, 33). Similarly, poverty schools you in the arts of dissembling to conceal weaknesses or make excuses (2014, 34). Gradually, you may become inured to others' disdain for your unreliability and dishonesty. Being criminalized is a further risk of living in subsistence poverty. If an unexpected turn of events, say, a health crisis or unemployment, leaves you with a financial deficit, the risk of criminality looms large. As Card puts it, "You 'borrow' without asking" (2014, 34). Likewise, people living in such extreme and persistent poverty are at risk of losing their homes and becoming homeless. The added vulnerability that comes with life on the streets may persuade you to acquire a weapon. But your weapon puts you in danger of seriously injuring, perhaps killing, someone and thus in danger of being prosecuted and punished if the verdict goes against you (2014, 33). Agents taking measures to survive the privations of severe poverty may end up snared in a downward spiral of crime, incarceration, stigma, and further crime.

---

[4] Card writes mainly from the standpoint of the post-closet era in many parts of the United States. However, she documents a practice known in South Africa (where gay marriage is legal) as "corrective rape," and homosexuality remains illegal and persecuted in much of the rest of Africa and in Russia.

In the case of the Holocaust, the remedy (if we can speak of one for that state-sponsored mass-murder juggernaut) was the surrender of the Axis powers in Europe, the closing of the camps, and the provision of humanitarian aid and reparations to the victims. The evils of misogyny, homophobia, and subsistence poverty are different. They exist worldwide, and there is no concerted, multinational campaign to conquer them. Because Card doubts that any determined effort to eradicate dire poverty will emerge any time soon, she asks what would enable victims of this evil to avoid the traps and temptations embedded in it. In other words, "What would significantly enhance both skilled and remainder survival" for the poorest of the poor? In Card's view, fostering hope is key: first, by ensuring the health of children and adequate care for them and, second, by protecting impoverished individuals from violence and criminalization (2014, 36–37). If people living in subsistence poverty were not hopeless, Card reasons, they would be able to focus their survival skills on taking advantage of available educational and occupational opportunities, and surviving would not condemn them to a remainder of shame, denial, or self-deception. Perhaps a parallel set of recommendations could be developed to alleviate the harms of misogyny and homophobia. But in the case of homophobia, Card recommends political activism and cultural interventions to detoxify the environment (2016a). Although I'm sure she would also advocate political activism and cultural intervention to defuse misogyny, in *The Atrocity Paradigm* she opts (surprisingly) to offer a suite of "fantasies" (2002, 132–35). That she takes refuge in fantasy in this regard strikes me as an excellent gauge of her assessment of the remoteness of any effective remedy for the abuses of misogyny in the patriarchal world we've inherited.

Clearly, nonvictims have obligations to agitate for policies and practices that bring a halt to evils or that at least diminish the gravity and the reach of the damage they cause. Is there anything to be said about the possibilities for victims to exercise their agentic powers in ways that might be conducive to truly surviving? I'll begin by offering some observations about autonomy and agency in section 3. Then, in section 4, I consider whether a conception of survival agency might be constructed based on Card's work on surviving evils.

3. Autonomy and Agency

The concepts of autonomy and agency are a bit slippery partly because of their close relationship and partly because they are terms of art. For the most part, philosophers of action use the terms *autonomy* and *agency* interchangeably to refer to self-governance or self-determination. Minimally, then, autonomy and agency consist of the capacity to act intentionally. When social scientists identify agency with the capacity for independent action, they sometimes mean to adopt this philosophical conception, but sometimes they mean to contrast agentic action with action governed by social structures. The latter injects the elements of power and resistance into the concept of agency. Along these lines, some philosophers and social scientists, usually those pursuing a progressive social and political agenda, adopt a stronger view of agency. They invoke the concept of agency to reference an individual's or a collectivity's capacity to move regnant institutions, norms, and practices toward greater justice. This conception departs from most philosophical accounts of autonomy, for accounts of autonomy typically focus on explicating the capacity to act on your desires and values (in some accounts, your authentic desires and values) and to disregard whatever capacities might be needed to bring about positive social change.

Feminist moral and political philosopher Serene Khader modifies and blends the two conceptions of agency that I've just sketched. According to Khader, "We may think of agency as the capacity to make decisions and shape one's world in accordance with what one cares about" (2011, 31). To the minimalist view from philosophy of action Khader adds the thought that agency requires that the individual is making choices that enact values and goals that matter to her and align with her interests, in contradistinction to desires and goals she simply happens to have. In this respect, Khader's conception overlaps with accounts of autonomy that require that the motivations for your conduct be authentically your own. It is uncertain, however, whether Khader embraces the strong view of agency that incorporates the power to influence the course of large-scale events or the structures undergirding social relations. Although her account of agency includes the capacity to shape your world, this capacity might be construed in a quite narrow way such that a woman who is capable of rejiggering her domestic relations so as to put a stop to being beaten at home would count as exercising agency. After all, a person's experiential or proximate world may be quite small.

I would concur with this restrained understanding of the relation between agency and social influence. The ability to have a localized, domain-specific, advantageous impact on your social environment suffices, I think, for agency, because the alternative of requiring the capacity to impact society in grander ways would implausibly deagentify too many people. But I would stress that this view of agency does not coincide with prevailing views of autonomy, which are value neutral or nonsubstantive. Only the most prescriptive, substantive accounts of autonomy—those that require autonomous individuals to act in morally admirable ways, in self-respecting ways, or in ways conducive to their own flourishing—coincide with this conception of agency.

I turn now to another line of thought found in Khader's work and in other recent work on women and oppression. This line of thought complements the view of agency I've just endorsed and also diverges from most accounts of autonomy. Whereas theorists of autonomy may distinguish between personal and moral autonomy, they often argue for the continuities between them.[5] In contrast, theorists of agency routinely speak of agencies rather than agency and underscore the differences among diverse types of agency.

Disparate settings define some types of agency—for example, political agency and sexual agency. Political agency concerns an individual's ability to participate in democratic processes by exercising rights, by organizing or joining social movements, or by agitating for a cause by some other means.[6] Sexual agency refers to control over your participation in possible sexual encounters, including your consent or refusal to engage and your choices about erotic activities and safety precautions.

Particular objectives define other types of agency. For example, Khader distinguishes welfare agency from feminist agency. Whereas welfare agency is the ability to enhance your own welfare, say, by obtaining better nutrition or adequate health care, feminist agency is the ability to "identify and change sexist norms" (Khader 2014, 224). Similarly, Alisa Bierria distinguishes transformative agency from insurgent agency. Both are types of resistance to oppression. Insurgent agency, however, "temporarily destabilizes, circumnavigates, or manipulates [oppressive] conditions in order to reach specific ends" (Bierria 2014, 140). In contrast, transformative agency aims to "overturn conditions of systemic oppression," often by working jointly with likeminded others (139). If I'm not mistaken, Bierria's insurgent agency has much in common with Khader's welfare agency, and Bierria's transformative agency parallels while also expanding on Khader's feminist agency.

This relation between transformative agency and feminist agency might raise the question of whether both Bierria and Khader are mandating the strong account of agency I rejected. But I doubt that their positions are vulnerable to the charges of grandiosity and undue exclusion that persuade me to adopt a more moderate conception. Provided that Khader would acknowledge the piecemeal changes in gender norms that women create one household, one workplace, or one relationship at a time to be expressions of feminist agency while also acknowledging that effecting major legal or cultural changes in gender relations is an expression of feminist agency, I see no problem with her view. Provided that Bierria regards transformative agency as one form of agency among others that are less demanding, as she clearly does, I see no problem in recognizing transformative agency as one type of agency.

---

[5] Philosophers also recognize economic autonomy and autonomous states; however, discussions of these concepts have rather tenuous connections to discussions of personal and moral autonomy.

[6] In some contexts, notably in political science, political agency refers to the relationship between constituents and their elected representatives. The latter are cast in the role of agents—individuals who act on behalf—of the former.

Discussions of agency suggest that some types presuppose some degree of publicly secured or self-appropriated empowerment. Thus, people who have no right to vote, no right to seek public office, and no right to organize around political issues lack political agency. In such repressive circumstances, only those courageous individuals who are powerfully motivated by steadfast political commitments snatch political agency out of the grip of the authorities and disobey the law to promote their political goals. Despite official denial of their rights, Nelson Mandela exercised political agency under apartheid and Martin Luther King Jr. exercised political agency in the Jim Crow South.

Similarly, women lack sexual agency if they cannot exert control over whether they have sex, whom they have sex with, whether they or their partners use contraception, and which sex acts they perform. Women who have been trafficked into sex work have little, if any, sexual agency. The sexual agency of girls who don't use contraceptives for fear of alienating their male partners or appearing to be loose women, thereby risking unwanted pregnancy at a young age, is severely compromised (for discussion, see Stoljar 2000). But many women seize sexual agency by refusing to engage in anything but mutually respectful forms of intimacy and insisting on choosing partners of whichever gender(s) appeal to them. Just as empowerment is a matter of degree and depends on social as well as individual resources, so too these types of agency are a matter of degree and vary depending on socially conferred options as well as personal gifts and traits of character.

Some types of agency are aimed specifically at gaining empowerment either temporarily in order to cope with a particular situation—Bierria's insurgent agency—or long-term by bringing about emancipatory social change—Bierria's transformative agency. In this connection, however, it is important to bear one of Khader's points in mind. Empowerment in one domain, such as access to basic necessities, does not entail empowerment across the board, such as achieving greater gender equality. Welfare agency and feminist agency can come into conflict, as can insurgent and transformative agency.

4. Survival Agency?

Any conception of survival agency befitting Card's theory of evils must secure victims' ability to act so as to preserve their lives and prevent their health and character from collapsing into irremediable disrepair. Yet because gray zones are designed to rob victims of precisely these capacities, few could exercise survival agency unless they had auxiliary capacities. For example, victims of evils need the capacity to identify an alterable feature of the situation in which they are confined, together with the capacity to alter it in a life-, health-, and character-preserving way. Alternatively, they need the capacity to spot fissures in the evil regime together with the capacity to reposition themselves in less dangerous sites within those regimes. Each of these modes of survival agency belongs in Bierria's category of insurgent agency. Whatever victims may accomplish stops way short of vanquishing the evil, and the benefits gained by exercising these forms of agency are always at risk of reversal unless or until the evil is brought to an end. In a moment, I'll say why I think that survival agency should prioritize personal survival over moral survival. But first I take up Card's views about surviving and morality.

At first blush, it seems that Card would classify survival agency as a species of moral agency, for she holds that moral remainder survival is a necessary component of true survival. In Card's view, this dimension of survival requires victims to preserve or improve their moral character. Since many victims of evil never lose their moral compass, this requirement does not seem patently unreasonable. Although their strength of conscience may prove to be deleterious to their health remainder survival, it may be advantageous to their moral remainder survival.

Still, Card acknowledges that, driven to desperation, victims of evils may lose their grip on ordinary categories of right and wrong. Her accounts of the evil of subsistence poverty and the evil of homophobia underscore, for example, how evils can sabotage honesty. Nonetheless, because survival is a matter of degree and relative to different domains, a victim's commitment to moral norms might remain fairly strong in her family relations but deteriorate significantly in her relations to others. Moreover, morally impaired victims are not barred from exercising skilled survival agency, for skilled survival need not be constrained by moral norms.

To truly survive an evil (or multiple intersectional evils), you need to be able to refrain from courses of action that would undermine your morally desirable attributes. Because reducing agency to acting intentionally neither identifies the aims of survival agency nor acknowledges the moral dimension Card imputes to survival, this conception is too general and too thin to accommodate her view.

Yet, inflating agency into a capacity to mitigate or halt current evils or to prevent future evils seems to put a greater onus on victims to solve historically intractable social and economic problems than Card would countenance. Throughout, Card's work demonstrates her sensitivity to the appalling quandaries in which evils embroil victims, along with her attentiveness both to the ways in which evils can drag victims into the moral muck and to the ways they can spur victims to feats of bravery or altruism that defy the most forbidding obstacles. Invariably careful not to gloss over the unsavory side of human psychology and alert to the unyielding constraints that evils impose on victims, Card would, I believe, favor a view of survival agency that is no less cognizant of those factors.

Khader's modest, but more than minimalist, account of agency is promising as a starting point from which to work out a conception of survival agency that Card could endorse. Recall Khader's view: agency is "the capacity to make decisions and shape one's world in accordance with what one cares about" (2011, 31). As a general rule, it is safe to assume that people care about their access to basic necessities, including safety as well as subsistence goods. If so, it stands to reason that remainder survival with respect to life and health matters to them. However, whether or how much people subjected to the extreme danger and the double binds of gray zones also care about their good character might vary quite a bit from person to person and/or depending on the type of evil that's been foisted on them.

In this regard, Card goes so far as to acknowledge that as a result of a (very unlucky) childhood attachment to a morally defective caregiver and the persistence later in life of the malign effects of that attachment, a person can develop a practical identity constituted by badness and hence desire to act under the guise of the bad (2016b, 52–54). This concession to the impact of inadequate childrearing notwithstanding, Card argues against the claim that moral remainder survival is dispensable for victims of evils. That is, she rejects the view that this aspect of survival is more a luxury than a need when a person is trapped in a gray zone (2012, 49–50). In what follows, I'll urge (1) that it's highly speculative whether a victim's good character will be permanently shattered or will be amenable to repair in the aftermath of an evil or at some point during a seemingly ineradicable evil, and (2) that victims often cannot repair their moral character on their own. In my view, this uncertainty and interdependency have implications for theorizing survival agency.

I'm not at all sure what causes character erosion or ruin. Card describes cases in which victims' moral character seems to have been irreparably damaged and cases in which victims' moral character seems to have survived despite their ruthless survival maneuvers. Indeed, she also presents the case of a Polish Catholic man who had a history of thievery and incarceration, but who brought food and other supplies to a Jewish family he discovered hiding in the sewers of Lvov during the Holocaust and who improved his character in the process (2016c). Some people adhere staunchly to moral precepts regardless of circumstances; some people totally abandon moral considerations under pressure; some people rise to the occasion and become newly committed to leading morally good lives.

To account for such divergent outcomes, Card suggests that luck is a significant determinant of a victim's ability to sustain or build a good moral character. If she is right that luck is so salient a factor in this regard, no taxonomic system for classifying survival tactics according to whether or not they are compatible with the remainder survival of the victim's good character would be tenable. For this reason, and also because I think the probable outcome for a victim's character is one of the profoundly disturbing imponderables of gray zones, I'm convinced that it's not so clear after all that survival agency must be a species of moral agency.

As I mentioned earlier, Card argues that becoming involved in criminal activities, which in many cases are conducted in partnership with criminal organizations, is one of an assortment of potentially noxious consequences of the evil of severe poverty.[7] Yet, it is well known that codes of honor function within criminal gangs that specialize in a variety of despicable but profitable enterprises. Likewise, it is well known that, despite the odds against them, some poverty-stricken youths who've been recruited into these organizations eventually break free and subsequently lead morally commendable lives. Although their initial survival strategy underwrites a constricted and distorted rectitude that is dictated by the conduct code of a particular criminal organization, later on they construct a survival strategy that fully satisfies Card's moral remainder criterion of true survival.

An analogy with the prospects for combat soldiers' postwar moral character is helpful here. I am not confident that the prospects for soldiers who have seen combat are any better or worse than the prospects for ex–gang members or, for that matter, for victims of evils more generally. Although serving in the military is a socially sanctioned form of employment, undergoing horrific hardships and performing horrific acts on the battlefield stretch many soldiers' moral fiber to the breaking point. Some evils plunge victims into circumstances that resemble the unpredictability and ferocity of war zones and that generate demands that resemble the extremity of those made on soldiers in the midst of warfare. Since soldiers' ability to recalibrate their values and motivational systems to civilian life seems to depend in part on the availability of post-service support systems for veterans, it seems likely that the same holds true for former gang members struggling to lead law-abiding lives. If so, access to such assistance should not be a matter of luck but rather should be guaranteed as a matter of justice.[8]

Good moral character seldom survives and flourishes in a social vacuum, and in the aftermath of evil or in the process of escaping from evil, social scaffolding can make the difference between some victims' renewed or newly fashioned good moral character and others' weakened or warped moral character. In this vein, Card acknowledges that control over their future moral character may not be within individual victims' agentic power. In some cases, she notes, access to mental health care can be decisive with respect to a victim's success in constructing a good moral character or surrender to a bad moral character (2016c).

In light of this relational dimension of moral remainder survival and the possibility that others will come forward to assist victims in restoring

---

[7] It goes without saying that many people organize or join criminal enterprises for reasons other than trying to escape from or at least cope with the evil of severe poverty. My comments in this essay are restricted to those individuals who pursue careers in crime as a strategy for surviving this evil.

[8] Sometimes families and friends provide support systems that are adequate to combat veterans' and former gang members' needs. But when such informal support isn't available or isn't sufficient, society must establish and secure access to institutionalized support systems that answer to the needs of these individuals.

or reconstructing their moral character, I'm inclined to discount how much jeopardy a victim's character is in when she's consumed by the need to try to survive an evil. If this is a sensible concession to the severity of intolerable harms and to the resilience of moral character in supportive social contexts, it follows that a defensible account of survival agency should prioritize skilled survival and remainder survival with respect to life and health over remainder survival with respect to moral character. In many cases, I conclude, victims of evils can postpone addressing the state of their moral character until after an evil is past or until they get a respite from a non-terminal, possibly interminable, evil or access to whatever support services they need.

5. Surviving Trafficking and Sexual Violence

Few if any periods of human history have been free of the evil of mass sexual violence during armed combat. As I write, ISIS—the self-proclaimed Islamic caliphate—is perpetrating such an evil in the territory it has occupied. The main targets are Yezidi women and girls, who are abducted in military campaigns in northern Iraq, sold or given to ISIS fighters and other men, and subsequently raped over extended periods of time. The ISIS perpetrators are shameless in their self-serving piety as revivers of the institution of sexual slavery. The organization has publicly proclaimed purportedly Sharia-sanctioned rules governing buying, selling, gifting, and emancipating Yezidi women and girls (Callimachi 2015). The testimony of women and girls who have escaped from their captors gives the lie to this sanctimonious nonsense. In this section, however, I focus not on the abominations of trafficking in persons and mass sexual abuse but rather on the survival agency of the victims of these crimes against humanity.

Pretense is a survival strategy that victims deploy in several ways. Despite their deep religious faith, some victims report pretending to go along with their captors' demands that they convert to Islam. One woman describes how she avoided betraying her faith while feigning compliance with Islamic practices: "We were forced to read the Quran and we started to pray slowly. We started to behave like actors" (Human Rights Watch 2015). Some abductees try to use Islamic sexual mores to defend themselves. Because Islam forbids sex with a pregnant woman, some women claim to be pregnant: "There was an American man there, who did not speak Arabic. He told me that I must marry him to become Muslim. He asked me to wash myself and then marry him. I told him that I was pregnant and could not have sex, so he brought me to a doctor and when he found out that I lied he beat me" (Salim 2015; also see Amnesty International 2014). Whether deviously pretending to comply with the demands of their captors or protesting their unfitness for sex, many Yezidi women and girls do their best to preserve their integrity and defend themselves under brutal conditions.

In addition to these subterfuges, some captives try to make themselves sexually undesirable by smearing themselves with dirt and refusing to bathe. Others try futilely to fight off their captors. Ultimately, however, escape is the main survival strategy the victims report. The daring, resourcefulness, and determination of the escapees is striking:

> I wore the black abaya and run [sic] away. I found some taxis and got into one asking the driver to take me to see my uncle at the border with Turkey. An ISIS car stopped the taxi and questioned the man and myself. They asked me what I was doing alone, without children outside the house. Then the taxi driver told the men that my uncle had an accident and he was helping me to get to him. They let us go, and the man drove me to Tel Abyad at the border with Turkey, where I was rescued.

> In a house one day I found a phone, which was probably left by one of the fighters. I took it and called my father, who worked in Erbil. My father paid a smuggler $4,000 to get me out of Tal Afar and into safety to the Peshmerga.

> I tried to escape once, but the soldiers found me in the streets, and brought me back. The man beat me hard, and lashed me with an electrical cable. He told me that if I did not want to stay there and marry him he would sell me to somebody worse. He gave me three days to think about it. The next day, when he was not there, his wife came to me, and told me that she could help me escape to a Kurdish family living in the neighborhood. She took me there when her husband was out and I asked the Kurdish family to help me, I begged them. I stayed with them for five months. Then one day we could finally arrange with my father to meet at the border with Turkey. The Kurdish man gave me his daughter's ID and drove me to the border, where I was finally rescued. (Salim 2015)

Although each of these women was lucky in being able to rely on others' assistance with her escape, each is intrepid in pursuit of her freedom, adroit at taking advantage of escape routes, and unshakable in her resolve to return to her family and community.[9]

Although it is important to acknowledge the survival agency that individual Yezidi women exercise, it is also important to acknowledge the social support for the recovery of the victims provided by the Yezidi community. Unlike in many other sexual-violence atrocities, a Yezidi spiritual leader, Baba Sheikh, has advocated welcoming women and girls who have been raped while in ISIS captivity back into the community. There is speculation that the Yezidis are compelled to behave so magnanimously because they are such a tiny minority that the alternative would be ethnic suicide. But I doubt this is the whole story.

---

[9] I don't want to paint an unduly rosy picture, however. Some captives despair: "We were 21 girls in a room, two of them were very young, 10–12 years. One day we were given clothes that looked like dance costumes and were told to bathe and wear those clothes. Jilan killed herself in the bathroom. She cut her wrists and hanged herself. She was very beautiful" (Amnesty International 2014; also see Human Rights Watch 2015).

One report tells of a husband's fear that his nineteen-year-old wife might be suicidal and of his devoted attention to her in the aftermath of her ISIS-inflicted ordeal, and also of a grandfather's tender concern and care for his sixteen-year-old granddaughter (Amnesty International 2014). Although the same report notes the shame and stigma customarily associated with sex outside marriage or sex with a man of a different faith, it is undeniable that Yezidi activists and families are taking great risks and going to enormous expense to rescue girls and women who have been abducted, and there is no credible evidence of recriminations against women and girls who have come home. Arguably affection for beloved wives and daughters, regard for female Yezidi coreligionists, and empathy for the female victims of ISIS are winning out over age-old taboos. There is reason to hope, then, that these victims will eventually prevail and survive morally as well as physically and psychologically.

Survival agency is the weapon of last resort for victims of evils—people who are as disempowered as possible by an evil deed, evil practices, evil social structures, or evil environments. To save themselves, victims must discover fortuitous, situational opportunities for self-protection. To notice and exploit these opportunities, victims must have appropriate traits of character, personality traits, and skills. Although I agree with Card that moral remainder survival is a vital component of true survival, I question whether victims assailed by the inexcusable harms evils inflict can anticipate which courses of conduct are incompatible with moral remainder survival, and therefore I question whether they must put achieving this end on a par with life and health remainder survival while subjected to an evil. Indeed, I think that one way to construe Bierria's emancipatory agency—a way that is in keeping with Card's theory of evils—would be to include in it a capacity to bring about a world in which the probability of developing a good moral character in childhood would be maximized and no one would be deprived of the opportunity to restore her good character or reconfigure her character for the better as an adult. Otherwise, as Card knew so well, victims of evils can only entrust their moral fate to luck.

Acknowledgments

Thanks to Lori Gruen and the participants in a Society for Analytic Feminism session at the 2016 APA Central Division meetings for helpful comments on a draft of this essay.

References

Amnesty International. 2014. "Escape from Hell: Torture and Sexual Slavery in Islamic State Captivity in Iraq." https://www.amnesty.org.uk/sites/default/files/escape_from_hell_-_torture_and_sexual_slavery_in_ islamic_state_captivity_in_iraq_-_english_2.pdf, accessed May 13, 2016.

Bierria, Alisa. 2014. "Missing in Action: Violence, Power, and Discerning Agency." *Hypatia* 29, no. 1:129–45.

Callimachi, Rukmini. 2015. "Enslaving Young Girls, the Islamic State Builds a Vast System of Rape." *New York Times* (August 14), A1 and A12–13.

Card, Claudia. 1999. "Groping Through Gray Zones." In *On Feminist Ethics and Politics*, edited by Claudia Card, 3–26. Lawrence: University Press of Kansas.

———. 2000. "Women, Evil, and Gray Zones." *Metaphilosophy* 31, no. 5: 509–28. Chapter 4 in this collection.

———. 2002. *The Atrocity Paradigm: A Theory of Evil*. New York: Oxford University Press.

———. 2012. "Surviving Long-Term Mass Atrocities." *Midwest Studies in Philosophy* 36:35–52. Chapter 7 in this collection.

———. 2014. "Surviving Poverty." In *Poverty, Agency, and Human Rights*, edited by Diana Tietjens Meyers, 21–42. New York: Oxford University Press.

———. 2016a. "Surviving Homophobia: Overcoming Evil Environments." Carus Lecture, delivered by Victoria Davion, APA Central Division Meeting, Chicago.

———. 2016b. "Taking Pride in Being Bad." In *Oxford Studies in Normative Ethics*, vol. 6, edited by Mark Timmons, 37–55. New York: Oxford University Press. Chapter 15 in the present collection.

———. 2016c. "Gratitude to the Decent Rescuer." Carus Lecture, delivered by Diana Tietjens Meyers, APA Central Division Meeting, Chicago.

Human Rights Watch. 2015. "Iraq: ISIS Escapees Describe Systematic Rape." https://www.hrw.org/news/2015/04/14/iraq-isis-escapees-describe-systematic-rape, accessed May 13, 2016.

Khader, Serene J. 2011. *Adaptive Preferences and Women's Empowerment*. New York: Oxford University Press.

———. 2014. "Empowerment Through Self-Subordination? Microcredit and Women's Agency." In *Poverty, Agency, and Human Rights*, edited by Diana Tietjens Meyers, 223–48. New York: Oxford University Press.

Meyers, Diana Tietjens. 2016. *Victims' Stories and the Advancement of Human Rights*. New York: Oxford University Press.

Salim, Seivan. 2015. "Escaped." http://www.mapofdisplacement.com/escaped/, accessed May 13, 2016.

Stoljar, Natalie. 2000. "Autonomy and the Feminist Intuition." In *Relational Autonomy*, edited by Catriona Mackenzie and Natalie Stoljar, 94–111. New York: Oxford University Press.

CHAPTER 11

INSTITUTIONAL EVILS, CULPABLE COMPLICITY, AND DUTIES TO ENGAGE IN MORAL REPAIR

ELIANA PECK AND ELLEN K. FEDER

Introduction

Among the most difficult moral challenges is reckoning with collectively perpetrated wrongs, a problem that Claudia Card confronts in her study of evils. Card's discussion of evils, delivered primarily in *The Atrocity Paradigm* (2002) and *Confronting Evils: Terrorism, Torture, Genocide* (2010), includes a rigorous account of evils perpetrated by groups and institutions, as opposed to evil acts committed by individuals in relative isolation. In her assessment of complex evils, Card takes up the challenge begun by Hannah Arendt's study of Adolph Eichmann (Arendt 2006) and provides an account of moral responsibility for the sort of intolerable harm that, we learned, is not committed only by "monsters" but can become ordinary. Card's analysis of evils departs from other contemporary conceptions that frame an evil act as an intentional, malevolent wrong; instead, Card emphasizes that evils may go unnoticed by many, expressed in local, everyday institutions and practices (2010, xii). She calls for a "demythologized" understanding of evil, one that directly acknowledges and confronts the fact that the effects of collectively perpetrated evils may not be specifically intended by anyone (Card 2010, 4–5, 8).

Assessing collectively perpetrated evils leads Card to investigate the nature of individuals' responsibilities for varying degrees of engagement in evils. She asks, "How well do we develop habits of reflection on what we are actually doing together, habits of inquiry into the history and consequences of institutions in which we participate or from which we benefit?" (Card 2010, 63–64). She insists upon the importance of expanding the categories of moral responsibility for evil to include not just obviously

Criticism and Compassion: The Ethics and Politics of Claudia Card.
Edited by Robin S. Dillon and Armen T. Marsoobian.
Chapters and book compilation © 2018 Metaphilosophy LLC and John Wiley & Sons Ltd.

culpable perpetrators of harm but also those who participate in an evil practice or institution. Complicity, she emphasizes, captures the sort of moral responsibility many individuals bear in collectively perpetrated evils. Persons may be complicit in a collectively perpetrated evil if they benefit from, contribute to, or participate in its perpetration (Card 2010, 63–66, 78, 83). The fact that a person is complicit in an evil practice or institution does not necessarily mean that he or she is an evildoer, or even that he or she is morally blameworthy (Card 2010, 37, 63–64). Indeed, Card explains that in collectively perpetrated evils "responsibility is distributed among many agents, many of whose acts are not harmful enough to be evils, although they contribute to real evils" (2010, 69). Complicity, therefore, should not be demonized but should be thoughtfully considered and addressed, particularly if individuals are to respond honorably to the evils that their complicity has supported (Card 2010, 4, 7, 24).

Though Card maintains that not all complicity is culpable, her study of collectively perpetrated evils does reveal the importance of assessing how complicity may be morally blameworthy (2010, 65, 78, 87). She rarely makes explicit her views regarding what is required of persons who are culpably complicit in institutional evils, but she does repeatedly convey the importance of such inquiries. A chapter of *The Atrocity Paradigm* is devoted to a study of the moral emotions that drive reparative efforts (Card 2002, 188–210), and in *Confronting Evils* Card remarks that one of her motivations for studying evils is her hope that a greater appreciation for the ordinariness of some evils may move people to take responsibility for their contributions to evils, and respond honorably (2010, 3–4, 7–9). Her work reveals an interest in how persons that are culpably complicit in evils should make amends for the harms to which they have contributed.

Our goal is to consider the moral responsibilities of persons who are culpably complicit in collectively perpetrated evils, focusing on a central act of reparative work, namely, apology. The unnecessary medical "normalization" of babies and children born with atypical sex anatomies provides an opportunity to examine an evil perpetrated by complicit agents.[1] After examining this evil on Card's terms, we conclude that doctors who engage in the practice of the unnecessary, nonconsensual "normalization" of persons born with intersex anatomies are culpably complicit. Card's analysis of culpable complicity directs us to identify an obligation to apologize in cases of culpable complicity in institutional evils. The account Card provides is helpful for making a demand for apology intelligible even in the face of objections that apology is not needed from those not obviously or singly blameworthy. We conclude that if, as she demonstrates, complicity in

---

[1] These unnecessary and nonconsensual "normalizing" interventions are not to be confused with interventions that adults with intersex conditions and people who are transgender may choose later in life, when they are able to provide fully informed consent.

an institutional evil may be culpable, then culpably complicit persons must apologize for the harm their complicity has supported.

Institutional Evils in Context: The Medical Management of Intersex Anatomies

Card defines evils as reasonably foreseeable intolerable harms, produced by inexcusable wrongs (2010, 16). In light of her interest in collectively perpetrated evils that may appear "ordinary" (Card 2010, xii), we ask whether unnecessary medical interventions on babies and young children with intersex conditions satisfy her definition of an institutional evil or evil practice. For nearly the past century, infants and young children born with atypical sex anatomies, that is, genitalia, chromosomes, hormones, and/or gonads that do not fit typical, binary notions of male or female, have been subjected to non-medically necessary normalizing interventions, including cosmetic genital surgeries, removal of healthy gonads, and sex reassignment (generally involving the long-term administration of hormones). Doctors have often misrepresented the urgency of such procedures and overemphasized the importance of physical "normality" for a child's development (Kessler 1990). Many also advised parents to conceal the nature of their children's conditions from them, which has led to emotional trauma (e.g., Coventry 1999; Hughes et al. 2006, 555).

Beginning in the mid-1990s, individuals subjected to normalizing interventions in early childhood or adolescence began to speak out about the harms they had suffered (see, e.g., Chase and Coventry 1997). Many came to understand that they had grown up uninformed or lied to, by doctors and parents, about the anatomies with which they were born. The narratives of persons subjected to normalizing interventions include painful accounts of confusing hospitalizations, appointments with specialists, and multiple operations; many describe ongoing trauma following repeated genital examinations, which sometimes included being photographed by medical teams. Persons have described the physical and emotional scars left by these practices, including painful or absent sexual response, depression, sterility, and difficulty forming relationships. Individuals also express great shame surrounding the sense that their bodies are or were inadequate, and anger that they were coerced into a standard of normality not in their best interest (Liao, Wood, and Creighton 2015; see, e.g., Amanda 2015; Blair 2015; Inter 2015; Garcia 2015).

Card's account of evil institutions and practices clarifies the nature of the wrong consisting of the unnecessary normalizing interventions performed on persons born with atypical sex anatomies, and the procedures' attendant harms. For Card, though evils may be perpetrated by individuals acting in relative isolation—she gives the example of domestic battery—evils often result, over time, from a collectively implemented policy or within an institution led by guiding norms (2010, 17–18, 27–28, 63–64). These evils may not be specifically intended; indeed, Card suspects that non-malevolent evils are commoner than malevolent ones (2010, 4, 24). Some evils take the form of what Iris Marion Young calls structural oppression, which is embedded within interconnected practices and norms rather than intentionally or tyrannically inflicted (Card 2010, 69). Such evils may have consequences that, although reasonably foreseeable, are neither anticipated nor intended by any specific individuals (Card 2010, 18, 65). Doctors engaged in the performance of unnecessary normalizing interventions for atypical sex anatomies act as members of medical institutions established to help and heal, and rely on a standard of care that they have been taught to trust. Evaluating the evil of unnecessary normalizing interventions therefore requires assessing, not just specific harms at the hands of individual doctors, but also the intolerable harm caused by the practice as a whole.

Card's understanding of evils centralizes the notion of intolerable harm, the severity and (often) irreversibility of which distinguishes evils from lesser wrongs (Card 2010, 5, 7). For Card, harm becomes intolerable when it "gravely, irreversibly, or irreparably jeopardizes access to basics that are ordinarily needed to make a life (or a death) tolerable or decent, from the point of view of the person whose life (or death) it is" (2010, 46). Card provides examples of such harm, including the elimination of "spheres in which one can exercise effective choice" and subjection to "severe and prolonged pain, humiliation, [and/or] debilitating fear" (2010, 46).

Narratives by patients powerfully attest to the intolerable harm that has resulted from the standard of care that was formalized in the 1950s (see, e.g., Chase and Coventry 1997; Jones et al. 2016). Konrad Blair recounts that soon after he was born, "the supervising physicians told my parents that plastic surgery was necessary to make me, an infant of questionable sex, 'look like a female'" (2015, 91). Blair's doctors performed a phalloectomy, which left him with significant scarring and lasting sexual difficulties (Blair 2015, 90–91). Blair recalls the stress of the unanswered questions that plagued him; no one ever explained why he had had the surgery he vaguely remembered as a toddler, or why, throughout his childhood, "medical residents still wanted to examine me, or why I had to be humiliated and ashamed, again and again" (2015, 90–91). It was not until Blair asked— repeatedly—for his complete medical records that he learned that he had been unnecessarily subjected to cosmetic surgery as a child, and discovered the reason that he had needed to take medicine for most of his life. The records revealed what the doctors and hospital had tried to conceal; finally Blair understood why, despite being "female," he had never felt at ease in his body or in the marriage to a man that, for his doctors, had marked his treatment a "success." The records told him that his life could have been otherwise (Blair 2015, 90–91).

The intensity of the stress and anger Blair describes is echoed in most of the other narratives that have been published since the late 1990s. Unlike Blair, Amanda had participated in the decision to have a vaginoplasty, the surgical construction of a vaginal opening. Looking back, however, it didn't seem like much of a choice:

> I chose this fake hole when I was a teenager because I didn't know there was another option. I was told from day one to be a female, to be heteronormative, to act like all the other girls, and the only way I could fully accomplish this is by looking the part. A fake hole would be necessary, I thought, to go along with the rest of the lies. Sometimes I think about how the doctors told me to lie about my surgeries and my scars. Sometimes I wonder what my parents would have told the world if I had died during [surgery]. Maybe they would have said "we were just trying to make her fuckable." (Amanda 2015, 98)

The compliance Amanda describes, tied to a sense of trust in physicians' and parents' good intentions, or just a reliance on "how things are," emerges in other narratives as well. Laura Inter did not have surgery as a child, though it was insistently recommended to her as a young adult. That she was able to refuse it may have been born of her unsettling experience of repeated exams throughout childhood:

> From the time I turned one, I was subjected to genital examinations twice a year, during which the endocrinologist would touch my genitals and look to see how they were developing. These unnecessary and intrusive examinations had a profound effect on me.... I found it confusing, and terribly uncomfortable, and I just felt it wasn't right.... I grew up with a feeling of being "inadequate," of having a sense that something was wrong with me, though I didn't know exactly what. These exams lasted until I was about 12 years old. Years later, as I began my adult, sexual life, I realized how much those displays had affected me emotionally. (Inter 2015, 95)

These narratives—remarkably consistent with those published more than a decade earlier, and echoed by narratives continuing to emerge in a variety of national contexts—speak to the severity of the harms perpetrated at the hands of a medical institution, through a practice meant to heal. The harm persons born with intersex conditions have suffered meets the definition of intolerability that Card lays out (2010, 46).

For Card, intolerability is one of the major characteristics that set evils apart from lesser wrongs. But to call unnecessary normalizing interventions an evil, we must also address the question of foreseeability. For the purpose of determining whether the harms entailed by unnecessary normalizing interventions satisfy the criterion of "reasonably foreseeable," we need not establish that intolerable harm was foreseeable to all perpetrators, at all times (Card 2010, 29). Card explains that when evil practices and institutions are implemented collectively, not all agents occupy the same epistemic position; some people may have more access or less access to knowledge that the practice in which they are engaged is causing harm (2010, 27–28). Therefore, she argues, "It may suffice to say that a morally indefensible rule or practice or institution is evil if *anyone* can reasonably foresee its intolerably harmful consequences.... Extending that idea over time, we could also make sense of saying that a practice was an evil even at times when no one *then* could foresee or appreciate the harm that it does, if others at later times can appreciate that it does intolerable harm for which there is no moral excuse" (Card 2010, 29). Card indicates that one can make judgments about the evil quality of an institution or practice after the fact, even if people acting at the time of the evil's inception cannot be held responsible for failing to recognize the evil in which they were partici-pating. This is not to say that individuals acting in the early years of such a practice are evil (as we will discuss later, in our discussion of culpable complicity); Card argues that establishing the evil status of an institution or practice is not the same as determining that complicit persons have been culpable evildoers (2010, 37). Nor is it to say that we cannot be mistaken, today, when we judge past practices to be evils. Rather, we do the best we can to evaluate evil practices that may have gone unnoticed or unseen in the past. For Card, therefore, showing that intolerable harm is foreseeable today in cases of unnecessary normalizing interventions is sufficient to say that the practice was always an evil (2010, 29).

Contemporary statements of recognition of the moral and medical vio-lations entailed by unnecessary interventions support the assessment that this practice constitutes an evil. The United Nations and the Council of Europe have acknowledged that "children's fundamental human rights to physical and psychological integrity and self-determination may be vio-lated" by these nonconsensual interventions (Council of Europe Com-missioner for Human Rights 2015; United Nations Human Rights Office of the High Commissioner 2015). A national ethics council in Switzer-land has also formally recognized the risk of harm and has insisted that surgery should be deferred until a patient can provide informed consent or refuse treatment (Swiss National Advisory Commission on Biomedical Ethics 2012). In 2016, the U.N. Committee Against Torture responded to calls from advocacy groups by demanding that the United States provide a report on how many children born with intersex conditions have been sub-jected to "sex assignment surgery" (United Nations Human Rights Office of the High Commissioner 2016). In February 2017, the European Parlia-ment released a statement in which it referred to the physical, psycholog-ical, sexual, and reproductive harms suffered by "intersex persons subject to genital mutilation" and called on member states to develop specific poli-cies to provide mental health support to such persons (European Parlia-ment 2017). Notably, these acknowledgments of harm have mostly come from groups outside the medical community. While the 2006 Consensus Statement by the U.S. and European pediatric endocrine societies provided some hope for change within medical practice (Hughes et al. 2006), anecdotal evidence from physicians (Feder 2014, 133–52) and the increasing numbers of critical statements by U.N. committees suggest that little has changed. Nonetheless, these statements, together with the patient narratives now widely available, make the harms of unnecessary normalizing interventions foreseeable on Card's account of evils. The remaining factor left to evaluate is that of inexcusability.

Card argues that evils, unlike lesser wrongs, are utterly without excuse. She details two types of possible excuses. The first is the metaphysical excuse, which alleviates culpability because an actor was in a state of justified (that is, not culpable) ignorance or was compelled by some external force (Card 2010, 16). While a metaphysical excuse could be claimed by an agent acting in genuine ignorance or unquestionably compelled to commit a wrong, it does not appear that Card's notion of metaphysical excuses could mitigate the evil quality of a practice or an institution that has caused intolerable harm. An evil institution or practice cannot be understood to act out of ignorance or compulsion; it can therefore claim no metaphysical excuse.

The second type of excuse that Card details, what she calls a "moral excuse," demands more careful consideration. A moral excuse, justifying wrongful action, mitigates blameworthiness without denying that a wrong has been committed, and without denying that someone or some group was responsible for it. Card gives the example of a midwife, stopped for speeding, who explains to an officer that she violated the law because she is on her way to deliver a baby (2010, 21). Moral excuses, then, mitigate culpability, but only if they are good excuses, ones that hold moral weight. "It is not sufficient," Card writes, "that the agent thinks there is a good reason. There must be one (and it must be the agent's reason), a reason defensible on reflection and in terms of moral values" (2010, 17). Inexcusable wrongs, by contrast, are those in which culpability is not diminished by any good reason (Card 2010, 17, 23). Though perpetrators may claim to have some good reason for their actions, we may determine upon reflection that this reason does not carry sufficient moral weight to justify the practice.

The evidence—and the striking absence of medical or ethical argument to the contrary—suggests that there is no moral excuse for the practice of unnecessary normalizing interventions (individual doctors' claimed excuses will be addressed later, in our discussion of culpable complicity). Despite the fact that these procedures have been performed for several decades, the idea that normalizing interventions will allow children born with intersex conditions to lead "better" lives remains, as many have indicated, unsubstantiated (e.g., Liao, Wood, and Creighton 2015). Patients' narratives support the idea that the risk of harm is too great to justify such interventions.

Normalizing surgeries and associated interventions have caused reasonably foreseeable intolerable harm, and the excuses given for it are insufficient; they do not justify the practice, morally, in light of the evidence. On Card's account, the standard of care that promotes the use of unnecessary normalizing interventions counts as an evil, one that some have begun to call intersex genital mutilation (IGM) (see, e.g., Swiss National Advisory Commission on Biomedical Ethics 2012; European Parliament 2017). Card's analysis of complicity provides essential tools for considering the responsibility of individuals engaged in evil practices that have been promoted within institutional contexts, such as unnecessary normalizing interventions.

Complicity in Evil Practices and Institutions

To help make sense of the dispersed responsibility in collectively perpetrated evils, Card discusses complicity, the study of which is a critical component of her account of evils. Persons can be complicit in an evil by association with it, because they benefit from it, or because they are participants in or contributors to it (Card 2010, 63–66, 78, 83). When considering whether an individual is complicit in an institutional evil, we may ask whether the person's choices causally contributed to harm, and whether the harm could have been prevented if some individuals within the institution had chosen differently (Card 2010, 65). We should investigate whether the individual *knew* that his or her choices were contributing to harm (Card 2010, 65). Finally, we can ask whether the person was or was not obligated to choose differently; this obligation would arise based on some special role within the institution, which could leave an individual with an additional responsibility to prevent harm (Card 2010, 65). Though not dispositive, these factors can help establish whether a person has been complicit in a collectively perpetrated evil.

Card explains that the nature of institutions is such that they may foster conditions under which culpable complicity in evil is more likely. The commission of evils may become routinized within an institution and be made to seem unremarkable. Individuals may follow procedural rules without questioning the mission toward which they work; worse, taking "the status quo to be natural, normal," such individuals may defend questionable practices "against attack" (Card 2010, 70). Following Arendt, Card observes that in a bureaucratic institution—which may compartmentalize tasks, diffuse responsibility, encourage anonymity, and elevate loyalty and efficiency—it is easier to ignore the evil in which one is engaged (2010, 70). Card writes, "We often act (or fail to act) from weakness or inertia. We may go along uncritically with practices we suspect are questionable, giving others the benefit of our doubts" (2010, 63). Though the individual actions of such persons may not, themselves, be evils, they may, taken cumulatively, amount to an evil (Card 2010, 7, 65). Complicit agents may therefore be blameworthy for the intolerable harms that they ignore or facilitate (Card 2010, 64).

When harm has resulted from the deeds of one person, that person's culpability is often relatively clear. But when persons are complicit in an evil perpetrated by many agents, it can be much more difficult to determine whether an individual is culpable. Card explains: "A major difference between the evils done by individuals … and institutional evils is the role of culpability. An individual whose deed is metaphysically and morally inexcusable is culpable. But the indefensibility of a norm does not settle the question of whether a responsible agent who applies or benefits from that norm is culpable. Individual culpability depends on such things as what options and what knowledge an individual has and the costs, including moral costs, attached to those options" (2010, 18). Card recognizes that a variety of roles may be played by agents involved in collectively perpetrated evils, each of which may allow for distinctive possibilities for knowledge and action (2010, 27–28, 63–64). Such differences will affect assessments of individuals' culpability. Many people involved in institutional evils contributed to harm, not because they made a conscious decision to do so, but because they failed to critically examine their reasons for acting, or how their actions made them participants in an evil (Card 2010, 22–23). Indeed, Card explains, there are likely to be institutional evils for which no one is culpable, or few people are (2010, 64–66). Trying to describe all individuals as "wrongdoers" fails to capture the different degrees of responsibility at work in a collectively perpetrated evil.

Culpable Complicity and Unnecessary Normalizing Interventions for Intersex

Doctors who recommend and perform unnecessary medical interventions are complicit in an evil practice; many of them have inflicted intolerable harm, and all have contributed to sustaining a standard of care we have shown is an evil. But as Card shows us, noting the complicity of doctors does not fully explain the nature of their moral responsibility for engaging in an institutional evil. It remains to be seen how we should view these doctors as moral actors, whom we would normally wish to hold accountable for evils to which they have contributed. To evaluate whether doctors' complicity in this practice is culpable, we must consider whether the intolerable harms they inflicted were foreseeable, and whether doctors have a good moral excuse for their actions, which might mitigate their blameworthiness (Card 2010, 64).

While Card directs us to call a practice like unnecessary normalizing interventions an evil even if intolerable harm was not foreseeable at its inception (2010, 29), we should consider whether this lack of foreseeability mitigates individual doctors' culpability during the early years in which practices for normalizing atypical sex conditions were developed. Historian Alice Dreger discusses the emergence of this standard of care. She explains that in the nineteenth and twentieth centuries, rising access to gynecological and medical care led to a surge in the medical identification and treatment of people with intersex conditions. Increased knowledge about persons with intersex conditions, Dreger writes, posed "powerful challenges to biomedical claims about the natural, inviolable distinctions between men and women" (2000, 28). As a response to this challenge, physician William Blair Bell recommended in 1915 that surgery be used to make persons born with intersex conditions conform to their "true" sex, to be determined and constructed by doctors. Dreger comments, "Only two true sexes would still exist, with a limit of one to each body, and the medical man would still be the interpreter…[and] the amplifier [of] true sex. This— the assignment to and the surgical construction of a single, believable sex for each ambiguous body—was the way of the future.… Medicine had won out over the threat of the hermaphrodite" (2000, 166). In the midtwentieth century, doctors and medical institutions began to promote the idea that surgical and hormonal normalization was necessary for patients' well-being, a concept that integrates assumptions and concerns regarding parental love, sexual performance, social acceptance, and the subjugation of deviance (Dreger 2000, 181–84).

The history Dreger offers complicates the question of whether individual, complicit doctors could have foreseen intolerable harm in the early years during which physicians engaged in efforts to "correct" bodies displaying "confused sex" (2000, 185). When assessing foreseeability, we should ask: To what degree did doctors recognize the risk of harm to their patients? What evidence or information was available to help them understand that risk? To what extent did physicians distinguish the use of medical practice to relieve individual versus social ills? Certainly, doctors' judgments would have been colored by social anxieties about persons with atypical bodies, and a suspicion of sexual deviance (Dreger 2000, 27–28). If such concerns led doctors to believe that their patients' well-being depended on normalization, these doctors may not have been able to anticipate the intolerable harm likely to occur as a result of their attempts to prevent harms they arguably believed would result from atypical sex anatomies.[2] Furthermore, in this period, no persons who had undergone normalizing interventions as babies would yet have come forward with complaints about their medical treatment. If they had, we can fairly judge the doctors

---

[2] We do not address here the question of whether the treatment is in fact for the benefit of the individual patient (as medical treatment is typically understood) or is motivated by other factors, such as relief of parental anxiety or even as a response to disgust, experienced by or projected onto parents or society as a whole (see Feder 2014, 75). The application of the tools Card offers would serve to enhance an exploration of this dimension of the moral problem in question.

they confronted as culpable for acting in a way they could have foreseen was harmful. But if doctors' assumptions were not challenged by harmed patients or their advocates, it is not clear that intolerable harm was foreseeable by all, or even most, doctors engaged in early normalizing interventions. Their ignorance of the potential for harm might mitigate some of these doctors' culpability.

There is reason to think, however, that many doctors might still be culpable for their engagement in normalizing interventions even in the mid-twentieth century, when treatment protocols were being formalized. Dreger explains the widespread failures to study the risks of unnecessary normalizing interventions, going back to their earliest use (2000, 192–94). On Card's account, doctors and medical institutions at this time might very well be culpable for failing to inquire about the potential for intolerable harm (Card 2010, 23). Today, the abundance of evidence means that one may reasonably censure physicians' failures to pursue robust follow-ups of their patients (see, e.g., Liao, Wood, and Creighton 2015). Medical professionals who continue to support the unnecessary normalization of people born with intersex conditions may be judged as we judge parents who smoke around their small children; in the 1940s, they would not have been expected to know the dangers of second-hand smoke. Today, there is no such excuse.

Tracing the history behind normalizing interventions on persons with atypical sex anatomies is helpful for assessing the question of foreseeability. It also allows for a better investigation into whether the doctors concerned have moral or metaphysical excuses, which would also mitigate their culpability on Card's account. One might argue that powerful social norms regarding sex and gender count as metaphysical excuses for doctors' treatment of persons with intersex conditions; doctors might claim ignorance of wrongdoing, resulting from their reliance on the soundness of prevailing standards. Resources for evaluating such claims might be found in the growing literature on structural oppression and epistemic injustice, which has addressed the ways in which social norms and practices may affect the implicit attitudes of individuals, and their moral responsibility for harm (see Young 1990, Fricker 2007, Medina 2013). The practice of unnecessary normalizing interventions is embedded in complex social norms that link notions of healthy human beings with two categories of sex: male and female. Such assumptions are not themselves evils but may be more accurately described as "blind spots" in what José Medina has called "social scripts" (2013, 68). In the context of such norms, we might understand why doctors find it difficult to imagine allowing a child with an intersex condition to grow up without medical intervention.

Card shows us, however, that even people with "blind spots" may be judged as culpable for the infliction of intolerable harm (2010, 64). She also clarifies that in cases of institutional evil there may come a time when a metaphysical excuse no longer applies (Card 2010, 19). When engaging in procedures that are medically unnecessary or non-medically urgent, as are normalizing interventions, doctors and medical institutions have a responsibility to identify evidence of harm and to interrogate their reasons for acting in light of the risks. This is true even when a normalizing practice of this sort aligns with the (structurally oppressive) norm that to be a healthy human being one must have a body that conforms to specific social standards. Particularly today, but in the past as well, unhesitating reliance on assumptions and "social scripts" is not a metaphysically valid excuse for doctors' culpable complicity in the evil practice of the unnecessary normalization of persons with intersex conditions. Doctors who perform these interventions demonstrate what Medina calls "intellectual laziness" and "epistemic arrogance," leading them unquestioningly to abide by norms without critical inquiry (2013, 68–69, 146). Card clarifies the moral violation that such laziness and arrogance entails: "When it is clear that others may be threatened with serious harm, failing to think is no excuse if we are in good health, free from other pressing demands on our attention, and have the time and opportunity" (2010, 23).

In addition to having no good metaphysical excuse for promoting and performing unnecessary interventions on persons with atypical sex anatomies today, doctors also have no good moral excuse. Though doctors who recommend unnecessary interventions may insist that the "normalcy" promised by these interventions will make a child's life easier (Parens 2006, xiv; Preves 2003, 62–63), Card's view of evils reveals the flaw inherent in the claim that a person who "means well" is excused from moral responsibility. Card explains, "'No moral excuse' does not mean 'no humanly understandable reasons'" (2010, 16). When great harm is at stake, doctors must question the urge to put social acceptance over the rights of patients to informed consent and to have their healthy bodies left intact. We can understand doctors' actions without treating "good intent" as exculpatory. These doctors have been culpably complicit in an evil practice; we may therefore inquire about their responsibilities to recognize and repair the intolerable harms for which they are culpable.

Responding to Culpable Complicity

Rarely does Card explicitly discuss responses to the culpable complicity of individuals in collectively perpetrated evils. She does, however, repeatedly indicate the importance of doing so. Card dedicates chapter 9 of *The Atrocity Paradigm* to a study of the moral emotions relevant to responding to evils, asking, "How is it possible to repair the harms of such evils?" (2002, 200). She offers a limited discussion of a variety of emotional responses to the perpetration of harm—guilt, remorse, regret, and repentance—that may motivate "confessions, apologies, restitution, and reparations" and "constructive steps toward rebuilding relationships or correcting social injustices" (Card 2002, 207–8).

In *Confronting Evils* (2010), Card explains that she initially intended to follow *The Atrocity Paradigm* of 2002 with a book on responses to evils, including apology and reparative efforts (2010, 9). Though she never wrote that book, she maintained an interest in asking which responses to evils are honorable (Card 2010, 4, 8). Her interest in distinguishing evils from lesser wrongs was at least partly driven by her concern with the need to respond to contemporary evils with greater alacrity. Card writes: "Why distinguish evils from lesser wrongs? One reason is to help set priorities when resources are limited for preventing wrongs and repairing harms.... Lesser wrongs can be easier to repair. But evils are urgent. Life and basic quality of life are at stake.... The harm of evils is intolerable, often irreversible, frequently uncontainable. Progress in containing, terminating, preventing, and repairing what can be repaired is apt to be incremental. But even slow progress can save lives" (2010, 7). Card's study of complicity therefore directs us to inquire about the moral responsibilities of persons culpably complicit for their contributions to an evil practice.[3] In what follows we consider the act of apology, which appears to hold special promise for the repair of harms effected by unnecessary normalizing interventions.

The Reparative Work of Apology

Apology and reconciliation after wrongdoing have recently become topics of psychological and philosophical interest (see Kort 1975; Gill 2000; Walker 2006; Smith 2008). In *On Apology* (2004) psychiatrist Aaron Lazare provides a detailed account of what good apology entails, that is, apology that holds the potential to effect repair, as opposed to obscure what has happened or excuse the perpetrator.[4] Apology requires that wrongdoers admit that they did wrong and accept responsibility for the harms caused by their wrongdoing (Lazare 2004, 75). A good apology consists of a wrongdoer's acknowledgment of the offense, a description of the wrong (displaying the wrongdoer's understanding of its nature), identification of the wronged party or parties, recognition of the harm and its impact, and confirmation that "the grievance was a violation of a...moral contract between the parties" (Lazare 2004, 75). Though circumstances may change

---

[3] Card also indicates a need to assess appropriate responses from the non-culpably complicit. Following Young, she writes, "Even non-culpable complicity can give rise to an appropriate sense of responsibility to participate in efforts at repair" (Card 2010, 78). Such efforts would not necessarily centralize apology but would involve forward-looking efforts to change harmful habits and attitudes (Young 1990, 151).

[4] For an apology to be good, it need not succeed in providing repair to victims, nor must the apologizer be forgiven. "Good" refers to the formulation of the apology, which must include certain elements (though not always explicitly), as detailed by Lazare (2004) and Walker (2006). These elements, Lazare and Walker attest, are most likely to provide repair to those affected by wrongdoing.

the sequence and form of these steps, and not every step need always be explicit (though often most should be), these are the building blocks of a good apology.

Apology, and, when appropriate, other reparative acts like long-term emotional or financial support, may provide restitution to victims, wrong-doers, and communities affected by harm. Margaret Urban Walker argues that victims are entitled to know that others grasp the fact of the wrong done to them, the perpetrator's culpability, and the reality of the harm the victims suffered; an offender's apology can provide all of this, and more (2006, 19). In its avowal of the wrongdoer's culpability, apology clarifies that the harm was not the victim's fault. The apology importantly assures victims that they are safe from further harm, and may restore their ability to trust others not to harm them (Lazare 2004, 59–61; Walker 2006, 93–94).

Good apology also acknowledges a victim's worth, dignity, and person-hood, which, Walker explains, were denied, even subtly, in the commission of harm (2006, 92). She insists that in the absence of efforts to repair harms to victims, "we may be outraged, or crushed by the sense that no one cares and we do not matter"; by apologizing, wrongdoers confirm that victims do matter (Walker 2006, 92–95). This is part of the wrongdoer's duty to fulfill what she calls "burdens of accountability," which arise due to shared expectations that others will comply with the moral standards to which we are also bound (Walker 2006, 67). Apology is an essential part of repairing our moral relationships when we fail to be accountable to others and we engage in wrongdoing.

Ethicist Lee Taft argues that the ideal outcome of good apology is to provide healing for *both* victims and wrongdoers (2005, 71). Offering an apology often requires moral courage, because it requires that one iden-tify oneself as a wrongdoer; therefore, engaging in apology is a virtuous act that, by aiming at repairing harms one has inflicted, has the capacity to restore the conceptions of wrongdoers of themselves as morally decent beings (Taft 2005, 71). Walker adds that apology may also allow individ-uals or groups who have participated in wrongdoing (like members of an evil institution) to be reconciled with the community that suffered or iden-tified harm. She proposes that apology allows wrongdoers or offending groups to affirm the moral standards of the community, acknowledging that what was done violated those standards (Walker 2006, 89, 200–201). Ideally, acceptance by wrongdoers of responsibility for violating the com-munity's standards may allow them to be trusted, once more, by that com-munity (Walker 2006, 96, 200–201). Good apology therefore holds promise for providing repair to all parties negatively affected by wrongdoing.

The Culpably Complicit Person's Apology

Academic discussions of apology generally centralize a singly blamewor-thy wrongdoer, one whose relation to harm is obvious (e.g., Kort 1975;

Lazare 2004; Walker 2006; Smith 2008). Where culpable complicity accurately describes an individual's involvement in an evil, there is less guidance on the ethical standards governing apology and participation in moral repair. Card, however, provides resources for thinking about the ways that complicity can be culpable and thus require apology. In the face of intolerable harm, the need to apologize is not diminished by an agent's "good intentions"; an individual's duty to engage in reparative work is not attenuated by the fact that others were also engaged in the evil (Card 2010, 78). Nor does the absence of legal liability obviate responsibility for repairing harms caused by one's complicit engagement in an evil practice. With respect to unnecessary normalizing interventions, apology from culpably complicit doctors would be a significant first step in the reparative work necessitated by decades of intolerable harm. By evaluating, through Card's lens, what apology can do when given by doctors culpably complicit in these practices, we hope to illuminate why apology is morally required of individuals culpably complicit in an institutional evil or evil practice.

The account by Konrad Blair of seeking, and ultimately receiving, an apology for his medical treatment reflects the importance of the repair that apology can provide to persons who have undergone unnecessary normalizing interventions. In his narrative, Blair explains that he reached out to his doctors, asking them to acknowledge that "what was done in the past was not the right thing to do, and [to] promise that things would be different for children like me in the future" (2015, 92). Blair subsequently received the first apology ever issued by a leading medical institution for the medical treatment of a child with an intersex condition. The doctors recognized that their methods were harmful; they acknowledged that there are other, better methods and expressed a commitment to share this knowledge with other doctors (Blair 2015, 92). Blair explains just how much the letter from the doctors meant: "Their response represented hope, hope for me and for future patients, hope that one day the medical procedures to which I was subjected would become a thing of the past. I felt that finally, a child's voice mattered, that what I had experienced mattered.... The apology restored my dignity, and allowed me to accept myself as the man I was supposed to become. It opened a door for me to speak out and be an activist so that others can be spared what was done to me" (2015, 92).[5] Blair expresses the healing he derived from the acknowledgment by his doctors of their wrong and the harm done to him. But in addition to showing the healing that apology can give to victims, the apology given to Blair showcases the particular power of an apology from a person culpably complicit in an

---

[5] Blair recently shared with one of the editors of the journal issue in which his essay appeared that he no longer felt positively about the apology he received. The apology changed his life, but it did not guarantee that others would be spared the treatment he had experienced. Blair argued that if the apology had been heartfelt, his physicians would no longer allow what had happened to him to happen to other children under their care (Blair, personal communication 2016).

institutional evil. By apologizing, these doctors chipped away at the authority of the standard of care that promotes unnecessary normalizing interventions, and they submitted the evil institution of which they were a part to the judgment of the community (Walker 2006, 200). The apology given to Blair was a way of taking responsibility, but it was also a way of requesting, as Walker insists is important in cases of institutional wrongs, that the truth about a particular wrong be established "for the record" (2006, 10). Whereas doctors might be expected to defend their application of the standard of care, their apology demonstrates the medical institution's vulnerability to fault. It shows that complicit persons could become aware of the wrongfulness of these practices, despite the features of the institution that make such recognition less likely (Walker 2006, 200; Card 2010, 63, 70).

Apology can, therefore, promote broader ethical reformation. This was what Blair sought when he requested that his doctors express a shared commitment to ensuring that "things would be different" in the future (2015, 92). The type of apology given to Blair upsets the narrative that medical practices are unimpeachable or should be unquestioningly trusted; it marks the kind of thinking that could have prevented these harms in the first place. The understanding conveyed by such an apology could be translated into the production of improved practices, habits, and standards of ethics (Walker 2006, 10; Card 2002, 178). Such an apology can provide needed hope that what Walker calls "morally habitable conditions" can be restored (2006, 209). Ultimately, apology may stimulate changes to widely held attitudes, and even to the rules governing social and political institutions.

Confronting Resistance to Asking for Apology from Culpably Complicit Persons

We suspect that there will be some resistance to the idea that persons who are complicit in an institutional evil have a responsibility to apologize. Much of this resistance may have its origin in a misunderstanding of the nature of culpable complicity; persons may claim that when an institution incurs blame for evil, individuals complicit in that institution should not be blamed and do not need to apologize. Failure to understand the nature of culpable complicity can lead persons not to apologize, or to apologize badly.

In the case of the institutional, sanctioned practices associated with unnecessary normalizing interventions, the medical providers who enact these practices are individuals whose intimate relationship with their patients can make them look singly culpable. It may be most intuitive for victims in this case to look at a particular doctor or particular doctors who performed a harmful procedure and identify them as "sole perpetrators." Failing to recognize a collectively perpetrated evil may lead to a failed process of repair because victims, wrongdoers, and scholars will not fully identify what the apology needs to do. Doctors who are culpably complicit in these practices may resist any interaction that requires them to admit fault on their part. Such doctors may decline to apologize on the grounds that they did not deliberately or maliciously cause harm.

This was the case in an interaction between intersex activist Sean Saifa Wall and his former doctor Terry Hensle, who had overseen Wall's gonadectomy as a young adolescent. When Wall approached Hensle to seek acknowledgment of the harm done to him, Hensle recoiled at the suggestion that he ought to feel remorse (see Pou 2015). Even as Hensle recognized that Wall experienced harm, and that Hensle "absolutely" would proceed with Wall's care differently now that he has a better understanding of the physical and emotional risks of unnecessary gonadectomy, Hensle insisted that he had no reason to regret his actions, because he had not acted out of malice (see Pou 2015). Hensle seemed to think that Wall's treatment would be wrong now but could not be judged wrong in the past, because it had been undertaken in good faith.

The resistance by Hensle to provide an apology is born of an idea that his good intentions excuse him from making amends for past harms. His claim that he intended to heal but now understands that he caused harm indicates his awareness of the factors that make him culpably complicit on Card's account. Hensle resists, not the idea that the practices in which he engaged caused harm, but the idea that this makes him blameworthy. He appears to identify Wall's confrontation as an indication that he is being called singly culpable, and seeing correctly that he is not solely responsible, he expresses neither remorse nor repentance. This resistance to identify a need to engage in reparative efforts consists of a failure on the part of the doctor to understand that he was culpably complicit in a larger institutional evil.

We suspect that in cases like this such misunderstandings are common. Because the community of specialists who treat intersex infants and children is relatively small, and the harms so great, culpable complicity in the treatment of intersex may be particularly difficult to recognize. If doctors do not understand that they may be culpably complicit in an evil practice, they are more likely to think that a call for apology is a call for them to admit intentional evildoing on their part, something they are very likely to resist. Card's analysis provides resources for working through the resistance to apology based on conceptions of collectively perpetrated evils that exempt individuals from apology because they are not singly culpable. Understanding complicity as Card does may open possibilities for doctors to identify their culpability for participation in an evil, and to apologize for their roles in that evil, without shattering their conceptions of themselves as healers.

One might argue that apology is not required of *individual* doctors, because these harms were "really" caused by a whole institution, of which individual doctors were only a small part. This claim is similar to the view that "following the rules" is an excuse for unethical conduct. But Card helps us appreciate the dangerous misconception that culpably complicit doctors are excused from responsibility because their actions aligned with the standard of care in which they were trained. Evil practices and institutions do not act on their own but are implemented and sustained by those complicit in them (Card 2010, 63). To be complicit is not to be coincidentally tied to an evil institution, which perpetrates harm as a response to orders by an evil leader. Rather, institutional evils often occur *because* of the special dynamics of the institution, which may be structured in such a way that unquestioning adherence to the rules of the institution is encouraged.

Thus, to say that we ought only to request apology from the "monsters" of the institution, or to blame the "rules," is to miss the point entirely. Implicit or explicit support by doctors of the standard of care constitutes their connection to the institutional evil of unnecessary normalizing interventions. Though we should not condemn every doctor who applied the harmful standard of care, we can assign varying degrees of responsibility to those doctors who failed to question it; indeed, the increasing evidence of harms suggests that the failure to attend to the evidence constitutes culpable complicity. Integrating Card's analysis of complicity into a discussion of apology highlights the problems with the idea that complicit individuals are innocent and a "whole institution" is *actually* to blame. Card shows that to be culpably complicit is to be blameworthy for one's role in a collectively perpetrated evil; thus, to be culpably complicit is to have a duty to apologize.

Why is assessing the resistance to a call for apology so important? Failures to understand the nature of individuals' culpable complicity can lead to no apology at all, or the offering of bad apologies, which neglect the features of apology we've learned are needed (Lazare 2004, 75).[6] Stories of bad apologies in the case of unnecessary normalizing interventions often involve a statement by a doctor that he or she is "sorry" for the pain felt by the sufferer, which may indicate the doctor's sympathy or empathy, rather than an acceptance of responsibility (Lazare 2004, 25). A doctor might also apologize to the wrong person, ignoring the victim of harm, or perhaps apologize in a way that seeks to minimize the degree of his or her responsibility. We find this in the case of Kimberly Zieselman, who, after sending a written request for an apology from her doctors, received an e-mail message stating that too much time had passed to take action, acknowledging only what was referred to as her "unsatisfactory experience." When

---

[6] There is a risk that this very essay (and other applications of Card's theory of collectively perpetrated evils) may result in opposition to calls for apology because readers reject, misunderstand, or take offense at Card's conceptions of evil and complicity in evil practices. We are concerned with these risks, but have tried to show the value of Card's approach despite them.

she responded with an offer to sign a waiver of legal liability in exchange for more dialogue, the hospital—where she had not only been treated as an adolescent but was also being provided care as an adult at the time of her request—told Zieselman to seek medical help elsewhere (Zieselman 2015, 125).

Bad apologies exacerbate and increase victims' pain, rather than heal it (Walker 2006, 205). Victims may experience lasting anger, hurt, and mistrust against those doctors who continue to deny or justify the wrong (Walker 2006, 205). Furthermore, the failure to engage in reparative efforts that genuinely recognize the harms effected implicitly validates the standard of care that promoted harm in the first place. This failure is a type of what Walker calls "normative abandonment": it tells the victim that "no one cares" and that he or she "does not matter" (2006, 95). On Walker's account of failed apology, the unsympathetic e-mail that Zieselman received was not only a morally unacceptable extension of the first wrong against her; it constitutes a new wrong (Walker 2006, 205). The great risk of harm resulting from bad apology (or no apology) leads Walker to argue that even if there is no guarantee that an apology will succeed, a wrongdoer must try (2006, 209). Good apology, as a means of providing moral repair, is required of persons culpably complicit in the practice of the unnecessary normalization of people born with intersex conditions.

Conclusion

The harms caused by the evil of unnecessary normalizing interventions have resulted from the culpable complicity of many medical providers over many years. Doctors have ignored the evidence of risk, failed to question the standard of care, and neglected to address the wrongs and harms of which they should have become aware. The actions and inactions of these doctors do not make them blameworthy in the classic sense; they did not maliciously cause harm, nor did they act alone. Physicians working today have engaged in these practices in accordance with a standard of care upon which they were taught to rely. But as Card's discussion of complicity powerfully demonstrates, doctors' complicity in the evil of normalizing interventions is culpable.

Card helps us see that to be culpably complicit is not to be a monster, it is not to be fully culpable, and it is not to be solely blameworthy for evildoing. She moves us to recognize, however, that to be culpably complicit is, unequivocally, to be morally blameworthy. Neither good intentions nor past ignorance excuse culpable persons from duties to engage in repair. Card's work clarifies why demands for apology that fail to elucidate the nature of the culpably complicit person's blameworthiness are likely to be met with opposition; doctors will not react well to accusations of "guilt."

To demand and engage in reparative work for complicity in collectively perpetrated evils requires understanding the nuances of complicity, and culpable complicity, that Card helps us assess.

By inquiring about culpably complicit persons' duty to apologize, we respond to Card's insistence that we have a responsibility "to be alert to the evils of our own time and appreciate the dangers of complicity in them" (Card 2010, 24), and her call for "habits of reflection" on those things we do together (Card 2010, 64). Though acting together does mean that harm will often occur, offering apology for one's complicity in complex cases of institutional evil—those very cases to which Card devoted herself—is a powerful means of repairing intolerable harms that might otherwise go unaddressed. In apologies for the normalizing interventions to which persons born with intersex conditions have been subjected, we find a promise of restoration for individuals and groups harmed by an institutional wrong. Such apologies provide a basis for building moral communities in which persons may come together to repair the damage wrought by harms perpetrated by many, a task that makes use of the best tools with which Card left us.

Acknowledgments

The Resolve project by InterACT: Advocates for Youth first inspired this project. We thank Kimberly Zieselman, Amy Oliver, Andrea Tschemplik, and Alice Dreger for their helpful suggestions. We are especially grateful for the careful readings and criticism of Robin Dillon and Armen Marsoobian.

References

Amanda. 2015. "The Truth in Writing." *Narrative Inquiry in Bioethics* 5, no. 2:98–100.

Arendt, Hannah. 2006 [1963]. *Eichmann in Jerusalem: A Report on the Banality of Evil.* New York: Penguin Books.

Blair, Konrad. 2015. "When Doctors Get It Wrong." *Narrative Inquiry in Bioethics* 5, no. 2:89–92.

Card, Claudia. 2002. *The Atrocity Paradigm: A Theory of Evil.* New York: Oxford University Press.

———. 2010. *Confronting Evils: Terrorism, Torture, Genocide.* New York: Cambridge University Press.

Chase, Cheryl, and Martha Coventry (eds.). 1997. "Intersex Awakening." Special issue of *Chrysalis: The Journal of Transgressive Identities* 2, no. 5.

Council of Europe Commissioner for Human Rights. 2015. "Human Rights and Intersex People." Last accessed December 18, 2016, at https://wcd.coe.int/ViewDoc.jsp?p=&Ref=CommDH/IssuePaper(2015) 1&Language=lanEnglish&Ver=original&Site=COE&BackColor

Internet=DBDCF2&BackColorIntranet=FDC864&BackColorLogged =FDC864&direct=true.

Coventry, Martha. 1999. "Finding the Words." In *Intersex in the Age of Ethics*, edited by Alice Dreger, 71–78. Frederick, Md.: University Publishing Group.

Creighton, Sarah M., Lina Michala, Imran Mushtaq, and Michal Yaron. 2014. "Childhood Surgery for Ambiguous Genitalia: Glimpses of Practice Changes or More of the Same?" *Psychology and Sexuality* 5, no. 1:34–43.

Dreger, Alice. 2000 [1998]. *Hermaphrodites and the Medical Invention of Sex*. Cambridge, Mass.: Harvard University Press.

European Parliament. 2017. "European Parliament Resolution of 14 February 2017 on Promoting Gender Equality in Mental Health and Clinical Research." P8_TA-PROV(2017)0028. Last accessed March 13, 2017, at http://www.europarl.europa.eu/sides/getDoc.do?pubRef-//EP// TEXT+TA+P8-TA-2017-0028 + 0+DOC+XML+V0//EN.

Feder, Ellen K. 2014. *Making Sense of Intersex: Changing Ethical Perspectives in Biomedicine*. Bloomington: Indiana University Press.

Fricker, Miranda. 2007. *Epistemic Injustice: Power and the Ethics of Knowing*. New York: Oxford University Press.

Garcia, Diana. 2015. "The Secret Inside Me." *Narrative Inquiry in Bioethics* 5, no. 2:92–95.

Gill, Kathleen. 2000. "The Moral Functions of an Apology." *Philosophical Forum* 31, no. 1: 11–27.

Hughes, I. A., C. Houk, S. F. Ahmed, and P. A. Lee. 2006. "Consensus Statement on Management of Intersex Conditions." *Archives of Disease in Childhood* 91, no. 7:554–63.

Inter, Laura. 2015. "Finding My Compass." *Narrative Inquiry in Bioethics* 5, no. 2:95–98.

Jones, Tiffany, Bonnie Hart, Morgan Carpenter, Gavi Ansara, William Leonard, and Jayne Lucke. 2016. *Intersex: Stories and Statistics from Australia*. Cambridge: Open Book.

Kessler, Suzanne J. 1990. "The Medical Construction of Gender: Case Management of Intersexed Infants." *Signs* 16, no. 1:3–26.

Kort, Louis F. 1975. "What Is an Apology?" *Philosophy Research Archives* 1:80–87.

Lazare, Aaron. 2004. *On Apology*. New York: Oxford University Press.

Liao, Lih-Mei, Dan Wood, and Sarah M. Creighton. 2015. "Parental Choice on Normalising Cosmetic Genital Surgery." *British Medical Journal* 351.

Medina, José. 2013. *The Epistemology of Resistance: Gender and Racial Oppression, Epistemic Injustice, and Resistant Imaginations*. New York: Oxford University Press.

Parens, Erik. 2006. "Introduction: Thinking About Surgically Shaping Children." In *Surgically Shaping Children: Technology, Ethics, and the*

Pursuit of Normality, edited by Erik Parens, xiii–xxx. Baltimore: Johns Hopkins University Press.

Preves, Sharon E. 2003. *Intersex and Identity: The Contested Self*. New Brunswick, N.J.: Rutgers University Press.

Smith, Nick. 2008. *I Was Wrong: The Meaning of Apologies*. New York: Cambridge University Press.

Swiss National Advisory Commission on Biomedical Ethics. 2012. "On the Management of Differences of Sex Development: Ethical Issues Relating to 'Intersexuality.'" Opinion No. 20/2012. Last accessed December 20, 2016, at http://www.nek-cne.ch/fileadmin/nek-cne-dateien/Themen/Stellungnahmen/en/NEK_Intersexualitaet_En.pdf.

Pou, Jackie. 2015. "The World of Intersex Children and One Person's Journey Between Two Sexes." *ABC News*. Last accessed December 20, 2016, at http://abcnews.go.com/Health/world-intersex-children-persons-journey-sexes/story?id=28667285.

Taft, Lee. 2005. "Apology and Medical Mistake: Opportunity or Foil?" *Annals of Health Law* 14:55–94.

United Nations Human Rights Office of the High Commissioner. 2015. "Fact Sheet: Intersex." Last accessed December 18, 2016, at https://unfe.org/system/unfe-65-Intersex_Factsheet_ENGLISH.pdf.

———. 2016. "List of Issues Prior to Submission of the Sixth Periodic Report of the United States Of America." Last accessed December 24, 2016, at http://tbinternet.ohchr.org/_layouts/treatybodyexternal/Download.aspx?symbolno=CAT%2fC%2fUSA%2fQPR%2f6&Lang=en.

Walker, Margaret Urban. 2006. *Moral Repair: Reconstructing Moral Relations After Wrongdoing*. New York: Cambridge University Press.

Young, Iris Marion. 1990. *Justice and the Politics of Difference*. Princeton: Princeton University Press.

Zieselman, Kimberly. 2015. "Invisible Harm." *Narrative Inquiry in Bioethics* 5, no. 2:122–25.

PART TWO

FEMINIST ETHICAL THEORY AND ITS APPLICATIONS

CHAPTER 12

AGAINST MARRIAGE AND MOTHERHOOD

CLAUDIA CARD

The title of this essay is deliberately provocative, because I fear that radical feminist perspectives on marriage and motherhood are in danger of being lost in the quest for equal rights. My concerns, however, are specific. I am skeptical of using the institution of motherhood as a source of paradigms for ethical theory. And I am skeptical of legal marriage as a way to gain a better life for lesbian and gay lovers or as a way to provide a supportive environment for lesbian and gay parents and their children. Of course, some are happy with marriage and motherhood as they now exist. My concern is with the price of that joy borne by those trapped by marriage or motherhood and deeply unlucky in the company they find there. Nevertheless, nothing that I say is intended to disparage the characters of many magnificent women who have struggled in and around these institutions to make the best of a trying set of options.

Backgrounds

My perspective on marriage is influenced not only by others' written reports and analyses but also by my own history of being raised in a lower-middle-class white village family by parents married (to each other) for more than three decades, by my firsthand experiences of urban same-sex domestic partnerships lasting from two and one half to nearly seven years (good ones and bad, some racially mixed, some white, generally mixed in class and religious backgrounds), and by my more recent experience as a lesbianfeminist whose partner of the past decade is not a domestic partner. My perspective

Criticism and Compassion: The Ethics and Politics of Claudia Card.
Edited by Robin S. Dillon and Armen T. Marsoobian.
Chapters and book compilation © 2018 Metaphilosophy LLC and John Wiley & Sons Ltd.

on child rearing is influenced not by my experience as a mother, but by my experience as a daughter reared by a full-time mother-housewife, by having participated heavily in the raising of my younger siblings, and by having grown to adulthood in a community in which many of the working-class and farming families exemplified aspects of what bell hooks calls "revolutionary parenting" (hooks 1984, 133–46).

bell hooks writes, "Childrearing is a responsibility that can be shared with other childrearers, with people who do not live with children. This form of parenting is revolutionary in this society because it takes place in opposition to the idea that parents, especially mothers, should be the only childrearers. Many people raised in black communities experienced this type of community-based child care" (hooks 1984, 144). This form of child rearing may be more common than is generally acknowledged in a society in which those whose caretaking does not take place in a nuclear family are judged by those with the power to set standards as unfortunate and deprived. Although bell hooks continues to use the language of "mothering" to some extent in elaborating "revolutionary parenting," I see this revolution as offering an alternative to mothering as a social institution.

Because it appears unlikely that the legal rights of marriage and motherhood in the European American models of those institutions currently at issue in our courts will disappear or even be seriously eroded during my lifetime, my opposition to them here takes the form of skepticism primarily in the two areas mentioned above: ethical theorizing and lesbian/gay activism. I believe that women who identify as lesbian or gay should be reluctant to put our activist energy into attaining legal equity with heterosexuals in marriage and motherhood—not because the existing discrimination against us is in any way justifiable but because these institutions are so deeply flawed that they seem to me unworthy of emulation and reproduction.

For more than a decade, feminist philosophers and lesbian/gay activists have been optimistic about the potentialities of legal marriage and legitimated motherhood. This should be surprising, considering the dismal political genealogies of those institutions, which have been generally admitted and widely publicized by feminist thinkers. Yet, in the project of claiming historically characteristic life experiences of women as significant data for moral theory, many are turning to women's experiences as mothers for ethical insight. Not all focus on marriage and motherhood. Feminist philosophers are taking as valuable theoretical paradigms for ethics many kinds of caring relationships that have been salient in women's lives. Marilyn Friedman, for example, has explored female friendship in *What Are Friends For?* (1993). Sarah Hoagland (1988) offers value inquiry based on experiences of lesbian bonding in many forms. *Mothering*, edited by

Joyce Trebilcot (1983), includes essays representing critical as well as supportive stances regarding motherhood. These works, however, are exceptions to a wider trend of theorizing that draws mainly positive inspiration from the experiences of women as mothers. Thus, Sara Ruddick's *Maternal Thinking* (1989), which acknowledges the need for caution, is devoted to developing ethical ideas based on experiences of mother-child relationships. Nel Noddings's *Caring* (1984) and Virginia Held's *Feminist Morality* (1993) likewise take inspiration from the experience of "mothering persons" and other caregivers, and to some extent, Annette Baier does likewise in *Moral Prejudices* (1994). These last four philosophers urge an extension of mothering values to more public realms of activity.

In *Black Feminist Thought* Patricia Hill Collins also speaks of "a more generalized ethic of caring and personal accountability among African-American women who often feel accountable to all the Black community's children" (1991, chap. 6). Her models for an "ethic of caring and personal accountability," however, differ significantly from the models characteristic of the work of so many white feminists in that her models already involve a wider community that includes "othermothers" as well as "bloodmothers," models elaborated by bell hooks as instances of "revolutionary parenting" (hooks 1984, 133–46). My skepticism is not aimed at such "revolutionary parenting," which I find has much to recommend it. Yet "parenting" by a wider community is a form of child care not currently enshrined in Northern legal systems. It is not the model guiding lesbian and gay activists currently agitating for equal rights before the law. For more communal child care, the language of "mothering" and even "parenting" is somewhat misleading in that these practices are not particularly "mother-centered" or even "parent-centered" but are centered on the needs of children and of the community.

Audre Lorde, who wrote about her relationship with her son (1984, 72–80), has left us with reflections on yet another model of parenting, that of a lesbian relationship struggling against the models of heterosexual marriage and patriarchal motherhood in her social environment. Nevertheless, she does not attempt to generalize from her experience or to treat it as a source of inspiration for ethical theory.

When confronted with my negative attitudes toward marriage and motherhood, some recoil as though I were proposing that we learn to do without water and oxygen on the ground that both are polluted (even killing us). Often, I believe, this reaction comes from certain assumptions that the reader or hearer may be inclined to make, which I here note in order to set aside at the outset.

First, my opposition to marriage is not an opposition to intimacy, nor to long-term relationships of intimacy, nor to durable partnerships of many sorts.[1] I understand marriage as a relationship to which the State is an essential third party. Also, like the practices of footbinding and suttee, which, according to the researches of Mary Daly (1978, 113–52), originated among the powerful classes, marriage in Europe was once available only to those with substantial social power. Previously available only to members of propertied classes, the marriage relation has come to be available in modem Northern democracies to any adult heterosexual couple neither of whom is already married to someone else. This is what lesbian and gay agitation for the legal right to marry is about. This is what I find calls for extreme caution.

Second, my opposition to motherhood is neither an opposition to the guidance, education, and caretaking of children nor an opposition to the formation of many kinds of bonds between children and adults.[2] Nor am I opposed to the existence of homes, as places of long-term residence with others of a variety of ages with whom one has deeply committed relationships. When "the family" is credited with being a bulwark against a hostile world, as in the case of many families in the African and Jewish disaporas, the bulwark that is meant often consists of a variety of deeply committed personal (as opposed to legal) relationships and the stability of caring that they represent, or home as a site of these things. The bulwark is not the legitimation (often precarious or nonexistent) of such relationships through institutions of the State. The State was often one of the things that these relationships formed a bulwark against.

Marriage and motherhood in the history of modem patriarchies have been mandatory for and oppressive to women, and they have been criticized by feminists on those grounds. My concerns, however, are as much for the children as for the women that some of these children become and for the goal of avoiding the reproduction of patriarchy. Virginia Held, one optimist about the potentialities of marriage and motherhood, finds motherhood to be part of a larger conception of family, which she takes to be constructed of noncontractual relationships. She notes that although Marxists and recent communitarians might agree with her focus on noncontractual relationships, their views remain uninformed by feminist critiques of patriarchal families. The family from which she would have society and ethical theorists learn, ultimately, is a postpatriarchal family. But what is a "postpatriarchal family"? Is it a coherent concept?

---

[1] Betty Berzon claims that her book *Permanent Partners* is about "reinventing our gay and lesbian relationships" and "learning to imbue them with all the *solemnity* of marriage without necessarily imitating the heterosexual model" (1988, 7), and yet by the end of the book it is difficult to think of anything in legal ideals of the heterosexual nuclear family that she has not urged us to imitate.

[2] Thus I am not an advocate of the equal legal rights for children movement as that movement is presented and criticized by Purdy (1992), namely, as a movement advocating that children have exactly the same legal rights as adults, including the legal right not to attend school.

"Family" is itself a family resemblance concept. Many contemporary lesbian and gay partnerships, households, and friendship networks fit no patriarchal stereotypes and are not sanctified by legal marriage, although their members still regard themselves as "family."[3] But should they? Many social institutions, such as insurance companies, do not honor such conceptions of "family." Family, as understood in contexts where material benefits tend to be at stake, is not constituted totally by noncontractual relationships. At its core is to be found one or more marriage contracts. For those who would work to enlarge the concept of family to include groupings that are currently totally noncontractual, in retaining patriarchal vocabulary there is a danger of importing patriarchal ideals and of inviting treatment as deviant or "second class" at best.

"Family," our students learn in Women's Studies 101, comes from the Latin *familia*, meaning "household," which in turn came from *famulus*, which, according to the *OED*, meant "servant." The ancient Roman *paterfamilias* was the head of a household of servants and slaves, including his wife or wives, concubines, and children. He had the power of life and death over them. The ability of contemporary male heads of households to get away with battering, incest, and murder suggests to many feminists that the family has not evolved into anything acceptable yet. Would a household of persons whose relationships with each other transcended (as those of families do) sojourns under one roof continue to be rightly called "family" if no members had significant social support for treating other members abusively? Perhaps the postpatriarchal relationships envisioned by Virginia Held and by so many lesbians and gay men should be called something else, to mark that radical departure from family history. But it is not just a matter of a word. It is difficult to imagine what such relationships would be.

In what follows, I say more about marriage than about motherhood, because it is legal marriage that sets the contexts in which and the background against which motherhood has been legitimated, and it defines contexts in which mothering easily becomes disastrous for children.

Lesbian (or Gay) Marriage?

A special vantage point is offered by the experience of lesbians and gay men, among whom there is currently no consensus (although much strong feeling on both sides) on whether to pursue the legal right to marry a same-sex lover (Blumenfeld, Wolfson, and Brownworth, all 1996). When heterosexual partners think about marriage, they usually consider the more

---

[3] See, for example, Weston (1991), Burke (1993), and Slater (1995). In contrast, Berzon (1988) uses the language of partnership, reserving "family" for social structures based on heterosexual unions, as in chap. 12, subtitled "Integrating Your Families into Your Life as a Couple."

limited question whether they (as individuals) should marry (each other) and if they did not marry, what the consequences would be for children they might have or raise. They consider this in the context of a State that gives them the legal option of marriage. Lesbians and gay men are currently in the position of having to consider the larger question whether the legal option of marriage is a good idea, as we do not presently have it in relation to our lovers. We have it, of course, in relation to the other sex, and many have exercised it as a cover, as insurance, for resident alien status, and so forth. If it is because we already have rights to marry heterosexually that right-wing attackers of lesbian or gay rights complain of our wanting "special rights," we should reply that, of course, any legalization of same-sex marriage should extend that "privilege" to heterosexuals as well.

The question whether lesbians and gay men should pursue the right to marry is not the same as the question whether the law is wrong in its refusal to honor same-sex marriages. Richard Mohr (1994, 31–53) defends gay marriage from that point of view as well as I have seen it done. Evan Wolfson develops powerfully an analogy between the denial of marriage to same-sex couples and the antimiscegenation laws that were overturned in the United States just little more than a quarter century ago (Wolfson 1996). What I have to say should apply to relationships between lovers (or parents) of different races as well as to those of same-sex lovers (or parents). The ways we have been treated are abominable. But it does not follow that we should seek legal marriage.

It is one thing to argue that others are wrong to deny us something and another to argue that what they would deny us is something we should fight for the right to have. I do not deny that others are wrong to exclude same-sex lovers and lovers of different races from the rights of marriage. I question only whether we should fight for those rights, even if we do not intend to exercise them. Suppose that slave-owning in some mythical society were denied to otherwise free women, on the ground that such women as slave-owners would pervert the institution of slavery. Women (both free and unfree) could (unfortunately) document empirically the falsity of beliefs underlying such grounds. It would not follow that women should fight for the right to own slaves, or even for the rights of other women to own slaves. Likewise, if marriage is a deeply flawed institution, even though it is a special injustice to exclude lesbians and gay men arbitrarily from participating in it, it would not necessarily advance the cause of justice on the whole to remove the special injustice of discrimination.

About same-sex marriage I feel something like the way I feel about prostitution. Let us, by all means, *decriminalize* sodomy and so forth. Although marriage rights would be *sufficient* to enable lovers to have sex legally, such rights should not be *necessary* for that purpose. Where they *are* legally necessary and also available for protection against the social oppression of same-sex lovers, as for lovers of different races, there will be enormous pressure to marry. Let us not pretend that marriage is basically a good thing on the ground that durable intimate relationships are. Let us not be eager to have the State regulate our unions. Let us work to remove barriers to our enjoying some of the privileges presently available only to heterosexual married couples. But in doing so, we should also be careful not to support discrimination against those who choose not to marry and not to support continued state definition of the legitimacy of intimate relationships. I would rather see the state *de*regulate heterosexual marriage than see it begin to regulate same-sex marriage.

As the child of parents married to each other for thirty-two years, I once thought I knew what marriage meant, even though laws vary from one jurisdiction to another and the dictionary, as Mohr notes, sends us around in a circle, referring us to "husband" and "wife," in turn defined by "marriage." Mohr argues convincingly that "marriage" need not presuppose the gendered concepts of "husband" and "wife" (1994, 31–53). I will not rehearse that ground here. History seems to support him. After reading cover to cover and with great interest John Boswell's *Same-Sex Unions in Premodern Europe* (1994), however, I no longer feel so confident that I know when a "union" counts as a "marriage." Boswell, who discusses many kinds of unions, refrains from using the term "marriage" to describe the same-sex unions he researched, even though they were sanctified by religious ceremonies. Some understandings of such unions, apparently, did not presuppose that the partners were not at the same time married to someone of the other sex.

Mohr, in his suggestions for improving marriage law by attending to the experience of gay men, proposes that sexual fidelity not be a requirement (1994, 49–50). What would remain without such a requirement, from a legal point of view, sounds to me like mutual *adoption*, or guardianship. Adoption, like marriage, is a way to become next-of-kin. This could have substantial economic consequences. But is there any good reason to restrict mutual adoption to two parties at a time? If mutual adoption is what we want, perhaps the law of adoption is what we should use, or suitably amend. And yet the law of adoption is not without its problematic aspects, some similar to those of the law of marriage. For it does not specify precisely a guardian's rights and responsibilities. Perhaps those who want legal contracts with each other would do better to enter into contracts the contents of which and duration of which they specifically define.

As noted above, my partner of the past decade is not a domestic partner. She and I form some kind of fairly common social unit which, so far as I know, remains nameless. Along with such namelessness goes a certain invisibility, a mixed blessing to which I will return. We do not share a domicile (she has her house; I have mine). Nor do we form an economic unit (she pays her bills; I pay mine). Although we certainly have fun together, our relationship is not based simply on fun. We share the sorts of mundane details of daily living that Mohr finds constitutive of marriage (often in her house, often in mine). We know a whole lot about each other's lives that the neighbors and our other friends will never know. In times of trouble, we are each other's first line of defense, and in times of need, we are each other's main support. Still, we are not married. Nor do we yearn to marry. Yet if marrying became an option that would legitimate behavior otherwise illegitimate and make available to us social securities that will no doubt become even more important to us as we age, we and many others like us might be pushed into marriage. Marrying under such conditions is not a totally free choice.

Because of this unfreedom, I find at least four interconnected kinds of problems with marriage. Three may be somewhat remediable in principle, although if they were remedied, many might no longer have strong motives to marry. I doubt that the fourth problem, which I also find most important, is fixable.

The first problem, perhaps easiest to remedy in principle (if not in practice) is that employers and others (such as units of government) often make available only to legally married couples benefits that anyone could be presumed to want, married or not, such as affordable health and dental insurance, the right to live in attractive residential areas, visitation rights in relation to significant others, and so forth. Spousal benefits for employees are a significant portion of many workers' compensation. Thus married workers are often, in effect, paid more for the same labor than unmarried workers (Berzon 1988, 266; Pierce 1995, 5). This is one way in which people who do not have independent access to an income often find themselves economically pressured into marrying. Historically, women have been in this position oftener than men, including, of course, most pre-twentieth-century lesbians, many of whom married men for economic security.

The second problem is that even though divorce by mutual consent is now generally permitted in the United States, the consequences of divorce can be so difficult that many who should divorce do not. This to some extent is a continuation of the benefits problem. But also, if one partner can sue the other for support or receive a share of the other's assets to which they would not otherwise have been legally entitled, there are new economic motives to preserve emotionally disastrous unions.

The third issue, which would be seriously troublesome for many lesbians, is that legal marriage as currently understood in Northern democracies is monogamous in the sense of one *spouse* at a time, even though the law in many states no longer treats "adultery" (literally "pollution") as criminal. Yet many of us have more than one long-term intimate relationship during the same time period. Any attempt to change the current understanding of marriage so as to allow plural marriage partners (with plural contracts) would have economic implications that I have yet to see anyone explore.

Finally, the fourth problem, the one that I doubt is fixable (depending on what "marriage" means) is that the legal rights of access that married partners have to each other's persons, property, and lives makes it all but impossible for a spouse to defend herself (or himself), or to be protected against torture, rape, battery, stalking, mayhem, or murder by the other spouse. Spousal murder accounts for a substantial number of murders each year. This factor is made worse by the presence of the second problem mentioned above (difficulties of divorce that lead many to remain married when they should not), which provide motives to violence within marriages. Legal marriage thus enlists state support for conditions conducive to murder and mayhem.

The point is not that all marriages are violent. It is not about the frequency of violence, although the frequency appears high. The points are, rather, that the institution places obstacles in the way of protecting spouses (however many) who need it and is conducive to violence in relationships that go bad. Battery is, of course, not confined to spouses. Lesbian and gay battery is real (see Renzetti 1992; Lobel 1986; Island and Letellier 1991). But the law does not protect unmarried batterers or tend to preserve the relationships of unmarried lovers in the way that it protects husbands and tends to preserve marriages.

Why, then, would anyone marry? Because it is a tradition, glorified and romanticized. It grants status. It is a significant (social) mark of adulthood for women in patriarchy. It is a way to avoid certain hassles from one's family of origin and from society at large—hassles to oneself, to one's lover (if there is only one), and to children with whom one may live or whom one may bring into being. We need better traditions. And women have long needed other social marks of adulthood and ways to escape families of origin.

Under our present exclusion from the glories of legal matrimony, the usual reason why lesbians or gay men form partnerships and stay together is because we care for each other. We may break up for other kinds of reasons (such as one of us being assigned by an employer to another part of the country and neither of us being able to afford to give up our jobs). But when we stay together, that is usually because of how we feel about each other and about our life together. Consider how this basic taken-for-granted fact might change if we could marry with the State's blessings. There are many material benefits to tempt those who can into marrying, not to mention the improvement in one's social reputation as a reliable citizen (and for those of us who are not reliable citizens, the protection against having a spouse forced to testify against us in court).

Let us consider each of these four problems further. The first was that of economic and other benefits, such as insurance that employers often make available only to marrieds, the right of successorship to an apartment, inheritance rights, and the right to purchase a home in whatever residential neighborhood one can afford. The attachment of such benefits to marital status is a problem in two respects. First, because the benefits are substantial, not trivial, they offer an ulterior motive for turning a lover relationship into a marriage—even for pretending to care for someone, deceiving oneself as well as others. As Emma Goldman argued in the early twentieth century, when marriage becomes an insurance policy, it may no longer be compatible with love (1969). Second, the practice of making such benefits available only to marrieds discriminates against those who, for whatever reason, do not marry. Because of the first factor, many heterosexuals who do not fundamentally approve of legal marriage give in and marry any-how. Because of the second factor, many heterosexual feminists, however, refuse legal marriage (although the State may regard their relationships as common law marriages).

Now add to the spousal benefits problem the second difficulty, that of the consequences of getting a divorce (for example, consequences pertain-ing to shared property, alimony, or child support payments and difficulties in terms of access to children), especially if the divorce is not friendly. Inti-mate partnerships beginning from sexual or erotic attraction tend to be of limited viability, even under favorable circumstances. About half of all married couples in the United States at present get divorced, and probably most of the other half should. But the foreseeable consequences of divorce provide motives to stay married for many spouses who no longer love each other (if they ever did) and have even grown to hate each other. Staying married ordinarily hampers one's ability to develop a satisfying lover rela-tionship with someone new. As long as marriage is monogamous in the sense of one *spouse* at a time, it interferes with one's ability to obtain spousal benefits for a new lover. When spouses grow to hate each other, the access that was a joy as lovers turns into something highly dangerous. I will return to this.

Third, the fact of multiple relationships is a problem even for relatively good marriages. Mohr, as noted, argues in favor of reforming marriage so as not to require sexual exclusiveness rather than officially permitting only monogamy. Yet he was thinking not of multiple *spouses* but of a monoga-mous marriage in which neither partner expects sexual exclusiveness of the other. Yet, one spouse per person is monogamy, however promiscuous the spouses may be. The advantages that Mohr enumerates as among the perks of marriage apply only to spouses, not to relationships with additional sig-nificant others who are not one's spouses. Yet the same reasons that lead one to want those benefits for a spouse can lead one to want them for addi-tional significant others. If lesbian and gay marriages were acknowledged in Northern democracies today, they would be legally as monogamous as heterosexual marriage, regardless of the number of one's actual sexual part-ners. This does not reflect the relationships that many lesbians and gay men have or want.

Boswell wrote about same-sex unions that did not preclude simultaneous heterosexual marriages (1994). The parties were not permitted to formalize unions with more than one person of the same sex at a time, however. Nor were they permitted to have children with a person of the other sex to whom they were not married. Thus, in a certain restricted sense, each formal union was monogamous, even though one could have both kinds at once.

Christine Pierce argues, in support of the option to legalize lesbian and gay marriages, that lesbian and gay images have been cast too much in terms of individuals—*The Well of Loneliness* (Hall 1950), for example—and not enough in terms of relationships, especially serious relationships involving long-term commitments (Pierce 1995, 13). Marriage gives visibility to people "as couples, partners, family, and kin," a visibility that lesbians and gay men have lacked and that could be important to dispelling negative stereotypes and assumptions that our relationships do not embody many of the same ideals as those of many heterosexual couples, partners, family, and kin (Pierce 1996). This is both true and important.

It is not clear, however, that legal marriage would offer visibility to our relationships as they presently exist. It might well change our relationships so that they became more like heterosexual marriages, loveless after the first few years but hopelessly bogged down with financial entanglements or children (adopted or products of turkey-baster insemination or previous marriages), making separation or divorce (at least in the near future) too difficult to contemplate, giving rise to new motives for mayhem and murder. Those who never previously felt pressure to marry a lover might confront not just new options but new pressures and traps.

My views on marriage may surprise those familiar with my work on the military ban (Card 1995). For I have argued against the ban and in favor of lesbian and gay access to military service, and I argued that even those who disapprove of the military should object to wrongful exclusions of lesbians and gay men. In the world in which we live, military institutions may well be less dispensable than marriage, however in need of restraint military institutions are. But for those who find legal marriage and legitimate motherhood objectionable, should I be moved here by what moved me there—that it is one thing not to exercise an option and another to be denied the option, that denying us the option for no good reason conveys that there is something wrong with us, thereby contributing to our public disfigurement and defamation, and that these considerations give us good reasons to protest being denied the option even if we never intend to exercise it? I am somewhat but not greatly moved by such arguments in this case. The case of marriage seems to me more like the case of slavery than like that of the military.

Marriage and military service are in many ways relevantly different. Ordinarily, marriage (like slavery) is much worse, if only because its impact on our lives is usually greater. Marriage is supposed to be a lifetime commitment. It is at least open-ended. When available, it is not simply an option but tends to be coercive, especially for women in a misogynist society. For those who choose it, it threatens to be a dangerous trap. Military service is ordinarily neither a lifetime nor open-ended commitment; one signs up for a certain number of years. During war, one may be drafted (also for a limited time) and, of course, even killed, but the issue has not been whether to draft lesbians and gay men. Past experience shows that gay men will be drafted in war, even if barred from enlistment in peace. When enlistment is an option, it does not threaten to trap one in a relationship from which it will be extremely difficult to extricate oneself in the future. There is some analogy with the economically coercive aspect of the marriage "option." Because those who have never served are ineligible for substantial educational and health benefits, many from low- (or no-) income families enlist to obtain such things as college education and even health and dental insurance. However, the service one has to give for such benefits as an enlistee is limited compared to spousal service. Being killed is a risk in either case.

In such a context, pointing out that many marriages are very loving, not at all violent, and proclaim to the world two people's honorable commitment to each other seems to me analogous to pointing out, as many slave-owners did, that many slave-owners were truly emotionally bonded with their slaves, that they did not whip them, and that even the slaves were proud and honored to be the slaves of such masters.

Some of the most moving stories I hear in discussions of gay marriage point out that the care rendered the ill by families is a great service to society and that the chosen families of gay AIDS patients deserve to be honored in the same way as a family based on a heterosexual union. The same, of course, applies to those who care for lesbian or gay cancer patients or for those with severe disabilities or other illnesses. But is this a service to society? Or to the State? The State has a history of depending on families to provide care that no human being should be without in infancy, illness, and old age. Lesbians and gay men certainly have demonstrated our ability to serve the State in this capacity as well as heterosexuals. But where does this practice leave those who are not members of families? Or those who object on principle to being members of these unions as sanctified by the State?

To remedy the injustices of discrimination against lesbians, gay men, and unmarried heterosexual couples, many municipalities are experimenting with domestic partnership legislation. This may be a step in the right direction, insofar as it is a much more voluntary relationship, more specific, more easily dissolved. Yet, partners who are legally married need not share a domicile unless one of them so chooses; in this respect, eligibility for the benefits of domestic partnership may be more restrictive than marriage. And the only domestic partnership legislation that I have seen requires that one claim only one domestic partner at a time, which does not distinguish it from monogamous marriage (see Berzon 1988, 163–82).

Whatever social unions the State may sanction, it is important to realize that they become State-defined, however they may have originated. One's rights and privileges as a spouse can change dramatically with one's residence, as Betty Mahmoody discovered when she went with her husband to Iran for what he had promised would be a temporary visit (Mahmoody with Hoffer 1987). She found after arriving in Iran that she had no legal right to leave without her husband's consent, which he then denied her, leaving as her only option for returning to the United States to escape illegally (which she did). Even if a couple would not be legally recognized as married in a particular jurisdiction, if they move from another jurisdiction in which they *were* legally recognized as married, they are generally legally recognized as married in the new jurisdiction, and they are held to whatever responsibilities the new jurisdiction enforces. The case of Betty Mahmoody is especially interesting because it involves her husband's right of access. Spousal rights of access do not have the same sort of contingency in relation to marriage as, say, a right to family rates for airline tickets.

Marriage is a legal institution the obligations of which tend to be highly informal—i.e., loosely defined, unspecific, and inexplicit about exactly what one is to do and about the consequences of failing. In this regard, a marriage contract differs from the contract of a bank loan. In a legal loan contract, the parties' reciprocal obligations become highly formalized. In discharging the obligations of a loan, one dissolves the obligation. In living up to marriage obligations, however, one does not dissolve the marriage or its obligations; if anything, one strengthens them. As I have argued elsewhere, the obligations of marriage and those of loan contracts exhibit different paradigms (Card 1988, 1990). The debtor paradigm is highly formal, whereas the obligations of spouses tend to be relatively informal and fit better a paradigm that I have called the trustee paradigm. The obligations of a trustee, or guardian, are relatively abstractly defined. A trustee or guardian is expected to exercise judgment and discretion in carrying out the obligations to care, protect, or maintain. The trustee *status* may be relatively formal—precisely defined regarding dates on which it takes effect, compensation for continuing in good standing, and the consequences of losing the status. But consequences of failing to do this or that specific thing may not be specified or specifiable, because what is required to fulfill duties of caring, safekeeping, protection, or maintenance can be expected to vary with circumstances, changes in which may not be readily foreseeable. A large element of discretion seems ineliminable. This makes it difficult to *hold a trustee accountable for abuses* while the status of trustee is retained, and it also means that it is difficult to prove that the status should be terminated. Yet the only significant sanction against a trustee may be withdrawal of that status. Spousal status and parental status fit the trustee model, rather than the debtor model, of obligation. This means that it is difficult to hold a spouse or a parent accountable for abuse.

Central to the idea of marriage, historically, has been intimate access to the persons, belongings, activities, even histories of one another. More important than sexual access, marriage gives spouses physical access to each other's residences and belongings, and it gives access to information about each other, including financial status, that other friends and certainly the neighbors do not ordinarily have. For all that has been said about the privacy that marriage protects, what astonishes me is how much privacy one gives up in marrying.

This mutual access appears to be a central point of marrying. Is it wise to abdicate legally one's privacy to that extent? What interests does it serve? Anyone who in fact cohabits with another may seem to give up similar privacy. Yet, without marriage, it is possible to take one's life back without encountering the law as an obstacle. One may even be able to enlist legal help in getting it back. In this regard, uncloseted lesbians and gay men presently have a certain advantage—which, by the way, "palimony" suits threaten to undermine by applying the idea of "common law" marriage to same-sex couples (see, e.g., Faulkner with Nelson 1993).

Boswell argued that, historically, what has been important to marriage is consent, not sexual relations. But, consent to what? What is the point of marrying? Historically, for the propertied classes, he notes, the point of heterosexual marriage was either dynastic or property concerns or both. Dynastic concerns do not usually figure in arguments for lesbian or gay marriage. Although property concerns do, they are among the kinds of concerns often better detached from marriage. That leaves as a central point of marriage the legal right of cohabitation and the access to each other's lives that this entails.

It might still be marriage if sexual exclusivity, or even sex, were not part of it, but would it still be marriage if rights of cohabitation were not part of it? Even marrieds who voluntarily live apart retain the *right* of cohabitation. Many rights and privileges available to marrieds today might exist in a legal relationship that did not involve cohabitation rights (for example, insurance rights, access to loved ones in hospitals, rights to inherit, and many other rights presently possessed by kin who do not live with each other). If the right of cohabitation is central to the concept of legal marriage, it deserves more critical attention than philosophers have given it.

Among the trappings of marriage that have received attention and become controversial, ceremonies and rituals are much discussed. I have no firm opinions about ceremonies or rituals. A far more important issue seems to me to be the marriage *license*, which receives hardly any attention at all. Ceremonies affirming a relationship can take place at any point in the relationship. But a license is what one needs to initiate a legal marriage. To marry legally, one applies to the state for a license, and marriage, once entered into, licenses spouses to certain kinds of access to each other's persons and lives. It is a mistake to think of a license as simply enhancing everyone's freedom. One person's license, in this case, can be another's prison. Prerequisites for marriage licenses are astonishingly lax. Anyone of a certain age, not presently married to someone else, and free of certain communicable diseases automatically qualifies. A criminal record for violent crimes is, to my knowledge, no bar. Compare this with other licenses, such as a driver's license. In Wisconsin, to retain a driver's license, we submit periodically to eye exams. Some states have more stringent requirements. To obtain a driver's license, all drivers have to pass a written and a behind-the-wheel test to demonstrate knowledge and skill. In Madison, Wisconsin, even to adopt a cat from the humane society, we have to fill out a form demonstrating knowledge of relevant ordinances for petguardians. Yet to marry, applicants need demonstrate no knowledge of the laws pertaining to marriage nor any relationship skills nor even the modicum of self-control required to respect another human being. And once the marriage exists, the burden of proof is always on those who would dissolve it, never on those who would continue it in perpetuity.

Further disanalogies between drivers' and marriage licenses confirm that in our society there is greater concern for victims of bad driving than for those of bad marriages. You cannot legally drive without a license, whereas it is now in many jurisdictions not illegal for unmarried adults of whatever sex to cohabit. One can acquire the status of spousehood simply by cohabiting heterosexually for several years, whereas one does not acquire a driver's license simply by driving for years without one. Driving without the requisite skills and scruples is recognized as a great danger to others and treated accordingly. No comparable recognition is given the dangers of legally sanctioning the access of one person to the person and life of another without evidence of the relevant knowledge and scruples of those so licensed. The consequence is that married victims of partner battering and rape have less protection than anyone except children. What is at stake are permanently disabling and life-threatening injuries, for those who survive. I do not, at present, see how this vulnerability can be acceptably removed from the institution of legal marriage. Measures could be taken to render its disastrous consequences less likely than they are presently but at the cost of considerable state intrusion into our lives.

The right of cohabitation seems to me central to the question whether legal marriage can be made an acceptable institution, especially to the question whether marriage can be envisaged in such a way that its partners could protect themselves, or be protected, adequately against spousal rape and battery. Although many states now recognize on paper the crimes of marital rape and stalking and are better educated than before about marital battering, the progress has been mostly on paper. Wives continue to die daily at a dizzying rate.

Thus I conclude that legalizing lesbian and gay marriage, turning a personal commitment into a license regulable and enforceable by the state, is probably a very bad idea and that lesbians and gay men are probably better off, all things considered, without the "option" (and its consequent pressures) to obtain and act on such a license, despite some of the immediate material and spiritual gains to some of being able to do so. Had we any chance of success, we might do better to agitate for the abolition of legal marriage altogether.

Nevertheless, many will object that marriage provides an important environment for the rearing of children. An appreciation of the conduciveness of marriage to murder and mayhem challenges that assumption. Historically, marriage and motherhood have gone hand in hand—ideologically, although often enough not in fact. That marriage can provide a valuable context for motherhood—even if it is unlikely to do so—as an argument in favor of marriage seems to presuppose that motherhood is a good thing. So let us consider next whether that is so.

Why Motherhood?

The term "mother" is ambiguous between a woman who gives birth and a female who parents, that is, rears a child—often but not necessarily the same woman. The term "motherhood" is ambiguous between the experience of mothers (in either sense, usually the second) and a social practice the rules of which structure child rearing. It is the latter that interests me here. Just as some today would stretch the concept of "family" to cover any committed partnership, household, or close and enduring network of friends, others would stretch the concept of "motherhood" to cover any mode of child rearing. That is not how I understand "motherhood." Just as not every durable intimate partnership is a marriage, not every mode of child rearing exemplifies motherhood. Historically, motherhood has been a core element of patriarchy. Within the institution of motherhood, mother's primary commitments have been to father and only secondarily to his children. Unmarried women have been held responsible by the State for the primary care of children they birth, unless a man wished to claim them. In fact, of course, children are raised by grandparents, single parents (heterosexual, lesbian, gay, asexual, and so on), and extended families, all in the midst of patriarchies. But these have been regarded as deviant parentings, with nothing like the prestige or social and legal support available to patriarchal mothers, as evidenced in the description of the relevant "families" in many cases as providing at best "broken homes."

Apart from the institution of marriage and historical ideals of the family, it is uncertain what characteristics mother-child relationships would have, for many alternatives are possible. In the good ones, mother-child relationships would not be as characterized as they have been by involuntary uncompensated caretaking. Even today, an ever-increasing amount of caretaking is being done contractually in day-care centers, with the result that a legitimate mother's relationship to her child is often much less a caretaking relationship than her mother's relationship to her was. Nor are paid day-care workers "mothers" (even though they may engage briefly in some "mothering activities"), because they are free to walk away from their jobs. Their relationships with a child may be no more permanent or special to the child than those of a babysitter. Boswell's history *The Kindness of Strangers* (1988) describes centuries of children being taken in by those at whose doorsteps babies were deposited, often anonymously. Not all such children had anyone to call "Mother." Children have been raised in convents, orphanages, or boarding schools rather than in households. Many raised in households are cared for by hired help, rather than by anyone they call

"Mother." Many children today commute between separated or divorced parents, spending less time in a single household than many children of lesbian parents, some of whom, like Lesléa Newman's Heather, have two people to call "Mother" (Newman 1989). Many children are raised by older siblings, even in households in which someone else is called "Mother."

My point is not to support Newt Gingrich by glorifying orphanages or other hired caretakers but to put in perspective rhetoric about children's needs and about the ideal relationships of children to mothers. Much ink has been spilled debunking what passes for "love" in marriage. It is time to consider how much of the "love" that children are said to need is no more love than spousal attachments have been. Children do need stable intimate bonds with adults. But they also need supervision, education, health care, and a variety of relationships with people of a variety of ages. What the State tends to enforce in motherhood is the child's access to its mother, which guarantees none of these things, and the mother's answerability for her child's waywardness, which gives her a motive for constant supervision, thereby removing certain burdens from others but easily also endangering the well-being of her child if she is ill supplied with resources. Lacking adequate social or material resources, many a parent resorts to violent discipline in such situations, which the State has been reluctant to prevent or even acknowledge. This is what it has meant, legally, for a child to be a mother's "own": her own is the child who has legal rights of access to her and for whose waywardness she becomes answerable, although she is largely left to her own devices for carrying out the entailed responsibilities.

By contrast, children raised by lesbian or gay parents today are much more likely to be in relationships carefully chosen and affirmed by their caretakers.[4] Even though that would no doubt continue to be true oftener of the children of lesbian and gay parents in same-sex marriages than of the children of heterosexual parents, marriage would involve the State in defining who really had the status of "parent." The State has been willing to grant that status to at most two persons at a time, per child. It gives the child legal rights of access to at most those two parties. And it imposes legal accountability for the child's waywardness on at most those two parties. Under the present system that deprives lesbian and gay parents of spousal status, many lesbian and gay couples do their best anyway to emulate heterosexual models, which usually means assuming the responsibilities without the privileges.[5] Others I have known, however, attempt to undermine the assumption that parental responsibility should be concentrated in one

---

[4] An outstanding anthology on the many varieties of lesbian parenting is Arnup (1995). Also interesting is the anthropological study of lesbian mothers by Lewin (1993). Both are rich in references to many resources on both lesbian and gay parenting.

[5] Lewin (1993) finds, for example, that lesbian mothers tend to assume all caretaking responsibilities themselves, or in some cases share them with a partner, turning to their families of origin, rather than to a friendship network of peers, for additionally needed support.

or two people who have the power of a child's happiness and unhappiness in their hands for nearly two decades. Children raised without such models of the concentration of power may be less likely to reproduce patriarchal and other oppressive social relationships.

The "revolutionary parenting" that bell hooks describes (1984) dilutes the power of individual parents. Although children retain special affectional ties to their "bloodmothers," accountability for children's waywardness is more widely distributed. With many caretakers (such as "othermothers"), there is less pressure to make any one of them constantly accessible to a child and more pressure to make everyone somewhat accessible. With many caretakers, it is less likely that any of them will get away with prolonged abuse, or even be tempted to perpetrate it.

In my childhood, many adults looked out for the children of my village. I had, in a way, a combination of both kinds of worlds. My parents, married to each other, had the legal rights and the legal responsibilities of patriarchal parents. Yet, some of those responsibilities were in fact assumed by "othermothers," including women (and men) who never married anyone. Because it could always be assumed that wherever I roamed in the village, I would never be among strangers, my parents did not think they always needed to supervise me, although they were also ambivalent about that, as they would be legally answerable for any trouble I caused. I used to dread the thought that we might move to a city, where my freedom would probably have been severely curtailed, as it was when we lived in a large, white middle-class urban environment during World War II. In the village, because everyone assumed (reasonably) that someone was watching us, we children often escaped the intensity of physical discipline that I experienced alone with my mother amid the far larger urban population.

There are both worse and better environments that can be imagined for children than stereotypical patriarchal families. Urban environments in which parents must work away from home but can neither bring their children nor assume that their children are being watched by anyone are no doubt worse. Children who have never had effective caretakers do not make good caretakers of each other, either. Feminism today has been in something of a bind with respect to the so-called postpatriarchal family. If both women and men are to be actively involved in markets and governments and free to become active members of all occupations and professions, when, where, and how is child care going to be done? The solution of many feminists has been, in practice, for two parents to take turns spending time with the children. There is an increasing tendency today for parents who divide responsibilities for the children to pay others to do the child care, if they can afford it, when their turn comes. To the extent that this works, it is evidence that "mothering" is not necessary for child care. Children who have had effective caretakers may be better at taking care of themselves and each other, with minimal supervision to protect them against hazards to life and health, than is commonly supposed. Charlotte

Perkins Gilman's solution in *Women and Economics* (1966) and *Herland* (1992) was twofold. On one hand, she would turn child care into one of the professions that everyone with the requisite talents and motivations is free to enter. At the same time, she would *make the public safe* even for children, by an ethic that incorporated aspects of good caretaking. Virginia Held's *Feminist Morality* also suggests the latter strategy. A danger of this strategy, of course, is instituting paternalism among adults but spelled with an *m* instead of a *p*. Still, the idea of improving the safety of the public environment is compelling. If it were improved enough, there might be no need for motherhood—which is not to say that children would not need to bond with and be supervised by adults.

In *Feminist Morality* Virginia Held maintains that the mother-child relationship is the fundamental social relationship, not in a reductive sense but in the sense that so much else depends on one's relationships to primary caretakers (Held 1994, 70). This idea, also urged by Annette Baier (1994), seems to me in a certain sense incontrovertible and its general appreciation by philosophers long overdue. The sense in which it seems to me incontrovertible is that when one does in fact have a primary caretaker who has, if not the power of life and death, then the power of one's happiness and unhappiness in their hands for many years in the early stages of one's life, the influence of that experience on the rest of one's life is profound. It seems, for example, to affect one's ability to form good relationships with others in ways that are extremely difficult to change, if they are changeable at all. Yet, there is another sense in which the observation that the mother-child relationship is fundamental may be misleading. It may be misleading if it suggests that everyone really needs a single primary caretaker (or even two primary caretakers) who has the power of one's happiness and unhappiness in their hands for many years during the early stages of one's life. Perhaps people need that only in a society that refuses to take and share responsibility collectively for its own consciously and thoughtfully affirmed reproduction. In such a society, conscientious mothers are often the best protection a child has. But if so, it is misleading to say that such a relationship as the mother-child relationship is the, or even a, fundamental social relationship. It has been even less fundamental for many people, historically, than one might think, given how many children have been raised in institutions other than households or raised by a variety of paid caretakers with limited responsibilities.

Because mothers in a society that generally refuses to take collective responsibility for reproduction are often the best or even the only protection that children have, in the short run it is worth fighting for the right to adopt and raise children within lesbian and gay households. This is emergency care for young people, many of whom are already here and desperately in need of care. There is little that heterosexual couples can do to rebel as individual couples in a society in which their relationship is turned into a common law relationship after some years by the State and in which they are given the responsibilities and rights of parents over any children they may raise. Communal action is what is required to implement new models of parenting. In the long run, it seems best to keep open the option of making parenting more "revolutionary" along the lines of communal practices such as those described by bell hooks. Instead of encouraging such a revolution, legal marriage interferes with it in a state that glorifies marriage and takes the marriage relationship to be the only truly healthy context in which to raise children. Lesbian and gay unions have great potentiality to further the revolution, in part because we *cannot* marry.

If motherhood is transcended, the importance of attending to the experiences and environments of children remains. The "children" if not the "mothers" in society are all of us. Not each of us will choose motherhood under present conditions. But each of us has been a child, and each future human survivor will have childhood to survive. Among the most engaging aspects of a major feminist treatise on the institution of motherhood, Adrienne Rich's *Of Woman Born* (1976), are that it is written from the perspective of a daughter who was mothered and that it is addressed to daughters as well as to mothers. This work, like that of Annette Baier, Virginia Held, bell hooks, Patricia Hill Collins, and Sara Ruddick, has the potential to focus our attention not entirely or even especially on mothers but on those who have been (or have not been) mother*ed*, ultimately, on the experience of children in general. Instead of finding that the mother-child relationship provides a valuable paradigm for moral theorizing, even one who has mothered might find, reflecting on both her experience as a mother and her experience of having been mothered, that mothering should not be necessary, or that it should be less necessary than has been thought, and that it has more potential to do harm than good. The power of mothers over children may have been historically far more detrimental to daughters than to sons, at least in societies where daughters have been more controlled, more excluded from well-rewarded careers, and more compelled to engage in family service than sons. Such a finding would be in keeping with the project of drawing on the usually unacknowledged historically characteristic experiences of women.

In suggesting that the experience of being mothered has great potential for harm to children, I do not have in mind the kinds of concerns recently expressed by political conservatives about mothers who abuse drugs or are sexually promiscuous. Even these mothers are often the best protection their children have. I have in mind the environments provided by mothers who in fact do live up to contemporary norms of ideal motherhood or even exceed the demands of such norms in the degree of attention and concern they manifest for their children in providing a child-centered home as fully constructed as their resources allow.

Everyone would benefit from a society that was more attentive to the experiences of children, to the relationships of children with adults and with each other, and to the conditions under which children make the transition to adulthood. Moral philosophy might also be transformed by greater attention to the fact that adult experience and its potentialities are significantly conditioned by the childhoods of adults and of those children's relationships to (yet earlier) adults. Whether or not one agrees with the idea that motherhood offers a valuable paradigm for moral theorizing, in getting us to take seriously the significance of the child's experience of childhood and to take up the standpoint of the "child" in all of us, philosophical work exploring the significance of mother-child relationships is doing feminism and moral philosophy a great service.

Acknowledgments

Thanks to Harry Brighouse, Vicky Davion, Virginia Held, Sara Ruddick, anonymous reviewers for *Hypatia*, and especially to Lynne Tirrell for helpful comments and suggestions and to audiences who heard ancestors of this essay at the Pacific and Central Divisions of the American Philosophical Association in 1995.

References

Arnup, Katherine, ed. 1995. *Lesbian Parenting: Living with Pride and Prejudice*. Charlottetown, P.E.I.: Gynergy Books.

Baier, Annette C. 1994. *Moral Prejudices: Essays on Ethics*. Cambridge: Harvard University Press.

Berzon, Betty. 1988. *Permanent Partnerships: Building Lesbian and Gay Relationships That Last*. New York: Penguin.

Blumenfeld, Warren J. 1996. "Same-Sex Marriage: Introducing the Discussion." *Journal of Guy, Lesbian, and Bisexual Identity* 1(1): 77.

Boswell, John. 1988. *The Kindness of Strangers: The Abandonment of Children in Western Europe from Late Antiquity to the Renaissance*. New York: Pantheon.

———. 1994. *Same-Sex Unions in Premodern Europe*. New York: Villard.

Brownworth, Victoria A. 1996. "Tying the Knot or the Hangman's Noose: The Case Against Marriage." *Journal of Gay, Lesbian, and Bisexual Identity* 1(1): 91–98.

Burke, Phyllis. 1993. *Family Values: Two Moms and Their Son*. New York: Random House.

Card, Claudia. 1988. "Gratitude and Obligation." *American Philosophical Quaterly* 25(2): 115–27.

———. 1990. "Gender and Moral Luck." In *Identity, Character, and Morality: Essays in Moral Psychology*, ed. Owen Flanagan and Amelie Oksenberg Rorty. Cambridge: MIT Press.

———. 1995. *Lesbian Choices*. New York: Columbia University Press.

Collins, Patricia Hill. 1991. *Black Feminist Thought: Knowledge, Consciousness, and the Politics of Empowerment*. New York: Routledge.

Daly, Mary. 1978. *Gyn/Ecology: The Metaethics of Radical Feminism*. Boston: Beacon.

Faulkner, Sandra, with Judy Nelson. 1993. *Love Match: Nelson vs. Navratilova*. New York: Birch Lane Press.

Friedman, Marilyn. 1993. *What Are Friends For? Feminist Perspectives on Personal Relationships and Moral Theory*. Ithaca: Cornell University Press.

Gilman, Charlotte Perkins. 1966. *Women and Economics: The Economic Factor Between Men and Women a Factor in Social and Evolution*, ed Carl Degler. New York: Harper.

———. 1992. *Herland*. In *Herland and Selected Stories by Charlotte Perkins Gilman*, ed. Barbara H. Solomon. New York: Signet.

Goldman, Emma. 1969. "Marriage and Love." In *Anarchism and Other Essays*. New York: Dover.

Hall, Radclyffe. 1950. *The Well of Loneliness*. New York Pocket Books. (Many editions; first published 1928.)

Held, Virginia. 1993. *Feminist Morality: Transforming Culture, Society, and Politics*. Chicago: University of Chicago Press.

Hoagland, Sarah Lucia. 1988. *Lesbian Ethics: Toward New Value*. Palo Alto, CA: Institute of Lesbian Studies.

hooks, bell. 1984. *Feminist Theory from Margin to Center*. Boston: South End Press.

Island, David, and Patrick Letellier. 1991. *Men Who Beat the Men Who Love Them: Battered Gay Men and Domestic Violence*. New York: Harrington Park Press.

Lewin, Ellen. 1993. *Lesbian Mothers*. Ithaca: Cornell University Press.

Lobel, Kerry, ed. 1986. *Naming the Violence: Speaking Out About Lesbian Battering*. Seattle: Seal Press.

Lorde, Audre. 1984. *Sister Outsider: Essays and Speeches*. Trumansburg: Crossing Press.

Mahmoody, Betty, with William Hoffer. 1987. *Not Without My Daughter*. New York: St. Martin's.

Mohr, Richard D. 1994. *A More Perfect Union: Why Straight America Must Stand Up for Gay Rights*. Boston: Beacon.

Newman, Leslea. 1989. *Heather Has Two Mommies*. Northampton, MA: In Other Words Publishing.

Pierce, Christine. 1995. "Gay Marriage." *Journal of Social Philosophy* 28(2): 5–16.

Purdy, Laura M. 1992. *In Their Best Interest? The Case Against Equal Rights for Children*. Ithaca: Cornell University Press.

Renzetti, Clair M. 1992. *Violent Betrayal: Partner Abuse in Lesbian Relationships*. Newbury Park, CA: Sage Publications.

Rich, Adrienne. 1976. *Of Women Born: Motherhood as Experience and as Institution*. New York: Norton.

Ruddick, Sara. 1989. *Maternal Thinking: Toward a Politics of Peace.* Boston: Beacon.

Slater, Suzanne. 1995. *The Lesbian Family Life Cycle.* New York: Free Press.

Trebilcot, Joyce, ed. 1983. *Mothering: Essays in Feminist Theory.* Totowa, N.J.: Rowman and Allanheld.

Weston, Kath. 1991. *Families We Choose.* New York: Columbia University Press.

Wolfson, Evan. 1996. "Why We Should Fight for the Freedom to Marry: The Challenges and Opportunities That Will Follow a Win in Hawaii." *Journal of Lesbian, Gay, and Bisexual Identity* 1(1): 79–89.

CHAPTER 13

GAY DIVORCE

THOUGHTS ON THE LEGAL REGULATION OF MARRIAGE

CLAUDIA CARD

Advocates usually pose the issue of marriage for same-sex partners as one of *recognition,* as though such marriages were already here and the only issue is whether the law should recognize them. "Recognition" has a positive ring. Yet what is at stake is not just recognition but *regulation* by the state, including the power to determine what counts as a marriage. "Marriage" is systematically ambiguous between a committed personal relationship antecedent to legal definitions and a union legitimated by external authority, such as a religious or governmental body. Hopefully, the phrase "legal regulation of marriage" surmounts that ambiguity and makes clear the topic of this essay.

My position on the regulation of marriage has been, and remains, that the law should no more declare which durable intimate sexual unions between freely consenting adults are legitimate and which are not than it should declare which newborns are legitimate and which not. My objection is not to durable intimate unions as extralegal relationships between consenting adults. The target of my criticism is the vague, open-ended, state-enforceable legal marriage contract, rarely entered into voluntarily by any who are adequately informed of its consequences.

Yet opposition to legal marriage does not settle what we should do here and now, given that marriage (a) is part of what John Rawls called "the basic structure of society" (1999, 6–7) and (b) has had recently attached to it in the United States critical *auxiliary* benefits (such as health coverage) that should be available independently but are currently economically

Criticism and Compassion: The Ethics and Politics of Claudia Card.
Edited by Robin S. Dillon and Armen T. Marsoobian.
Chapters and book compilation © 2018 Metaphilosophy LLC and John Wiley & Sons Ltd.

beyond the reach of many except through marriage.[1] We face a kind of situation that Rawls used to say (in class lectures) presents the most difficult
questions of moral philosophy, namely, how to determine what to do when
every option confronting us is riddled with injustice, thanks to prior wrongful deeds of others. In such situations the objective, as he saw it, should be
to try to identify the path of least injustice. I try to be guided by that objective in what follows.

Briefly, here are some of the injustices. First, consider injustices in the
option of *advocating* legal regulation of marriage for same-sex partners.
Auxiliary benefits currently attached to marriage can make the difference
between having a place to live and being rendered homeless or, in some
cases, between life and death. This should not be so. Marriage should not
make this kind of difference to the satisfaction of basic needs. Yet currently
in the United States it does. Lack of access to adequate health coverage is
suffered not only by many lesbian and gay partners (and dependants) who
are not members of the professions but by the poor in general who for
whatever reason are not married. This is not a problem in countries with
universal health care. But the United States does not appear headed in that
direction soon. Thus legal regulation of same-sex marriage in the United
States at present supports a profoundly unjust distribution of benefits.

But it is important to appreciate also that even these benefits are insufficient to enable an abused spouse to exit a marriage and protect children,
if need be, before any of them suffers intolerable harm. Abusive marriages
easily become lethal. A major problem with marriage in many jurisdictions
is its burden-of-proof requirement that to terminate it when one spouse
does not consent, the other must justify before the law the request for
a divorce. Abused partners are commonly unable to produce convincing
objective evidence of abuse, for a variety of reasons. No-fault divorce in
many states means only that spouses who *mutually agree* are no longer
guilty of the crime of collusion (as they were when my parents divorced
in 1969 in Wisconsin). Relief from that criminal charge is not sufficient,
however, to allow a spouse to terminate a marriage unilaterally without
showing grounds acceptable to the state (such as, in the state of New York,
that one's spouse has been in prison for more than three years or that one
has not lived with or slept with one's spouse in at least a year). As long as the
state retains a divorce-granting power that prevents unilateral dissolution

---

[1] Rawls lists "the monogamous family" (1999, 6) as an example of a major social institution that could be part of the basic structure of a society. In the United States, it seems fair to
say that legal marriage is part of the basic structure, given how it is written into Social Security
rules and so much else. On auxiliary benefits attached to legal marriage in the United States,
see Chauncey 2004, 71–77, Callahan 1999, and Wolfson 2004, 13–15. A good recent history
of marriage, longer than Chauncey's, is Cott 2000. A good recent anthology of short essays
is Shanley 2004. Graff 2004 provides a moral practically oriented treatment.

at will—historically, a major distinction between marriages and less formal unions—marriage is a trap for abused partners and their children. The abusive spouse is commonly unwilling to let go and is able to conceal abuse from third parties, often with forced collusion of the abused spouse. Linda Marciano, popularly known as Linda Lovelace, forced to star in the film *Deep Throat*, was compelled by her abuser to marry him so she could not be made to testify against him in court (Lovelace and Grady 1983). This is an oppressive trap.

Next, consider the injustices of *refusing* to support the legal recognition of marriage for same-sex partners. This option condones the arbitrary denial to lesbians and gays and their dependants of benefits made available to heterosexual couples that can make the difference between major hardship and a decent life, or at the extreme, between life and death. Further, the right to marry is currently enshrined in the Universal Declaration of Human Rights (1948) in language that does not specify the genders of the partners. Denial of that right to any group of law-abiding rational adults is dangerous in that it may lead to denying lesbians and gays other human rights. Further, it makes lesbian and gay partners socially less visible, thereby facilitating the survival of oppressive stereotypes, which can have their own lethal consequences.

Thus, whether one supports extending legal regulation of marriage to same-sex partners or refuses to support its legal regulation at all, at the present time, people's lives are at stake. People will die, either way. They will be killed by a spouse, or they will not receive health care needed for survival. These worst-case scenarios are common enough to take seriously. Consequences will often be less dire but still intolerable. It need not be the same people who face these alternatives. But, interestingly, it *can* be. Behind a Rawlsian "veil of ignorance," which screens out knowledge of particular facts that would enable one to distinguish oneself from others, one should take seriously the possibility of being in either position: that of a dangerously abused spouse or that of an unemployed (or underemployed) and seriously ill or injured dependant without access to decent health coverage.

Behind that veil of ignorance, one is to choose principles on the assumption that once the principles are chosen and the veil removed, people will generally comply with the requirements of institutions in the basic structure of society, which, in turn, will, for the most part, satisfy those principles. This is why Rawls calls "justice as fairness" a "strict compliance" theory and an "ideal theory" (1999, 7–8, 215–16, 308–9). *A Theory of Justice* (Rawls 1999) does not address the reasoning of parties behind the veil for choosing principles to rectify widespread deep injustices. When we do confront such injustices, the path of sanity should at least include the long-range objective of creating a better set of options. But that aim leaves open the question of what our short-range objective should be, what to do here and now. The next two sections explore further the dilemma of what to do now and conclude that we should take marriage off our political agenda for the next few years, maybe longer, and put our energies, beginning now, into improving our options. But I begin with the ideal, which appears unattainable in the near future.

The Ideal: Deregulate, Not Further Regulate

My ideal regarding marriage is not that the law regulating it become perfectly just, which I think is not possible. My ideal is that the law not define or in any other way regulate durable intimate unions between freely consenting adults. According to George Chauncey's retelling of the story of the evolution of marriage-as-we-know-it in his highly informative (and delightfully readable) short book *Why Marriage?* the legal regulation of marriage in Europe is a relatively recent matter of the past few centuries (Chauncey 2004, 77–86). For a long time, state and church battled over who was to be the regulator. Before that, and for most of human history, marriage was unregulated by either. It was left to individuals to work out among themselves. Such anarchy in the absence of legal regulation of much else was hardly a rosy situation. Spouses commonly did not choose each other. Women had little protection against being stolen to become brides, even if already married.[2] Many women were more economically dependent on men than they need be today. State regulation of marriage could offer them and their children some protection against being left destitute. The reality, however, was that many were (and continue to be) left destitute anyway. In the context of a legal system that offers some protection against kidnap and coercion and enables women to become relatively independent of families economically, motives to form durable intimate unions do not translate as readily into motives to turn those unions into legal contracts. What motivate many to turn their relationships into legal marriages are a variety of penalties, including social stigma, attached to not doing so in a context in which (legal) marriage has become part of the basic structure of society.

My ideal is for legally regulated marriage to be no longer part of that basic structure, much as legitimate birth is no longer part of it. In the United States, birth certificates of children born to women who are not married are no longer stamped "illegitimate." They are not, however, stamped "legitimate" instead. There is today rightly no stamp at all regarding legitimacy on birth certificates. Like all analogies, the analogy with birth certificates is imperfect. A case-by-case stamp of illegitimacy is not explicitly placed upon same-sex relationships, although the judgment is implicitly there, because the state does officially *legitimate* heterosexual ones case

---

[2] See, for example, the story of the theft of the mother of Genghis Khan in Weatherford 2004.

by case with first a license and then a certificate for all who marry. These procedures of licensing and certification should ideally go the way of the stamp of illegitimacy on birth certificates. (I set aside the interesting question of whether births should be certified at all.) In short, marital status, like legitimacy of birth, would ideally disappear as a legal status.

The slogan "every child is a legitimate child" really means only that no child is *il*legitimate. Likewise, if the state ceased to sanction marriages, it would not follow that all kinds of intimate unions, no matter how bizarre, would suddenly be legitimate, as slippery slope arguers fear. Rather, the concept of legitimacy would cease to apply. Some such relationships might be deplorable, for a variety of moral reasons. But any that violated laws against assault, fraud, kidnap, and so on could and should be dealt with under existing laws addressing those crimes. Presumably, "doing it with dogs" could be dealt with under laws pertaining to cruelty to animals.

To those who regard marriage romantically as signifying to the world at large the eternal commitment of two people in love, I say, "Contemplate equally seriously the nightmare of legal divorce." A dash of realism needed in the debate over same-sex marriage might be to think of it as the gay divorce issue, for part of the baggage of marriage is the liability to being divorced and the requirement of getting a divorce in order to signify similarly one's eternal commitment to a new partner. "Divorced," like "married," is a matter of public record, available to anyone interested enough to inquire, whereas there is no public record of one's extra-legal intimate relationships. And roughly half of all marriages do end in divorce.

Contemplate the prospect having to sue for divorce because your spouse does not agree to it (even if she or he is not generally abusive). Contemplate the likely legal battles over property, custody, and visitation rights that often underlie a spouse's unwillingness to agree. Marriage and divorce can be such nightmares that I have difficulty wrapping my mind around the evident fact that so many same-sex couples in the United States have demonstrated their desire to marry by participating in public ceremonies. (It would be interesting to know how many are not survivors of a contested legal divorce.) The influence of dire economic circumstances I do understand. But the romanticism of much of the rhetoric of marriage, when what is at issue is a *legal* status, is misplaced. The really "good marriages" I know are good in spite of the law, not because of it. For every story of those who live happily together for twenty-five years or more, it is possible to produce other stories of those irreversibly injured or murdered by a spouse, or driven to kill in self-defense.

Were the law to restrict access to marriage, it would make better sense to do so on the basis of an applicant's past abuses (domestic violence, for example, or the unrectified abuse of a prior partner's credit cards) or on the basis of clear evidence that the applicant lacks the willingness to respect basic rights (a record of criminal violence, for example) than to do so on the basis of the gender of one's proposed partner, which tells us nothing about that person's fitness to be granted legally enforceable intimate access to other human beings. Yet proponents of marriage for same-sex partners fondly cite the Supreme Court decision (*Turner v. Safley* 1987) that declared *unconstitutional* the "arbitrary exclusion" of prisoners from marrying, as though that were a progressive move (Wolfson 2004, 8–9). Perhaps it is for felons whose crimes were nonviolent. I do not know which exclusions the law counts as arbitrary. But I know of no jurisdiction that prohibits felons convicted of violent crimes, even domestic abusers, when *not* in prison, from remarrying as often as they like, provided they are not already married, are free of STDs, and so on. Proponents of marriage for same-sex partners might do better not to suggest that their case is analogous to that of felons.

My infamous potboiler, "Against Marriage and Motherhood" (Card 1996), which argued against the political institutions of marriage and motherhood, urged lesbians and gays not to put energy into the battle for same-sex marriage, not to join heterosexuals in discriminating against those who are not married and in trapping abused partners in lethal relationships. I hinted that there might be a certain propriety, however, in heterosexuals, who benefit from the discrimination, putting *their* energies into the issue. Inheritance laws that specify what relationships one must bear to the deceased to inherit when there is no will (as is often the case with those who die young) and Social Security laws that specify what relationship one must bear to the deceased to qualify for death benefits are unjust to same-sex couples but can be profitable to heterosexual kin. It seems especially appropriate for heterosexuals who appreciate these injustices to work for their removal, to spend their ill-gotten gains in battles to undo the injustice.

But choosing to do this by fighting to gain legal regulation of marriage for same-sex partners leaves unaddressed equally serious injustices to people who choose not to marry but also have no affordable access to such things as health coverage or no way to leave Social Security death benefits to the party of their choice. It takes as givens practices that deserve to be challenged and undone. A more inclusive strategy would work to separate from marriage the auxiliary benefits that ideally the state would provide everyone but that are currently economically accessible to many only through employers and at the discretion of insurance companies, who are given free rein by the state to specify whatever relationship they like that one must bear to an employee in order to qualify. It is a virtue of Chauncey's treatment (2004) of this subject that he makes clear these injustices and alternative ways to remove them. Ideally, we should work for equity in inheritance laws, Social Security, and the like. At least, it has to be admitted that appealing to health coverage and so on is a tainted argument for legal recognition of marriage for same-sex partners. Marriage should not have to be anyone's path to those benefits.

Yet it would not be an *altogether* bad thing if the state were to recognize same-sex marriages. Even for gays and lesbians who never married, just possessing the right in a society in which marriage is part of the basic structure of society would be laden with positive meaning, apart from auxiliary advantages and disadvantages of marriage. It would be more difficult for others to maintain that there is anything morally wrong with or abnormal about same-sex intimacy or to deny lesbians and gays other rights. It would be more difficult to maintain that lesbians and gays cannot be trusted to occupy positions of caretaking of the vulnerable, such as children or the elderly. Refusing to support legal recognition of same-sex marriage leaves these issues to be addressed in other ways. That is a cost, for they surely do have to be addressed.

A point of clarification. The denial of certain auxiliary benefits such as health insurance for dependants to same-sex partners is not only an *injustice*, in that it is an arbitrary (unjustified) inequality. It is also an *evil*, insofar as a reasonably foreseeable consequence is intolerable harm to some of those dependants. Thus it is both unjust and evil for insurance companies to deny coverage to dependants of gays and lesbians. I rely here on a distinction between evils and other wrongs, which I develop and defend elsewhere (Card 2002). In broad outline, evils are culpable wrongs that foreseeably produce intolerable harms. Wrongs are not evils when they produce less serious harms, if they are harmful at all (in any sense of *harm* definable independently of *wrong*). Many wrongs (many inequities, for example) are not actually harmful, or not very.[3] Petty theft is wrong, unjust, but not an evil. Murder and torture are evils.

The denial to same-sex couples of the right to marry is an injustice. But, unlike the denial of health coverage to dependants, it is not an evil, as long as unmarried couples can cohabit and be left in peace to establish and live out their durable intimate relationships. That point may not be obvious, however. For it looks as though once the auxiliary benefits such as health coverage for dependants are attached to marriage, denying marriage to lesbians and gays produces the reasonably foreseeable intolerable harm of cutting their dependants off from those benefits. Evils, as I have defined them, have two basic components: culpable wrongdoing and intolerable harm, linked by reasonable foreseeability and a causal relationship. But every event has multiple causes. The morally relevant causal relationship is not always evident, and it may not be evident in this case. Which of the many causes of harm to dependants who lack health coverage is responsible for that harm? Which of them "produces" it, in the morally relevant sense?

The denial of access to marriage does have the consequence of cutting many dependants off from health insurance. But marriage law is simply the means used to deny such benefits to the dependants of lesbians and

---

[3] For extended argument in support of this contrast between evils and other wrongs, see Card 2002, 96–117.

gays. The morally critical causal nexus is between denying the benefits and the harm, rather than between denying access to marriage (to which such benefits have been attached in some places, such as the United States) and the harm, for the following reasons.

First, the benefits are not essential to marriage; they can be detached from it and made more generally available. A state need not give insurance companies or employers the right to restrict health coverage to the dependants of only its married employees, nor need the state depend on private insurance companies or employers to provide health coverage.

Second, even if gays and lesbians could marry and thereby access those benefits, dependants of those who choose not to marry would still be exposed to the intolerable harms that flow from being cut off from such benefits. It could be justifiable for a state to allow such benefits to be attached (via employers and insurance companies) to marital status at such a cost only if marriage were a rational choice for anyone with dependants. But not only is marriage not an option for everyone, it is not a rational choice for everyone for whom it is an option, not even everyone with dependants. It is wrong for the state to allow those benefits to be so attached to a status that is not available to everyone and that not everyone to whom it is available could rationally choose. Responsibility for the harm, therefore, lies in the denial of the benefits, rather than in the denial of the right to marry.

Although the denial of marriage to same-sex partners is not an evil, legal marriage itself is an evil, to the extent that it facilitates the infliction and cover-up of reasonably foreseeable intolerable harm to those unlucky enough to find themselves trapped with violently abusive spouses.[4] What makes marriage an evil when it is not merely an injustice is that it hinders an abused spouse from exiting an abusive relationship before intolerable harm is done. An evil institution need not have as its purpose the infliction of intolerable harm. It is sufficient that intolerable harm be reasonably foreseeable, that there be no realistic way to prevent that harm short of abolishing the institution, and that there be people in a position to abolish the institution. American slavery did not have as its purpose to make slaves suffer cruelly and die young. Yet those harms were reasonably foreseeable, and there was no adequate way to protect slaves against them. But there were people who could have outlawed slavery. That is enough to make the institution evil. Marriage without unilateral divorce is in a similar position. There is no way to enforce laws against domestic cruelty without intolerable intrusion into the lives of spouses. The possibility of cruelty, unlike insurance benefits, is not detachable from the institution of marriage. The best one can do in an abusive marriage is divorce, when doing so is an option. Yet, unilateral divorce is not always an option, and even divorce may be insufficient when there are children.

---

[4] For more extended discussion of the evil of terrorism in the home, see Card 2002, 139–65.

The "foreverness," or at least indefiniteness, of the marriage commitment and the presumption, backed by the power of the state, that the *burden of justification* lies on whoever would dissolve the union as long as one spouse wishes to keep it, have been central, historically, to distinguishing marriage from other intimate unions. Unilateral divorce, now available in some states, is a progressive move, bringing marriage closer to other civil unions. If there are no children, unilateral divorce may be sufficient to extricate an abused spouse from a legally binding relationship that gives the abuser intimate access. If there are children, matters are less simple. Laws governing guardianship are at present highly interwoven with marriage law. The marriage may be over, but there may still be a relationship giving an abuser a dangerous legal right of access that would never have existed without a history of marriage. If it is not necessary to establish abuse to get the divorce, it may still be necessary to establish abuse to prevent an abuser who is a legal guardian from retaining a legal right of access to the children, and through the children, often enough in effect, access to oneself also if one remains their guardian. It is still in many cases impossible or nearly so to establish with objective evidence the facts of severe abuse (whether to oneself, the children, or both) that might lead a judge to prohibit an abuser from further contact.

But this is old ground. I have not seen reason to change my mind on marital cruelty issues. People who disagree tend to do so on empirical grounds, not philosophical ones. They tend to believe, on the basis of personal observation and despite voluminous evidence to the contrary, that domestic violence is not a great problem. Or, that it is not that difficult to prove. Or, that it is not so difficult to get out of an abusive relationship. Or, that marriage does not add significant obstacles to doing so. Or, that women who choose not to leave do so voluntarily.

My position has been not only that ideally the legal regulation of marriage would disappear but that, since that disappearance seems politically unlikely in the foreseeable future, we should at least not support legal marriage for anyone, gay or straight. Widespread worsening of the political scene during and since the 2004 U.S. presidential campaign may call for some modification in, or qualification or clarification of, that stance.

The Reality: A Set of Undesirable Options

There are two plausible directions that modification of my prior position might take. One is to support a temporary battle for equality in the legal regulation of partnerships, whether same-sex or heterosex, as part of a general battle against arbitrary discrimination, but with the long-range objective of eventually abolishing all state regulation of intimate unions. The other direction is to try to get the marriage issue taken off the political agenda (whether one favors extending marriage or abolishing it) and turn our energies now to fighting evils that we may have a greater opportunity to address constructively, including the evil of people being left without health care in the wealthiest nation of the world, in the hope that when it becomes feasible to put marriage back on the agenda, our options will have improved. If we made progress with the issue of political torture by governments, for example, which is probably as widely condemned as it is practiced, we might find it easier to get constructive attention to the fact that marriage facilitates the private torture of women. Of these directions, I favor the second, taking marriage off the agenda for a while and turning our energies to other battles.

In today's political climate, religious fundamentalism has become a force of significance. Appealing to the fundamentalist vote, political conservatives recently exploited the marriage issue to divert public attention from such widely recognized evils as political torture by governments and basic health issues, including environmental degradation. The marriage issue has been used to reentrench homophobia, gain the support of an electorate for an overall political agenda that many might otherwise not have supported, and divert not only liberals but almost everyone from attending to such matters as the constitution of the Supreme Court, the immorality of U.S. failure to support the World Court, and other issues of global justice and U.S. foreign policy. For lesbians and gays, a result has been to make official in even more jurisdictions than before, and to reentrench, our status as second-class citizens.

There are two currently troubling issues. First, the marriage issue has been used by the political Right to focus voters' attention away from volatile issues that are consequential for everyone, married or not, not just for lesbians and gays. Second, the marriage issue has backfired with truly frightening consequences to lesbians and gays in the United States. We are worse off now than before, and the future appears grimmer.

To begin with the second issue, the specter of gay marriage mobilized social conservatives to redefine marriage to explicitly exclude same-sex partners, and there is now the possibility of a Constitutional amendment to the same effect. Such initiatives probably would not have been taken even by conservatives had lesbians and gays not made marriage a public issue. Publicly embracing marriage in mass ceremonies and standing in long lines for marriage licenses were all that was needed to mobilize the anti-gay vote, since such marriages, suddenly more than a theoretical possibility, make lesbian and gay life more visible and make it harder for fundamentalists to teach children that we are abnormal or immoral.

Given my views on marriage, some might wonder why I would not regard the conservative vote as a step forward. Marriages between same-sex partners are now officially and explicitly impossible in at least eleven states, since the November elections. Does that not mean less likelihood, at least for gays and lesbians, of being trapped in abusive relationships in those states?

Probably so. But excluding us is hardly a step toward the abolition of marriage. It is a step in the reverse direction, reentrenching marriage in its traditional forms. Heterosexual victims of domestic violence continue to perish. Any gain for abused lesbian or gay partners may be outweighed by the exclusion's larger implications regarding lesbian and gay citizenship. Arbitrary denials of the right to marry are nothing for marriage resisters to celebrate, because those denials contribute to defining people who are arbitrarily excluded as second-class citizens.

The Universal Declaration of Human Rights (1948; Art. 16, sec. 1), states: "Men and women of full age, without any limitation due to race, nationality, or religion, have the right to marry and to found a family. They are entitled to equal rights as to marriage, during marriage, and at its disso-lution."[5] Although the Declaration does not explicitly mention the genders of partners, its statement is perfectly compatible with the presumption ... that those genders might be the same. The wording "men and women have the right to marry" is utterly ambiguous between that reading and one that assumes heterosexual partners. Insofar as the gender-neutral reading is plausible, the denial of marriage to same-sex partners is a denial of human rights. If it is a human right from which gays and lesbians are excluded, we should contemplate seriously the possibility that we might also be denied other human rights. For the implication of that exclusion is that we are not fully human.

How can one not recall the Nuremberg Laws of 1935, which banned marriages between German citizens and anyone not a German citizen and went on to strip German Jews of their citizenship (Gutman 1990, 1076–77)? The Nuremberg Laws did not prohibit marriages among Jews, and the recent definitions of marriage do not, of course, prohibit gays and lesbians from entering into heterosexual marriages. But the law does not tell anyone else, within certain degrees of kinship, of a certain age, not already mar-ried to someone else, and free of STDs, whom they can or cannot marry. To that extent, the new definitions of marriage are analogous to the Nurem-berg Laws that prohibited intermarriages. Nuremberg went further. It was a major step toward the Final Solution in destroying the legal personhood of Jews. Insofar as the restriction of marriage to heterosexual unions is an injury to the legal personhood of lesbians and gays, it is to be deplored independently of any value or disvalue that one may attach to marriage.

Must I now reverse my position on whether lesbians and gays should fight for marriage? Not necessarily. But there are serious costs in refusing to fight for same-sex marriage rights. Hence the attractiveness of the com-promise of fighting for marriage now but with the long-range objective of eliminating the evils mentioned above. When explicit exclusions are in place regarding participation in unjust institutions that help define

---

[5] See, also, Roosevelt (n.d.).

the basic structure of society, there is a danger of contagion, that the exclusions will not be confined to just those practices but will spread to others, including practices that are in other respects just and desirable, such as being licensed to be a member of various professions. Supporting an evil practice by working to remove the arbitrary exclusion of lesbians and gays from it, then, needs to be weighed against risking the evil of a proliferation of exclusions if that one is not removed, which would further corrode the legal personhood of lesbians and gays.

Explicit arbitrary exclusions of lesbians and gays are dangerous, as others have long noted, for the same kinds of reasons that miscegenation laws were dangerous. Miscegenation laws explicitly banned interracial marriages in many states until the Supreme Court declared them unconstitutional (*Loving v. Virginia* 1967). They were part of a larger pattern of discrimination that socially disfigured African Americans, making it easier to discriminate against them in other areas. It took action by the highest court in the land to end those laws. Supreme Court support for gays and lesbians in any decade soon appears dismal.

Many critics have noted apparent analogies between marriage for same-sex partners and interracial marriage. Yet denial of marriage to same-sex partners is not quite analogous to miscegenation laws. Miscegenation was criminal. The case that led to the Supreme Court decision was preceded by an actual arrest and criminal charges against an interracial couple from Virginia who went to another state to marry and then returned home (Wolfson 2004, 69–70). At present, lesbian or gay partners in the United States who marry (going to Canada, for example) are not vulnerable to criminal charges for having done so when they return home. But that could change.

When racially mixed marriages are not criminal but are subject to severe social penalties, existing laws against harassment and other crimes can be used to combat the discrimination. It is not necessary, in that case, to agitate for a new definition of marriage that explicitly recognizes interracial unions. But when anti-miscegenation laws exist, it becomes arguably imperative to fight for their removal, as long as marriage remains a basic social institution. Likewise, it can be argued, it becomes imperative to fight laws that explicitly prohibit same-sex marriage, or, what is for all practical purposes the same, states that invalidate such licenses or certificates, or situations in which no one with legal authority to do so will issue the needed licenses or certificates.

The Supreme Court did not stop at finding unconstitutional the *criminalization* of interracial marriage. It found unconstitutional the *exclusion* of interracial partners from marrying, which had been done by the expedient of making such marriages criminal. It was not that the law explicitly defined marriage as the union of two persons of the same race. Interracial partners could and did marry, when they found someone willing to issue the license and someone to perform the relevant ceremony. They just risked being charged with a crime for having done so. It was something like abortion before *Roe v. Wade*. You could do it, if you could find someone willing to perform the procedure. But that person risked being charged with a crime. The situation with lesbians and gays is different. It does not matter who we find willing to perform the ceremony. The result in most of the United States does not count as marriage. Short of abolishing marriage, there is no way to remove that exclusion without opening lesbian and gay intimate unions to legal regulation.

Yet a worry is that agitating for marriage in the current political climate may move religious fundamentalists to take advantage of their newfound power to go further and implement more exclusions of lesbians and gays from the basic structure of society. Consider who will be appointing the next several Supreme Court justices.

It might be replied that, as feminists have learned about responding to rape, you do not necessarily get hurt worse for fighting back. *Au contraire,* fighting back may be your only hope of *not* getting raped. Those who discover they can get away with doing as they please are more likely to do it than those who meet with resistance. Consider how long it might have taken to abolish slavery or end segregation had people not been willing to endure things getting worse before they got better. But, of course, the wisdom of your methods of resistance depends on whether you are confronting multiple or armed rapists or someone alone and unarmed. Religious fundamentalists confronting lesbians and gays today are like multiple and armed rapists. Here, there is something to be said for lying low, being realistic about where one can effectively channel one's energies.

Do I blame lesbians and gays who helped to make gay marriage a public political issue? One could as easily blame me for having urged lesbians and gays not to fight for marriage as feeding right into the conservative agenda. The best strategy, from hindsight, might have been to let the issue alone. The relatively liberal regime of President William Jefferson Clinton in the 1990s gave uptake to lesbian and gay demands, fostering hope that discriminatory social practices might change. As it turned out, "don't ask, don't tell" made things worse in the military than they were before, and improvement does not appear to be on the horizon.

But, it may be objected, if you find a practice unjust, should you not protest it? That depends. Not necessarily. The consequences of doing so are not irrelevant to the wisdom of doing so, and it is important not to contribute, if possible, to making the overall situation worse for decades to come. You can in many ways resist *supporting* a practice without protesting it publicly, even if others misread your silence as support. There are relatively quiet ways to refuse support: refuse to marry, to attend weddings or congratulate newlyweds, to give wedding gifts, and so on, and patiently explain why when people ask out of sincere interest. If you teach, put the topic on the syllabus to raise consciousness regarding the philosophical issues. If you are already married, refuse, if you can afford to, to enjoy benefits wrongfully denied others, as John Stuart Mill refused to exercise rights the law unjustly gave him upon marrying Harriet Taylor.

If we were being shot for our sexual orientations, then, of course, we should protest publicly. We should always protest gay-bashing and other hate crimes. Perhaps likewise we should continue to protest against marriage in general, for the sake of those to whom it is fatal. But when we are arbitrarily denied the benefits of an already highly questionable (if not downright evil) institution, such as marriage, it may be better to focus our energies on basic issues that are more likely to gain enough support to make a difference, such as universal health coverage, preserving Social Security and making it more just, making our foreign policy more humane, fostering good relations with other nations, addressing world poverty and disease, and so on. Progress in these areas may or may not improve our social image as lesbians and gays. But it would benefit us as human beings, as well as benefiting countless others.

I take seriously the consequences of what we may do, because I am not a stoic. I think so-called externals matter and that they are not totally beyond our control. But neither am I a utilitarian: consequences are not everything. There is, further, a well-known problem with appeals to consequences in politics. Political consequences are so very difficult to predict with any reasonable degree of accuracy when power can shift as it can in a democracy, when myriads of individual choices, each somewhat unpredictable, determine outcomes. Thus, although it is fairly clear that marriage will not disappear in the foreseeable future, it is not clear, empirically, whether there is a greater likelihood of success in time to save lives in the project of removing the arbitrary exclusion from marriage of same-sex partners than there is of success in the projects of universal health coverage, making Social Security more just, making our foreign policy more humane, living in more environmentally sustainable ways, fostering good relations with other nations, and so on.

Progress on any of these projects looks grim. But progress on any or all of the latter issues would be an unambiguous move in the direction of justice. Removing the marriage exclusion, although it might save lives, would not be such an unambiguous move. For that reason, I conclude that it is probably better to put marriage on the back burner, at least for the next few years (if not longer). When we take it off at some propitious future moment, if efforts regarding universal health care and Social Security have meanwhile paid off, the option of phasing out marriage altogether (with appropriate grandparent clauses) may be both more feasible and more attractive. At any rate, we should have an improved set of options.

Acknowledgments

Thanks to Cheshire Calhoun, Victoria Davion, Holly Kantin, Francis Schrag, Russ Shafer-Landau, and audiences at the American Philosophical Association Eastern Division meetings (2004) and the University of Wisconsin Law School (2005) for helpful comments and questions.

References

Callahan, Joan. 1999. "Speech That Harms: The Case of Lesbian Families." In *On Feminist Ethics and Politics*, ed. Card.

Card, Claudia. 1996. "Against Marriage and Motherhood." *Hypatia* 11 (3): 1–23.

———. ed. 1999. *On Feminist Ethics and Politics*. Lawrence: University Press of Kansas.

———. 2002. *The Atrocity Paradigm: A Theory of Evil*. New York: Oxford University Press.

Chauncey, Jr., George. 2004. *Why Marriage? The History Shaping Today's Debate over Gay Equality*. New York: Basic Books.

Cott, Nancy F 2000. *Public Vows: A History of Marriage and the Nation*. Cambridge, Mass.: Harvard University Press.

Graff, E. J. 2004. *What Is Marriage For?* Boston: Beacon.

Gutman, Israel, ed. 1990. *Encyclopedia of the Holocaust*. New York: Macmillan.

Lovelace, Linda, with Mike Grady. 1983. *Ordeal*. New York: Bell.

Loving v. Virginia. 1967. 388 U.S. I.

Rawls, John. 1999. *A Theory of Justice*. Rev. ed. Cambridge, Mass.: Harvard University Press.

Roosevelt, Eleanor, et al. n.d. *Universal Declaration of Human Rights* in English, Spanish, French, Chinese, Russian, and Arabic. Bedford, Mass: Applewood Books.

Shanley, Mary Lyndon, ed. 2004. *Just Marriage*. New York: Oxford University Press.

Turner v. Safley. 1978. 482 U.S. 78.

Universal Declaration of Human Rights. 1948. http://www.un.org/Overview/rights.html (accessed March 16, 2005).

Weatherford, J. McIver. 2004. *Genghis Kahn and the Making of the Modern World*. New York: Crown.

Wolfson, Evan. 2004. *Why Marriage Matters: America, Equality, and Gay People's Right to Marry*. New York: Simon and Schuster.

CHAPTER 14

CHALLENGES OF GLOBAL AND LOCAL MISOGYNY

CLAUDIA CARD

Two main ideas motivate the Law of Peoples. One is that the great evils of human history—unjust war and oppression, religious persecution and the denial of liberty of conscience, starvation and poverty, not to mention genocide and mass murder— follow from political injustice, with its own cruelties and callousness. The other main idea … is that once the gravest forms of political injustice are eliminated by following just (or at least decent) social policies and establishing just (or at least decent) basic institutions, these great evils will eventually disappear.
John Rawls, The Law of Peoples, 6–7

John Rawls's hypothesis that grave political injustices underlie the great social evils motivated his life's work, not just his last book. Evils discussed throughout his work include the atrocities of slavery and the Inquisition. Rawls's hypothesis implies that the worst evils that target women and girls will disappear once the gravest political injustices are gone. This idea is hard to assess. Misogynous evils are often rooted in failures of cooperation, enforcement, and perception, rather than in a political constitution, legislation, or foreign policy. Some sexism stems from background cultures not obviously incompatible with (liberal) just institutions. But the worst *evils* are not immune to institutional forces. Often women are left to defend themselves without organized help, not only within societies but in global traffic and in wars. That could change.

Perhaps Rawls was right that *if* the worst political injustices *were* eliminated, the great evils that have plagued humanity would disappear. Yet those worst injustices may not be eliminable unless people are willing to fight back using measures that include force and violence and are willing to do so in nonstate organizations when states fail them, as peoples go to war against unjust aggressors after less drastic measures have failed. If such nonstate organizations were understood to value reciprocity and to be

Criticism and Compassion: The Ethics and Politics of Claudia Card.
Edited by Robin S. Dillon and Armen T. Marsoobian.
Chapters and book compilation © 2018 Metaphilosophy LLC and John Wiley & Sons Ltd.

capable of governing themselves by Rawlsian scruples, that thought might be less disturbing than it is otherwise apt to be.

If Rawls's ideas are to be a helpful resource for thinking about women's self-defense and mutual defense, that will probably not be through straight-forward applications of his own projects. His projects were, first, what justice means in the basic structure of a society (*A Theory of Justice* and *Political Liberalism*), and second, what justice means in the foreign policy of a reasonably liberal well-ordered society (*The Law of Peoples*). Justice in foreign policy he divided into "ideal theory" for relations with other well-ordered peoples (governed by shared public conceptions of justice) and "nonideal theory" for relations with states not well-ordered. In nonideal theory we find his principles for war against outlaw states, which "refuse to comply with a reasonable Law of Peoples" (*LP*, 5). Rawls saw need for nonideal theory also within society but never developed that project. Perhaps the nonideal part of his Law of Peoples can be a resource for thinking about responding to evils when the subject is not state-centered, neither a society's basic structure nor its foreign policy. It is plausible that defense against great evils other than those of aggressive states should be governed by analogues of scruples that Rawlsian well-ordered societies observe in defending themselves against outlaw states.

This essay explores those hypotheses in relation to women's self-defense and mutual defense against evils of misogyny. It extrapolates and adapts to this case values, concepts, and methods from Rawls's life's work, especially his writing on war.

Global and Local Misogyny

Despite its exemplary Constitution, the United States, like most societies, has laws, practices, customs, and attitudes that create environments hostile to women's and girls' development and thriving. In his later work Rawls explicitly addresses the family as a source of female oppression (*CP*, 587, 595–601). In response to protest by Susan Moller Okin (1989) that making parties in the Original Position heads of families left families internally opaque to claims of justice, Rawls changed that aspect of his theory. He also ventured the hypotheses that were women treated equally in the family, population growth would cease to be a major issue and that such a change would have a positive impact on unlawful immigration and the evils attendant upon current policies for dealing with it (*LP*, 9).

Special attention to the family by Rawls and a majority of his feminist critics and defenders is easily justified, as Okin argued, in terms of the early formative impact of families on the child's development of a sense of justice. Yet families are not a centerpiece of my concern. Family is not the stage for many of the worst forms of misogyny. Many victims of the worst misogyny are not particularly attached to men. These victims include women who do not rear children, women with careers (not necessarily as caregivers) and economic independence, and women who are intimate with women. In "Renaissance" Europe, women not attached to men—"dispensable" women, economically independent midwives and healers—were the most vulnerable to being burnt as witches (Daly 1978, 178–222). In India, widows were burnt. Today, many women who resist traditional expectations regarding marriage are vulnerable to "honor killings." Globally, it is very young women who are sold and enslaved for sexual service.[1]

Families are often sexist without being misogynous. "Misogyny" (literally, "woman-hating") is the term feminists apply to the most deeply hostile environments of and attitudes toward women and girls and to the cruelest wrongs to them/us, regardless of whether perpetrators harbor feelings of hatred. Sexism includes misogyny but encompasses a spectrum of bad attitudes and behaviors, including male arrogance, male-centeredness (not only in men), sex discrimination, and female subordination. Not all sexism is culpable. Misogyny tends to be highly culpable and grossly oppressive.

By "misogyny," I have in mind evils perpetrated with aggressive (often armed) use of force and violence against women: rape and domestic battering, kidnap for sexual slavery, forced prostitution, "honor killing," stoning, simulated suicide by burning, widow burning, and horrors without special names, such as throwing acid in a woman's face to disfigure her. Most global are the overlapping evils of rape (including forced prostitution) and domestic battering. More local are the systematic, irreversible, and disabling mutilation of girls (as in clitoridectomy and infibulation), coerced sati (widow burning, not altogether of the past), and "honor killing."

Evils

My work on evil has been motivated by concerns to identify evils and avoid the perpetration of further evils in responding to them. On what I call "the atrocity paradigm," evils are reasonably foreseeable intolerable harms produced by inexcusable wrongs (Card 2002, 3–26; 2010, 3–35). There is no need for malicious motives, such as sadism or spite. A practice is evil when there is morally no excuse for it and acting in accord with it foreseeably does intolerable harm.

Not all injustices are evils, only those that are inexcusable and do intolerable harm. What makes harms intolerable is not altogether subjective. A

---

[1] "An estimated *2.5 million people* are in forced labour (including sexual exploitation) at any given time as a result of trafficking"; "The majority of trafficking victims are *between 18 and 24 years* of age"; "43% of victims are used for *forced commercial sexual exploitation*, of whom 98 per cent are women and girls" (emphases in the original). For these and more statistics on human trafficking and the proportions of victims who are women and girls, see UN GIFT (Global Initiative to Fight Global Trafficking), at http://www.unglobalcompact. org/docs/issues_doc/labour/Forced_labour/HUMAN_TRAFFICKING_-_THE_ FACTS_-_final.pdf (accessed May 2013).

reasonable conception of intolerable harm is that it is a significant deprivation of basics ordinarily required for a life (or a death) to be decent for the
person whose life (or death) it is. Such basics include nontoxic air, water,
and food; sleep; the ability to move one's limbs; the ability to make choices
and act on some of them; freedom from severe and unremitting pain and
from debilitating humiliation; affective bonds with others; a sense of one's
human worth. Although not exhaustive, that list is enough to show that
intolerable harm does not totally depend on individual preferences. Intolerable harm interferes with one's ability to function decently as a human
being.

A wrong can be inexcusable in two ways, which I call "metaphysical"
and "moral." There is metaphysically no excuse when there was no diminished capacity for choice in the wrongdoer (no insanity or other relevant
disability, for example). There is morally no excuse when no significant
morally good reasons provide a partial defense. When there is some moral
excuse, there are significant reasons in favor of the deed that carry moral
weight, although not enough to justify it on the whole. Nonmoral reasons
may favor the deed. And a reason that might carry moral weight for some
deeds may carry none for others. An inexcusable deed or practice is morally
indefensible. On the atrocity paradigm, evils are inexcusable in both ways,
metaphysically and morally.

On these understandings, rape, domestic battering, and murder (as in
"honor killing," simulated suicide, and coerced sati) are generally evils,
as social practices and in individual instances. Disfiguring and disabling
women or girls can be evils as well, depending on forms, contexts, and consequences. Stoning, like burning, tortures many victims to death, and is
especially evil.[2]

Principles for Individuals

What uses of force and violence are justifiable for defense by women
against evils of misogyny? I ask "what is justifiable?" rather than "what is
just?" because, as Rawls noted in class lectures, full justice may be unre-
alizable when currently available options are shaped by past wrongful
choices. When no fully just options remain, it may be possible to reduce
the amount or seriousness of deprivations of justice, or to contain them,
prevent spreading or worsening. A best choice can be the lesser of unjust
options or the creation of options that set a course for future justice. Even
a best option can leave what Bernard Williams called "remainders," including injustices that can never be adequately redressed (1974, 179).

Uses of force and violence include matters of individual choice and matters of policy or practices involving cooperation. Rawls's theory of justice

---

[2] A detailed account of a 1986 stoning is in Sahebjam 1990.

for society's basic structure includes distinct principles for these different cases: two principles for social practices or institutions and one principle (fair play) for individuals. In *The Law of Peoples*, the distinction between justifying a practice or policy and justifying a particular choice seems not to figure, unless in the "supreme emergency exemption" if that exemption is understood as an unpunishable violation of policy (rather than a policy itself). Rawls's theorizing about the Law of Peoples remains at the level of policies and practices. His principle of fair play presupposes principles at that level. And so the question arises: how are individuals to approximate fairness in the absence of relevant social practices, institutions, or organizations for self-defense?

At the root of Rawls's idea of fair play is the idea of reciprocity. Rawls's principle of fair play, incorporating reciprocity, is borrowed from H.L.A. Hart, who described it as a "mutuality of restrictions" (1955, 185; cf. *TJ*, 96). According to that principle, it is *sufficient* for one's obligation to follow rules of a just practice that one freely accepted benefits of others having done so. This principle leaves much unspecified. It does not say what is *necessary*. It does not say there is no obligation if the practice is unjust (would that depend on how unjust?), if one lacked choice about accepting benefits (would it depend on the nature of the benefits?), or if one did not benefit although it was reasonable to expect that one would, nor does it say how many must cooperate in order to generate duties to reciprocate. It is unclear how much women would be obligated by accepting (without exactly being forced to do so) benefits of existing practices and institutions.

Consider the following true stories, on which I have written elsewhere (Card 2010, 141–45). One is that of Francine Hughes of the "burning bed," who in 1977 poured gasoline on her sleeping former husband and ignited it, killing him, after years of being battered by him despite her efforts to enlist law enforcement protection (McNulty 1980). The other is that of Inez García, who in 1974 pursued and shot with intent to kill at two men who had just raped her. Right after the rape (but before the shooting), she received a phone call from one of them warning her to leave the area and threatening her otherwise. She killed one; the other escaped (Salter 1976; Wood 1976).

What these survivors did may have been justified, but it is not likely to be described as fair or just (however deserved their actions). Neither does it seem fair or just to evaluate their choices simply by Rawls's principle of fair play, although one could apply it as follows. They had benefited somewhat by living under the rule of law, which argues in favor of letting courts, not victims, decide perpetrators' fates. But the law also failed to protect them well against rape and battery. A more appropriate standard for evaluating their responses might be whether they chose the lesser of injustices. Would it not be a worse injustice to let such evils continue unopposed by anything more than incompetent or unwilling law enforcement agencies? Clearly, there is need for creative thinking on how, using the apparatus of law, to combat such incompetence and unwillingness. That process is slow. Women are poorly represented in it. Meanwhile, many endure irreversible harm or are at risk of being killed. Of options available to them, which represent the lesser injustices?

There are also questions of justice regarding how others should respond to what the women did. States may have no choice but to charge and try them for murder. But how should women respond? One, an attorney, responded by successfully defending García.

Hughes and García were each found guilty of murder, with the verdicts overturned on appeal. Hughes (in Michigan) was declared not guilty by reason of insanity. García (in California) was found justified in self-defense. None of these verdicts may be totally satisfying. If "guilty" seems unjust to the women, "not guilty" raises the question whether individuals should be allowed to execute assailants who have not been tried and are not at that moment engaged in an assault. It is tempting to adapt John Stuart Mill's observation: "If society lets any considerable number of its members grow up mere children ... society has itself to blame for the consequences" (2003, 153). This is interesting from Mill: an argument not from utility but from fairness. Adapting his reasoning, we might argue that a society that fails to protect any considerable number of its members has itself to blame when they do what they judge needful to protect themselves. That does not imply that they act justly. It does suggest where the greater injustice might lie.

Containing Unavoidable Injustice

In war some agents confront options none of which is fully just. Rawls's *Law of Peoples* contains his only extended discussion of war. Here, he invokes the idea of the social contract by way of a "second original position" (*LP*, 32) to yield a hypothetical agreement that representatives of liberal peoples could make with each other, the content of which could be agreed to also by representatives of nonliberal decent peoples situated within their own appropriate original position. The agreement includes principles for engaging with states that are not well-ordered, including outlaw states. These, Rawls's principles of war, might be best conceived as principles for containing injustice, principles "of " justice only because motivated by concern for justice, hope for future justice, and values underlying justice.

Rawls's approach to war seems actually to respond to these questions: in a people's defense against unjust aggression, (1) what scruples best contain, reduce, or at least do not aggravate injustice? (2) what principles pave the way for outlaw states to become well-ordered so that relationships of justice with them are possible? Rawls uses the language of "just war" (*LP*, 90ff.), which sounds as though he thinks war can be just, whether in execution or in cause. Yet that terminology may persist only because of tradition. Both "just war theory" and Rawls's principles are for the conduct of war by societies that value justice. It is consistent with Rawls's best insights to acknowledge that the most to be hoped for in the conduct of war is containment of injustice and movement toward justice. Principles of "just war" then become scruples for managing war's inevitable injustices, identifying the lesser of unjust options and paving the way for (at least, not putting obstacles to) a future in which no states are outlaws.

Suppose we approach Rawls's thoughts on war and justice with the following two ideas. First, there is in reality no such thing as true justice in fighting a war, even if its cause is just; rather, there are degrees of injustice. Second, some wars need to be fought because the alternatives are morally worse. What is justifiable depends on alternatives in a way that what is just does not. Justice is determined more abstractly by relationships that are not always realizable. Fighting a war when alternatives are worse can be a choice of the lesser of unjust options, attempting at least to contain injustice and ideally set a stage for future justice.

So understood, Rawls's thoughts on war are suggestive for addressing a "war" on women.

"War" on Women

Mary Kaldor argues that the "new wars"—since the Cold War—"involve a blurring of distinctions between war (usually defined as violence between states or organized political groups for political motives), organized crime … and large-scale violations of human rights" (2001, 2). Extending her reasoning, one can argue that many ancient massive violations of human rights warrant classification as "wars" at least as much as the Cold War, drug wars, and wars on terrorism. Such classifications change (blur) the meaning of "war"—a price of the moral recognition of relevant analogies. Millennia of global misogyny bear enough analogies to hostilities, aims, and consequences of wars perpetrated by heads of state to warrant speaking of a "war" (or "wars") of aggression against women, some of it consciously organized, some coordinated by way of norms internalized early by individuals. In these ways, sex wars resemble race wars. A decade before Kaldor's work, Harvard Medical School psychiatrist Judith Lewis Herman wrote, "There is a war between the sexes. Rape victims, battered women, and sexually abused children are its casualties. Hysteria is the combat neurosis of the sex war" (1992, 32). She compared female "hysteria" to "shell shock" in soldiers during World War I. Both today are recognized as posttraumatic stress disorder. "War between the sexes," however, suggests a more balanced distribution of responsibility for aggression than we find. For the most part, women have not fought back very aggressively. War *between* the sexes would be progress. What we find is better described as a war on women.

The aggression has been mainly by men (not without female support), and groups instituted by men, against females on account of their sex. As with outlaw states, this aggression is not justifiable self-defense, despite some rhetoric of "honor." It is to advance and secure prudential and other interests that lack moral grounding. Collaborating women are also victims. Some male resisters become victims. Others profit but are not aggressive. Some are bystanders. Some beneficiaries are not very aware that their profits come at women's expense. Those aware who choose to "do nothing" are collaborators; those unaware but who should be are at least complicit. Many men in these categories are intimate with and feel benevolent toward women. The "war" is not by all men as hostile aggressors against all women. Aggressors, however, are mainly men and victims mainly women.

There are environments where women are less likely to be targets of aggressive violence based on their sex. Some men would not knowingly advance themselves at women's expense, let alone do so violently. Still, women court danger when they venture outside those environments. And many men are not very aware of when they advance at women's expense.

Misogynous evils mostly lack national boundaries. With the exception of certain war crimes, such as mass rape, they tend not to victimize entire peoples. Nor are perpetrators always a people. But peoples are guilty of failing to do well at protecting women and girls. Eventually, many women, individually and in groups, confront needs to defend themselves.

Most misogynous practices do not fit the conventional model of war Rawls has in mind in his Law of Peoples. His parties to war are well-ordered peoples and outlaw states, not individuals.[3] Opposing aggressive outlaw states are well-ordered peoples, whose societies are relatively compliant with a shared public conception of justice. So described, well-ordered peoples sound innocent and clearly distinct from their enemies. Women are seldom innocent. They are often sleeping with the enemy. Their loss of innocence is frequently traceable to misogynous evils they have suffered. Many inhabit something like what Primo Levi called "gray zones," in which victims become complicit in the evils from which they, too, suffer (1989, 36–69; Card 2002, 211–234).

Well-ordered peoples, however, are less innocent than they sound when described as above. Even "relatively well-ordered peoples" (*LP*, 89) contain and tolerate what are for women "outlaw environments" in which a commitment to justice for women and girls does not exist or is not very effective.

"Outlaw" here does not mean what gender critics have meant. It does not describe rebels against conventional gender practices. On the contrary, it describes conventional gender practices that are deeply unjust, "noncompliant," as Rawls would put it, with principles of justice.

If global misogyny is not unproblematically conceived as martial, neither are domestic misogynous evils unproblematic as causes for armed

---

[3] On why Rawls reserves the term "peoples" for liberal and decent societies and does not apply it to outlaw states, see helpful discussion by Philip Pettit in Martin and Reidy 2006, esp. 42–48.

humanitarian intervention. What people does such a good job of protecting its females that it would be justified in militarily intervening for that purpose into the affairs of another? Such "glasshouses" questions are raised about humanitarian intervention generally. In response, some propose that international bodies such as the United Nations be given sole power to authorize interventions. But glasshouses questions can be asked of international bodies. At issue are long track records of failing to protect women and girls against inexcusable intolerable harms, not inevitable failures due to error or ignorance.

Ideal Contracts, Original Positions, and Hypothetical Agreements

Despite analogies between a war where parties are peoples or states and a "war" on women, there are obvious disanalogies. So, I have heretofore put the analogous "war" in scare quotes (dropped hereafter). Fighting back in a war on women is like fighting a war on terrorism in which the terrorists are not states. Some of it *is* war on terrorism that targets women. Unlike states, the sexes are not agents. The sexes might be regarded as groups in virtue of shared interests. But the sexes do not *act* as groups (although subgroups act). Peoples at war, in its conventional sense, act through representatives. Outlaw states act, although they do not represent their peoples. There are no representatives of the sexes, considered as such. Were we to employ Rawls's imaginative device of a veil of ignorance for choosing principles to govern women's responses to misogynous evils, the parties would have to represent individuals, as in Rawls's first use of the idea of the "original position" (hereafter, OP). So, why not simply leave it a task of parties in Rawls's first and second uses of the OP to propose principles for responding to misogyny? Is it helpful to use the OP to generate principles specifically to guide women's responses to misogyny? I will suggest a way that it is.

It should, indeed, be a task of parties in both of Rawls's OPs to propose principles governing responses to misogynous crimes. The Law of Peoples includes the principle: "Peoples are to honor human rights" (*LP*, 37). But there is no enforcement provision other than humanitarian intervention, the particulars of which are not given. Parties in the first OP would want women protected, too. But how would their reasoning go?

When the task is nonideal theory for within a society, parties in the OP must know that their society may be permeated even in law enforcement by misogyny and that many may in reality not be committed to principles reasonable to choose behind the veil. Do circumstances of justice, then, obtain? How should parties conceive the point of their task?

It might be thought that *well-ordered* peoples would not have that problem. But misogynous evils are not confined to outlaw states, burdened states, and benevolent dictatorships. The division of societies into those well-ordered and those not sounds simpler than the reality. Being well-ordered is a matter of degree in how well-governed a people is, how well-developed, well-applied, widely shared, and comprehensive its public conception of justice. Rawls refers to "relatively well-ordered peoples" (*LP*, 89). No society is thoroughly well-ordered. "Relatively" does not even imply "very." Misogynous subcultures exist within many a relatively well-ordered people as do areas of conduct in which an otherwise relatively well-ordered people is not at all well-ordered.

Individuals, too, can be inconsistent. People who try to be guided by justice toward those they respect often treat others as inferiors. This phenomenon applies to race and gender. Many men in relatively well-ordered societies are not motivated to grant women the respect they grant other men (or, *some* other men).

So the question arises: whom would parties in the OP represent when proposing (nonideal theoretical) principles to address such evils as those of misogyny? In what Rawls calls his second use of the OP, parties represent only well-ordered peoples, not outlaw states or burdened societies. Analogously, in Rawls's first OP, if the task were to choose principles for a *partially* compliant society, parties should represent not *all* individuals but only those of presumable compliance. They need to know roughly the collective strength of that group to estimate how much compliance to expect on the other side of the veil, in order to assess whether circumstances of justice obtain, so they can set a realistic task.

Rawls understands circumstances of justice as conditions under which cooperation is both useful and necessary: everyone is vulnerable but no one so powerful as to be able to dominate the rest for long. In ideal theory, parties in the first OP know this about their society. In nonideal theory, must parties know that noncompliance is not so widespread that cooperation is hopeless? Is that enough to give point to their task for parties who know they might turn out to be victims of well-entrenched misogyny? What if cooperation *has been* hopeless? Might the task then shift to proposing principles for coalition building, to ground hope of sufficient cooperation? In any case, victims can be justified as a matter of self-respect in fighting even hopeless battles.[4] If they care about self-respect, presumably they care about principles for fighting even hopeless battles.

Rawls's use of the contract idea in his sketch of a Law of Peoples does not receive the elaboration of reasoning that we find in *A Theory of Justice*. Perhaps the contract idea is less useful for nonideal theory. More interestingly, perhaps the parties' task changes.

Something like Nietzsche's view of early justice is suggestive for nonideal theory: "Justice on this elementary level is the good will among parties of approximately equal power to come to terms with one another, to reach an 'understanding' by means of a settlement—and to *compel* parties of lesser power to reach a settlement among themselves" (Nietzsche 1967, 70–71).

---

[4] I owe this thought to Richard Mohr's work on gays and dignity (1988, 315–337).

Nietzsche, unlike Rawls, presents the compact as historical, not hypothetical, and as among those who know they are powerful, not among parties behind a veil who may know only that cooperation is not hopeless. But Nietzsche also presents his speculative compact as among parties of good will, suggesting that it may not be merely a modus vivendi, and as including provision for coercing others. A Rawlsian hypothetical contract for non-ideal theory might likewise be conceived as among parties of goodwill and as including principles for using force against those whose goodwill cannot be presumed. This is how Rawls does conceive it for the case of war.

Rawls admits to a certain agnosticism regarding the likelihood of success in implementing a Law of Peoples and, ultimately, bringing about a world in which all societies are members of a Society of Well-Ordered Peoples. What sustains him is the human possibility of success here. This allows him hope. His agnosticism may derive from doubts about whether circumstances of justice obtain at the global level. His hope may be more an aspect of his nontheistic religion than a sociologically grounded stance (*A Brief Inquiry*, 261–269).

Rawls does not assume that the basic structure of society and relations among peoples are the only subjects of justice. But they are the only ones he addresses. Defense of women should doubtless be incorporated into justice for both subjects. Given the histories of peoples, however, that will not much encourage women. A more promising idea might be to seek circumstances of justice among women, or groups of women, or try to cultivate circumstances in which cooperation among women would be fruitful (as it surely seems necessary).

Women and girls do not form a society. They form a kind of group, joined (if not united) across the boundaries of peoples by common and overlapping interests. This group is not yet capable of action, although subgroups are. What social units are appropriate subjects of principles for the self-defense and mutual defense of women and girls against evils of misogyny? Feminist groups have not achieved stability, let alone membership, comparable to states. An interesting approach embraced by radical feminists of the 1970s, exemplified earlier in Virginia Woolf's "society of outsiders," is separatism. Woolf was moved in her last, most radical book to have her female outsider proclaim, "In fact, as a woman I have no country. As a woman I want no country. As a woman my country is the whole world" (1938, 109). Women need principles for forming social units of defense against global and local misogyny. Meanwhile, women need principles now for defending themselves and each other as individuals.

Principles for Individual Self-Defense in a War on Women

Instead of going much into the reasoning of parties in his second use of the OP (which generates the Law of Peoples), Rawls sets out a list of principles, including principles for war. Let us consider how adaptable those war principles are to the case of women, when their case is not subsumed under the basic structure of the society of a well-ordered people or its foreign relations.

Following just war theory, Rawls begins his discussion of war by first taking up justifications for going to war (*jus ad bellum*) and states a version of the principle of just cause, in two parts. The first part is negative: "No state has a right to war in the pursuit of its *rational* as opposed to its *reasonable* interests" (*LP*, 91, emphasis in original). His distinction between rational and reasonable interests roughly tracks Immanuel Kant's distinction between merely prudential interests and morally grounded interests.[5] Reasonable interests take others into account; merely rational interests need not. The second part of Rawls's *jus ad bellum* principle is positive: "*Any* society that is non-aggressive and that honors human rights has the right of self-defense" (*LP*, 92, emphasis in original). Later he mentions humanitarian intervention but does not elaborate or clarify.

Adapting Rawls's just cause principle to the case of women requires distinguishing women's merely prudential (rational) interests from morally grounded (reasonable) interests and altering the part about a nonaggressive society. The first part of the principle is satisfied when the interests protected are the morally grounded interests of security and freedom. Women are not justified in resorting to violence over conflicts regarding forms of discrimination that hamper their pursuit of merely rational (prudential) interests (say, merely personal ambitions) that are not at the same time reasonable interests (morally grounded). In the second part of the principle, a plausible substitute for "society that is nonaggressive" might be: "one who lacks a history of unjust aggression and whose principles would not permit it" so that the principle becomes: Anyone who lacks a history of unjust aggression, whose principles would not permit it, and who honors human rights has the right of self-defense. Thus, complicity under duress need not negate a justification for self-defense.

Next Rawls offers six principles for the conduct of war (*jus in bello*). The first states that "the aim" is "a just and lasting peace among peoples, and especially with the people's present enemy" (*LP*, 94). Adapting this principle, the plausible aim would be a just and lasting peace between (among) the sexes. But the part about peace with one's current enemies is not clearly adaptable. When the parties are not group agents, one's most obvious current enemies are the individuals one is most likely to harm deliberately in war. Perhaps the aim should be reconceived for both the Law of Peoples and the case of women as a peace that paves the way to reducing significantly the injustices that led to war.

---

[5] For Kant's distinction between prudence and morality, see the first and second sections of *Groundwork of the Metaphysics of Morals* (Kant 1996, 49–93).

Rawls's second *jus in bello* principle is: "Well-ordered peoples do not wage war against each other...but only against non-well-ordered states whose expansionist aims threaten the security and free institutions of well-ordered regimes and bring about the war" (*LP*, 94). This principle seems redundant, given the *jus ad bellum* principle: well-ordered peoples are not aggressively expansionist. Here what Rawls may want to emphasize is that well-ordered peoples resolve conflicts among themselves even over *reasonable* interests without violence. An analogue for women might be that women governed by a sense of justice resolve conflicts with individuals who are not outlaws even over *reasonable* interests without violence. We need, then, to define "outlaw individuals." A plausible approximation is "individuals who are prepared to *use violence*, in a society that fails to restrain them from doing so, in pursuit of interests that are not reasonable."

Rawls's third principle distinguishes degrees of responsibility among three groups: "The outlaw state's leaders and officials, its soldiers, and its civilian population" (*LP*, 94). Adapting it, we can distinguish levels of responsibility for aggressive violence against women. Parallel distinctions might be those who have greatest control over whether, how, and what kinds of aggression are perpetrated (compare "leaders and officials"), those who are instruments of aggression but lack such control (compare "soldiers" who are not leaders or officials), and those under the authority of members of the first group but who are not instruments of violence (compare "civilians"). Further distinctions may be needed regarding bystanders and beneficiaries. Rawls's fourth principle is: "Well-ordered peoples must respect, so far as possible, the human rights of the members of the other side, both civilians and soldiers" (*LP*, 96). This principle seems straightforwardly adaptable and even to follow from the fifth principle.[6]

Rawls's fifth principle is that well-ordered peoples are to foreshadow during war the kind of peace they aim for and the kind of relationships they seek. This duty, he notes, falls largely on leaders and officials. Although there are no current analogues of leaders, the basic idea is important for women. What kinds of relationships with men should women aim for and foreshadow? Women have been steered into relationships that give men constant intimate access to them, often to the detriment of peace. The relationship lacking has usually been one of adequate respect. Women should try to foreshadow a peace in which men have less of that intimate access and are more respectful. This idea rules out sexual seduction by women as a war tactic.

Rawls's sixth principle is that "practical means-end reasoning must always have a restricted role in judging the appropriateness of an action or

---

[6] It is puzzling that Rawls mentions the human rights only of civilians and soldiers, apparently omitting leaders and officials. Perhaps he was subsuming leaders and officials under "soldiers"?

policy" (*LP*, 96). His intent seems to be to emphasize that the preceding principles restrict the role of means-end reasoning in war. In his gloss on this principle Rawls invokes the exception of "supreme emergency," discussing it only briefly, relying for illustration on Nazism's threats to "civilized life everywhere" (*LP*, 98–99). Like ticking bomb torture, "supreme emergency" is a dangerous idea, liable to gross abuse. If it has validity nevertheless, we should appreciate that it undercuts the human rights of the fourth principle and the "foreshadowing peace" of the fifth. As applied to women's resistance, "supreme emergency" measures, which violate normal restrictions on means-end reasoning, should be not only needed quickly but reasonably judged necessary and, under the circumstances, sufficient for an objective of supreme importance transcending that of any individual and limited in severity by the severity of the evils to be prevented. Still, it is good to be skeptical of the idea of a "supreme emergency exemption."

Insofar as Rawls's principles say not what is *justifiable* but only what is not, they are scruples. Only the second part of the just cause principle and the "supreme emergency exemption" (not a principle but an exception) are explicitly about what is justifiable. The unnamed elephant in the vicinity is the use of force and violence to kill and maim. The idea is that killing and maiming can be justifiable if these principles are observed. Adapting that conclusion to women's resistance yields the idea that killing or maiming perpetrators of the evils of misogyny can likewise be justifiable if analogues of Rawls's principles are observed.

Did the actions of Hughes and García fall within those limits? Did they avoid doing evil in response to evils they faced? They inflicted harm clearly intolerable from their victims' points of view. But were they justified? And if not, had they any moral or metaphysical excuse?

Consider just cause. If the interests defended were the morally grounded interests in security and freedom, not some merely prudential interest (or, say, an interest in revenge), they satisfied the first part of this principle. If the women lacked histories of unjust aggression, were not committed to unjust aggression, and honored human rights, they satisfied the second part. Of course, what is at issue is whether their responses failed to honor human rights. Perhaps it is sufficient for this principle that they lacked histories of commitment to aggressive injustice or of failing to honor human rights.

If Hughes and García are regarded as ordinary civilians (as the courts regarded them), their acts are difficult to construe as self-defense, given how assault and battery are defined in criminal law. Hughes's batterer was asleep. García's rapists had done their deed; she was free to go. But military combat rules are reasonably more permissive. Soldiers can attack at night when the enemy might be asleep. They do not have to retreat whenever retreat is possible. Hughes and García defended against *patterns* of violence, not simply particular episodes. Neither could depend on state protection. Regarding them as more like military combatants than like civilians seems fair. Another way to look at Hughes is that she defended herself against a coerced relationship, which did not dissolve when the enforcer slept.

Were their aims a lasting peace with those who currently terrorize women? The analogy breaks down if the peace at issue is between groups at war. Hughes was not fighting batterers in general, nor was García fighting rapists generally. Each fought only her own assailant(s). Nor was either fighting as a member of a group. Yet, their deeds were potentially precedent setting, sending the message that men cannot be confident of being able to get away with misogynous violence, a message compatible with peace. Whether that is the dominant message depends also on whether women who do likewise are exonerated. Most women who respond as they did go to prison, many for the rest of their lives. Still, the first message remains partially valid (the men killed did not get away with it) and might have a salutary effect.

Did either woman fail to make relevant distinctions regarding responsibility? Hughes tried first to enlist help from law enforcement. Although García succeeded only in killing the 300-pound man who stood guard while the other assaulted her, she tried to kill both and regretted only that she did not succeed in killing the other man. (He was never charged with a crime.) Neither woman harmed others.

Was either woman guilty of a human rights violation? Did Hughes violate the right not to be tortured? As her batterer was asleep in a drunken stupor, there may be no way to know what he felt. She should have been aware of the danger that she might be torturing him.[7] Although she was protecting children also, her objective was, I would say, insufficiently important and transcendent to make plausible a "supreme emergency exemption," that is (here), a violation of restrictions on means-end reasoning that proscribe torture. Further, her incendiary deed, although sufficient, may have exceeded what was needful, a conclusion calling for judgment regarding her long-range options. In any case, it appears not to have been premeditated, which enabled Michigan to find her temporarily insane.

García took advantage of the fact that her rapists would not expect her to pursue them armed. Had they expected that, they would have been armed and she would likely have been the one killed. Given women's socialization to nonviolence and failures in law enforcement, the rapists' expectation was epistemically justified. As combatants in a war on women, they had no moral title to rely on that expectation.

Neither woman's response seems, on these reckonings, inexcusably wrong, morally or metaphysically. In the absence of nongovernmental

---

[7] Thanks to Jeffrey Reiman for noting that the possibility that she was torturing him was something she should have known.

organizations for defense of women, individuals like these survivors are all we have to consider. But ultimately the more important issue is organizing for effective use of force and violence in women's defense.

Guerrilla Feminism

In the 1970s and 1980s guerrilla feminists in the United States carried to another level defense of women against misogyny. Typical tactics were property assaults—public graffiti, physical destruction of pornography, trashing pornography shops. There may have been organized violence against targeted individuals. In 1989, the journal *Lesbian Ethics* carried an interesting piece titled "Guerilla Feminism," consisting of information about actions in Massachusetts "from newspaper clippings and other material sent to *LE* anonymously" ("Guerilla Feminism" 1989, 79–90). Reports of violence against persons appear in a concluding paragraph:

> In Iowa, a huge group of women kidnapped a man who had raped dozens of women. They castrated him in a cornfield. Closer by, a man who had raped at least 10 women was captured by a band of women. They stamped 'rapist' all over his body. They super-glued his hands to his penis and his balls to his legs. (1989, 90)

This is vigilantism, or freedom-fighting, depending on your perspective.

A pair of short stories by Melanie Kaye/Kantrowitz, "The Day We Didn't Declare War" and "The Day We Did" suggests that more drastic violence against persons may have been contemplated (1990, 85–96), even implemented. The first story describes an organization calling itself "The Godmothers." The Godmothers made services available to women who were being assaulted in their homes. This organization put new and better locks on doors, sent pairs of Godmothers to stay with women in their homes, and put up warning signs on doors that the assailant was being monitored by The Godmothers. And they did monitor assailants. The second story describes a formal meeting at which Godmothers entertained more drastic measures in response to series of rapes in a local park after police failed to arrest anyone. That story ends without revealing what the Godmothers decided. In a later collection of essays, Kaye/Kantrowitz wrote, "In Portland we formed a group called the Godmothers who would protect battered women in their own homes" (1992, 48).

Women in the self-defense movement and in a group called WAR (Women Against Rape) organized in many cities to teach women and girls martial arts through groups like Chimera Self Defense, which has active branches today. Chimera was formed in the 1970s by women with black belts in martial arts who were getting raped on Chicago streets. Physical skill, they concluded, was only part of self-defense. Their courses consist of 50 percent attitude training.

These are small-scale organizations compared to political states. But like the Portland Godmothers and guerrilla feminists of Iowa and Massachusetts, they demonstrate sensitivity to reciprocity. When men are trained for combat and taught how to kill, is it not justifiable for women to form groups to teach those skills systematically to women, who might need them for protection against men so trained? Might it be justifiable to teach women to notice when breaking a law might save life or limb (perhaps one's own) without endangering the innocent? Such projects might be regarded as supplements, rather than alternatives, to projects for improving the law, although tension between these kinds of projects is likely.

Yet, a serious issue remains. Civil law has trials to determine who is guilty of an offense, and states have international norms for identifying combatants. Nonstate organizations have only their own relatively subjective improvisations for identifying the enemy, which can make their identifications and subsequent targetings seem to others unpredictable or indiscriminate.[8] The difficulty of identifying enemies fairly is a general problem for terrorists, insurgents, and all who would engage them in scruple-governed combat. Rawls's just war principles need to be supplemented with further principles and discussion to address that issue.

Acknowledgments

Earlier drafts of this essay were read and commented on by Adam Pham, Harry Brighouse, Jeffrey Reiman, Eric Senseman, Regina Schouten, and the editors of this book. I am grateful for their suggestions and also to Jeffrey Reiman for sharing with me in advance his review of my book *Confronting Evils* (2010), in which he comments on my discussion of Hughes and García.

Works by Rawls, with Abbreviations

A Brief Inquiry into the Meaning of Sin and Faith, with "On My Religion" (*BI*), ed. Thomas Nagel. Cambridge, MA: Harvard University Press, 2009.

Collected Papers (*CP*), ed. Samuel Freeman. Cambridge, MA: Harvard University Press, 1999.

The Law of Peoples (*LP*). Cambridge, MA: Harvard University Press, 1999.

Political Liberalism (*PL*), expanded ed. New York: Columbia University Press, 2005.

A Theory of Justice (*TJ*), rev. ed. Cambridge, MA: Harvard University Press, 1999.

---

[8] I discuss this and other issues raised by terrorism in Card 2010, 123–148, which discusses Hughes and García.

Other References

Card, Claudia (2002) *The Atrocity Paradigm: A Theory of Evils*. New York: Oxford University Press.

—— (2010) *Confronting Evils: Terrorism, Torture, Genocide*. Cambridge: Cambridge University Press.

Daly, Mary (1978) *Gyn/Ecology: The Metaethics of Radical Feminism*. Boston: Beacon Press.

—— "Guerilla Feminism" (1989) *Lesbian Ethics* 3(3): 79–90.

Hart, H.L.A. (1955) "Are There Any Natural Rights?" *Philosophical Review* 64(2): 175–191.

Herman, Judith Lewis (1992) *Trauma and Recovery*. New York: Basic Books.

Kaldor, Mary (2001) *New and Old Wars: Organized Violence in a Global Era*. Stanford: Stanford University Press.

Kant, Immanuel (1996) *Practical Philosophy*, ed. and trans. Mary J. Gregor. 2nd ed. Cambridge: Cambridge University Press.

Kaye/Kantrowitz, Melanie (1990) *My Jewish Face and Other Stories*. San Francisco: Spinsters/Aunt Lute Books.

—— (1992) *The Issue Is Power: Essays on Women, Jews, Violence and Resistance*. San Francisco: Aunt Lute Books.

Levi, Primo (1989) *The Drowned and the Saved*, trans. Raymond Rosenthal. New York: Vintage.

Martin, Rex, and Reidy, David (eds.) (2006) *Rawls's Law of Peoples: A Realistic Utopia?* Oxford: Wiley-Blackwell.

McNulty, Faith (1980) *The Burning Bed*. New York: Harcourt Brace Jovanovich.

Mill, John Stuart (2003) *Utilitarianism and On Liberty*, ed. Mary Warnock. 2nd ed. Oxford: Blackwell.

Mohr, Richard (1988) *Gays/Justice*. New York: Columbia University Press.

Nietzsche, Friedrich (1967) *On the Genealogy of Morals*, trans. Walter Kaufmann and R. J. Hollingdale. New York: Vintage.

Okin, Susan Moller (1989) *Justice, Gender, and the Family*. New York: Basic Books.

Pettit, Philip (2006) "Rawls's Peoples." In Rex Martin and David Reidy (eds.), *Rawls's Law of Peoples: A Realistic Utopia?* (38–55). Oxford: Wiley-Blackwell.

Sahebjam, Freidoune (1990) *The Stoning of Soraya M.*, trans. Richard Seaver. New York: Arcade.

Salter, Kenneth (1976) *The Trial of Inez García*. Berkeley: Editorial Justa.

Williams, Bernard (1974) *Problems of the Self*. Cambridge: Cambridge University Press.

Wood, Jim (1976) *The Rape of Inez García*. New York: Putnam.

Woolf, Virginia (1938) *Three Guineas*. New York: Harcourt, Brace & World.

CHAPTER 15

TAKING PRIDE IN BEING BAD

CLAUDIA CARD

In the street jargon of inner city gang members of the 1980s described by sociologist Jack Katz, "bad" is worn as a badge of pride.[1] It appears to signify simultaneously "good" and "bad"—good, as worthy of the admiration of certain parties, and bad, insofar as that worthiness is based on such criteria as toughness, meanness, cruelty, hard-heartedness, and a willingness and competence to carry out really bad deeds. A reputation for being a "badass" in this context is a source of self-esteem and of others' respect. But self-esteem and respect, unqualified, are thought to be goods. Are the gang members, then, really acting under the guise of the good, after all? I will argue that they are not. The esteem or respect in this case, however good it feels (no doubt it *feels* good), is based on bad traits of character. Further, an aspiring badass who does bad things only *in order to gain* the respect of comrades will not deserve it. A real badass doesn't care what others think. To deserve their respect, one must not act for the sake of it. Rather, one must become a certain kind of person. Being motivated by the desire to become a person who would *deserve* esteem or respect does not undermine one's desert of it.

Socrates thought we always act under the guise of the good (Plato, *Protagoras*, Stephanus pp. 352–6C). Aristotle disagreed with Socrates' idea that we think what we are doing is good at the time that we do it, and struggled in Book. VII of the *Nicomachean Ethics* with how to make sense of acting against one's better judgment. Kant agreed with Aristotle that we can do wrong knowingly. Frailty is the first of his three degrees of evil. However, in the worst degree, Kant also thought we tend to deceive ourselves into

[1] Jack Katz, *Seductions of Crime: Moral and Sensual Attractions in Doing Evil* (New York: Basic Books, 1988).

Criticism and Compassion: The Ethics and Politics of Claudia Card.
Edited by Robin S. Dillon and Armen T. Marsoobian.
Chapters and book compilation © 2018 Metaphilosophy LLC and John Wiley & Sons Ltd.

thinking our will is good, since what duty requires can be also to our advantage. These ways of acting under the guise of the bad are not at issue in the case of taking pride in being bad. Weakness is nothing to be proud of.

Kant's theory of radical evil in human nature is not radical enough to comprehend taking pride in being bad. Pride so grounded seems to presuppose what Kant called *diabolical* evil, doing evil for evil's sake, for which he found no basis in human nature.

Taking pride in being bad is taking pride in being a certain kind of person, in having those qualities of character that enable one to be good at being cruel, hard-hearted, merciless, ruthless, manipulative, making people suffer, terrifying people, and so forth. Such a person also lacks or keeps under control qualities that would interfere, such as a vulnerability to compassion. The agent who takes pride in being bad is not doing bad things simply as a means to gaining something that is *independently* conceived as good. The independence is important. Being worthy of the approval of fellow badasses is not conceived as good independently of the bases of their approval, admitted bads. If something is valued *in virtue of its badness*, or of its enabling one to be bad, then acting from a desire for it is acting under the guise of the bad.

I will try to make sense of the idea of valuing something in virtue of its badness, not merely as a means to an independently conceived further good. If to value something simply *meant* to find it good, then it would be self-contradictory to value something in virtue of its badness. To defend the idea of acting under the guise of the bad, we need to distinguish between valuing something and judging that it is valuable, i.e., worthy of being valued. The judgment that something is good carries a claim to objectivity not carried simply by the activity of valuing. To value something, it is enough to find it important to oneself. If I am right, acting under the guise of the bad is fairly common. But actually, "bad" is not a strong enough term. What I am going to talk about is taking pride in being downright evil.

The gang members' desire to be worthy of each other's esteem is not to be equated with some general desire for approval, as though one could substitute worthiness of the approval of one's priests or teachers and be satisfying the same desire. The desire to be worthy of approvals that are grounded in a certain way can outlive one's relationships with those whose approval one initially sought to deserve. The thought that one *would* deserve their approval takes on a life of its own. It is analogous to Immanuel Kant's view of the motive of persons of good will.

In the opening paragraph of the first section of the *Groundwork of the Metaphysics of Morals*, Kant observes that "an impartial rational spectator can take no delight in seeing the uninterrupted prosperity of a being graced with no feature of a pure and good will, so that a good will seems to constitute the indispensable condition even of worthiness to be happy."[2] The unstated implication is that persons of good will *would* be a source of delight to that spectator. This delight would naturally be coupled with (or even identical with) approval, esteem, perhaps even love. Thus Kant's observation seems to imply that a good will is necessary to make us worthy of an impartial spectator's admiration, approval, esteem, or love (G 4:303, Gregor 49).

Kant may have been thinking of God as the "impartial spectator." He argued in the second Critique that only God would have the power to bring it about that persons of good will are rewarded with happiness (CPrR 5: 124–32; G 239–46), offering this belief as support for the rationality of theistic faith, in place of the traditional proofs, which, he argued in the first Critique, fail. The motive of duty makes one worthy to be rewarded with happiness by an omnipotent, omniscient, and perfectly just rational spectator. Importantly, happiness is *not the motive* of a good will. (That motive would make one prudent.) The goal is, rather, to be *worthy* of happiness—a reward that would symbolize its bestower's esteem. (Even happiness thereby acquires a stoic value for Kant, for what it symbolizes about another's esteem for one's will.)

Likewise, to be worthy of the approval or esteem of those whose esteem is based on such qualities as cruelty, hard-heartedness, ruthlessness, and so forth, one must have as one's motive the desire to be a badass, to be the kind of person who enjoys the exercise of such qualities apart from their utility, is good at exercising those qualities, and takes pride in doing so.

The desire to be worthy of the approval of comrades in crime no more undermines the judgment that one is really acting under the guise of the bad than the desire to be worthy of the approval of an impartial rational spectator undermines Kant's judgment that a person of good will is acting under the guise of duty. To be worthy of the impartial rational spectator's approval, one must act under the guise of duty, not for the sake of approval. Likewise, to be worthy of the approval of other badasses is to be cruel because one values cruelty, takes pride in being cruel, ruthless, hard-hearted, mean, and so on. An appropriate answer to the question "why do you do that?" need not be the very abstract "because it shows how bad I am" but can take a more specific form, such as "because it shows how heartless [cruel, ruthless, merciless, etc.] I am," leaving it to be understood that these are ways of being very bad.

Taking pride in being evil has no place in Immanuel Kant's theory of evil, which is presented in Book 1 of *Religion Within the Boundaries of Mere Reason* (1797).[3] A radically evil will, as Kant understands it, is simply

[2] Immanuel Kant, *Practical Philosophy*, trans. Mary Gregor (Cambridge: Cambridge University Press, 1996), p. 49. Further references are given in parentheses in the text.

[3] In *Religion and Rational Theology*, trans. and ed. Allen W. Wood and George Di Giovanni (Cambridge: Cambridge University Press, 1996), pp. 69–97. Further references are given in parentheses in the text.

a commitment to prioritizing self-love over morality, so that in cases of conflict, one would as a matter of principle, do the self-interested thing rather than act as duty requires.

Kant's explicit denial that we ever do evil for evil's sake, which is what he means by the idea of *diabolical* evil, is unequivocal:

> *Sensuous nature* ... contains too little to provide a ground of evil in the human being ... an *evil reason* as it were (an absolutely evil will), would on the contrary contain too much, because resistance to the law would itself be thereby elevated to incentive ... and so the subject would be made a *diabolical* being.—Neither of these two is however applicable to the human being. (R 6:35; Wood and Di Giovanni, p. 82)

Again:

> The depravity of human nature is ... not to be named *malice,* if we take this word in the strict sense, namely as a disposition (a subjective *principle* of maxims) to incorporate evil *qua evil* for incentive into one's maxim (since this is *diabolical*) ... (R 6:37; Wood and Di Giovanni, p. 84)

Kant's idea is that when we do evil, we do it for the sake of a non-moral good, namely, the good of self-interest, prudence—not under the guise of evil, wrongness, or badness itself.

It is more than a little confusing that in that same essay Kant says that certain human vices are called *diabolical*—"*envy, ingratitude, joy in others' misfortune,* etc.*"* We need to read the "called" as "called by others," not as an endorsement by Kant of that judgment. Thus, he notes that "in their extreme degree of malignancy (where they are simply the idea of a maximum of evil that surpasses humanity) ... they are called *diabolical vices*" (R 6:27; Wood and Di Giovanni, p. 75). He elucidates by describing a kind of self-love based on comparing oneself with others, noting that "out of this self-love originates the inclination *to gain worth in the opinion of others,* originally, of course, merely equal worth." There is room for development in a different direction than the one Kant pursues, as we will see. Kant offers an account of these "vices of culture" that finds them rooted in a self-love that is originally good. Thus, he writes that they are:

> inclinations, in the face of the anxious endeavor of others to attain a hateful superiority over us, to procure it for ourselves over them for the sake of security as preventive measure. (R 6:27; Wood and Di Giovanni, p. 75)

Acting from these "diabolical vices" is thus a matter of doing evil for the sake of one's security.

To appreciate the contrast in Kant of radical evil with diabolical evil, it is helpful to look more closely at his theory of evil in human nature.

Kant's Theory of Radical Evil in Human Nature

Kant finds within human psychology no initial predisposition to what is bad or wrong. But he does not argue that there would be anything self-contradictory in such a predisposition. The Australian philosopher Stanley Benn argued in his classic essay "Wickedness" that there is ultimately no logical or even psychological incoherence in the idea of choosing evil for its own sake, once we acknowledge the distinctions between desiring (or valuing) something and finding it desirable (or worthy of being valued) and the distinction between finding a position reasonable and holding it as one's own reason.[4] Kant does acknowledge those distinctions. And so, to reject the idea that humans ever act for the sake of wrongness, immorality, or evil, he needs an account of human moral psychology that simply provides no basis for such action. That is what he offers.

Kant analyzes human moral psychology, first, in terms of three pre-dispositions, all basically good (R 6:26–6:28; Wood and Di Giovanni, pp. 74–76), which he calls the predispositions to animality, to humanity, and to personality. *Animality* is a predisposition to be motivated by "physical or merely *mechanical* self-love," for self-preservation, propagation of the species, and even for "community with other human beings." *Humanity*, he writes, is also a kind of self-love but one that involves comparison with others (not what he meant by "humanity" in the *Groundwork*). The predisposition to humanity can give rise to jealousy, rivalry, and those "vices of culture," such as envy and joy in others' misfortunes. Finally, *Personality* is the predisposition to be moved by the moral law. Absent from this list is any predisposition to be moved by *immorality* as such. And so, an evil will, for Kant, is not analogous to a good will.

The three predispositions, he says, are inborn, meaning that they are *given*, not *chosen* by us. What *is* up to us is how to rank these incentives in cases of conflict. We choose which to make the condition of the others. A good will ranks duty above interest and inclination. A radically evil will makes self-interest supreme. Self-interest is good as long as it is qualified by a commitment to pursue it only within the bounds of duty. A radically evil will is not committed to that restriction. But neither, Kant thinks, is such a person committed to immorality as such.

Kant distinguishes two levels of the will's action. At the level of "intelligible action," I adopt (although not in the world of time and space) a supreme principle for myself, such as the Categorical Imperative (the principle of personality). At the level of empirical action (in time and space), I can perform an action in accordance with the supreme principle I have adopted (R 6:31; Wood and Di Giovanni, p. 79), for example, by telling the truth even when tempted not to. John Silber calls the adoption of a

---

[4] Stanley Benn, "Wickedness," *Ethics* 95 (1985): 795–810.

supreme principle a legislative act.[5] Kant thinks of that act as *only* intelligible, whereas he thinks of choices that apply the legislation as having an intelligible and an empirical aspect. Both deeds are products of a free will.

A radically evil will, for Kant, performs a legislative act in the *intelligible* world, outside time and space. Evil does not consist fundamentally in empirical violations of the moral law, such as telling lies, even though one whose will is evil surely will perform such acts sooner or later. And so, because prudence and morality can coincide, we can be radically evil even while our empirical choices happen not to violate the moral law. We do the outwardly right thing, but for the wrong reason. Radical evil consists in a preparedness to violate the moral law when its requirements conflict with pursuing one's interests.

Next, Kant distinguishes three stages of "the natural propensity to evil in human beings" (R 6:29–30; Wood and Di Giovanni, pp. 77–78). Unlike the predispositions, the propensity to evil describes choices. In the first stage, frailty, we adopt the right supreme principle but give in to a conflicting desire or inclination. We have not enough strength of character to abide by our own principles. We are not yet *radically* evil because our will is still good in what it legislates. Yet, observers may know only that we do wrong, not whether from weakness or on principle.

In the second stage, impurity, we act from mixed motives. One might slide from frailty into impurity, as the motive of duty is insufficient for a frail will, and so one buttresses it by relying partly on self-interest. As long as we act in accord with duty, to observers there may appear nothing wrong. But we act partly for the wrong reasons. We are honest not only because duty requires it but also from fear of a bad reputation. Although this is not yet radical evil, Kant finds it more dangerous than weakness. This may seem paradoxical. Weak agents actually do wrong acts in the world, whereas those with impure motives may not, owing to a fortuitous coincidence of duty with interest. But impurity begins a process of corruption in the will, setting one on a slippery slope at the bottom of which one has reversed the priorities of a good will. It is at this third stage, when self-interest has become one's supreme principle, that evil is finally rooted in the will. One's will has become radically evil.

Although Kant's good will is the will to do duty for duty's sake, he denies, more than once, that there is such a thing in human beings as a will to immorality as such. If that is what is meant by "acting under the guise of the bad," Kant denies that we ever do it. There is thus an asymmetry between a good will and a radically evil one. "Hence the difference," he writes,

> whether the human being is good or evil, must not lie in the difference between the incentives that he incorporates into his maxim (not in the material of the

---

[5] John Silber, "The Ethical Significance of Kant's Religion," in Immanuel Kant, *Religion Within the Limits of Reason Alone*, trans. Theodore M. Greene and Hoyt H. Hudson (New York: Harper & Row, 1960).

maxim) but in their *subordination* (in the form of the maxim): *which of the two he makes the condition of the other.* It follows that the human being (even the best) is evil only because he reverses the moral order of incentives ... he makes the incentives of self-love and their inclinations the condition of compliance with the moral law. (R 6:36; Wood and Di Giovanni, p. 83, emphases in the original)

On the question *why* one would ever subordinate the moral law (duty, the Categorical Imperative) to self-interest, Kant finds it a mystery, incomprehensible, inexplicable:

This propensity to evil, remains inexplicable to us, for, since it must itself be imputed to us, this supreme ground of all maxims must in turn require the adoption of an evil maxim.... yet the original predisposition ... is a predisposition to the good; there is no conceivable ground for us, therefore, from which moral evil could first have come in us (R 6:43; Wood and Di Giovanni, p. 88).

Commenting on the scriptural narrative of Eve and the serpent (a "spirit"), he writes:

The absolutely *first* beginning of all evil is thereby represented as incomprehensible to us (for whence the evil in that spirit?); the human being, however, is represented as having lapsed into it only *through temptation,* hence not as corrupted *fundamentally* (in his very first predisposition to the good) but, on the contrary, as still capable of improvement. (R 6:43–44; Wood and Di Giovanni, pp. 88–89)

An explanation of evil in terms of empirical causes would not satisfy the inquirer who seeks a rationale for the choice, as it would remove the agent's responsibility if it were the only account. But an account in terms of the will is, he says, ultimately inaccessible. If the question is why we have made a principle our *supreme* principle, we cannot, by hypothesis, cite any principle more fundamental. Kant is not puzzled about why anyone makes the moral law supreme, for he thinks rational autonomy requires it. But he finds that we cannot know why anyone fails to do so.

Kant's treatment of the ultimate springs of moral and immoral motivation as a mystery is deeply unsatisfying. First, if it is a mystery why anyone does not prioritize the moral law over self-interest, it should be equally a mystery why others do. That some do not proves that the capacity for rational autonomy does not make the choice for morality inevitable.

Second, if a principle is supreme, then, by definition, there cannot be any rationale for adopting it other than its being the principle that it is. But then we lack explanation for why some people *fail* to make the moral law their supreme principle. The "explanation" that they are being irrational is unsatisfying if we want to know why. If there is an empirical explanation, then the legislative act that subordinates morality to self-interest is not "purely intelligible" but is also an empirical deed. How, in that case, are we to understand that the legislator is nevertheless free?

I want to build on Kant's account in a way that preserves responsibility in most of us and yet dissipates, to a great extent, the mystery of why some of us become good and others evil. Kant's view seems excessively generous and optimistic because it is too narrow in the possibilities it envisions for immoral motivation. Specifically, he fails to acknowledge a predisposition to become attached to others. We are motivated not only by drives to obtain things for ourselves as individuals and scruples limiting how we do it, but also by attachments to others and subsequent desires to be worthy of their approval. Kant notes that we *compare ourselves with* others and in doing so come to care what they think of us. But this caring does not stem from attachment. Comparing ourselves is not a matter of caring for others.

Today, there is evidence that a predisposition to attachment exists even in infants. Recognizing such a predisposition, it becomes possible to argue that prioritizing self-interest over duty is not the worst way that we can be motivated to do evil. Attachments to others can become powerful motivators. Attachments can form when we are too young to evaluate them. However, as reflective adults, we can choose whether to detach or remain attached.

If we subsume all the interests one has and everything one cares about under the heading of self-interest, prudential good, we thereby trivialize Kant's denial that we ever act under the guise of the bad, in the sense of doing evil for evil's sake. For then, acting on any of one's interests would necessarily be acting under the guise of what is good for oneself. We would also lose the contrast between the motives of duty and of self-interest. We would have no way to explain how it is possible to act imprudently. We would lose the contrast between self-interest and many motives. As Bishop Joseph Butler pointed out in his famous sermon on human nature, "this is not the language of [human] kind, or if it were, we should want words to express the difference between the principle of an action proceeding from cool consideration that it will be to my own advantage, and an action, suppose of revenge or friendship, by which a [person] runs upon certain ruin to do evil or good to another."[6]

If the motive of duty is not just another manifestation of self-interest, there is room to argue that the same is true of some evil motives. They need not be self-interested, either, even if there is a reference embedded in them to what one hopes to be worthy of. Just as one may be motivated by revenge or friendship to do what will prove a great setback to one's general well-being, one may be motivated by the desire to excel at being bad to do what will also involve major costs to one's overall well-being. It can require great self-discipline to excel at being bad.

To make sense of acting under the guise of the bad, we need an alternative to Kant's theory of radical evil. My theory of evil, which I call the

[6] Joseph Butler, *Five Sermons* (Indianapolis, IN: Hackett, 1983), p. 47.

atrocity paradigm, leaves open what can count as a motive to evil-doing. And so, I turn briefly to the essentials of that theory.

The Atrocity Paradigm: A Theory of Evil

In atrocities, most salient are the harms people suffer. Since atrocities are my paradigms of evil, I begin with the noun, evils (plural) and center the idea of great harm. In lieu of a definition of "atrocity," I offer examples: the Holocaust, the 9/11 bombings, torture at Abu Ghraib, the institution of slavery. I define evils as reasonably foreseeable intolerable harms produced (supported, maintained, etc.) by inexcusable wrongs. So conceived, evils have two basic elements: a harm component and an agency component, neither reducible to the other.

Important concepts to clarify are "intolerable" (in "intolerable harms") and "inexcusable" (in "inexcusable wrongs"). I understand "intolerable" in a normative sense, not what you cannot in fact tolerate (which varies from person to person) but more like what no one should have to tolerate. Unfortunately, many people tolerate the intolerable daily, because they have to. Intolerable harms include deprivations of basics ordinarily required for a life (or a death) to be decent, for the person whose life or death it is. They would include access to non-toxic food, water, and air; freedom from severe and prolonged pain or suffering or deep humiliation and from disabling or even severely disfiguring diseases; the ability to stand, sit, and lie down; the ability to form attachments to others and interact with some of them; the ability to make choices and act on some of them; the ability to hope. So much for "intolerable." Next, "inexcusable."

Wrongs can be inexcusable in two ways. One way is by lacking a *metaphysical* excuse. A metaphysical excuse interferes with your ability to act— mental or physical disability, for example. The other kind of excuse, more interesting for my purposes, is a *moral* excuse. You have a moral excuse when you have a partially justifying reason, one that carries some moral weight, although not enough to justify your deed on the whole (what is justified on the whole needs no excuse). Evils lack both kinds of excuse.

That a wrong is inexcusable tells us nothing about its actual motive except that it carries no moral weight. A wrong can be inexcusable even when it has no motive at all—e.g., some omissions such as result from carelessness. These are failures of attention, not bad motives. The atrocity theory leaves it open whether an evil deed is motivated at all, motivated by an evil principle, by an evil interest, by the desire to be a badass, or some combination of the last three.

A principle subordinating morality to prudence is not the worst practical principle we can imagine, if the person whose principle it is does not have evil desires or interests. Interests and desires are evil when their objects include inexcusably wrongful inflictions of intolerable harm. An interest in being the instrument of another's undeserved suffering is not on a par with desires for wealth or fame, which can be pursued within moral bounds. A principle is immoral, for Kant, if it fails to respect anyone's humanity. Subordinating anyone's humanity to one's personal interests is surely immoral. But just how immoral can depend on what one's interests are.

Three ways to disagree with Kant's theory of evil are (1) to acknowledge evil desires, interests, or inclinations not rooted in predispositions to good, (2) to acknowledge immoral principles other than that of subordinating morality to self-interest, and (3) to acknowledge a desire to be worthy of the favorable opinion of others whose values are known to be bad.

Cruelty is a problem for Kant's ethics. As Nietzsche saw, cruelty can be a source of pleasure. One can take pride in one's cruelty. Richard Henry Dana, Jr. reports, in *Two Years Before the Mast*, that his ship captain said, as he administered the lash "swinging half round between each blow, to give it full effect" to the back of a crew member for having asked why another crew member was flogged, "If you want to know what I flog you for, I'll tell you. It's because I like to do it!—because I like to do it!—It suits me! That's what I do it for!"[7]

Solving Kant's Mystery

What motivates cruelty may be a certain normative self-conception ("it suits me"), that is, the desire to be a certain kind of person, one who would be worthy of the admiration or esteem of certain others. Wanting to be worthy of their admiration or esteem need not be grounded in a judgment of their moral worthiness. It can be grounded in an emotional attachment that one who has it may not understand and of which that person may be unaware.

There is a kind of self-interest more basic than the prudence that Kant usually has in mind when he refers to self-interest or self-love. Prudence is wisdom in the pursuit or protection of goods that we can obtain or secure for ourselves. But some of our interests are not in what we can obtain. They are interests in *being certain kinds of selves*, living up to certain self-conceptions, having a certain character. As Kant scholar Christine Korsgaard puts it, they are about who we are, not what we can get.[8]

The desire to be the kind of person who is attractive to or worthy of certain parties' esteem (admiration, praise, approval) is a possible motive for adopting or rejecting morality as a limit on the pursuit of more specific interests. Jack Katz's book *Seductions of Crime* with its examples of youthful inner city gang members who take pride in being bad, seems to illustrate such motivation. They do terrible things (including murder), apparently not

[7] Richard Henry Dana, Jr., *Two Years Before the Mast: A Personal Narrative of Life at Sea* (New York: Penguin, 1981), p. 155.

[8] Christine Korsgaard, *Sources of Normativity* (Cambridge: Cambridge University Press, 1996), pp. 250–51.

just for material gain or idle entertainment but to be worthy of the esteem of colleagues.

The idea that what underlies morally good character is one's desire to be worthy of the esteem of an all-powerful, omniscient, perfectly just being suggests a more general answer to Kant's mystery about why some of us make the moral law our supreme principle and others do not. The more general answer is that our fundamental practical principles have roots in our wishes to be persons who are attractive to or worthy of the love or esteem of someone who is or was, at critical times in our lives, important to us. If the persons whose esteem one seeks to deserve are lesser beings than God, it should not be surprising that one's supreme practical principles are less than moral. Even if your perception is false, if you perceive someone whose esteem you wish to be worthy of as a person who values cruelty, ruthlessness, and so forth, then you may seek to become that kind of person, to model yourself on that perception. You would not think you deserved the esteem that you value if you wanted to be that kind of person only as a means to feeling good. In fact, as Butler's famous stone argument shows, being that kind of person would not feel good unless that's what you wanted to be. Just as Kant's people of good will would not deserve the approval of the impartial spectator if they were motivated by the desire for it, those who take pride in being bad would not deserve the approval of which they hope to be worthy if they want to be bad only in order to get that approval.

This solution to Kant's mystery concerning the roots of human evil can be reached by combining two bodies of theory from different disciplines. One is Christine Korsgaard's philosophical analysis of the sources of normativity, which builds on and extends Kant's moral psychology.[9] The other is American psychologist Lorna Smith Benjamin's theory of social behavior, which combines interpersonal psychology with attachment theory in psychoanalysis.[10]

Korsgaard on Self-Conception as a Source of Normativity

Korsgaard develops a Kantian view of the sources of normativity that locates their roots in one's self-conception (she calls it one's "practical identity"). She takes issue with the narrowness of Kant's range of possible fundamental practical principles. Where he recognizes only one such principle

---

[9] Korsgaard, *Sources of Normativity*, esp. chs. 3 and 9, on "practical identities" and on evil.

[10] Lorna Smith Benjamin, "An Interpersonal Theory of Personality Disorders," in *Major Theories of Personality Disorder*, ed. J. F. Clarkin and M. F. Lenzenweger (New York: Guilford Press, 1996), pp. 141–220; Harry Stack Sullivan, *The Interpersonal Theory of Psychiatry* (New York: Norton, 1953); George Herbert Mead, *Mind, Self, and Society* (Chicago: University of Chicago Press, 1943); John Bowlby, *The Making and Breaking of Affectional Bonds* (New York: Routledge, 1989; orig. 1979), esp. pp. 126–60 and *Attachment and Loss: Vol. I, Attachment* (London: Hogarth, 1969).

besides the Categorical Imperative, namely, the principle of prudence, she finds several.[11] Whether the law that one wills categorically is the moral law or something else, she argues, will depend on one's self-conception, which is a jumble of conceptions of one's identity, in which some elements are more central than others.

By a self-conception, she means something practical, "a description under which you value yourself...under which you find your life to be worth living and your actions to be worth undertaking."[12] "Finding to be worth living or worth undertaking" sounds more objective than what she needs to make the point. It is enough that your self-conception is what gives meaning and shape to your life, a conception under which your life makes sense and you are motivated to continue it, protect it, and so on. She gives as examples thinking of oneself as a citizen of Kant's realm of ends (as a member of humanity), "as someone's friend or lover, as a member of a family or an ethnic group or a nation," as "the steward of her own interests" (an egoist) or as "the slave of her passions" (a wanton). How you think of yourself will determine whether it is the moral law, the law of some racial group, the law of egoism, or the law of the wanton that will be the law that you are to yourself.[13]

Most of our identities, she notes, are contingent: "You are born into a certain family and community, perhaps even into a certain profession or craft. You find a vocation, or ally yourself with a movement. You fall in love and make friends. You are a mother of particular children, a citizen of a particular country, an adherent of a particular religion...."[14] With this framework, she proposes something like Kant's conception of radical evil but adds to Kant's principle of prudence various other principles associated with our contingent practical identities. These become alternative possible supreme principles, to which morality might be subordinated.[15] She accepts Kant's idea that an evil will has the wrong priorities. But what is given priority over morality need not be prudence. It could be the good of a specific group, such as one's racial group or one's gender. One could be as willing to sacrifice, even to die, for the sake of that good as others are willing to do for the sake of moral ideals. She concludes that although "evil *may* take the form of ungoverned self-interest or selfishness...it takes many other forms as well," and that the selfish form, in which people "care only for what they get and not at all for who they are," is relatively uncommon.[16]

---

[11] Korsgaard, *Sources of Normativity*, pp. 98–99. Compare Benn's discussion of "heteronomous wickedness" and "conscientious wickedness" ("Wickedness," pp. 800–804).

[12] Korsgaard, *Sources of Normativity*, p. 101.

[13] Korsgaard, *Sources of Normativity*, p. 101.

[14] Korsgaard, *Sources of Normativity*, p. 120.

[15] Korsgaard, *Sources of Normativity*, p. 243.

[16] Korsgaard, *Sources of Normativity*, pp. 250–51.

This analysis opens up the possibility that the identity one constructs for oneself might be that of a badass.

On caring for who one is, as opposed to caring for what one can get, she continues, "Self-conception is the source of some of our sweetest pleasures—knowing ourselves to be loved or to have done well; and our greatest (and often self-inflicted) torments—believing ourselves to be worthless, unlovely, or unlovable."[17] Thus she brings her understanding of self-conception close to the idea of being moved by the desire to be worthy of the love or esteem of others who are important to us, to whom we are attached and with whom we may identify.

We are easily aware of self-concepts under such descriptions as someone's friend or lover, member of a family or ethnic group or nation. But if a self-concept is analyzed in terms of norms and values *implicit* in our conduct, we may not be aware of it. It can be hard work to learn to recognize that we have in fact identified with someone (even someone with whom we would not have knowingly chosen to identify) and that certain norms and values—some of which we would not endorse reflectively—have in fact implicitly governed our behavior.

Interpersonal psychology lends support and amplification to Korsgaard's view that normativity is rooted in one's self-concept, but without assuming that we know in detail who we have become or that the knowledge is easily acquired. According to interpersonal psychology, your self-concept, insofar as it regulates your behavior, is greatly the product of interaction with others who have been important to you, perhaps as sources of protection or security, even if they are no longer around or even living, even if you are unaware of having modeled yourself on them, as you once perceived them. Attachment theorists in psychoanalysis extend the exploration of interaction to the intrapsychic domain.

Benjamin's "Important Persons and their Internalized Representations" (IPIRS)

Using psychoanalytic concepts and building on John Bowlby's "attachment theory," Lorna Smith Benjamin argues that attachment to an internalized important other can elucidate behavior that otherwise appears simply perverse, irrational, perhaps even diabolical.[18] In her system, internalizing an important other can take the form of imitation (of the person's treatment of others, such as oneself), recapitulation (of one's early responses to the person), or introjection (treating oneself as the person used to treat one).

John Bowlby defines attachment behavior as "any form of behavior that results in a person attaining or retaining proximity to some other

---

[17]Korsgaard, *Sources of Normativity*, p. 251.
[18]Benjamin, "Interpersonal Theory," pp. 181–210.

differentiated and preferred individual, who is usually conceived as stronger and/or wiser." He finds that such behavior "characterizes human beings from the cradle to the grave" but that in adults it tends to be "especially evident when a person is distressed, ill, or afraid."[19] Children, he finds, retain representations of relationships with caregivers as internal working models, using them to evaluate potential interactions with others.[20]

Benjamin's hypothesis is that the quest for proximity also plays out intrapsychically in adults in relation to these internal working models. She calls the models "important persons and their internalized representations," for short, "IPIRs." I'll just call them "internalized models." Her idea is that imitation and introjection of the behavior of an important person and recapitulation of our responses to that person, get us *psychic* proximity, "the mental equivalent of reunion with the mother after separation stress," providing "an 'intrapsychic hug'," and that, likewise, "the need for psychic proximity to the IPIR increases under stress."[21]

If attachments can be renegotiated or rejected, as Benjamin argues they can be (this is how therapy works, in her view), they can also be reflectively endorsed, leading in some cases to the willful perpetration of evils. Knowingly choosing to continue to be worthy of the admiration of an internalized model who is perceived to have immoral values looks like an endorsement of immorality. Was Kant was wrong, then, to insist that evil in us is never truly diabolical?

One might question whether one who internalizes an evil model is endorsing immorality as such. It might be objected that the cruel model is valued or identified with not *for the sake of* the cruelty but in spite of it. The person internalized is or was once perceived as an important source of support, perhaps one's only source. That support was presumably a good thing. Still, if that support is no longer needed, then one's continuing, on reflection, to endorse and copy that model looks like an endorsement of being an evil person. In reality, the original model may not have been an evil person or valued evil as such. All that is required to generate someone who takes pride in being bad is that this is how the model appeared to those who internalized it.

Early models are internalized before one is able to assess their character, before one can realize what one is doing. Benjamin cites Harry Harlow's experiments with the unfortunate baby monkeys who tried to

[19] Bowlby, *Making and Breaking*, p. 129.

[20] Kenneth Craik, *The Nature of Explanation* (Cambridge: Cambridge University Press, 1943), quoted in Inga Bretherton and Kristine A. Munholland, "Internal Working Models in Attachment Relationships: A Construct Revisited," in *Handbook of Attachment: Theory, Research, and Clinical Applications*, ed. Jude Cassidy and Philip R. Shaver (New York: Guilford Press, 1999), pp. 90–91; J. Z. Young, *A Model for the Brain* (London: Oxford University Press, 1964); Bowlby, *Attachment and Loss*, pp. 80–83.

[21] Benjamin, "Interpersonal Theory," pp. 189–90.

bond with extremely cruel "mothers"—"diabolical devices that included having a huggable cylinder that unpredictably projected sharp spikes, and another that sometimes would spring loose and violently throw the baby across the cage"—when that was all they had.[22] She notes that the baby monkeys clung even more tenaciously to the violent "mothers" than other baby monkeys did to their terry cloth "mothers," suggesting that this may be because "the tendency to cling to a protective 'parent' is enhanced when there is danger, irrespective of the source of the danger," since infants do not appreciate that the parent is the source of the danger.[23] One's early models and protectors are a matter of luck, not choice; choice comes only later, if at all, in deciding whether to affirm or reject the fallout.

Kant's position that evil in human beings is not diabolical now seems partly right and partly wrong. It seems right that there is no need to suppose a fundamental predisposition to the bad in human nature. But people can knowingly choose to do evil without believing it prudent, and it is possible to come to value being bad. A predisposition to form attachments to others, missing in Kant's moral psychology, could explain why some people come to take pride in being bad. The predisposition to form attachments can explain the persistence across generations of such dangerous principles as racism and nationalism. Yet, it is important to recognize also that there is room for choice later on as adults. Attachments can be renegotiated and even rejected, upon reflection. One who becomes aware of an underlying attachment to an immoral internalized model as a source of attractions to wrongdoing can choose whether to *reaffirm the attachment* or disengage. Disengaging could require serious reconstruction of one's self-concept.

Perhaps a life of immorality creates habits that outlive the attachments that initially gave rise to it. Perhaps we can become attached eventually to the behavior itself. In affirming an unfortunate attachment, however, we affirm not simply wrongdoing but a relationship that rewards us with a feeling of worthiness of love or esteem. Some failures to disengage may indicate weakness rather than positive affirmation. What seems most right about the Kantian denial of diabolical evil, from the point of view of attachment theory, is that attachment even to an immoral model is not *initially* diabolical, in Kant's sense of that term. It is not motivated initially by a prior proclivity for wrongdoing. The attachment may have been necessary for the survival of a developing agent too young to judge. However, an adult capable of appreciating the past who chooses to continue to identify with an immoral model, despite the imprudence as well as the immorality of doing so, acts under the guise of the bad and has arguably no excuse.

If this psychoanalytic view is right, Kant's optimism about human freedom seems excessive (as does the pessimism of metaphysical determinists).

[22] Benjamin, "Interpersonal Theory," pp. 190–91.
[23] Benjamin, "Interpersonal Theory," p. 191.

Human beings are potentially free to accept or reject morality, to reject or endorse evil. The *actualizing* of the potentiality, however, depends not simply on the individual's will but on factors beyond the individual's control. Some of us are freer than others from our early internalized models, depending on such things as stress levels in our lives, how early caregivers treated us, and whether those caregivers facilitated or hindered our letting go. Whether our *initial* attachments are to people who have morally acceptable values is not within our control. Coming to appreciate the nature and role of those early attachments can also depend on a variety of contingencies, such as access to mental health care. And so, the possibility of becoming morally good or morally evil appears to be more a matter of luck than Kant thought, although also less mysterious than he thought.

On this analysis, acting under the guise of the bad becomes acting under the spell of a model who is perceived to find others worthy of approval, admiration, esteem, or love on the basis of their cruelty, meanness, hardheartedness, ruthlessness, and so forth. If it is objected that this analysis only pushes the issue back a step (that the question now becomes, how can the *model* have valued being bad?), one answer is that the model may not in fact value being bad—all that is necessary is that those who fall under the spell *perceive* the model as valuing badness, that it be logically possible to perceive someone that way. That perception can be enough to make those who come under their spell take pride in *actually* being bad.

CHAPTER 16

HATE CRIME LEGISLATION RECONSIDERED

MARCIA BARON

1. Introduction

It is a bittersweet pleasure to contribute to a collection on Claudia Card's work. Claudia inspired so many people, both as a philosopher and—for those of us lucky enough to get to know her—as a terrific mensch.[1] The paper of hers with which I'll engage here, "Is Penalty Enhancement a Sound Idea?" (2001), displays many of the qualities I love about both her and her work: her honesty, her open-mindedness, her readiness to rethink her view, her imaginativeness—all that plus (and contributing to) brilliance. Part of the honesty and open-mindedness is that she is exploring the issues as she writes, probing deeply, bringing others into the conversation, including people (such as Nietzsche) not usually associated with the topic.

I had not seen this paper when it first appeared but I heard Card speak on the topic at a 2005 conference at the University of Minnesota honoring Tom Hill. I was intrigued to hear her call into question the practice of classifying certain crimes as hate crimes and enhancing the penalties accordingly. The opposition that I knew of all came from libertarian quarters. The doubts Card raised were quite different. I continue to think (though with less conviction now) that penalty enhancements for hate crimes are a good idea. But I want to think it through, with Claudia.

2. Hate Crime Legislation

Hate crime legislation, writes Card, "applies to criminal offenders who intentionally select as their victims members of certain groups who are

---

[1] She was also a wonderful friend.

Criticism and Compassion: The Ethics and Politics of Claudia Card.
Edited by Robin S. Dillon and Armen T. Marsoobian.
Chapters and book compilation © 2018 Metaphilosophy LLC and John Wiley & Sons Ltd.

especially vulnerable to oppression on the basis of their race, color, sexual orientation, disability, or other deviance, or perceived deviance, from prevailing social norms" (Card 2001, 196). This characterization of hate crimes has two important features:

(1) X counts as a hate crime only if the victim is a member of a group that is especially vulnerable to oppression. Thus an attack on someone who is not a member of such a group would *not* count as a hate crime, given this characterization, even if the attacker hates the victim specifically qua member of a particular group.

(2) X does not count as a hate crime if the offender selects as a victim a member of such a group (that is, a group especially vulnerable to oppression, hereafter GEVO) *without regard to* the fact that the victim is a member of that group.[2] Thus, if D attacks V out of resentment for V's having gotten a job that D wanted, without regard to the fact that V is (say) gay, that won't count as a hate crime. It is crucial that V's being a member of such a group *was a reason* for D's attacking V (and not just a minor reason, either). Imagine that D attacks V out of resentment for V "and his like" (say, recent immigrants, in a climate of hostility toward recent immigrants) "taking away our jobs." That, I take it, could count as a hate crime. "Intentionally selects such a victim" has to mean that it is part of what one intends—part of the reason for selecting that victim—that V is a member of such a group.

I'll say more about (1) shortly but first want to comment on (2). That one intentionally selected as one's victim a member of a particular group (where that group counts as a GEVO), or more to the point someone whom one believes to be a member of that group, clearly should be required for the crime to count as a hate crime, but it is worth noting that this sets a rather low bar. Suppose D plans to burgle some house or other, and in addition to taking into account various practical considerations (ease of burgling without being noticed, ease of escape from the scene, likelihood of making off with items that are both valuable and easy to fence), D, regretting the likely toll, emotional and otherwise, on the victims, intentionally chooses Jews as his victims. Not that he hates Jews, but he likes them less than the others whose houses he could instead burgle (having narrowed down his options to just a dozen or so). If he is going to have to cause considerable unhappiness, better, he thinks, that his victims be Jews. This,

---

[2] A clarification concerning GEVOs: whether something is a GEVO is context sensitive. In the United States, especially in an era of intensified hatred thanks to Donald Trump and his followers, Muslims would constitute a GEVO. In some countries Muslims would not, though a particular sect might.

it seems to me, should not count as a hate crime.[3] If I am right, what is missing?[4]

For starters, hatred. I say "for starters" not because I think there is more needed besides hatred but because more specificity is needed. How must hatred enter in? One might answer by specifying that the defendant has to have been *motivated* by hatred. That would explain why the crime I described should not count as a hate crime: it was not done out of hatred. But I believe that answer sets too high a bar. We should not limit hate crimes to those motivated by hatred. Imagine a case where D attacked a gay man in order to impress a friend. The friend hates gay men; D doesn't. Even though D did not act out of hatred, this seems to be an instance of the sort of crime that we want to count as a hate crime if we are going to have that classification and enhance penalties accordingly.

So is it enough that D intentionally selected as his victim a member of a group of the relevant sort (namely, a GEVO)? I don't think so. Something more is needed and although it is hard to pinpoint exactly what, the notion of *enacting hatred* (which I borrow from R. A. Duff and S. E. Marshall (Duff and Marshall forthcoming)) seems pretty well suited to the task. To enact hatred is more than anything else to communicate something, and to communicate it not only to the victim but to others as well. At least implicitly it invites—or incites—others to embrace the hateful attitudes (Duff and Marshall forthcoming). D enacts hatred when he beats up the gay man, having selected him because he is gay; and he does so even though he is motivated by a wish to impress his bigoted friend. D is communicating something in doing this, and even though it is not his aim to invite others to embrace a hateful attitude toward gay men, he is by his actions implicitly inviting others to do so. He is also communicating something to the gay man himself and to other gay men (and presumably women, too), along the lines of "You are an abomination."[5]

---

[3] Card, following Frederick M. Lawrence (Lawrence 1999), distinguishes between the "discriminatory selection model" and the "animus model," the difference being that only the latter requires that the attacker be motivated by hatred (Card 2001, 197). Although the distinction as such doesn't seem to me problematic, the discriminatory selection model seems underdescribed. In particular, it leaves it unclear just what role hatred is supposed to play and raises for me the question I articulated above concerning the burglar who regrets causing unhappiness but prefers that such unhappiness be borne by Jews.

[4] I raise this not as a problem for hate crime legislation; it is easy enough to restrict the crimes for which such enhancement is an option, and burglary, embezzlement, and other crimes whose aim is not to harm another or to deface property but to acquire something could simply be ineligible. I bring it up rather as a question about the underlying rationale on which hate crime legislation can plausibly be based.

[5] The notion of enacting hatred is helpful in another way as well: as Duff and Marshall point out, that the defendant's action was motivated by hatred arguably is not an appropriate concern of a liberal republic's criminal law, for "such law is properly concerned with actions, not with the emotions that might lie behind them" (Duff and Marshall forthcoming, 5). An action may enact hatred, however, without being motivated by it; it expresses something

I said that a requirement that the crime was motivated by hatred sets too high a bar, but that is a bit misleading; it is not so much that the bar is too high as that the emphasis is on the wrong item. What matters for purposes of having a legal classification of hate crime is not what motivated the agent to act as she did but what the crime enacts.

I turn now to (1). It is important to observe that Card's characterization of hate crime legislation is at odds with the hate crime legislation she discusses (that of Wisconsin), and as far as I know with all hate crime laws in the United States.[6] The disparity between her account and the Wisconsin statute is that whereas Card characterizes hate crime legislation as applying to offenders who intentionally choose as their victims members of certain groups "especially vulnerable to oppression on the basis of their race, color, sexual orientation, disability, or other deviance, or perceived deviance, from prevailing social norms," the Wisconsin statute she discusses takes no notice of any such "special vulnerability." It requires only that the victim be "intentionally selected ... in whole or in part because of the actor's belief or perception regarding the race, religion, color, disability, sexual orientation, national origin or ancestry of that person."[7] An attack by an Asian American on a Caucasian, if the defendant intentionally chose as a victim a Caucasian, could count as a hate crime.[8]

I read Card's characterization as an idealization that captures why hate crime legislation seems (at least prima facie) to be a very good idea. The rationale for enhanced penalties is far more compelling if hate crimes are characterized as Card characterizes them. Although she does not indicate that it is idealized rather than a report of how it is understood in current statutes, given the disparity between it and the legislation she discusses, it makes sense to suppose that she so intended it.

I will follow her characterization, and in assessing objections will consider them as objections to hate crime legislation as she characterizes it rather than to current hate crime laws. I will therefore not take up the worry that enhanced penalties for hate crimes could be used disproportionally to

---

(whether or not the agent wished to, or felt or endorsed the something her action expresses; see Duff and Marshall forthcoming, 23–24). Also relevant, however, is the sort of hatred it is. See section 5, below.

[6] And because it is also at odds with Wisconsin's hate crime legislation as Card presents it, I don't think the explanation is that the law has changed since the time she wrote the paper. She writes that the Wisconsin legislation provides "for penalty enhancement in cases where offenders intentionally selected their victims, or intentionally targeted the property of victims, based on their perception of the victim's race, religion, color, disability, sexual orientation, national origin or ancestry" (2001, 198).

[7] http://docs.legis.wisconsin.gov/statutes/statutes/939/IV/645 (last accessed July 1, 2016).

[8] There is room for confusion here, so it is worth clarifying that the idea is not "intentionally chose S as her victim, where S happens to be Caucasian." It has to be, as explained above, that S intentionally chose this person (at least in part) because S was Caucasian.

enhance penalties for nonwhites attacking whites (moved perhaps by smoldering rage at whites' failure to recognize their social and economic advantages, and failure to realize how the legacy of slavery and Jim Crow laws lives on), and only rarely used to enhance penalties for crimes reflecting racist hatred on the part of whites.[9] If Card's understanding were the one accepted and carried out, this would not be a problem—except insofar as a policy emerges that is at odds with the law itself.[10]

3. Card's Concerns About Hate Crime Legislation

Card's main worries about enhanced penalties for hate crimes are as follows:

(1) Penalty enhancement for hate crimes "makes sense only if not all crimes have enhanced penalties," and therefore a contrast is presupposed between those crimes whose penalties are enhanced and other crimes. But, Card asks, is there really a morally significant difference, significant enough to warrant enhancing the penalties for hate crimes (2001, 207–8)?

(2) What message does the practice send? The message conveyed may be not what we were hoping for, namely, "that bias or bigotry is intolerable" but instead "that it is intolerable in those who commit crimes" (Card 2001, 196). In addition, Card worries that the practice "sends the message that those who do not commit crimes are absolved of responsibility for bias and bigotry in those who do" (196).

These are intriguing and important worries. I'll take up the first in sections 4 and 5 and the second in sections 6 and 7.

---

[9] Card mentions a conviction in Wisconsin of a black defendant for having incited a group of young black men who had just viewed the film *Mississippi Burning* to assault a young white man. The conviction of the assailants for a hate crime was upheld by the U.S. Supreme Court; by contrast, the conviction in Minnesota of white men for burning a cross in front of the home of African Americans was overturned. As Card notes, there is an explanation: the Minnesota statute criminalized something that was not already a crime; the Wisconsin statute only provided for an enhancement for something that was already a crime. Still, as she also notes, one wonders whether "it is just a coincidence that hate crime legislation in these cases ended up protecting white people against blacks and not protecting blacks against white haters" (2001, 198).

[10] Or unless the law is ruled unconstitutional on equal-protection grounds and therefore is replaced with the sort of legislation we in fact do have in the United States (and not only in the United States; see Duff and Marshall forthcoming, 32–33; for more detail on current law in the United Kingdom, see Law Commission 2014, chap. 2). I am grateful to Jeannine Bell for pointing out to me (in an e-mail exchange, June 13, 2016) that equal-protection considerations might bar hate crime legislation that limited its scope to cases where the victims were members of GEVOs.

4. What's So Special About Hate Crimes?

Since not all crimes can have enhanced penalties, Card reasons, there must be something about hate crimes that makes them worse than all other crimes—there must, that is, if enhanced penalties for hate crimes are warranted. The suggestion that there isn't might be advanced by noting that if all that is required for a hate crime is that the offender intentionally chose as a victim a member of a GEVO, it is hard to see what could make these crimes worse. But that is not the approach Card takes. She focuses on hate crimes that are motivated by hatred (presumably because they are more likely to have some feature that makes them worse than crimes that cannot qualify as hate crimes).[11]

One reason for wondering what is so special about hate crimes is, as Card highlights, the obvious fact that hate crimes are not the only crimes motivated by hatred. A might attack C (or burn down C's house, or kill his dog) because he hates him, without this being hatred based on C's (perceived) race, ethnicity, religion, ancestry, nationality or national origin, sexual orientation, or disability.[12] A might hate C because he resents the fact that C is so successful when A isn't, or because C won the heart of A's sweetheart (or as A might think of it, "stole" him), or because C got the job A wanted (or the job A had but lost when it was decided that C would be more suited to it). Particularly in scenarios where C in no way sought to undermine A and did not even know (for example) that this person was A's sweetheart (think here of the mayor of Casterbridge in Thomas Hardy's novel of that name), A's hatred is so egregious that it is not clear that it would be worse if A hated C because of C's ethnicity.[13] If the hatred is just as egregious, one is hard pressed to say how a crime motivated by one sort of hatred would be more egregious than an otherwise similar crime motivated by another sort.[14] So this is one serious obstacle to finding some feature of hate crimes that makes them worse than other crimes: the latter may also be motivated by hatred, and it is by no means obvious that they are motivated by a less objectionable hatred. If they are not, it is difficult to see how they could merit a penalty enhancement. (But not impossible; see section 5.) As Card asks, "Why privilege being victimized as a member of a hated group over being victimized for being the particular individual that one is or simply for

[11] Card does not consider the possibility of a different role for hatred, to the effect that it would have to be enacted (or communicated) rather than that it would have to be the defendant's motivation. Her assumption that its role would have to be the latter makes it harder to discern a compelling rationale for hate crime legislation.

[12] In listing these I am following the Wisconsin statute. http://docs.legis.wisconsin .gov/statutes/statutes/939/IV/645 (last accessed July 1, 2016).

[13] That said, it is also not clear to me that it wouldn't be.

[14] I don't mean to commit to these being different sorts of hatred; I'm phrasing it thus as shorthand for "hatred of S qua member of a GEVO" versus "hatred of S for some other reason."

being a human being who may be perceived as luckier than one's assailant or…as representative of establishment values that are loathed by the perpetrator?" (2001, 206).

Moreover, Card suggests, putting the spotlight on hatred—even apart from the question of whether crimes committed from one kind of hatred are worse than crimes committed from another—is morally problematic. In a section entitled "Who Becomes a Hater?" she recalls Nietzsche's observation that those who were victimized are more likely to hate their persecutors (2001, 200). Without fully endorsing Nietzsche's claim that it is the weak who hate, not the powerful, she worries that if "it is not the powerful or privileged who are likely to be the most intense haters, and if the hatred of those who have experienced long oppression can erupt in seriously harmful crime, then penalty enhancement legislation runs the risk of enhancing the penalties of some who have already been wrongly 'punished,' that is, those who are already especially vulnerable to oppression" (2001, 202–3).

The problem is particularly acute for the typical hate crime legislation that does not limit the relevant groups to GEVOs, but even hate crime legislation as Card characterizes it is vulnerable to the objection she develops. For, as she emphasizes, the oppressed often attack others who are oppressed. Such violence can come in the form of attacks on others in the same group or on those in another vulnerable group. Particularly when it is of the latter form, it could qualify as a hate crime if the victim is selected because of her membership in a particular GEVO.[15]

We are all too familiar with the phenomenon. Whether to feel better about oneself by saying "At least I'm not one of *them*" and working oneself up into (and tapping into others') hatred of those in that other group, thereby increasing one's sense of distance from (and elevation above) them, or out of resentment that (allegedly) those in that other group get all the

---

[15]Could it also qualify if it is an attack on someone in the same group? Card's account of hate crime legislation does not rule it out; nothing is said as to whether (for example) an African American police officer's use of excessive force against another African American, if enacting hatred against African Americans, could count as a hate crime. Card does not specify that the perpetrator of a hate crime has to be of a GEVO different from that of the victim, and she speaks to the issue only by observing that "black on black crime is not ordinarily discussed in addressing the hate crimes issue, because it is not perceived as a bias crime or a crime of bigotry" and adding parenthetically, "Whether it should be is another question" (2001, 202). Robin Dillon has suggested to me that some instances should be, drawing from the film *Boyz 'n the 'Hood* an example of an African American cop who pulls over an African American teenager and threatens to shoot him for "being one of those niggers." Had he shot the boy, Dillon suggests, that should indeed count as a hate crime. I think that plausible, but I worry that crimes by one member of a GEVO against another are too often going to be misinterpreted as enacting hatred against the person qua member of that GEVO. Many such actions may instead be actions reflecting anger at comembers for "bringing down" the group. Insofar as they reflect hatred, they reflect hatred not of the person qua member of that GEVO but qua member of that GEVO who is harming the group by "confirming" negative stereotypes.

jobs or are in some other way more successful, members of one oppressed group may hate those in another; and sometimes this hatred erupts into violence against members of that group (or attacks on their shops or cars or homes). There is no suggestion here that the fact that the offenders are themselves oppressed justifies or excuses their actions, but, Card wonders, do they really deserve an *enhanced* penalty? It is disturbing if hatred that is thought to warrant an enhanced penalty is hatred arising from oppression. Card quotes Andrew Sullivan, who "finds the most intense hate to be 'the hate of the hated'" and argues that "'hate-crime laws may themselves be an oddly biased category—biased against the victims of hate'" (Card 2001, 203). The "thought that he may be to some extent right" gives her serious pause about "the whole idea of penalty enhancement legislation" (203).

In sum, Card argues—or more accurately, raises the concern—that hate crimes are not really worse than other crimes and takes it that if they are not, there is no basis for a penalty enhancement. They are not worse, because it is by no means clear that a crime committed out of hatred for people qua members of a particular (oppressed) group makes it worse than a crime committed out of hatred of a particular individual (or a less focused hatred, such as that of Theodore Kaczynski, the Unabomber). Moreover, it is not clear that singling out for an enhanced penalty crimes committed out of hatred is wise anyway, particularly if those who become haters are more often than not victims of hatred themselves. In addition, canvassing other possible explanations of how they might be thought worse, Card claims that it is not the case that hate crimes harm more than (for example) crimes of horizontal violence by one member of a GEVO against another. "Is there good reason," she asks rhetorically, "to suppose that more harm is done by ... crimes of bigotry" than by "crimes exhibiting horizontal hostility?" (2001, 204).

5. Critique: What Sort of Comparative Judgment, if Any, Does Penalty Enhancement Presuppose?

Before addressing the question posed by my heading, I want to consider a possible reply to the rhetorical question from Card that I just quoted.

One might respond by saying "Yes, there *is* good reason, because harm is done to the group toward which the hatred is directed as well as to the specific victim of the crime." There's no gainsaying that; certainly harm is done to the group (or at least to its members) as well as to the specific victim. When a gay teenager is beaten up for being gay, when racist epithets are spray-painted onto a house or car, when a cross is burned in front of the home of African Americans, it is not just the teenager, the owner of the car, and those who reside in the house who are harmed.

Although this is a possible line of reply, I don't think it is the best reply. Hate crimes are a subset of crimes that cause group harm. Rape harms women[16] as a group (as Card helped bring out with her influential "Rape as a Terrorist Institution" [Card 1991]), and that is true of rape that would not plausibly count as a hate crime.[17] There seems to be something more going on in the case of hate crimes, and I don't think that the "something more" is best construed as "more harm." Thus I'm not convinced that the possible response I've sketched to Card's rhetorical question is the best reply. Instead of arguing that the harm wrought by hate crimes is (Card to the contrary) worse than that wrought by other sorts of crimes, I want to call into question her assumption that penalty enhancement presupposes a comparative judgment to the effect that hate crimes are worse than other crimes.

It might seem obvious that it does presuppose it: if a crime warrants penalty enhancement, it has to be worse than those crimes that do not. Not that every instance of the type that gets an enhanced penalty has to be worse than every instance of the type that does not. But (it might be argued) there has to be something about hate crimes in general that makes them (by and large) worse than other crimes.

This much is right: there has to be something about hate crimes in general which sets them off from other crimes, and in virtue of which an enhanced penalty is warranted. But it does not have to be the case that they are worse. They need not be worse all told; and although they have to be *pro tanto* worse, that would not be enough to warrant penalty enhancement.

Then what could warrant it? I see two promising (and overlapping) answers. First, arguably it is warranted by the particular kind of hatred involved in hate crimes—hatred not just of this person because of some history between the hater and the hatee, or because of resentment or envy, or even because of what the person represents to the hater (success, having an easy life when the hater's is very hard), but what Duff and Marshall refer to as "civic hatred." If someone hates the person qua member of a group she thinks inferior to her and "her kind" (or sinister and taking over "our" country) and if this group is a GEVO, there is special reason for the state to

---

[16] I am speaking here of the rape of girls and women but do not mean to ignore the fact that males are also victims of rape. I doubt, however, that the rape of males could count as a terrorist institution; nor does it seem likely that the rape of one man could count on some other ground as harming men as a group. The rape and sexual molesting of boys might so count, at least when committed in certain institutional contexts, notably by male authority figures such as priests and coaches. It would be a valuable Cardian project to explore how broadly applicable the notion of rape as a terrorist institution is. Does it apply only to certain types of rapes, and if so, which types?

[17] One might argue, however, that if we think of hatred as civic hatred, the vast majority of rapes (of females, anyway) should indeed count as hate crimes. Without spelling out her reasons (and without utilizing the notion of civic hatred), Card indicates that rape "could arguably be considered a hate crime in a jurisdiction that recognized the category of gender in its list of victims selected on the basis of their group identity" (2001, 211). See also Card 1991.

take an interest in a crime enacting such hatred. As Duff and Marshall put it, "If I am acting as an individual who hates another individual, nothing of great civic moment hangs on my conduct or hatred. I wrong her, but I lack the power to give effect to my exclusionary attitude; I cannot secure her exclusion from the community." A hate crime has a different character, insofar as it is "directed against victims who are, as a group, already vulnerable or threatened.... If, for some idiosyncratic reason, I hate people with red hair, and enact that hatred in my behaviour towards them, this is a wrong, and constitutes an individual threat to the safety of redheads with whom I come into contact; but it does not threaten their membership of the polity—their civic status. If, however, my hatred is directed, and enacted, against a group identified by a characteristic that is more widely seen and treated as contemptible or hateful, as disqualifying from proper citizenship, its enactment is genuinely threatening" (Duff and Marshall forthcoming, 7). I take it that the contrast here lies not in its enactment being more genuinely threatening in the latter case than in the former but rather in what it threatens: only in the latter case is the civic status of members of the group in question imperiled. The state should of course take an interest in the safety of all individuals within its borders (and of its citizens when abroad), but it should take an additional interest in threats to the civic status of members of GEVOs. And thus one ground for enhanced penalties for hate crimes is that in addition to the harm they do to the (primary) victims, they also imperil the civic status of some members of the polity. Thus, enhanced penalties for hate crimes need *not* presuppose a comparative judgment to the effect that hate crimes are worse than (most) other crimes, since the basis can instead be that they have a further dimension that should be of concern to the state.[18]

That was the first alternative to the position that what warrants the legal category and the enhanced penalty for hate crimes is that hate crimes are worse than other crimes. The second, closely related, alternative is that hate crimes send a message, a message that needs to be firmly and clearly countered. A message that redheads are inferior beings is not such a message (at least not in any society with which I am familiar), and an attack on a redhead by someone who chose his victim because the victim is a redhead and because he thinks redheads are (say) polluting "his" people should not count as a hate crime (except in a society where redheads constitute a GEVO). By contrast, attacks on gays and lesbians, on Muslim Americans, on African Americans, on people thought by the attacker to be illegal immigrants, do send a message that needs to be countered. They send such a message in part because of the long history of contempt for the groups (for example, gays and lesbians, African Americans). In the case of African

---

[18]One might say, "But then it is worse"; but that would be a further step, contingent on acceptance of an additive view.

Americans, it is a history dating to Reconstruction, when the "problem" of the emancipation of slaves was dealt with by a terror campaign of intimidation, a campaign waged especially by the Ku Klux Klan but abetted by many others, including law enforcement officials.

Hate crimes today should be viewed as part of an ongoing campaign of intimidation. With respect to other groups, hate crimes send such a message because of current intense animosity and mistrust or fear (seen by many as rendering more understandable violence against members of such groups). A firm denunciation of the hate crime—not just of the specific harm done but also of the message conveyed—is needed because of the content of the messages, for example, that homosexuals are being punished by God, with hints that violence against them may be God's will. Messages to the effect that crimes against people of certain ethnicities or sexual orientation or religious affiliation are less egregious than otherwise similar crimes against those in the "mainstream" (because, for example, it is—allegedly—understandable that a white man would be upset by nonwhites moving into "his" neighborhood) need to be countered.[19] Arguably, one apt way to counter them is to label such crimes hate crimes, enshrine this label in the criminal law, and attach an enhanced penalty to the crimes.

Thus this approach too, focusing on the need to counter the message sent by hate crimes, avoids taking the position that hate crimes are worse than other crimes. Rather, the idea is that they call for state action, for recognition that they are hate crimes, and for an enhanced penalty to counter the message that such crimes are more understandable than similar crimes against (say) white, heterosexual, second-generation-or-later U.S. citizens.

Card is of course well aware of the position that the legal category of hate crimes and enhanced penalties for hate crimes are called for to counter the message sent by hate crimes; in fact she notes that she was initially "attracted to the idea of penalty enhancement legislation for hate crimes as a way to send a strong social message against racism, sexism, anti-Semitism, and homophobia" (2001, 195). Her worry, as noted above in section 2, is that enhanced penalties do not do a good job of relaying that message. The message conveyed by hate crime legislation, Card suggests, may be not that "bias or bigotry is intolerable" but instead that "it is intolerable in those who commit crimes" (196). In addition, she worries that the practice of enhancing penalties for hate crimes "sends the message that those who do not commit crimes are absolved of responsibility for bias and bigotry in those who do" (196). I turn next to this objection to enhanced penalties for hate crimes.

---

[19]See Hampton 1988 for a helpful explication of this idea—as a way of working out a viable form of retributivism—in terms of vindicating the victim's value.

6. Card's Likely Response

Card might grant my point that penalty enhancement need not presuppose a comparative judgment to the effect that hate crimes are worse than other crimes. But she would question—indeed, as noted above, has questioned—whether penalty enhancement is a good way to counter the message sent by hate crimes, and could likewise question whether civic hatred is helpfully countered by penalty enhancement for hate crimes.

The message that is in fact sent may be only that bigotry is intolerable in those who commit crimes, not intolerable in other forms. Moreover, penalty enhancement may serve to make us complacent, to deem ourselves morally in the clear, and thus to shirk our responsibility both to recognize our own biases and to address the many facets of widespread bigotry.

> Is the support by white liberals in America for making blatantly racist crimes into hate crimes with enhanced penalties an attempt by white America to distance itself from racism? Is it a way of not confronting its own responsibility for racism but of deflecting attention from the advantages, in everything from college admissions to real estate purchases, that the attitudes reflected in such crimes make available to white people generally? Who benefits from recognizing as a hate crime the gay-bashing murder of Matthew Shepard? Does it not relieve of responsibility for homophobia all the homophobes in America who do not dirty their own hands with murder? (Card 2001, 213)

Penalty enhancements could be serving as a way for those of us who are insufficiently concerned about injustices against members of certain GEVOs to deceive ourselves into thinking we are deeply concerned. We may have the illusion, moreover, that we are addressing bigotry when we are doing something akin to scapegoating: heaping an additional penalty on someone guilty of a crime, and thinking that by heaping this additional penalty we are correcting injustices. (Perhaps the enhanced penalties meted out provide us with the sense that we are making up for many years of turning a blind eye to violent attacks on gays and for the notorious long-standing condoning of lynchings, especially in Southern states in the United States, of black men.)

Recognizing these dangers, would it be better simply to drop hate crime legislation and strive to enforce existing laws evenhandedly? Would the best approach be simply to see to it that assault charges are filed and the suspect prosecuted with as much zeal when the victim is a member of a GEVO as when he or she isn't?

One worry about taking this approach is the pragmatic one: the long-standing practice of not prosecuting such crimes with as much zeal has not died, and it arguably needs to be counterbalanced by having a legal category of hate crimes, with enhanced penalties. (This parallels one argument for affirmative action: it is needed as a counterweight to implicit bias.) But even apart from that, even supposing we actually could and would enforce existing laws evenhandedly, there is another consideration: without the legal classification of hate crime, many a crime is not recognized for what it really is. An example from Bloomington, Indiana, is illustrative. In October 2015, a Turkish woman was sitting with her nine-year-old daughter at a table outside a cafe when Triceten Bickford, a young white man (and an Indiana University student) who did not know her and had not interacted with her in any way walked up to her, grabbed her by the neck, forced her head forward, and tried to remove her headscarf (thereby restricting her breathing).[20] Just before attacking her he allegedly shouted "White power" and "Kill them all"; he also shouted in the course of the attack anti-black racial slurs and "Kill the police."[21] This is not just a battery (nor even "just" a battery and strangulation).[22] It is morally and legally significant that he attacked her because she is Muslim. Yet, because Indiana, unlike most states in the United States, has no hate crime legislation, it cannot count as a hate crime under Indiana state law. According to Indiana law, the fact that this attack was an act of hatred against Muslims is legally irrelevant. I take it to be important that we call what he did a hate crime.[23]

Why is it important? In part to recognize that this was no mere "random" attack that could have happened to anyone. It would not have happened to a Caucasian, seemingly nonimmigrant, Hoosier. Relatedly, it tells us something about our social climate. Calling these hate crimes is an important step toward recognizing and addressing the bigotry.

Now, Card agrees that the label is important but points out that we can have the social category without the legal category (2001, 199). While that is true, the social category of hate crime lacks something if there is no legal category of hate crime. It is important to be able to say of Bickford, if he

---

[20] Fortunately, he was prevented from further harming her thanks to the intervention of a bystander, who together with the woman's husband held the violent man down until the police arrived.

[21] http://www.cbsnews.com/news/police-indiana-university-student-shouted-white-power -before-attacking-muslim; http://www.cbsnews.com/news/fbi-opens-hate-crime-investigation -into-attack-on-muslim-woman-in-indiana.

[22] Bickford is charged with both, strangulation being defined in the relevant statute as "applies pressure to throat or neck or obstructs nose or mouth" https://public.courts.in .gov/mycase/#/vw/CaseSummary/eyJ2ljp7lkNhc2VUb2tlbil6lk1qYzFNVGd3TmpFeE1EEQ XhPalk1TWpreE9ERXlObVE9ln19.

[23] This case also brings out—if one thinks it should count as a hate crime, as I do— why it is important not to require that the perpetrator be motivated by hatred. Bickford, who was intoxicated at the time and reports that he had failed to take his antianxiety medication that day, seems to be utterly baffled by his action. But whatever his motivation, it clearly enacted hatred against Muslims. It was not just odd behavior (such as throwing off one's clothes, running down the middle of the street, and yelling "Kill the police"). It was directed at a particular person, and for no reason other than her religion or ethnicity.

is convicted, that he committed a hate crime, and indeed to be able to say now, in advance of the trial, that he is charged with a hate crime.

The case is even clearer when we consider nonviolent crimes, such as spray-painting a house, or a tree in front of that house. Whatever one sprays can count as defacing (barring authorization to mark a tree to indicate that it needs to be trimmed or removed); but surely it matters whether what is painted is (say) an *A* in a circle (a sign denoting "anarchy") or, alternatively, a racist epithet on a tree in front of a home where (the perpetrator knows) African Americans live.

But, it might be said, the legal classification "hate crime" is one thing; the enhanced penalty, another. In reply, I want to grant that it is the classification that matters most. As I see it, the enhanced penalty is needed mainly just because otherwise the message "This is not only an assault/defacing of property but also a hate crime" would be a muddled message. So an enhanced penalty is called for; but enhancing it a great deal is counterproductive. Doing so may lead jurors to resist convicting (perhaps to construe as a "reasonable doubt" something far-fetched so as to be able to avoid concluding that the state has shown the defendant to be guilty beyond a reasonable doubt).[24] For this reason and to reduce the risks that Card brings up, enhancing penalties modestly is preferable to hefty enhancements.[25]

In sum, although the risks Card brings up certainly deserve our attention, I don't think they outweigh the benefits of having the legal classification of hate crime. Besides, there is *always* a risk that if we address injustices by doing *X*, we may delude ourselves into thinking that we have done all that we need to do. That there is this risk is a strong argument only against deluding ourselves into thinking that this is all that needs to be done (or that our own responsibilities have now been met), not against doing *X*. Enhanced penalties obviously will not by themselves address bigotry in all its forms; mainly they address the long-standing problem that violence against gays, African Americans, and members of other GEVOs is treated as less serious than violence against others. That by itself is important. In addition, however, announcing that these crimes are hate crimes is likely—I speculate—to gradually have a rippling effect, so that, for instance,

---

[24]It is disturbing, too, to see harsh penalties replace consistent enforcement of the law. We want to see rape taken more seriously by those in law enforcement than it now is, but I think I speak for many when I say what we want is *not* to see the harshest possible penalty meted out in those relatively few cases that are prosecuted and end in a conviction but rather to see more cases prosecuted. We want to see the cases handled differently from the moment that the crime is reported, without such hindrances as rape kits not processed in a timely fashion, and complainants who suspect a date rape drug was used being told that they can only be tested if they foot the bill themselves (see Cochran 2010).

[25]How much to enhance will depend in part on what sort of penalty the crime in question carries when it is not a hate crime.

schoolteachers less often turn a deaf ear to children referring disparagingly to someone as a "fag." One hopes it will be recognized that the same bigotry that is a basis for enhanced penalties for a crime is also to be treated as a problem by schoolteachers and principals.[26]

7. More Cardian Rejoinders

I said that there is always the danger that if we take measure X in an effort to address an injustice we will congratulate ourselves on our efforts and think we have done all that we need to do; but is there a greater danger with hate crime legislation? Card thinks so. Citing Joel Feinberg, she observes that "one of the functions of punishment generally is that of denouncing and disavowing the crime on the part of a society" and that "a significant function of punishment is the absolution of others from blame" (2001, 213). She takes it that one function of punishment is to absolve ourselves or society as a whole from blame. Is that really the case?

I don't think so, and I take Feinberg to be saying something a little different, both more plausible and less unsettling. Explaining the expressive function of punishment, he provides several illustrations. One of them is that in a case where the actor may be thought to represent (say) the nation or the military or the government, an important reason for prosecuting and punishing X is to make it clear that *we do not condone X*, let alone cheer it on. Thus among the reasons needless violence by police officers needs to be punished is to make it clear that the police force deplores this misuse of power (rather than simply regretting the injuries and deaths it causes). Punishment has symbolic significance, expressing "authoritative disavowal." This seems both accurate and as things should be: one purpose of punishment (obviously permissible only when the person punished has been proven beyond a reasonable doubt to be guilty) is to make it clear that the person was not authorized by superiors or the institution in question to do X.

It is not only where there is a particular need to show that the action does not represent our university, or police force, or synagogue (and so on) that the expressive function of punishment is in evidence; punishment serves to relay "symbolic nonacquiescence" on the part of our university or community. This too seems to me accurate and as it should be. Of course, there is room for hypocrisy; maybe the action *is* representative of our community. But taking a stand to show that we do not acquiesce can be helpful in clarifying for ourselves what we do stand for. Perhaps we have acquiesced in

---

[26] I found it deeply troubling when my son was in school (in the late 1990s and early 2000s) that although teachers certainly took seriously any racist epithets, a child's using the term "fag" or "queer" as a term of derision was not treated as a matter of concern. My efforts to bring the problem to the attention of teachers went nowhere.

the past by not speaking out, by tolerating (say) bullying of the immigrant children in our schools. In no longer tolerating it we clarify (and perhaps in effect revise) our community's or our institution's values.

A further expressive function of the law is "vindication of the law": "It is murder in Mississippi, as elsewhere," writes Feinberg, "for a white man intentionally to kill a Negro; but if grand juries refuse to issue indictments or if trial juries refuse to convict, and this fact is clearly recognized by most citizens, then it is in a purely formal and empty sense indeed that killings of Negroes by whites are illegal in Mississippi.... A statute honored mainly in the breach begins to lose its character as law, unless...it is *vindicated* (emphatically reaffirmed); and...the way to do this...is to punish those who violate it" (1970, 104). I would prefer to think of this along the lines of Jean Hampton's suggestion that we vindicate the value of the victim (Hampton 1988), but either way (vindicating the statute or the value of the victim) there is a message sent by prosecution, conviction, and punishment, and it is particularly important in the face of a history of failing to indict or convict in cases where the victim was African American.

Finally, Feinberg notes that in a case where "the wrongdoer must be one of a small number of suspects," punishment of one "relieves the others of suspicion and informally absolves them of blame" (1970, 105). Thus those who were suspects are now absolved.

Feinberg does not suggest (and I do not see any other reason for thinking) that punishment serves to absolve us of blame for our bigotry when we punish someone for a hate crime (or for anything else). His point, rather, is that when A is convicted of a crime, those others who had been suspected of that crime are now relieved of suspicion and informally absolved of blame—absolved specifically of blame for that crime. Others might still be blamed (and perhaps rightly so) for having, say, helped create a climate in which anger reigned or for having fought gun control measures. His point is not—and I think it would be implausible to claim—that punishment of a wrongdoer serves to absolve everyone else from any blame whatsoever for the crime in question, let alone to absolve everyone from blame period (or from blame for being violent, hateful, or bigoted). Without wishing to deny the phenomenon of scapegoating, I do not think it the case that punishment serves to absolve the community from all blame. Instead, punishment serves, and happily so, to send a message that we condemn this action. It sends the message that rather than viewing it as bad but not as bad as it would be had the victim been white, we acknowledge that it is every bit as bad, and with the added dimension of being a hate crime—of perpetuating an ongoing injustice against a particular group.

Of course, there is the danger that we are only mouthing the words. But sometimes (though by no means always) saying the words helps us to come to see the reality.

8. Concluding Thoughts

My defense of hate crime legislation is limited in certain ways and in need of qualification in others. First, it needs to be qualified by the crucial recognition that we punish too much. (I'm thinking here especially of the United States, though it is by no means the only country where this is true.) Punishments are on the whole too harsh; our prisons are ghastly places. Thus although I do (albeit somewhat tentatively) favor enhanced penalties for hate crimes, the point is a comparative one: defacement that involves an expression of hatred against a group that should count as a GEVO should be, other things equal, punished more harshly than other defacement (including expressions of hatred against a particular individual). Moreover, hate crime legislation is only one part of the solution. It is certainly no substitute for addressing the problems that give rise to "intense and dangerous" hatred (Card 2001, 205).

My defense is limited in that I have been discussing hate crime legislation in what I called an "idealized" form—that is, hate crime legislation as Card presented it. I find it far more difficult to provide a rationale for hate crime legislation in its usual form, where something counts as a hate crime because the victim was "intentionally selected ... in whole or in part because of the actor's belief or perception regarding the race, religion, color, disability, sexual orientation, national origin or ancestry of that person,"[27] and it counts as such even if the victim's (perceived) race or religion or ancestry (and so forth) was not such as to render him vulnerable to bigotry in that particular society. The rationale is clearer when hate crimes are limited to instances covered by Card's account, that is, where the victims are, or are perceived to be, "members of certain groups who are especially vulnerable to oppression on the basis of their race, color, sexual orientation, disability, or other deviance, or perceived deviance, from prevailing social norms" (Card 2001, 196). Yet whether it is feasible to so limit hate crimes without running afoul of equal-protection considerations is a further question.[28]

Finally, I have not undertaken or investigated empirical research that might serve either to confirm or to disconfirm Card's suspicion that hate crimes may be undertaken especially often by those who are themselves victims of hatred and oppression. Of course, that is less of a worry for hate crime legislation as she presents it than for the sort that allows as a hate crime a crime against someone qua Caucasian, but it is still a worry insofar as the hate crime could be committed by one member of a GEVO against a member of a different GEVO (or perhaps a member of the same GEVO).

---

[27] http://docs.legis.wisconsin.gov/statutes/statutes/939/IV/645 (last accessed July 1, 2016).

[28] There is also the worry that hate crime legislation so understood will unleash fights to get more groups recognized as GEVOs, including groups that would hardly seem to qualify as oppressed.

That the defendant was himself or herself a victim of oppression could, however, be taken into account at sentencing, and that to some extent addresses the problem. That said, I have been relying in this essay on my sense that hate crimes are at least as often perpetrated by those who are not members of anything plausibly regarded as a GEVO. Living in the United States in an era when presidential candidate Donald Trump whipped up (or at the very least brought to the surface) widespread civic hatred and rallied supporters with suggestions that to "make our country great again" we need to build a wall against Mexicans and close our doors to Muslims (with the exception of some Muslims he knows personally), I find it very hard to believe that it is the victims of hatred and oppression who are most likely to hate (or to commit crimes enacting hatred).[29] Spending summer 2016 in the United Kingdom, I saw a similar trend: most woes—for example, inadequate funding for the National Health Service—were blamed on immigrants. I see no sign that civic hatred is more common among members of GEVOs than among others; to the contrary. There is in any case a great deal of civic hatred in the air, and it seems to me important to undercut the messages that condone and even encourage hatred with a message that crimes enacting civic hatred are of particular concern, meriting a harsher penalty than would an otherwise similar crime. Having laws against hate speech would strengthen the message, but that is a topic for another occasion.

Acknowledgments

I am indebted to Robin Dillon for her encouragement and helpful comments, and to Jeannine Bell for answering some questions about hate crime legislation

References

Card, Claudia. 1991. "Rape as a Terrorist Institution." In *Violence, Terrorism, and Justice*, edited by R. G. Frey and Christopher W. Morris, 296–319. Cambridge: Cambridge University Press.
———. 2001. "Is Penalty Enhancement a Sound Idea?" *Law and Philosophy* 20:195–214.

---

[29]For an example of what Trump's campaign unleashed, and for similar bigotry in the United Kingdom encouraged and exploited by UKIP (the U.K. Independence Party) and others pushing (alas, successfully) for Brexit, see http://thinkprogress.org/politics/2016/06/24/3792046/rick-tyler-tennessee-make-america-white-again/ and http://www.theguardian.com/politics/2016/jun/26/racist-incidents-feared-to-be-linked-to-brexit-result-reported-in-england-and-wales (last accessed July 1, 2016). Thanks to Levi Tenen for telling me about the Rick Tyler campaign to "make America white again."

Cochran, Kelly. 2010. "A Story That's Far Too Common." *Indiana Daily Student.* May 16.

Duff, R. A., and S. E. Marshall. Forthcoming. "Criminalizing Hate?" In *Hate, Politics, Law*, edited by T. Brudholm and B. S. Johansen. Oxford: Oxford University Press.

Feinberg, Joel. 1970. *Doing and Deserving: Essays in the Theory of Responsibility*. Princeton: Princeton University Press.

Hampton, Jean. 1988. "The Retributive Idea." In J. G. Murphy and Jean Hampton, *Forgiveness and Mercy*, 111–61. Cambridge: Cambridge University Press.

Law Commission. 2014. *Hate Crime: Should the Current Offences Be Extended?* London: Stationery Office. http://www.lawcom.gov.uk/wp-content/uploads/2015/03/lc348_hate_crime.pdf

Lawrence, Frederick M. 1999. *Punishing Hate: Bias Crimes Under American Law*. Cambridge, Mass.: Harvard University Press.

CHAPTER 17

MISPLACED GRATITUDE AND THE ETHICS OF OPPRESSION

ROBIN MAY SCHOTT

Introduction

One of the final pieces that Claudia Card wrote before her death is an essay entitled "Gratitude to the Decent Rescuer," originally presented to the Workshop on Gratitude at the University of Birmingham, November 22–23, 2013, and read by Diana T. Meyers at the Central Division Meetings of the American Philosophical Association in St. Louis in February 2015.[1] Whereas typically in the philosophical literature there is a discussion of gratitude and the problems of the failures to honor obligations of gratitude, Card is more interested in the opposite fault of misplaced gratitude.

The notion of misplaced gratitude may seem odd. How could it be wrong to provide moral regard or honor to someone for her actions on one's behalf? Even if gratitude were undeserved and therefore unnecessary as a moral obligation, why would it actually be morally wrong? Card's interest in these questions is formed by her social indignation and her fundamental commitment to opposing oppression, exploitation, and injustice in all its forms. The phenomenon of misplaced gratitude becomes visible from this perspective, where one catches sight of what oppression does to people. Only then can one see that if, for example, a woman is grateful for not being battered by her husband, her gratitude is misplaced because it is based on socially normative beliefs and practices that in themselves undermine the possibility of justice and moral integrity.

---

[1] I refer to the version Diana T. Meyers presented, which she was kind enough to share with me.

Criticism and Compassion: The Ethics and Politics of Claudia Card.
Edited by Robin S. Dillon and Armen T. Marsoobian.
Chapters and book compilation © 2018 Metaphilosophy LLC and John Wiley & Sons Ltd.

The problems of misplaced gratitude troubled Card in her early work, which she addressed in "Gratitude and Obligation," originally published in 1988 and included in her book *The Unnatural Lottery: Character and Moral Luck* (1996). As she looped back to these concerns in her late work as well, I want to look more closely at the question, What does Card's analysis of misplaced gratitude tell us about her own philosophical methods and contributions?

Card's Feminist Lens

In her essay "Genocide and Social Death" (Card 2007), Card defends her work on genocide as being within the project of feminist philosophy. As the editor of the special issue of *Hypatia* entitled *Feminist Philosophy and the Problem of Evil* (2007), in which the essay originally appeared, I passed along to her the comments of two of the reviewers that her article was not explicitly about feminist philosophy.[2] Her answer to this objection was concise: her work on genocide was feminist because of the history of the project and the perspective from which it was carried out. Genocide targets both sexes. Because the violence of genocide is not specific to women's experience, there has been a risk that genocide is overlooked in feminist thought. Philosophers have thought mostly about the positions of perpetrators and have given little attention to the experience of civilians who are victims and survivors. Card argues for a feminist philosophy that looks to issues of ethics and social theory and is not only a study of women, feminism, or gender. From this perspective, work on what genocide does to individuals and to communities, how it destroys their social vitality, is part of feminist philosophy. She writes, "My lens is feminist, polished through decades of reflection on women's multifarious experiences of misogyny and oppression. What we notice, through a feminist lens, is influenced by long habits of attending to emotional responses, relationships that define who we (not just women and girls) are, and the significance of the concrete particular" (Card 2007, 72).

It was from this feminist lens that Card found her philosophical voice. She once told me that there was a ten-year period in her life when she did not publish, after she took up her position at the University of Wisconsin, Madison, and before she found out how to use her activism within the women's and lesbian movements for her work in philosophy. This feminist perspective opened up a range of phenomena previously overlooked in the tradition of moral thinking. Philosophers typically considered cases like whether parents should be grateful to the swimmer for rescuing their small child who is in danger of drowning; they did not consider cases like

---

[2] She subsequently mentioned to me that this was one of her most widely read and reprinted articles.

whether women should be grateful for not being battered. Not only did Card contribute to changing the moral horizon on which philosophical reflection takes place, she also contributed to changing the perspective from which one wielded analysis. As she writes in *The Unnatural Lottery*, "In the twentieth and twenty-first centuries, the most significant transitions in the descendants of European philosophy may come from the increasing access to academic education of people with social histories of disempowerments: the working classes, Jews, people of color with histories of oppression in white societies, women of all classes and ethnic backgrounds, people with disabilities, people living openly lesbian or gay lives" (Card 1996, 1). She goes on to note that this multifaceted pluralism is reflected in the topics to which philosophers attend, the audiences for whom one writes, the styles of philosophical critiques, and the points of view philosophers represent.

Unlike many feminist philosophers who have fought with the canonical thinkers who shaped philosophical traditions, Card drew inspiration and methods of analysis from these traditions to take on the moral complexities and problems of oppression and to develop a finely tuned analysis of the moral imagination of individuals who are either privileged or disempowered in situations of oppression. She was not reluctant to engage critically with the philosophers from whom she drew (such as Kant, Nietzsche, and Rawls), nor was she reluctant to turn the skills of her philosophical analysis and moral imagination against feminist moral theorists themselves.

Card's Critique of Care Ethics

One finds the problem of misplaced gratitude on the edges of Card's scathing and brilliant critique of feminist care ethics as a form of slave morality. (This was also my first encounter with her work.) Her point of departure is to give weight to issues of oppression and abuse, in intimate relations as well, and to hone insight into the risks oppression poses for individuals' survival and spiritual integrity (Card 1996, 89). Card argues that the oppression of both racism and sexism are basic evils, which she defines as treating people "in ways that no one should be treated, no matter what it does for anyone else" (1996, 91). There are dilemmas, however, for theorists who work on issues of oppression. On the one hand, one can understand the contours of what being on the losing side of moral luck does to moral character, what risks it poses to an individual's safety and integrity, through personal encounters with oppression. But anger and outrage that are rooted in experience may lack the patience to work systemically through philosophical arguments and objections. On the other hand, professional distance allows one to think abstractly and generally about the moral damage of oppression. Yet with this distance, issues of oppression may not beckon as powerfully as if one were in their midst. One of Card's achievements was to sustain a passionate engagement with issues of oppression coupled with close philosophical scrutiny. This combination of moral indignation and philosophical acumen shaped her encounter with care ethics.

While many feminist ethicists turn to care to uncover a "feminine approach to ethics" (Noddings 1984), as an alternative or complement to an ethics of justice, Card was sharply critical of what care as a basis for moral relations might imply (Card 1990, 101). Valorizing care threatens to include too much, such as relationships in which carers are exploited. These relationships ought to be dissolved and not sustained. In cases of intimate partner abuse or child abuse, caring relationships can be highly dangerous. When someone is abused or psychologically terrorized in an intimate relationship, he might use his energy to avoid missteps and trespasses, to avoid breaking off contact in order to protect himself from potential blame from the abuser. As Card notes, in such situations care may be a survival strategy that risks damaging one's own moral character and other central intimate relations (such as with one's children), but may be disguised as a virtue to oneself or the surrounding community (Card 1996, 53). In situations of exploitative power relations, the exploited persons often have finely tuned insights into the needs of their exploiters. "Women learn well to do this with men; slaves have learned to do it with masters" (Card 1990, 106–7). Card explicitly connects this critique of care ethics with Nietzsche's critique of slave morality, in which care (or in Nietzsche's account Christian charity and love) is a fantasy of the weak and impotent who are unable to exact justice, which requires power and autonomy (Card 1996, 60).

Card did not argue that abuse is the only paradigm case from which to theorize about moral relations. In *The Unnatural Lottery*, however, she noted that a local newspaper in Madison, Wisconsin, carried the story that fully one-fourth of all arrests were for domestic crimes (Card 1996, 86). In the light of these huge numbers, philosophers cannot take non-abusive intimate relationships as the only paradigm for care either. Hence, ethics must address the social and structural issues in which intimate violence is normalized. In this context, Card claims that misplaced gratitude is a moral fault. It is a fault in one's own moral character if one is grateful for not being abused, as it effectively acknowledges the ongoing potential for abuse in intimate relations without effectively resisting the abuse. In continuing care and contact instead of breaking off contact with the potential abuser, an individual becomes complicit in a situation of abuse. Misplaced gratitude is indicative of harm to one's moral character. Misplaced gratitude is also a black mark on the moral character of the society, in which the norms of family life and gendered behavior, the regulations and limitations of the police and the court system, and the necessities of economic survival have effectively given impunity to abusers, allowing the reproduction of such violence.

Care ethics risks including too much—as in the risk of caring for abusers. In Card's analysis, it also risks excluding too much. From the point of view of opposing oppression and exploitation, Card argues for the necessity of a justice perspective. Many injustices suffered in society are not perpetrated by people one knows or potentially could know (as is often assumed by care theorists) but are perpetrated by strangers whom one will never know. When Nina Simone sang, in the final verse of *Mississippi Goddam* (1964), "You don't have to live next to me, just give me my equality," she was enraged by the murder of Medgar Evers in Mississippi and the bombing of the Sixteenth Street Baptist Church in Birmingham, Alabama, that had killed four black children on September 15, 1963.[3] Perhaps proximate strangers committed these murders and hence were persons the victims potentially could know. Yet as Card notes, it is not care from such strangers that Simone is demanding but political rights—and the respect that is its precondition (Card 1996, 85). Respect is basic for just relations, and Card argues that justice is also more basic than care, in contrast to the care ethics approach of Nel Noddings.[4] While Noddings regards justice as a substitute for caring in some contexts where caring would be ideal but is unrealistic, Card suggests that the opposite is true. "The demands of perfect justice may be so great that perhaps the best we can do in many contexts is to assume responsibilities of caring where we are able, although justice would be ideal" (Card 1996, 96).

With respect to social relations that are just, issues of gratitude are generally not in play. One may grateful for living in a society that operates, or aspires to operate, according to principles of justice. One is not grateful, however, to someone for acting justly, as it is morally right to act in this way. Moreover, in a just society what is morally normative and normally practiced are in close allegiance with each other. Just social relations eliminate or diminish many of the flaws in moral character that appear under situations of injustice and oppression. Situation, as Simone de Beauvoir also noted, is central for moral character.

Ambiguity Is Not Enough

Card's interest in moral luck is rooted in her view that "how we become good or bad, how good or bad we become, and whether some of our choices turn out to have been justified are matters into which luck enters substantially" (Card 1996, 2). Human agency is limited, and we know how little control we have over factors that determine the basic conditions of our work, lives, and deaths. These factors also shape our moral opportunities,

---

[3] Although the FBI concluded in 1965 that four known Ku Klux Klansmen and segregationists had committed the bombings, no prosecutions ensued until 1977. https://en.wikipedia.org/wiki/16th_Street_Baptist_Church_bombing (accessed June 8, 2016).

[4] Card argues that Nel Nodding's monistic approach to care excludes a justice perspective in ethics, in contrast to Carol Gilligan's pluralistic approach to care ethics (Card 1996, 74).

and although they do not dictate what choices we make in the face of such opportunities, they may influence our character development, which does influence these choices. Card's inquiry into the role of moral luck in the formation of character contributes to an ethics of oppression. She asks, What implications and distortions does oppression have for the character and agency of those who are privileged as well as for those who live the hardships of oppression?

Beauvoir also addresses the role of situation for moral experience. When Card edited *The Cambridge Companion to Simone de Beauvoir* (2003), it was an occasion for her to clarify her own position with regard to Beauvoir's existential approach to oppression. Beauvoir's inquiry into the role of situation for human experience is, like Card's position, rooted in an acknowledgment of the fundamental structures of oppression—such as racism, colonialism, and sexism. Beauvoir exemplifies her nuanced phenomenology of oppression, in which she analyzes how oppression informs subjective embodied experience, both in her analysis of racism and in her analysis of sexism. For example, in *America Day by Day* Beauvoir—inspired by Richard Wright, Jean-Paul Sartre, and Frantz Fanon—describes the contours of the experience of whiteness and blackness in a racist society. While traveling through the South by bus and experiencing the segregation of blacks in bathrooms, restaurants, waiting rooms, and buses, Beauvoir writes, "it was our own skin that became heavy and stifling; its color making us burn"; "we are the enemy despite ourselves, responsible for the color of our skin and all that it implies" (Beauvoir 1999 [originally 1954], 204, 228; see Schott 2003a, 234). Beauvoir experienced the helplessness of whites, who do not feel responsible because they think they cannot do anything, when she didn't dare to offer her seat in the front of a bus to a black woman who had fainted: "The whole bus would oppose it, and she would be the first victim of their indignation" (Beauvoir 1999, 231). Every moment of the lives of blacks is penetrated by the social consciousness of being black, by the consciousness of the white world from which black takes its meaning (Beauvoir 1999, 67). Beauvoir's strength in these accounts is in providing nuanced descriptions of how such racist structures invade seemingly innocuous moments of everyday experience, in showing the complexities of consciousness, with its inner divisions and failures, for both blacks and whites.

Beauvoir's attunement to the failures of moral consciousness derives from her focus on the paradoxes, contradictions, and ambiguity at the heart of human relations. In *The Ethics of Ambiguity*, she argues that existentialism is the only philosophy that takes seriously the element of paradox and negativity in human existence. Human existence is fundamentally paradoxical, as is evident in the fact that humans have consciousness and intentionality but cannot escape their natural condition, cannot escape being an object or instrument for others, and ultimately are fated to die. Thus, failure is an inescapable element of the human condition. In Beauvoir's view, there is an inherent split or alienation in human existence, which makes possible different relations to freedom, for example, the escape from freedom or its affirmation. One can never completely flee from freedom, nor can affirming one's freedom overcome the primary split or alienation within human existence (Schott 2003b, 93–94). Instead of fleeing from the complexity of the human condition, we should "try to look the truth in the face ... to assume our fundamental ambiguity (Beauvoir 1948, 9; see Schott 2003a, 229). Hence, ambiguity is central for Beauvoir's understanding of the human condition. By connecting moral failure to social institutions, such as the institutions that animate racism, Beauvoir also implies that an individualistic approach to ethics is incomplete. Ethical analysis must incorporate features typically excluded from an individualistic-based ethics, with its focus on individuals' intentions, actions, or principles. Instead, ethics must incorporate analyses of social institutions and historical developments to make moral judgments that can transcend the ambiguity of individual moral values (Schott 2003b, 95–96).

Though Card is also attuned to how social institutions shape moral experience, she argues that a focus on ambiguity is insufficient to analyze the moral issues of oppressed agency. It may be that individual intentions, actions, or principles are shaped by the historical situation in which we find ourselves, but for Card that does not put out of play the centrality of moral judgments. In her view, ambiguity is not enough to solve moral problems. Moreover, in the context of extreme oppression, the fundamental ambiguity that is rooted in human existence is insufficient to delineate the complexities and ambiguities that mark these conditions. "The complicity of agents who suffer oppression embodies ambiguities that go beyond those of ordinary human agency.... The ethics of ambiguity might be extended to address ambiguities of oppressed agency in addition to ambiguities that are universal to the human condition" (Card 2003, 15). Card highlights the question of whether ambiguity is at play in extreme cases of oppression, such as during the Nazi Holocaust. Primo Levi, a survivor of Auschwitz, introduces the notion of the gray zone as a way of exploring the ambiguity of the kapos, prisoners who themselves assisted in the extermination by ushering the condemned into gas chambers and assisting in medical atrocities. Levi writes, "These were gray, ambiguous persons, ready to compromise" (1989, 49). But in Card's view, the ambiguity of these persons meant that "their very subjectivity, their capacity for choice, became an instrument for others' evil projects" (Card 2003, 16). Levi's discussion shows the need to delineate ethical ambiguities (such as when prisoners are forced to inflict the same violence on others that perpetrators inflict on them, thereby denying them their innocence) that are not universal but are a distinctive factor of oppression. Under Nazism, the choice of the Nazi leaders to exterminate the Jews was unambiguously wrong, and an ethics that merely focuses on universal conditions of ambiguity is not in a position to show the nonambiguous nature of evil intentions (Card 2003, 17–19).

Extreme situations that generate the use of the term "evil" suggest for Card that a phenomenology of oppression is not enough to analyze the moral landscape of oppression. One must develop an ethics of oppression that can show what is wrong without ambiguity in evil acts and intentions, and that is equipped to explore the problems of burdened agency. Card sees in Beauvoir's concept of ambiguity the risk that one tolerates what one should reject (Card 2003, 21). I have argued, however, that Beauvoir faced the limits of an agent-based analysis of evil and offered alternative pathways for addressing evil, including a discourse of historical dynamics (as in the absolute evil of lynching) and a discourse of symbolic representations (as in the representation of woman as evil) (Schott 2003a, 244). Card's insistence on maintaining an agential perspective in ethics even in situations of extreme oppression leads her again in her later work to explore the problems of gratitude and misplaced gratitude as a way of grappling with the moral virtues and flaws that occur under oppression.

Misplaced Gratitude Versus Gratitude

Although Card, like Beauvoir, has a keen eye for the complexities of ethics and for delineating moral flaws, her interest does not rest with an ethics of negativity that focuses on moral failure (Schott 2003b, 95). Rather, she examines moral flaws in order to clarify moral virtues. In her late paper "Gratitude to the Decent Rescuer" (2013) she explores how gratitude can go wrong, how it can be offensive, how it can be misplaced. Gratitude is misplaced if one is grateful for acts of "basic decency that are clearly morally required" (Card 2013, 2). It is misplaced if one is grateful "for not being wrongfully injured or harmed by someone who could have injured or harmed you" (2). Here Card returns to her earlier example of a wife's gratitude to her spouse for not beating her, or for not bringing home venereal disease, or for not becoming an alcoholic or a gambler. Such misplaced gratitude reflects a situation of abuse, in which morally wrong and distorted behavior has become accepted as the norm not only by the wife but also by many in her surrounding community. Misplaced gratitude is also dangerous because of its tendency to bind one to the abuser, and thereby to make one become complicit in one's own abuse.[5]

---

[5] One of the editors of this collection asked whether Card's notion of misplaced gratitude can be extended from intimate relations to broader social issues, such as foreign aid for food. In order to answer this question I consulted one of my colleagues at the Danish Institute for International Studies, Lars Engberg-Pedersen, who is an expert in international development, poverty reduction, and inequality. He answered that this reasoning would only make sense if one considered foreign aid to be part of ongoing relations of exploitation. It would be more correct to understand foreign aid in some cases as compensation for historical imperialism. Engberg-Pedersen's objection to the use of misplaced gratitude in relation to foreign aid is fourfold. (1) Gratitude does not typically characterize how recipients look upon aid. Mostly,

Yet gratitude is not always out of place and offensive. Gratitude is in order for acts that benefit one and exceed what is morally required. Card considers the example of the passengers on Flight 93 on September 11, 2001, who forced a crash landing in the countryside in Pennsylvania, thereby preventing a suicide bombing in Washington, D.C. These passengers had nothing to lose, and their acts may not have been supererogatory. One is grateful, however, not only for the fact that they did what they thought was right but also for the fact that they were not overcome by fear and retained the moral imagination and self-possession to act morally under stressful circumstances (Card 2013, 5–6). One can be grateful for acts of rescue that are morally required but are contrary to prudence. Card finds an exemplary instance of this in the case of the French villagers of Le Chambon, who protected many children from deportation to Auschwitz during the Nazi occupation of France by hiding them in their homes or fleeing with them into the forests. Although it might not be surprising that these villagers acted according to their conscience, it might be surprising what their conscience demanded of them. In examining these cases, Card illustrates that gratitude is in order for acts (1) when they are beyond the demands of morality; or (2) when they are beyond the common practices of morality (as when they exceed a statistical norm, like those of the villagers of Le Chambon [Card 2013, 11]); or (3) when they require exceptional qualities of character—such as endurance, moral imagination, self-possession, and courage under stressful conditions.

Even while Card accounts for examples where gratitude is in order, she also catches sight of potential flaws in such morally good attitudes and acts. Card considers this problem both from the perspective of the decent rescuer and from the perspective of the rescued. If the rescuer is not offended by gratitude, is it because the rescuer shares the judgment of others that one's acts and character are morally superior to other peoples' acts and characters? Should the rescuer hold such self-regard, however, it would express arrogance, which is a morally problematic attitude. Moreover, if the rescued expresses gratitude to the rescuer, does that indicate a low expectation about whether other people would act morally? Such an attitude expresses a pessimistic view of human beings, and Card considers this pessimism to

recipient countries are well aware of the political economy of donors themselves, which underlies foreign aid. (2) Poor countries wish to be treated as equal and independent partners. In such a context, were they to express gratitude for aid it would underline the equality between the countries, where economic help is not expected. (3) It is wrong to view imperialism as the only reason for misery in the world, and hence one should not understand foreign aid only in terms of compensation. (4) Most people do not believe that foreigners should help them. They are not global citizens but think in terms of tribe, community, and nation, and expect help from kin. Engberg-Pedersen adds that foreign aid in some cases might stimulate a feeling of dependence, but this is rarely due to gratitude. In cases of humanitarian relief, there may be no alternative to dependence.

be a version of Schopenhauer's view that true goodwill is as rare as a four-leaf clover (Card 2013, 12). She notes that with respect to what she calls the arrogance problem and the Schopenhauer problem, she does not yet have a satisfying solution.

Hence, even acts that are morally right (being a decent rescuer, expressing gratitude to a decent rescuer) might be bound up with morally wrong attitudes. Card takes it as her task to unravel these distinctions. Such morally wrong attitudes can be about concrete other persons (for example, other people who were in a position to rescue but who did not) or about persons more generally (for example, general expectations of morally inadequate behavior). What does Card mean when she presents the arrogance problem and the Schopenhauer problem as moral *problems* requiring solutions?

It helps to understand what Card means by moral problems by looking at her account of the extreme moral problems of evil. In *The Atrocity Paradigm*, she argues for a theory of evil that includes both a stoic and a utilitarian component (Card 2002, 95). She views Kant as maintaining a stoic view that wrongdoing is independent of its effects on others. When we wrong others, we fail to treat them as equals and fail to value their rationality as we value our own. Since Kant's stoicism implies that the suffering of victims is incidental to what makes evil deeds evil (Card 2002, 73), it needs to be combined with a utilitarian component that acknowledges the moral importance of harms that are suffered (2002, 16). One can extrapolate from her approach that in considering the arrogance problem and the Schopenhauer problem, one needs to consider both the reasons for people's behavior and the harms that may result.

One could then explicate Card's position as follows. If someone (even a decent rescuer) has an attitude of arrogance, the reason for action is not just to help a person in need but also to help a person in the expectation that no others are morally capable of such an act. Hence, the reason for acting mixes the motive to help with a demeaning view of other people. Such a demeaning view is not just a minor moral flaw mixed with otherwise moral behavior; such a view denies the equal moral worth of most other human beings. Card considers the distinction between whether such a person views her conduct as morally superior or views herself as a morally superior person as "a distinction without a difference" (Card 2013, 11–12). If such an individual reflected on how differently other people behaved, she would likely regard herself as morally superior. With the Schopenhauer problem, moral pessimism might lead to inaction rather than action, promoting passivity in relation to unjust or oppressive conditions. The harm this creates is not only in being complicit with such conditions; inaction can lead to a further loss of respect for oneself and others, and to ongoing suffering. In both cases, even good actions and attitudes can present moral flaws that threaten to jeopardize the moral quality of the act or attitude. Card notes that she does not yet have a satisfying solution (Card

2013, 13) to this problem, where "yet" suggests that the problem is not insoluble.

Despite ample grounds to abandon the view that moral ideals are realizable, Card steadfastly pursues the inquiry into moral behavior. In reference to the Holocaust, she contrasts Levi's notion of gray zones with the idea of "zones of light" (Card 2013, 6), where seeing light at the end of the tunnel, even if one does not emerge from that tunnel, enhances one's chances to survive by grounding hope. Card's own hope—which she maintains even after having completed two of her projected three volumes on evil—is grounded in a secular conception of morality. Existentially, as a response to Kant's question "What can I hope for?" Card maintains a commitment to hope in morality, in contrast to settling for moral ambiguity or insoluble problems.

How to Express Gratitude?

As Card notes, for some people the more pressing question may be not *whether* to express gratitude but *what form* gratitude should take. In her view, one should discuss this question in the context of the "logic of gratitude," which addresses the moral relations between benefactor and beneficiary (Card 2013, 14). Expressing gratitude can occur through publicly honoring the benefactor, which is to pay a person respect for some exceptional act or qualities. Honoring one's benefactor is based on the special relationship there is between benefactor and beneficiary, a way of saying, "I am yours" (Card 2013, 15). One can also express gratitude through reciprocating in the future or through paying forward and giving to other people the benefits that one has received oneself.

It may be, however, that Card's notion of the logic of gratitude is too narrow, based as it is on the dyadic relation between benefactor and beneficiary. It may be that one makes a decision to express gratitude and to prioritize what is required in the context of a wider network of relationships. This also opens up the question of whether one should express gratitude to those who enabled one to make morally right decisions about gratitude. In such a case, one is grateful to another not for her extraordinary acts or qualities but for her enabling one to express gratitude to a beneficiary in a way that puts demands on one's ordinary habits and priorities. This form of gratitude also highlights the many ways in which one is a recipient in moral relations that exceed the logic of benefactor and beneficiary. Moreover, just as misplaced gratitude involves a negative relation to one's self that harms one's moral integrity, so expressing gratitude that is in order also has an impact on one's relation to oneself. In both cases, gratitude to another person encompasses a much wider range of moral relations than in Card's account of exceptional acts or qualities.

While Card develops her reflections on whether and how to express gratitude in the context of the decent rescuer, one is tempted to consider whether it applies beyond this scope as well. Does the logic of gratitude apply in relations between colleagues and friends? If so, how could one express gratitude? In Card's view, gratitude is in order when it is for acts that are beyond the demands of morality, or beyond the common practices of morality, or when they require exceptional qualities of character. Would it be proper for me to express gratitude to her as a reader, when I was stunned by her critique of care ethics in 1990? As a member of an audience, when I was inspired by her keynote address on war rape at the conference of the International Association of Women Philosophers on Krieg/War in Vienna in 1996? As a colleague and friend who engaged with reciprocal and common invitations to anthologies, conferences, and workshops over nearly two decades? Do these experiences belong to the logic of gratitude?

While Card no doubt would have argued that her actions were not beyond the demands of morality, one can add that the attention and time she used for her colleagues and friends, and for younger colleagues and students past and present, certainly went well beyond common practices. They also display exceptional qualities of character that benefited her friends, colleagues, and students. Claudia Card displayed endurance in her commitment to her profession, including teaching and writing through much of her cancer treatment; courage in finding a strong voice as a feminist and lesbian philosopher and in forging a path for other scholars; grace and gratitude to her family and friends in the face of her own death; and the moral imagination to articulate and challenge the wrongs she experienced in her own life and the lives of her friends and colleagues and in the historical cases that provided the material for her reflections on evil. The special relationships created between Card and her students, family, friends, and colleagues sometimes changed the course of their life stories. This is one way of interpreting her notion that expressing gratitude through honoring another is a way of saying, "I am yours" (Card 2013, 15). When the death of a colleague and friend has put to rest the question of reciprocating in the future, one can express gratitude by learning from her methods of moral analysis as well as by giving to one's own younger colleagues, students, and friends the generosity of time and the seriousness of attention that she gave to us. Even so, Card would remind one to consider whether expressing such gratitude carries a tint of self-satisfaction, which risks putting the brakes on the ongoing practice of critical moral inquiry and diverting one's attention from the practice of paying it forward.

Concluding Reflections

In her study of misplaced gratitude and of gratitude that is in order and in her contribution to an ethics of oppression as distinct from a phenomenology of oppression, Card expands the horizon of moral inquiry by focusing on issues of oppression and injustice. This is true from her early work on women's oppression under patriarchal relations to her later work on the atrocity paradigm of evil, where she analyzes the evils of rape, terrorism, torture, and genocide (Card 2010). She has provided a powerful example of a feminist lens for analyzing what oppression does to moral character. She was particularly adept at unraveling the complex web of moral possibilities, of displaying her own moral imagination of how persons might, could, and would respond to moral choices even when they are under pressure (and the conditional tense of the verb flags her attempts to bring these moral dilemmas, choices, and pitfalls to life).

While Card focuses on the social and structural conditions that distribute luck and moral luck so differently and unfairly, she maintains a focus on the individual agent and how moral conscience operates, or fails to operate properly, in these situations. She rejects an ethics of ambiguity as Beauvoir proposed, since she considers an ontological perspective on the ambiguity of the human condition to be inadequate to address the particular ambiguities of extreme situations. One might suggest, however, that Beauvoir's account of a phenomenology of oppression could enrich Card's account of an ethics of oppression, by further probing the moral agent's self-relation. Moreover, catching sight of the network of relations that enable decisions about and expressions of gratitude (an insight garnered from care ethics) might suggest a wider notion of the distribution of moral agency.

In rejecting an approach to ethics that focuses on moral failures, Card finds herself in a predicament. She distinguishes moral flaws from moral virtues, in order to clarify what morality demands in particular situations. Yet her reflection on moral virtues also opens up a discussion of the moral pitfalls embedded in these virtues. Despite the difficulty—or in a flush of rhetoric one might be tempted to say impossibility—of finding good acts and attitudes that are good through and through, Card remained steadfastly devoted to the project of philosophical reflection on morality. Her faith in the power of moral reflection and in the role of moral philosophy as a normative project rather than a description of moral acts and attitudes sustained her secular approach to morality. This commitment grounded her hope for morality, even if one does not ever reach the moment where hope is justified in actuality. Hence, even though she repeatedly analyzes moral flaws, failures, and wrongs, she refuses to rest with the negative, but maintains her quest for moral good.

References

Beauvoir, Simone de. 1948. *The Ethics of Ambiguity*. Translated by Bernard Frechtman. New York: Philosophical Library.

Card, Claudia. 1999 [1954]. *America Day by Day*. Translated by Carol Cosman. London: Phoenix.

————. 1990. "Caring and Evil." *Hypatia* 5, no. 1:101–7.

————. 1996. *The Unnatural Lottery: Character and Moral Luck*. Philadelphia: Temple University Press.

————. 2002. *The Atrocity Paradigm; A Theory of Evil*. Oxford: Oxford University Press.

————, ed. 2003. *The Cambridge Companion to Simone de Beauvoir*. Cambridge: Cambridge University Press.

————. 2007. "Genocide and Social Death." In *Feminist Philosophy and the Problem of Evil*, edited by Robin May Schott, 71–86. Bloomington: Indiana University Press. Chapter 5 in the present collection.

————. 2010. *Confronting Evils: Terrorism, Torture, Genocide*. Cambridge: Cambridge University Press.

————. 2013. "Gratitude to the Decent Rescuer." Unpublished manuscript.

Levi, Primo. 1989. *The Drowned and the Saved*. Translated by Raymond Rosenthal. New York: Vintage.

Noddings, Nel. 1984. *Caring: A Feminine Approach to Ethics and Moral Education*. Berkeley: University of California Press.

Schott, Robin May. 2003a. "Beauvoir and the Ambiguity of Evil." In *The Cambridge Companion to Simone de Beauvoir*, edited by Claudia Card, 228–47. Cambridge: Cambridge University Press.

————. 2003b. *Discovering Feminist Philosophy: Knowledge, Ethics, Politics*. Lanham, Md.: Rowman and Littlefield.

————, ed. 2003c. *Hypatia:* Special issue entitled *Feminist Philosophy and the Problem of Evil*, 18, no. 1.

————, ed. 2007. *Feminist Philosophy and the Problem of Evil*. Bloomington: Indiana University Press.

CHAPTER 18

THE CHALLENGES OF EXTREME MORAL STRESS

CLAUDIA CARD'S CONTRIBUTIONS TO THE FORMATION OF NONIDEAL ETHICAL THEORY

KATHRYN J. NORLOCK

1. Introduction

In "Challenges of Local and Global Misogyny," her contribution to *A Companion to Rawls*, Claudia Card writes of her onetime adviser, "Rawls saw need for non-ideal theory also within society, but never developed that project. Perhaps the nonideal part of his Law of Peoples can be a resource for thinking about responding to evils when the subject is not state-centered" (Card 2014, 473). John Rawls is the widely cited author of the distinctions between ideal and nonideal theory as described in *A Theory of Justice* and further developed in *The Law of Peoples* (Rawls 1999). Interest in and development of nonideal theory, especially in political philosophy and especially in response to (and in rejection of) the views of John Rawls, has taken off over the past twenty-five years, richly expanding in the past ten years in particular.[1] Yet Card herself did not move to describe her own work in ethics as nonideal theory. She regularly cited Rawls in her ethical and sociopolitical writings, and she referred to the work of leading nonideal theorists today, including Charles Mills, Lisa Tessman, Amartya

---

[1] The expansion in philosophical literature on nonideal theory in the past decade is remarkable, attributable at least in part to responses to widely cited works, including Charles Mills's "'Ideal Theory' as Ideology" (2005) and Amartya Sen's *Idea of Justice* (2009). Social and political philosophers have entertained much more discussion of ideal and nonideal theory than philosophers of interpersonal ethics, although that, too, is changing; see especially the works of Lisa Tessman, including *Moral Failure* (2015) and "Expecting Bad Luck" (2009).

Criticism and Compassion: The Ethics and Politics of Claudia Card.
Edited by Robin S. Dillon and Armen T. Marsoobian.
Chapters and book compilation © 2018 Metaphilosophy LLC and John Wiley & Sons Ltd.

Sen, and Lisa Schwartzman. Despite her appreciation of the works of non-ideal theorists, Card did not explicitly identify herself as an author of or a contributor to nonideal theory, let alone to a specifically nonideal *ethical* theory; she does not engage directly with the concept of nonideal theory until her "Challenges of Local and Global Misogyny," written very near the end of her life. Nonideal theorists have cited Card's work, especially her fundamental and early challenge to Rawls's notion of a natural lottery, in the form of her "Unnatural Lottery," a quintessentially nonidealizing insight, but I have not yet found a work in which a nonideal theorist numbers Card in the set of nonideal theorists. In this essay, I provide reasons to enter Card into the set. She was a theorist of the nonideal not just in her last work but in decades of ethical theorizing.

One may think it is not necessary to identify Card as a nonideal theorist. I am interested in doing so, however, because I advocate for the worth of nonideal theory, and I believe it is important to understand how to do it better, and how to do so with the help of Card's contributions. Doing nonideal theory better includes maintaining self-conscious awareness that a multiplicity of feminist philosophers have been offering the conceptual apparatus for nonideal theory for decades. In the field of philosophy, the authors of an early boom in a theoretical literature become the experts; as nonideal theorists of the past ten years become the authorities credited with expertise in nonideal theory, it is incumbent upon those experts to recognize the shoulders on which they stand. Almost all nonideal theorists recognize an intellectual debt of sorts to John Rawls, the object of so much nonideal analysis and criticism; this collection in Claudia Card's honor is an opportune occasion to point out that Rawls's first female advisee should be recognized as a contributor as well; indeed, more than one of the women who were Rawls's advisees have been valuable contributors of nonideal conceptual tools.[2]

In this essay, I further argue that philosophers of ethics ought to more concertedly develop nonideal ethical theory (NET), as a distinctive contribution to, and as a subset of, nonideal theory more generally. I am influenced by philosophers including Tessman and Mills when I contend it is important for ethical theory, and it is important for feminist purposes, to carry forward the interrelationship that Mills (2005) identifies between nonideal theory and feminist ethics. For this collection in Card's honor, I think it is also important to point out that while Mills was quicker to overtly and succinctly identify that interrelationship, Card exemplifies it, frequently elaborating on elements of her ethics by noting that they are

---

[2] Most evidently, Elizabeth Anderson is a major author of nonideal theory; see especially *The Imperative of Integration* (2010). Barbara Herman's work in Kantian ethics has long offered provocative angles on Kant's otherwise perfectionist ideal theory; see especially *Moral Literacy* (2007).

informed by the experiences of the oppressed and by feminist philosophy. In NET, too, I draw attention to her work because she may help us to do it better, especially since, as I will show, her theorizing includes basic elements of NET indicated by Tessman, Mills, and others, and because I suggest that she offers two important and neglected elements to the insights of other nonideal ethical theorists.

In the first part of this essay, I develop my account of Card's ethical work as nonideal theory. I doubt this part will be controversial; I offer it to clarify Card's role in ethical theorizing of the recent past, partly in order to brief the unfamiliar reader on Card's ethics and nonideal theory, and partly to enter Card's contributions into the story of nonideal theory's emergence in philosophy—a history of a movement in its youth, but one I believe that nonideal theorists should start keeping track of better than we have.

In the second half, I recommend, to other NET philosophers, the prioritization of (i) Card's rejection of the "administrative point of view," explicated below, and (ii) Card's focus on "intolerable harms" as critical to excellent ethical theorizing. I conclude that there are worthwhile reasons to more concertedly develop NET, as such, and as a subset of nonideal theory generally, although, like Tessman and Mills, I hold that the border between ethical and sociopolitical theory is and ought to be porous, though not nonexistent (especially and not solely in nonideal theory). I end with the observation that NET may helpfully point toward reasons to take a pessimistic stance toward moral progress as elaborated in some classic texts in political philosophy; my appreciation of Card's insights yields a variety of pessimism that Card herself did not share.

2. Claudia Card's Place in Nonideal Ethical Theory

David Schmidtz rightly comments that the "contrast between ideal and nonideal theory is elusive" (2011, 773); I will be simplifying the contrasting elements for much of this essay. Accounts of nonideal theory, as developed by many different participants, enjoy "heterogeneity," as Laura Valentini argues (2012, 654), but there are certainly consistent elements. Valentini offers a conceptual map of "the debate on ideal and nonideal theory" as she sees it occurring between "political philosophers," who "have started to interrogate the methodology they use to develop normative prescriptions" (654). Such interrogation, she notes, is driven by concern that the "dominant—Rawlsian—paradigm is too detached from reality to guide political action," motivating "this methodological debate on the proper nature of political philosophy, and its ability to guide action in real-world circumstances" (654).

Similarly, Lisa Tessman (2010) points out, at times theorists of *ethics* pause in the work of doing ethical theory to ask, What do we want in a normative theory? The answer, in short, will include sensitivity to the actualities of contexts that (just *do*) include oppression. With others, Tessman concludes that we want ethical theory to be "[relevant] to actual agents in actual conditions and [applicable] to the problems created by oppression" (806), including moral failures in the presence of dilemma. Eduardo Rivera-López (2013) concurs that "any adequate moral theory should be sensitive to ... unfortunate facts," adding, "It seems obvious that the best or most appropriate actions, rules, and institutions in this nonideal world are *different from what they would be* in an ideal one" (3626).

Valentini and Rivera-López concentrate on Rawls's three main elements of the ideal/nonideal distinction:

(1) Nonideal theory as "partial compliance" theory, versus ideal theory's "full compliance," that is, "what duties and obligations apply to us in situations of partial compliance as opposed to situations of full compliance" (Valentini 2012, 654), and whether it makes a difference if we're referring to the partial compliance of others or that of ourselves (Rivera-López 2013, 3631–32; see also Murphy 2000).

(2) Nonideal theory as "realistic" theory, versus ideal theory as "utopian or idealistic theory," that is, "whether feasibility considerations should constrain" theorizing "and, if so, what sorts of feasibility constraints should matter" (Valentini 2012, 654).

(3) "Nonideal theory" as "transitional" theory, that is, "whether a ... theory should aim at identifying an ideal of societal perfection, or whether it should focus on transitional improvements without necessarily determining what the 'optimum' is" (Valentini 2012, 654), or as "comparative" instead of transitional to a "transcendent" ideal (Rivera-López 2013, 3633, extending Amartya Sen [2006] to ethical theory).

Valentini's and Rivera-López's accounts explicitly commit to revolving around Rawls's ideal theory in *political* philosophy. Charles Mills's widely cited essay "'Ideal Theory' as Ideology" (2005) starts with criticism of Rawls's political philosophy and notes that "feminist ethics has interestingly come to converge with feminist political philosophy" (165); Mills proceeds to endorse nonideal methods and goals for both, especially the method of rejecting idealizations that "obfuscate realities" (177). Tessman argues for avoiding idealizations in *morality*: "Theory must begin with an empirically informed, descriptive account of what the actual world is like" (2010, 807), keeping front and center that "there are irrectifiable wrongs" (809) and that we "should forego the idealizing assumption that moral redemption is possible, because it obscures the way that moral dilemmas affect the moral agent" (811). Tessman adds, "To see the moral agent as someone who will likely face complicated moral conflicts and emerge from them bearing moral remainders is an important way to de-idealize the moral agent" (811). All the nonideal theorists I find take "the perspective or standpoint of oppressed groups" (as Schwartzman [2009, 182] says; see also Tessman [2010, 819, n. 31]) or "historically subordinated groups" (as Mills [2005, 170] says).

Philosophers familiar with the work of Claudia Card will recognize that the elements of nonideal theory, so described, are hallmarks of her approach. Her early monographs (*Lesbian Choices* and *The Unnatural Lottery*) concern the subordination of women and the (inherently nonideal) oppressed moral agent threatened with moral damage and bad constitutive luck in a heteronormative and patriarchal world. Card's occupation in *The Unnatural Lottery* with the role that moral luck plays in the options available to moral agents, and the potential of oppressed individuals to ever *be* ideal, bespeaks a commitment to doing ethics from the point of view of a deidealized moral agent. Given her attention to double binds, and moral luck's occasionally generating only bad options, Card's deidealized agent is potentially doomed to partial compliance even with one's own idealized duties. As Cheshire Calhoun notes, "Whereas Nagel emphasized the luck that enters into our being *held* responsible, blamed, or praised, Card emphasizes the luck that enhances or undermines our capacity to *take* responsibility for ourselves" (2016, 30).

Importantly critical of dominant traditions in moral philosophy, Card notes in *The Unnatural Lottery* and in *The Atrocity Paradigm* that "feminist philosophers have long realized that the history of Western philosophical ethics has always been more specific than it usually pretends to be with respect to the perspectives it exemplifies. If philosophers reflect on the data of everyday life, Western philosophers have reflected on the lives of mostly relatively privileged, mostly Christian men of white European descent" (2002, 35). Card suggests this "presents a project for feminist philosophy: to articulate the world, critically, from the perspectives of women" (35). Her identification of the perspective of many canonical philosophers was not intended as a contrast with her own work as somehow closer to a neutral ideal. Instead, in *The Unnatural Lottery* Card defended her view that drawing on the experiences of women to develop theory engaged what she called "a *self-conscious particularism*—one that does not pretend to be universalist" and that in its self-consciousness "is more likely to avoid solipsistic and narcissistic arrogance" (1996, 14).

Taking the perspective of oppressed groups as her starting point for theorizing, Card particularly attends in *The Atrocity Paradigm* to "experiences of women as examples of dominated valuers" (2002, 36), and she thinks "about what our positions as dominated beings have led us to value" (36). Like Lisa Tessman, Card focuses on oppression rather than on concerns about equality, especially in her chapter tellingly called "Prioritizing Evils over Unjust Inequalities," which she says "do not get to the practices most important to resist" (2002, 99). Briefly in *The Unnatural Lottery* and at length in *The Atrocity Paradigm*, she attends to moral remainders, averring, "There are things that will never be made right" (1996, 87).

Identifying feasibility constraints and implying her theorizing is appropriately transitional instead of perfectionist, Card says, "Some ethical conflicts … cannot be resolved without wronging someone. In such situations,
our ethical possibilities are diminished in relation to what they would be
ideally. Here, the very ideals under which we act are compromised" (87). In
The Atrocity Paradigm, she importantly adds to Bernard Williams's influential account of moral remainders, noting that for Williams remainders
are just nonrectified wrongs. Card adds, "I find it natural [to see] emotional
attitudes and responses as also remainders" (2002, 169).

This is more important than it may at first appear: Card paid particularly
diligent attention to "emotional attitudes and responses as also remainders." The interior life of an individual's moral emotions were a motivating topic of her scholarship. She explained that in the course of writing
about evils, "my concerns here are with attitudes not toward life or humanity as such but toward individuals connected with particular evils" (2002,
167). The threat to individual character luck that oppression presents is
both a matter of concern for political groups *and* for the suffering human
heart. While appreciating the work of philosophers on state and community responses to atrocity, she stressed, "My concerns here are more with
responses by individuals who do not hold positions of political influence
but must find ways to go on feeling, thinking, and acting" (167). Her work is
emotional, and individualized for ethical reasons, as she regarded the pains
of others, reminding us of the emotional remainders we each carry. Attention to moral emotions informs the last line of *The Atrocity Paradigm*,
where she indicates that the internal life of individual victims of evil are the
source of any hope she has for an ethical future: "In survivors who refuse to
abdicate responsibility and somehow create ways to meet the challenges of
extreme moral stress, [or] remain ashamed when they think they have failed,
the chain of evil is broken" (2002, 234). The importance of the inner moral
life to her ethical theorizing is clearest when she concludes her discussion
of forgiveness, pointedly declining to recommend a perfectionist ideal, and
instead saying, "What is difficult but has the *potential* to bring change is
reaching out, taking risks, making explicit the complexities in one's heart"
(187).

If the above does not sound satisfyingly action guiding, that too is
consistent with the work that a good nonideal theorist must occasionally accomplish. As Lisa Tessman points out, much theory, including
nonideal theory, has been unduly focused on action guiding (2010, 803),
still idealizing the moral agent as one with options that can be exercised
toward a right choice; Tessman urges us to do more important jobs more
often, including attending to situations of moral failure and moral remainder, and "understanding moral life under oppression" (808). Of course,
Tessman and Card also occasionally attend to nonideal theory with an eye
to overcoming oppression, but part of challenging Rawlsian ideal theory, I
suggest, is the metaethical challenge to the possibilities for ethical action,

and the metaethical identification of threats posed to moral agents. Non-ideal theory is not just an instructional repair manual; it is good nonideal theory to identify those times when, for real-world reasons, what is broken cannot be fixed. Nonideal theory affirms the existence of nonideal conditions that render Rawls's ideal theory compromised and inapplicable.

I add to Tessman's observations that Card offers the valuable reminder of the complexities in one's heart, to direct our attention to the felt life of the individual in nonideal theory. I suggest that an overfocus on *overcoming* oppression in much social and political nonideal theory has been keen to identify action guidance and distributions of social justice at the expense of something that ethical theory does well, that is, identifying moral emotions *as* moral remainders and *as* obstacles to action guidance. Indeed, actions can leave emotions unresolved, as Card says in arguing for seeing some moral remainders as "emotional residues," that is, "rectificatory feelings regarding what otherwise proves unrectifiable by our actions.... These emotional residues ... reveal our appreciation that all has not been made right, or that not all is as it should be (or would be, ideally) between us" (2002, 169), in interpersonal interaction.

While Card's attention to these arguably nonideal elements in ethical theory are present in all of her works, only in the year preceding her death did she overtly address the nonideal nature of her lifelong interests. In "Challenges of Global and Local Misogyny," Card comments that it is "hard to assess" John Rawls's hypothesis in *The Law of Peoples* that "the worst evils that target women and girls will disappear once the gravest political injustices are gone" (2014, 472). She offers the doubtful note, "Misogynous evils are often rooted in failures of cooperation, enforcement, and perception, rather than in a political constitution, legislation, or foreign policy. Some sexism stems from background cultures not obviously incompatible with (liberal) just institutions" (472), and institutions do not guarantee compliant individuals; "individuals, too, can be inconsistent" (479). Here, it is clearer than ever that her interest in ethical theory in addition to, and as opposed to, political theory concerns the decent lives and moral struggles of individuals; Card notes that Rawls's moral parties to ideal theory "are well-ordered peoples and outlaw states, not individuals" (475). She motivates application of Rawls's notion of the nonideal to her ethical concerns with this suggestion: "Perhaps the non-ideal part of his *Law of Peoples* can be a resource for thinking about responding to evils when the subject is not state-centered, neither a society's basic structure nor its foreign policy" (473).

Although Card describes her essay as an extension of Rawls's principles, her attention to nonideal and material actualities raises pressing questions, especially with respect to the challenges of localized misogyny, such as the dilemmas faced by battered women whose law-enforcement resources are unresponsive or unavailable. Well-orderliness comes in degrees, she notes, and even in a generally orderly society such as the United States, failures

of law-enforcement systems to prevent or respond to domestic violence are
systemic. She finds it plausible that individuals who must defend themselves against great evils "should be governed by analogues of scruples that
Rawlsian well-ordered societies observe in defending themselves against
outlaw states" (2014, 473), such as refraining from behaviors that are not
justifiable, while pursuing best-available options as to what it is justifiable
to do in the course of resisting evils:

> I ask "what is justifiable" rather than "what is just" because, as Rawls noted in
> class lectures, full justice may be unrealizable when currently available options
> are shaped by past wrongful choices. When no fully just options remain, it may
> be possible to reduce the amount or seriousness of deprivations of justice, or
> to contain them, prevent their spreading or worsening.... Even a best option
> can leave ... "remainders," including injustices that can never be adequately
> redressed.... And so the question arises: how are individuals to approximate fair-
> ness in the absence of relevant social practices, institutions, or organizations for
> self-defense? (475)

In her essay, one of the last she published and the first to attend to nonideal
theory explicitly, especially in the above passage, we see in one place the
elements of nonideal theory I have identified so far, including attention
to oppression, deidealized moral agents, recognition of moral remainders,
and the appreciation that some wrongs are irreparable, so that nonideal
conditions remain.

3. Cardian Contributions: Administrative Perspectives and Intolerable Harms

I have come to think of Card's approach as "personalized," in contrast to
perspectives she describes as "de-personalized," such as the objective standpoint Nagel characterizes as the "view from nowhere" (1996, 26). Avoiding
depersonalized perspectives does not, of course, guarantee the best view.
It is one of Card's more overlooked but, for nonideal theory, more valuable insights that philosophy is often written from the perspective of an
administrator, which is not *de*personalized so much as *third*-personalized;
as Card says, such an "orientation embodies a perspective of observation—
what [Bernard] Williams calls 'the view from there' as opposed to 'the view
from nowhere'" (25–26). She writes, "Most essays on responsibility in contemporary Anglo-American moral philosophy look backward. They are
preoccupied with punishment and reward, praise or blame, excuses, mitigation, and so on" (25). When conceptual analyses of responsibility proceed
from, as Card describes it, this "backward-looking orientation," we find a
preference for holding wrongdoers responsible, for fear of letting them off
hooks. This stems from a (sometimes) well-intentioned concern for fairness,

yet one that demonstrates a widely held perspective of executors of punishment (1996, 25; see also 2002, 35) who will administer "justice" in a public sphere (Card evokes the image of a judge on a high bench, overlooking the court); her words here are reminiscent of Tessman's observation that Rawls's Ideal Theory is done "standing within the ideal" (Tessman 2010, 819, n. 31). The backward-looking orientation on responsibility, one that locates blame and sources of error, is sometimes necessary for judgments, so I do not mean to depict Card as dumping over desert entirely. One can even take the observational, objective perspective on oneself, identifying with those who would have one punish oneself more than one identifies with one's own wrongdoer.

Card's arguments caution, however, against assuming that the administrative point of view should be the starting point of ethical theory. While backward-looking theories of justice focus on the distribution of basic *goods*, Card's work urged attention instead to basic *harms*. And bearing in mind Card's comment above that she is concerned "more with responses by individuals who do not hold positions of political influence but must find ways to go on feeling, thinking, and acting," one can better understand her aside that "too often, criminal punishments have subjected convicted offenders to basic harms. That fact should make the justification of criminal punishment more difficult than philosophers have usually found it" (2002, 63). These twin elements—skepticism of the administrative perspective and attention to basic harms—infuse her last book, *Confronting Evils*, typified by the opening of her chapter "Ordinary Torture": "Philosophers who reflect on torture tend to focus almost exclusively on options and choices of potential torturers [i.e., administrators] and their ratifiers, to the relative neglect of the experience of the tortured.... Since torturers and ratifiers are the only free agents in the case, a focus on them might be thought ethically appropriate. Yet the experiences, positions, and agency of the tortured should not be neglected" (2010, 205). I draw attention to Card's identification of the administrative point of view, not to argue against the perspective of the oppressed as advocated by the nonideal theorists cited earlier, but to support their observations that the perspectives of oppressed groups constitute a good starting point for theory. As Card notes, "What feminist analysis of oppression tends to offer is the perspective of those who suffer the harm.... Were we to begin...with [harmers'] perspectives, it would be easy to fail to discover any evil at all, especially when the evil in question is collectively perpetrated. So let us *begin*, as feminists generally do, with the perspectives of the oppressed and the experience of being trapped by social structures" (72).

The arc of her work may have begun with the perspectives of the oppressed, but increasingly Card took the perspectives of victims of basic harm as instructive, whether or not she also identified them as oppressed. In other words, she appears to have shifted her attention to include some oppression in a wider set in which it belongs, a set describing something even more fundamental and urgent: the obstacles that evils, as basic harms, present to a decent life for any being capable of living decently, including even trees and ecosystems. Although oppressed people can suffer from unjust inequalities as well as basic harms (evils), she enjoined philosophers and feminists to prioritize the latter (basic harms that are evils) rather than, as so many of us had, the former. As she clarified, "Severe oppression is a paradigm evil," but "not all evils result from oppression" (2002, 99). "Inequalities are not themselves evils, although they tend to accompany the evils of exploitation and oppression" (99). While crediting Rawls's influence on her view, Card emphasized that "we need a conception of basic harms, not simply a theory of primary goods. Basic harms are not just deprivations of primary goods, even on Rawls' revised understanding of them. Not all such deprivations would render anyone's life, or a significant portion of it, impossible or intolerable" (63) from the perspective of the being whose life it is.

Let me return to my comment that Card's approach is "personalized," in contrast to perspectives she describes as "de-personalized," the better to explicate why we need a conception of basic, intolerable harms, or, as she said, "what no one should be made to suffer, no matter what it does for anyone else" (2002, 17). An evil is a basic harm committed by humans that "deprives, or seriously risks depriving, others of the basics that are necessary to make a life possible and tolerable or decent (or to make a death decent)" a *tolerable* life "is at least minimally worth living for its own sake and from the standpoint of the being whose life it is, not just as a means to the ends of others" (16). Card's conception of tolerability has both subjective and normative components; our perceptions are not infallible regarding our own worth or well-being, but in determining the intolerability of anyone's treatment, Card's point is that the *standpoint of the being whose life it is* ought to be a primary source of information, rather than the standpoint of the administrator (of punishment or harm or justice). The empirical stake that holds the concept of tolerability in place is the suffering individual's interest in a life worth living, and therefore Card's analyses of kinds of evils always include examples of actual individuals who have suffered.

Card's attention to basic harms and rejection of administrators' perspectives provide us with reasons for an empirical approach to ethics: actual individuals' perspectives ought to be the empirical basis of good ethics, because where basic harms are inflicted, they impose obstacles to lives worth living, so foreseeing and appreciating, ameliorating, or preventing these actual evils ought to be paramount for ethical theorists. Otherwise, we fail to attend to the conditions that allow for decent lives. Card does not argue that all philosophers should do ethics, but she does argue that all philosophers of ethics should prioritize evils as most urgent, and the suffering of victims of evils as most worthy of our attention and our efforts. As Tessman has commented, "In her focus on evils," Card is "actually an *extreme* nonideal theorist,"[3] and I think I know what she meant; Card took as her starting point for theory not just the "nonideal" conditions of the world but the *worst* conditions, because basic harms are such fundamental challenges to having lives and characters at all.

As a philosopher primarily concerned with the moral emotions, it is a relief to me to read, in Card's corpus, the outlines for a nonideal ethical theory, in part because Card's work places research on moral emotions into its proper context, and helps me to think about the moral emotions better. Research in the moral emotions may not pursue macroscopic sociopolitical questions of philosophy. (Indeed, more than one political theorist has suggested to me that we *only* need political theory and not philosophies of ethics!) Yet Card's work contributes to the reasons for Charles Mills's statement cited earlier that feminist ethics and politics tend to converge. The challenges to both political and philosophical agency are captured in that key phrase, "extreme moral stress." It's not just that the political is personal; it is also the case that the personal, including moral damage and character luck, provides obstacles to political and to ethical possibility. One may need to appreciate the relevance of extreme moral stress to both ethical *and* political realms in order to accomplish what Card called the prioritization of evils.

Further, in researching the moral emotions in particular, one ought to bear in mind the injunction that we not start from the point of view of the administrator of justice. Card's insight that identifying with suffering and nonideal characters is the more helpful starting point makes much more sense when I am sitting down to write about forgiveness and self-forgiveness. After all, if we start from the point of view of administrators of retributive justice, then self-forgiveness can only be suspect; some wrongdoer deserving of punishment may let himself off a hook! If, instead, I take seriously the injunction to start from the perspective of one with moral and emotional remainders, then I take to heart the perspective of one who suffers shame or guilt for her own wrongdoing, that is, for *my* past wrongs. Card's contributions to feminist and nonideal ethical theories then include the valuable reminders that we philosophers have not, often enough, identified with wrongdoers and carriers of shame in the course of our professionalization.

Card's contributions to feminist and moral philosophies include implications for future work to be done. More scholarship in ethics must consider the responses available to nonideal agents. More of the virtues involved in living with imperfection deserve working out. And more philosophers should identify themselves, not as judges or avenging angels, but as fellow strugglers with the challenge of moral stresses. Humility and

[3] Personal communication, January 4, 2016.

compassion are called for once we take Card's lead and reject the administrative viewpoint while prioritizing basic harms.

4. Conclusion: Did Card Need NET? Do We?

Ethical theorists contribute to nonideal theory in distinctive ways, but I
have not yet justified my call for nonideal ethical theory. Does NET enhance
our understanding, so much so that it merits its own place in the wider
world of nonideal theory? And if it merits special attention, then why didn't
Card herself identify with it?

I confess that I am almost positive Card usually saw no need to embrace
nonideal theory as separate from ethical or sociopolitical theorizing as
done by Rawls, Kant, or anyone else. She argued for the goods of empirically informed understanding and articulation of the world in critical and
feminist ways. If that is what ethics requires to be done well, then one might
say we don't need an ethics marked as nonideal theory; we just need to do
ethics better and thereby meet the moral challenges of responding to evils
(2010, 9). Card seemed to entertain hopes of meeting those challenges,
occasionally identifying herself as optimistic and her theorizing as transitional toward moral ideals, another indication that she didn't embrace
nonideal theory as *her* theory, as long as she took an optimistic view to the
possibilities for the realization of justice. For example, at the same time she
offers the actualities of local and global misogyny as challenges to Rawls's
view, she says, "But the worst evils are not immune to institutional forces.
Often women are left to defend themselves without organized help, not only
within societies but in global traffic and in wars. That could change" (2014,
472). This sounds a note of hope for organization, yet it is quickly followed by this observation: "Those worst injustices may not be eliminable
unless people are willing to fight back using measures that include force and
violence and are willing to do so in non-state organizations when states
fail them, as peoples go to war against unjust aggressors after less drastic measures have failed" (472). Card's form of optimism does not look to
Rawls's realistic utopia so much as something akin to "a counterfactual
social world," as Cheshire Calhoun says (2016, 5). As Mills so saliently
observes, not all ideals are idealizations raised to the level of ideology;
his observation is consonant with Calhoun's that reasoning about what a
morally preferable world might include entails reasoning about hypotheticals, and not all hypotheticals appeal to ideals (2016, 4).

I agree with Calhoun that it is difficult to reason about doing morality
differently unless one reasons hypothetically about how to get from *here* to
there. While engaging in hypothetical reasoning toward better practices, I
tend to resist optimism with respect to evils. I believe NET gets something
important right, namely, the feasibility constraints constituted by the nonideal conditions of a world in which victims inevitably suffer from evils. I

write elsewhere about the importance of the inevitability of evils; if I am right that evils are inevitable in a world with human beings, then NET is not, contra Rawls, transitional, and instead NET is helpfully pessimistic and a needed counternarrative to optimistic ideal theory. Institutions can be orderly, but their orderliness does not thereby yield compliant individuals, because to believe individuals will be compliant with orderly institutions *is* to idealize moral agents, as primarily rational, unencumbered by moral remainders, free from histories of violence or oppressive occupation, and so on. And Card's attention to the unnatural lottery reminds us all to, as Tessman says, deidealize moral agents.

In short, I endorse NET for the same reason that I suspect Card was slow to embrace it as appropriately descriptive of her views; NET is highly appropriate to pessimistic approaches to enduring moral change and social progress, more pessimistic than the approaches Card was trained in and applied, even in *The Atrocity Paradigm* and *Confronting Evils*. NET offers reminders to theorists of wider systems that individuals are inconsistent, bear emotional and moral remainders, and are often outmatched by the seriousness of the problems we face. Note that I am not merely drawing out a difference in claims of probability; I'm asserting—against Rawls' optimism with respect to logical possibility—that embodied individuals in the material world will continue on all-too-human paths in a way that forestalls those eminently logical possibilities. As Charles Mills says, "Nonideal theory recognizes that people will typically be cognitively affected by their social location," and nonideal theorists "map accurately (at least arguably) crucial realities that differentiate the statuses of the human beings within the systems they describe; so while they *abstract*, they do not *idealize*" (2005, 175). (Regarding Rawls's ideal theory in particular, Mills asks, if you were new to academic discourse, "Wouldn't your spontaneous reaction be: *How in God's name could anybody think that this is the appropriate way to do ethics?*" [169].)

Card's identification of the challenges of extreme *moral* stress provides reason to believe that NET is an important corrective to the continued predominance of optimistic and idealizing moral approaches. Nonideal theorists that, as Valentini says, revolve around Rawls are also well served by attention to the moral damages that complicate the possibilities for political action. Card reveals attention to the pessimism such theorizing gives rise to, in that final work on Rawls. It is an unusual experience for a regular reader of her work to encounter her using the word "hopeless," but it appears, at last, and fittingly for Card, in a passage that still holds out hopes for decent lives:

> In non-ideal theory, must parties know that non-compliance is not so widespread that cooperation is hopeless? Is that enough to give point to their task for parties who know they might turn out to be victims of well-entrenched misogyny? What if cooperation *has been* hopeless? Might the task then shift to

proposing principles for coalition building, to ground hope of sufficient cooperation? In any case, victims can be justified as a matter of self-respect in fighting even hopeless battles. If they care about self-respect, presumably they care
about principles for fighting even hopeless battles.... Women need principles for
forming social units of defense against global and local misogyny. Meanwhile,
women need principles now for defending themselves and each other as individuals. (2014, 479, 480, emphasis in original)

It is possible that Card's attention to individual, ethical, decent lives was
also the source of her often optimistic nonideal theorizing. Social and political progress is often temporary or illusory. Yet while continuing to fight
hopeless battles in a world that does not change, one can hope for realization of one's own self-respect. Caring for the interior life is within reach in
a way that ending global misogyny is not, even as the former may entail
working toward the latter.

It is a strength of what I am calling NET that it may justify pessimism
toward social and political progress, while at the same time grounding the
optimistic attention of ethical theorists like Card to self-respect. I do not
know if Card would have come to identify with nonideal theory if her life
had not been foreshortened. But I believe I have shown that her contributions to ethical theory are invaluable in assisting nonideal theorists in our
continued projects. As the story of nonideal theory gets written, I hope it is
written with some attention to the least of us, to the individuals with moral
shame, the victims of basic harm, and the fighters of hopeless battles.

References

Anderson, Elizabeth. 2010. *The Imperative of Integration*. Princeton:
    Princeton University Press.
Calhoun, Cheshire. 2016. *Moral Aims: Essays on the Importance of Getting
    It Right and Practicing Morality with Others*. New York: Oxford Univer-
    sity Press.
Card, Claudia. 1996. *The Unnatural Lottery: Character and Moral Luck*.
    Philadelphia: Temple University Press.
———. 2002. *The Atrocity Paradigm: A Theory of Evil*. New York: Oxford
    University Press.
———. 2010. *Confronting Evils: Terrorism, Torture, Genocide*. Cambridge:
    Cambridge University Press.
———. 2014. "Challenges of Local and Global Misogyny." In *A Compan-
    ion to Rawls*, edited by Jon Mandle and David A. Reidy, 472–86. Oxford:
    Wiley-Blackwell. Chapter 14 in the present collection.
Herman, Barbara. 2007. *Moral Literacy*. Cambridge, Mass.: Harvard Uni-
    versity Press.
Mills, Charles. 2005. "'Ideal Theory' as Ideology." *Hypatia* 20, no. 3:165–
    84.

Murphy, Liam. 2000. *Moral Demands in Nonideal Theory*. Oxford: Oxford University Press.

Rawls, John. 1999. *The Law of Peoples*. Cambridge, Mass.: Harvard University Press.

Rivera-López, Eduardo. 2013. "Ideal and Nonideal Ethics and Political Philosophy." In *International Encyclopedia of Ethics*, edited by Hugh LaFollette, 3626–34. Oxford: Blackwell.

Schmidtz, David. 2011. "Nonideal Theory: What It Is and What It Needs to Be." *Ethics* 121, no. 4:772–96.

Schwartzman, Lisa. 2009. "Non-ideal Theorizing, Social Groups, and Knowledge of Oppression: A Response." *Hypatia* 24, no. 4:177–88.

Sen, Amartya. 2006. What Do We Want from a Theory of Justice? *Journal of Philosophy* 103, no. 5:215–38.

———. 2009. *The Idea of Justice*. Cambridge, Mass.: Harvard University Press.

Tessman, Lisa. 2009. "Expecting Bad Luck." *Hypatia* 24, no. 1:9–28.

———. 2010. "Idealizing Morality." *Hypatia* 25, no. 4:797–824.

———. 2015. *Moral Failure: On the Impossible Demands of Morality*. Oxford: Oxford University Press.

Valentini, Laura. 2012. "Ideal vs. Non-ideal Theory: A Conceptual Map." *Philosophy Compass* 7, no. 9:654–64.

CHAPTER 19

RADICAL MORAL IMAGINATION AND MORAL LUCK

MAVIS BISS

In her study of women's biography Carolyn Heilbrun uses Sartre's words to define genius as "not a gift, but rather the way one invents in desperate situations" (1988, 44).[1] We recognize the courage of women, like Claudia Card, who lived against oppressive social norms when there were few examples to follow, but less is said about their inventiveness. Card understood that resistance to one's own oppression may require creativity and that one's ability to invent in desperate situations caused by sexism, racism, poverty, violence, or homophobia often requires others' cooperation and is always subject to luck.

In this essay I explore the implications of Claudia Card's analyses of moral luck and taking responsibility in her 1996 book *The Unnatural Lottery* for an account of "radical moral imagination," understood as the creation of new possibilities for moral action through the modification of meanings. Card writes, "Taking responsibility in the context of practices that we reject requires *doing it at the level of meaning and definition*" (1996, 148). I situate Card's arguments in relation to work by other feminist philosophers in order to address a number of questions about her understanding of the relation between moral agency and the process of creating or imposing meanings.

1. Radical Moral Imagination

How does Card's work on moral luck pertain to accounts of moral imagination? Within philosophical ethics the term "moral imagination" has been

---

[1] Sartre says this in the introduction of his biography of Jean Genet.

Criticism and Compassion: The Ethics and Politics of Claudia Card.
Edited by Robin S. Dillon and Armen T. Marsoobian.
Chapters and book compilation © 2018 Metaphilosophy LLC and John Wiley & Sons Ltd.

used to refer to an excellent form of moral perception or an aspect of moral judgment, but also to the radical revision of moral understandings and the capacity to generate new possibilities for realizing moral ends or exercising virtue. Card's work on moral luck combines the last two senses of moral imagination, for on her view it is partly through the radical revision of moral understandings that agents may create new possibilities for realizing ends and developing virtue. Overcoming bad moral luck may require transforming oneself and also transforming the meanings of one's actions through the modification of concepts and the creation of new social practices.

Other feminist philosophers who have theorized the relationship between meanings and possibilities for moral action have similarly suggested that the radical revision of moral understandings can create new possibilities by changing what is intelligible as an expression of virtue. Like Card, Miranda Fricker and Cheshire Calhoun investigate examples of "moral resisters" who contest distorted interpretations of their actions or identities in attempts to claim self-worth and express self-respect. Yet, Card's conception of taking responsibility, her understanding of the relationship between social recognition and moral success, and her approach to moral risk set her argument apart. To a greater extent than other theorists Card considers the impact of attempts to transform moral meanings on the development of the agent's character and her responsibilities, over time and in relation to other agents. This wider frame of reference captures more of what is at stake in the efforts of those who resist oppression by attempting to implement radically revised meanings.

2. Taking Responsibility, and Moral Luck

Card's analysis of moral luck in chapter 2 of *The Unnatural Lottery* focuses on constitutive moral luck, or luck in the development of character. She is specifically interested in the bad moral luck of having one's character damaged by oppression or abuse. In contrast to Bernard Williams's and Thomas Nagel's concern with the relationship between moral luck and the backward-looking "taking credit" (or accepting blame) sense of moral responsibility, Card considers the forward-looking perspective of agents who seek to take responsibility in the care-taking sense as a response to histories of bad moral luck. From this perspective, taking responsibility means committing to making oneself good.

Taking responsibility for oneself in response to bad constitutive luck is a form of resistance to oppression, but moral luck impacts one's ability to achieve this task in multiple ways. As Card explains, "We develop responsibility as a virtue by first *taking* responsibility in ways that outrun our apparent present worthiness to do so and then carrying through successfully. Luck is involved both in the motivation to take responsibility and in our ability to carry through" (1996, 27). One of the most inspiring aspects of Card's argument is also one of the most theoretically challenging: taking responsibility requires that I act to create the resources I need to become a person who can reliably take responsibility for herself. Card asks, "But how is it possible for us as damaged agents to liberate ourselves from the damage? And how can we act for our futures, not knowing just whom we may liberate?" (41). In response to these questions, she explains that we may have to work hard to create the internal and external conditions that make the development of a different self possible.

Card is deeply sensitive to the interactive nature of moral agency, continually emphasizing the ways in which relationships with others and others' responses to our actions shape our moral development and our possibilities for moral action. An agent's ability to take responsibility is not just a matter of individual will because it depends on how her attempts to create relationships and communities supportive of her development actually play out and on the meanings that are assigned to her actions by others. On Card's view, "The judgment that someone took responsibility can be withdrawn if the person fails to follow through" (1996, 28). This claim is developed in chapter 7 of *The Unnatural Lottery*, "What Lesbians Do," which details the limits of radical moral imagination. I turn now to Card's argument in that chapter.

Card understands coming out as a lesbian in the context of a heterosexist patriarchy as a paradigm of taking responsibility for oneself. In a society in which "lesbianism" is dominantly interpreted as deviant or criminal, taking responsibility for one's lesbian identity requires imposing radically revised meanings on one's actions and relationships. Recall that the relevant sense of responsibility is "committing oneself to standing behind something, to back it, support it, make it good...and following through" (1996, 28). Card elaborates the care-taking sense of responsibility in relation to the paradigm of coming out, explaining that taking responsibility for something with a welfare requires the ability to do things that further the end of well-being, such as providing guidance, protection, and support. A person who encounters extreme hostility in response to her attempts to change the meaning of lesbianism cannot actually take responsibility for herself in the care-taking sense by coming out because she cannot follow through on her commitment to provide protection and support to herself and those she loves.

There are two problems of reception here. For one, coming out requires uptake because it is an interaction: one comes out *to* a public. As Card put it, "I do not manage to identify myself to others in a particular way if they fail to or refuse to recognize me in that way" (1996, 146). Second, taking responsibility in the relevant sense "is not just a matter of mentally embracing something," because it is partly constituted by the ability to actually take care of self and others (150). Card writes, "Our freedom to act on meanings we can stand behind partly depends on our success in changing meanings. Since that is a social success, not an individual one, there is a genuine moral risk here" (150).

Keeping this dynamic in mind, I would like to ask some questions about Card's conception of the success conditions for taking responsibility. Card asserts: "It is absurd to think that you can change the meaning of something just by intending a different meaning when you use it yourself or with your friends" (150). Taking this statement out of context, one might think that the reasonableness of thinking that you and your friends can change the meaning of a practice depends on how many friends you have. Reading it in context, we still might think that the use of new, resistant meanings within a small community of resisters can make a significant difference in a person's ability to commit to and support her own development. Changing a meaning does not mean changing everyone's mind. Referring to groups like fundamentalist Christians who define outsiders as heretics, Card remarks: "Their definitions do not negate our responsibility-taking as long as they do not prevent us from standing behind our own definitions. To do that we need to be able to make something of them, give them effect, implement them" (149).

Card's analysis raises several questions about moral agency within fragmented moral communities and in situations of contested moral meaning. What counts as implementing or making something of a new definition? What are the conditions of success? When has a meaning changed? (When most people accept it? Or when a sufficient number accept it? Or when sufficiently powerful people accept it? Or when living according to it does not make one's life worse?) According to some accounts of radical moral imagination an agent succeeds when she achieves a more accurate understanding of the meaning of her experience or acts according to newly conceptualized criteria for virtuous action. Here, the achievement does seem to be brought about within the agent's own mind. By comparing Card's account to other models, I will show that there are at least two different types of moral achievement associated with radical moral imagination, each with its own success conditions. The comparison will also highlight Card's unique appreciation for the moral risks involved in attempts to live according to radically revised moral understandings.

3. Assessing Risky Undertakings

Miranda Fricker addresses moral imagination as part of an analysis of hermeneutical injustice, a specific form of epistemic injustice whereby individuals are systematically disadvantaged "in the practices through which social meanings are generated" (2007, 6). The ability to create meanings is morally significant because one cannot effectively resist one's own or others' oppression if one cannot understand it (151). Fricker argues that hermeneutical injustice occurs "when a gap in collective interpretative resources puts someone at an unfair disadvantage when it comes to making sense of their social experiences" (1). Yet in exceptional cases this disadvantage may be overcome through individual and collective exercise of moral imagination.

Fricker offers the narrator of Edmund White's semiautobiographical novel *A Boy's Own Story* (1982) as an example of an "epistemically marginalized" person who manages to reject the received social meaning of his identity. Coming of age in the 1950s, the narrator experiences dissonance between his experience of his homosexuality and the dominant social judgment of it. On Fricker's reading, this dissonance gives him the courage to challenge denigrations of his identity. Describing his response to a priest's announcement that homosexuality is a sin, White writes: "I think he had no notion of how little effect the word sin had on me. He might just as well have said, 'Homosexuality is bad *juju*.'" White replies to the priest: "But I feel very drawn to other men" (White 1983, 204).[2]

For Fricker, the most relevant aspect of this exchange is the boy's inner rebellion. An agent can succeed in resisting an oppressive interpretation of his desires and actions without changing the social meaning. The fact that the priest does not confirm the boy's self-image does not undermine the boy's success. In contrast to Fricker, Card's paradigm case is one in which the agent has already internally rejected negative constructions of her identity and is now trying to do something else. Indeed, the woman seeking to take responsibility for herself by coming out as a lesbian may have already developed a sophisticated critique of heteropatriarchy and its definitions of sexual identities. Card could certainly acknowledge that inner rebellion is a kind of moral achievement distinct from taking responsibility for oneself: a new meaning is articulated but not yet implemented. (Conceptual articulation and inner rebellion may also require uptake for psychological reasons; a person may not be able to sustain her sense of meaningfulness or sense of self without some good reception.)

Fricker's focus on epistemic achievement brackets many aspects of moral luck in the life of the agent who newly grasps the meaning of her experience or identity and then seeks to live according to these meanings.[3] Knowledge and understanding do transform one's possibilities for action, but the need for social cooperation also places real limits on what one can do and be. Further, Fricker's analysis is framed in terms of single moves

[2] I discuss Fricker's analysis of this example and her conception of moral imagination in greater detail in Biss 2013.

[3] Fricker writes, "Our narrator had history on his side inasmuch as the Sixties were on the horizon, when all sorts of sexual liberations were to be articulated, indeed demanded" (2007, 166). Here Fricker suggests a kind of moral luck enjoyed by the narrator, but the point is curious. How does a transformation that occurs later in time assist the narrator? The fact that a meaning will be implemented does not ease the difficulties faced by an agent struggling to articulate it internally or to implement it in the present social world.

or acts, whereas Card continually thinks in terms of the impact of discrete moves on the development of the agent and the unfolding of her responsibilities going forward.

A particular "progressive move in moral consciousness" (Fricker 2007, 104) may be necessary but not sufficient for taking responsibility for oneself, and attempts at taking responsibility through exceptional social moves can be quite morally risky. On Card's view we can become responsible for unforeseen and unintended consequences of risky undertakings, including attempts to implement new meanings (Card 1996, 35). Card revises Kant's principles of imputation (whereby the good consequences of meritorious actions and the bad consequences of unlawful actions can be imputed to the subject) to more adequately reflect the role of luck in determining responsibilities. She concludes, "When we have or take responsibility for something that turns out badly, that typically gives us further responsibilities. Since the process of responding to our previous choices (and failures to choose) can go on indefinitely, it may be impossible to say whether a person is 'justified' until that person can no longer choose" (39). Here Card extends the concept of justification from discrete actions to the life of the dynamic moral agent. Consistent with this approach, Card holds that where attempts to act on new meanings may expose oneself or others to harm, the morality of such attempts may only be assessable in retrospect. The proposal that radically imaginative moral moves should be considered in relation to the larger context of an agent's life and her community takes consequences seriously without suggesting that the right thing to do is whatever will maximize good consequences.

Card's assessment of risky undertakings is more complex than Fricker's because of Card's attention to aspects of moral life that are outside even the most imaginative agent's control. But even accounts of moral life that highlight ways in which our moral success is not fully up to us can miss some important aspects of moral luck that Card includes. We find such an account in Cheshire Calhoun's essay "Moral Failure," which is heavily influenced by Card's arguments in *The Unnatural Lottery* and appears in the collection *On Feminist Ethics and Politics* (1999), edited by Card. Calhoun argues that in social worlds structured by systems of domination an agent's most conscientious attempts to act morally may directly bring about a form of moral failure. Where conventionalized conceptions of virtue and moral principle serve systems of oppression, acting morally necessarily involves resistance to shared understandings. Yet acting according to revised meanings may render one's actions unintelligible or unjustified to many within one's community. The woman who openly embraces her lesbian identity and is read as exhibitionist rather than as self-respecting serves as a paradigm example of the problem Calhoun has in mind. On her view, the woman cannot successfully express self-respect if her actions are routinely misread because self-expression requires making one's own sense of things manifest to others. So although those who resist oppressive meanings "do the right thing," they fail with respect to another moral ideal—the ideal of participating in a shared scheme of moral meaning.

Calhoun emphasizes that moral failure caused by resistance to distorted moral understandings is *not* culpable error; however, regret and even shame may be appropriate responses to one's blameless inability to express virtue in action. How could this be? Echoing Card, Calhoun remarks: "Our actions have meanings in the social world, and individuals cannot change those meanings at will" (1999, 95). If my attempt to protest unfairness is interpreted as hysterical, then I am hysterical. It is not my fault, yet I have failed to count as good in my social world. Calhoun maintains that "who we are and, thus, our sources of shame are partly determined by who others take us to be" (95). If the point of taking responsibility as a response to bad constitutive moral luck is to make oneself good, it seems that failures of moral communication can undermine the efficacy of even virtuosic efforts to take responsibility through the creation of new meanings, including Card's own.

But here I think we should take a few steps back and problematize Calhoun's suggestion that a person's character is determined by others' interpretations of her. Most of us participate in several interlocking communities and engage in disagreements across and within these multiple communities. When an agent resists a distorted moral understanding that holds sway within one of her communities, her moral moves may well be both comprehended and applauded, though perhaps by only a small number of allies. In this case, the resister does successfully cooperate in a shared social scheme of meaning, and if the new meaning she seeks to implement is apt, *and she is sufficiently lucky*, she both does the right thing and expresses virtue.

Further, following Lynne Tirrell, we should acknowledge that uptake does not mean agreement. In an analysis of the ways in which semantic authority depends on community recognition Tirrell argues that the ability to make meaning within a community requires some overlap in normative commitments, but not perfect agreement. An agent gets her meaning to "stick" when a community grants her semantic authority by taking her expressive acts seriously: "Authority gets one the respectful attention of one's community, but guarantees neither its obedience nor its agreement in belief or action. Authority gets one's words and deeds woven into the fabric of a social life" (Tirrell 1993, 22). If a developing community of fellow resisters is available, then the person who challenges conventional moral understandings does not risk failure to participate in a shared scheme of moral meaning.

Although Calhoun does not address the issue of interlocking communities, I suspect that she would not consider participation in a community of resisters an adequate shield against the threat of blameless moral failure. By definition, the moral resister challenges understandings that are widely held. Thus, barring dramatic withdrawal from social life, others will regularly misunderstand her actions and reject her justifications. The fact that a moral resister has semantic authority within one of her communities cannot protect her from the failure to gain semantic authority in a larger community. Part of Calhoun's point is that having one's actions misread should be *unusual*—we expect a good life to be a life in which failures of moral communication are infrequent occurrences on the background of mutual intelligibility. So when it becomes common for a morally conscientious person to be misunderstood or judged unreasonable, the person suffers a moral loss because her life falls short of what we expect of a good life.

Calhoun's analysis blends claims about one-off communicative exchanges with claims about patterns of failed communication in a way that makes her framing of communicative failure as *moral* failure somewhat difficult to track. Pervasive communicative failure might constitute moral failure because it prevents a person's life from meeting the minimal threshold with respect to the moral ideal of social cooperation; however, this thesis is separate from the claim that the meaning of a discrete expressive act is determined by its reception. A person's actions may be misread by a particular other for many reasons unrelated to distorted social meanings. The fact that a friend thinks I have lied to her does not make me a liar, though this single failure of communication may have a devastating impact on my life, possibly even making it fall short of what we expect of a good life. I do not think that Calhoun would consider such social failures to be moral failures, but it is not totally clear why bad social reception factors into moral assessment more in some cases than others.

Card's conception of taking responsibility is useful for sorting out these issues, for several reasons. It explains why we may meet moral failure even if we are successful in communicating with some others within our communities. If I do not have the ability to provide support, then I cannot fully take responsibility in the care-taking sense. It also explains how bad reception experienced by the moral resister/innovator is different from other kinds of bad reception. The person whose apology is rejected because of the recipient's character flaw can stand behind her meanings. A person whose action is misinterpreted because she and her interlocutor do not share cultural assumptions may be responsible for coming to understand these differences and working toward shared understandings, but again, the problem is not that she lacks meanings that she can reliably stand behind.

The central question for Card is whether you can follow through on your initiative to take responsibility by fulfilling your commitments to yourself and others. You certainly may be able to follow through even if many others misunderstand or disagree with you, but you cannot do so if your efforts to implement new meanings put you and others in peril. Whereas Calhoun focuses on the moral resister and the community she challenges, Card makes the relationship between the moral resister and her loved ones central. The woman coming out as a lesbian must ask herself, What do others who trust me take me to be committing to? What do they trust me to do?[4] Successfully taking responsibility thus requires shared understanding with those to whom one has made commitments, and it requires competence in dealing with the consequences of one's choices.

I also think that for Card it is less clear that agents who seek to implement new meanings that better capture their own and others' worth always do the right thing and also less clear that being unintelligible to many others itself counts as a moral failure. For Card, consequences matter to the assessment of risky, morally imaginative moves. The fact that one acts according to an improved grasp of moral meaning does not exempt one from the moral risks that may have been assumed. Acting according to a radically revised meaning may not always be the right thing to do, because it could prove to have been too risky when the results are destructive to oneself or others. One may be unable to live up to the responsibilities generated by a risky choice. As I indicated above, Card presents a model of moral assessment that "includes how the agent's character and moral career develop" (1996, 38), and this model challenges Calhoun's claim that doing the right thing "is not a function of how others receive us" (Calhoun 1999, 95). Where coming out as a lesbian is dangerous, "it may be possible only in retrospect to assess with any confidence the morality of taking or foregoing such a risk" (Card 1996, 150). The conscientious moral agent is not committed to acting on principles of resistance at any cost, because she honors her commitments to caring for others and for her own moral development. A principled attempt to change moral meanings may turn out to have been the wrong thing to do.

This might sound jarring. Recalling Aristotle, one might hold that some risks are reasonable or noble while others are unreasonable or foolish, and conclude that a person only fails to do the right thing when she takes reckless risks and shies away from noble ones. If the right thing to do is to take the right risks, the actual reception of one's actions need not factor into moral assessment. But Card's point is that whether a particular risk is worth taking cannot be determined in advance, especially when past experience does not provide much guidance. Card is thinking of moments when moral understandings are unstable, although positive change is not yet obviously under way. She writes, "I often feel lucky to live at a time when the meanings of 'lesbian' are in as much flux as today" (1996, 142). Card saw that common understandings of lesbians *could* be challenged, but doing so was still morally risky, and hence any attempt to take responsibility by creating new meanings would make the agent vulnerable to bad moral luck.

Finally, Card's more open-ended approach to moral assessment indicates that Calhoun's verdict of moral failure due to failed communication is sometimes premature. A person's attempts to express her moral understandings in interpersonal interactions may initially be met with confusion

---

[4] I thank Vicky Davion for raising this point.

or hostility, but those who are confused or hostile may eventually come to acknowledge the meanings they previously rejected. At what point in a process of communication are we to judge an agent's attempts at moral self-expression and social cooperation to be failures? A moral resister's life may include large stretches of bad social reception yet ultimately lead to incredible development of self and community. Moral resisters may begin processes of meaning making that outlive them. And as Tirrell beautifully articulates, we may participate in the transformation of moral understandings across our interlocking communities even as we struggle to receive uptake: "We bring our whole selves to these communities, even where they cannot see us whole, so we are part of the ways that communities effect each other. Even communities of which we are not members can provide insights and inspirations, and can reshape the communities in which we participate" (1993, 25). The judgment of moral failure should not be applied to a person's expressive efforts when the possibility of future shifts in reception is still open.

Still, the moral resister who is currently struggling to build community may be burdened by her actions' negative social meanings and *fear* moral failure. Facing the prospect of bad luck, such an agent might worry that her efforts to take responsibility for her life will not be worth it (or will not feel worth it), although she does not experience regret, since she cannot know how her life is going to turn out. When the problem is not actual moral failure but fear of failure, the only solution is hope. Indeed, Card considers taking responsibility for one's own development going forward to be "incompatible with cynicism and despair" (1996, 146).

I previously asked what counts as implementing a meaning. But my preoccupation with success conditions may distract from what is most important in Card's analysis. The language of "success" and "failure" does not capture the complexity of the situations of many agents struggling to change meanings. It may be better to use less binary language, as this would allow theorists interested in exercises of radical moral imagination to retain more of the nuance of Card's work on moral luck.

Coda: A Duty to Resist Oppression?

Nowhere in her powerful account of taking responsibility as a way of overcoming and resisting oppression does Claudia Card claim that oppressed people have a duty to resist their own oppression. One reason for this may be that the language of duty and obligation encourages the thought that it is appropriate for others to hold one accountable for fulfilling the duty or to assign blame for a failure to fulfill the duty. Card writes, "Overcoming and resisting our own oppression require us to *take* responsibility for situations for which others could not reasonably hold us responsible (in the credit sense), despite our complicity" (1996, 41). An advocate of the duty to resist oppression might respond that others cannot or should not hold us responsible for fulfilling certain duties to self, so aversion to sanctioning negative judgments of people who have been damaged by oppression should not decide the question of whether there is a duty to resist oppression.

In Card's work we find other reasons to avoid framing resistance to oppression as a duty. Card takes as a starting place the perspective of a person who has suffered bad constitutive luck, specifically the bad luck of having her character formation distorted by oppressive institutions. The person who responds to bad moral luck by taking responsibility is acting to liberate herself from moral damage that has been done largely before she could have developed capacities for protecting herself from such damage. Card's emphasis on remaking the self by "constructing some of the conditions of our own integrity" (1996, 32) contrasts strikingly with the erosion analogy used by Carol Hay in her recent and influential Kantian argument for a duty to resist oppression (Hay 2011). Hay argues that agents have a duty to protect their rational capacities from the harmful cumulative effects of oppression, which act like drops of water gradually eroding a stone. The duty is *imperfect*, meaning that the agent is not obligated to resist oppression in every instance but must act to ensure that the gradual harms of oppression—the repeated "drops"—do not add up to marked damage. Whereas Card's agent builds her moral character up to overcome past damage, Hay's agent acts to protect her fully formed rational capacities from being worn down.

I am myself very sympathetic to Hay's project and the Kantian tradition, but Card shows that taking moral luck seriously requires attention to the developmental aspects of moral agency. Because Kant often speaks "as though a morally complete self were present each moment, flexing its will like an invisible muscle in a material vacuum," we should not expect his reflections on moral striving and self-respect to be fully adequate to the situation of those working to overcome moral damage (Card 1996, 39). There may be a duty to self to resist oppression, but it does not matter what duties we have if we are not currently positioned to take responsibility for making ourselves good.

The most decisive reason Card gives for not speaking of a duty to resist oppression is that with respect some ways of taking responsibility duty is irrelevant. She explains, "What I have in mind by taking responsibility for oneself in coming out as a lesbian is not a matter of justifying oneself to others or even of justifying oneself to oneself. It is not really about justification. It is about care-taking and about pride" (1996, 144). There is moral meaning and value in the kind of self-care that transforms the self and its possibilities that is not reducible to the value of fulfilling a duty. While the Kantian grounds the duty of self-respect in the value of one's shared rational nature that is there to be valued, taking responsibility for oneself is done for the sake of a better self and a good future, both of which do not yet exist.

References

Biss, Mavis. 2013. "Radical Moral Imagination: Courage, Hope and Artic-ulation." *Hypatia* 28, no. 4 (November): 937–54.

Calhoun, Cheshire. 1999. "Moral Failure." In *On Feminist Ethics and Pol-itics*, edited by Claudia Card, 81–102. Lawrence: Kansas University Press.

Card, Claudia. 1996. *The Unnatural Lottery: Character and Moral Luck*. Philadelphia: Temple University Press.

Fricker, Miranda. 2007. *Epistemic Injustice: Power and the Ethics of Know-ing*. Oxford: Oxford University Press.

Hay, Carol. 2011. "The Obligation to Resist Oppression." *Journal of Social Philosophy* 42, no. 1 (Spring): 21–45.

Heilbrun, Carolyn. 1988. *Writing a Women's Life*. New York: Ballantine Books.

Tirrell, Lynne. 1993. "Definition and Power: Toward Authority Without Privilege." *Hypatia* 8, no. 4:1–34.

White, Edmund. 1983. *A Boy's Own Story*. London: Picador.

CHAPTER 20

THE AMERICAN GIRL

PLAYING WITH THE WRONG DOLLIE?

VICTORIA DAVION

Preface

One of the most significant themes throughout the work of Claudia Card is that of character development. Card was interested not only in the physical survival of human beings in oppressive environments but also in the survival of their character within such environments. This concern is particularly evident in her work on sexism, homophobia, poverty, genocide, and evil (Card 1996a, 1996b, 2005, 2013, 2014). This essay is an extension of Card's life work in that it concerns character development under heteronormative patriarchy as pertaining to the American Girl Just Like You doll. Hence, it is an extension of ideas that were central to Card's work and very much in the spirit of it. I had the privilege of reading and discussing this piece with her with while she was in hospice in Wisconsin.

The essay is a feminist exploration of the American Girl Just Like You doll. It was inspired by my experiences of visiting the American Girl doll store in New York City last December with my eleven-year-old friend Grace, along with my subsequent experience of returning to the store with my mother and brother to buy a doll myself. When I visited the store for the first time, I was really disturbed about what I saw in addition to dolls for sale—preening little girls, a dollie beauty salon, and even a restaurant where one can eat with one's doll. I wasn't quite sure, however, why I was so upset by what looked to be just another company pushing dolls and doll accessories. What I did know at the time was that something was extremely troubling about this particular doll. So, I decided to seek some reasoning for my instinctive emotional reaction. This essay is a feminist explanation of why

Criticism and Compassion: The Ethics and Politics of Claudia Card.
Edited by Robin S. Dillon and Armen T. Marsoobian.
Chapters and book compilation © 2018 Metaphilosophy LLC and John Wiley & Sons Ltd.

I found the doll so disturbing; I shall argue that although the American Girl company advertises this line of dolls as empowering for little girls, a solid feminist analysis shows otherwise. In particular, I shall draw upon the views of Claudia Card, Sandra Lee Bartky, Marilyn Frye, Maria Lugones, and Sara Ruddick to argue that the Just Like You Doll is problematic in several ways. This is important for the following reasons: It challenges us to look once again at empowerment, particularly the empowerment of little girls, and also because of the extreme popularity of this doll (what I call the dollie craze). Many people argue that cultural change will be the result of socializing people differently, as Card does in "Against Marriage and Motherhood" (1996b), where she argues that the nuclear family is not necessarily the best institution for raising children. To the extent that toys with which young children play have an impact on socialization, toys are extremely important from feminist perspectives. While this is not new news, it means that the dollie craze should be of interest to feminists. In what follows, I shall describe my personal experiences with the Just Like You doll, analyze these experiences from feminist perspectives, and conclude that this doll is not empowering, does not at all encourage little girls to express their uniqueness (as the company maintains), and has troubling racial and ethnic implications.

I looked forward to a trip to New York City with Grace. I thought the fun would be mostly about going to museums, shows, and maybe a bit of shopping. Grace announced that something she really wanted to do was to visit the American Girl Store to buy outfits—I initially thought this clothing was to be for Grace herself. So when Grace said she wanted to visit the American Girl store to buy clothing I thought would be for her, I was really surprised when she emerged with her doll, one that supposedly has "Asian" features to look like her. I was even more surprised when we arrived at the American Girl Store, which is located across the street from Rockefeller Center and takes up more than a half block of prime real estate in Manhattan. The store itself is several stories high and has an astounding array of outfits and accessories for American Girl dolls. I saw more shoes than there are for women in department stores, more outfits than I could possibly imagine, books about dolls, doll underwear, a place where one can eat lunch with one's dolls for a hefty price, a doll hair salon featuring tiny barber chairs where little girls could take their dolls and watch technicians wash and set dolls' hair and pierce dolls' ears. There is even a doll day spa (how do you pamper a doll?), and doll personal shoppers for those who are wealthy enough and tired enough not to want to fight the crowds. It was near Christmas, and the store was jammed. My first instinct was to run away, but when confronted with the doll hair salon and the personal shopper area I became intrigued. What was this phenomenon, and why was it so popular? In what follows, I shall provide some brief background about the doll and a discussion of my experiences in buying one for myself.

1. The Doll: A Very Brief History

American Girl dolls are produced by the American Girl Company in Middleton, Wisconsin. The company, founded twenty-three years ago, produces a variety of dolls and accessories aimed at girls aged seven to twelve. The company was purchased by Mattel in 1998 and generated $463 million in revenue in 2009 (Salkin 2009). The company manufactures several categories of dolls, but my discussion here will be limited to the Just Like You line. According to American Girl's website advertisement,

> With its selection of more than 20 dolls featuring various combinations of skin tones, facial features, and hair and eye colors, the Just Like You line highlights the individuality and diversity of today's American Girls. Doll-sized clothing and accessories reflect the wide variety of lifestyles and interests of contemporary girls and encourage them to express their own unique style and personality. A few of the girl-friendly themes and activities represented in the product line include friends, sports, hobbies, school, personal care, holidays, and other special occasions. Each Just Like You doll arrives wearing a contemporary outfit and comes with a *Fun With Your Doll book*. To further enhance the play experience, a line of stylish Dress Like Your Doll clothing allows girls to dress like their favorite dolls. (American Girl 2012)

2. Doing a Doll

I decided that I would engage in some first-hand feminist research on this Just Like You doll. So, my mother and brother joined me in paying another visit to the American Girl store. The store was jam-packed with little girls chaperoned by adult women oohing and ahhing over the dolls and all the doll accessories, with an occasional adult man along for the ride, usually looking bored or just plain confused.

We found an eager doll technician, and I explained that I wanted to buy a Just Like You doll and some accessories. Step 1 was to find the "correct" doll from a large selection of generic dolls. I was led to a huge showcase with dolls of varied hair, skin, eye color, and "ethnic looks." The technician explained that the object was to try to find a doll that looked just like me. This meant trying to match skin, hair, eye color, and other ethnic features. I really couldn't find one that did me justice, but we settled on one with the same skin tone and basic eye and hair color. I could have her hair cut and get her ear pierced later—I only have one ear pierced, and she needed to look just like me. Interestingly, we picked out the same doll for me, a Middle Eastern Jew, as the one that was supposed to have "Asian features" for Grace, although I didn't realize this until later—so much for fine-tuning. I was then told that most girls want to buy unique outfits for their dolls so that they did not have to wear the generic one that all unadopted dolls wear. At this point it was clearly time to discuss price, something my technician never mentioned until I explicitly asked. The doll itself was $124, and she came with a star hoodie outfit (the one all generic dolls wear before finding homes), a book *Fun with Your Doll*, a dollie cell phone, a charms set, and earrings. For those wanting to dress like their dolls, a matching generic outfit is available for girls for $8, there is a party outfit for dolls ($28), and a matching party outfit for girls ($22—cheaper than the doll outfit for some reason). I could play camp with my doll with a doll camp bunk bed set ($145) and dress my doll in wildflower pajamas ($22, matching wildflower pajamas for girls are $22). Finally, a heart dress for dolls is available for $24, while a heart dress for girls costs $58. My head was spinning as I realized that this very basic stuff that the technician suggested just to get me started came to more than $526! And I could also buy other "unique" theme-based outfits that would make my doll into a snowboarder, gymnast, soccer player, cheerleader, volleyball player, softball player, basketball player, yoga enthusiast, tennis player, or golfer for about $30 per outfit. Note that one of the company's advertising points is that its doll outfits model the possibility for girls to be whatever they want. Of course, many families simply cannot afford to spend this kind of money on luxury items, a point discussed by Card in "Surviving Poverty" (2014). I shall return to this point later.

All of this, and I hadn't even visited the dollie hair salon to get her hair done or her ear pierced yet. So, I stuck with the generic outfit, but to stay in the spirit of things I bought a matching one of my own (I was able to squeeze into a girls' size large). Now that we had matching outfits, my doll was "just like me," according to the doll technician.

I stood at the dollie hair salon in the middle of dozens of little girls watching what looked like a cocktail bar, but instead of drinks it had

mini hair salon chairs bolted down to it. Behind the bar several certified doll hair technicians (complete with uniforms and name tags) were coiffing doll hair while little girls watched. I took a number and waited. The wait turned out to be much too long. I could, however, purchase a doll hair kit (brush, curlers, hairspray, and some other stuff) and my own dollie salon chair to take home. I got a chance to talk with some of the hair technicians. Almost all of them enthused about their jobs, but one of them rolled her eyes, perhaps sensing a comrade. I also strolled around the store watching people shop and I even talked to several adult women chaperoning little girls around the store. Their responses were telling. Some said that they thought the whole thing was ridiculous, but the pressure to give in to doll mania was extreme, and so they finally just gave up. Others were just as interested in the dolls as were the little girls they accompanied.

3. Feminism and the American Girl

What exactly disturbed me so much about this dollie craze? American Girl advertises this doll as a doll that can help little girls feel strong, powerful, unique, and ready to take on the world. The doll isn't at all like Barbie, she isn't bone thin with huge breasts, and doll outfits clearly encourage little girls to imagine themselves as active in sports and as career professionals. The word "feminist" is not used in any of the company's marketing (still the "F" word), but the company is clearly trying to market the idea that the Just Like You line is empowering for girls. The doll is of a healthy body type and is marketed as a kind of combination of best friend and sister. At first glance she appears extremely wholesome and not at all inappropriately sexy. She also doesn't particularly encourage little girls to play mommy. In my experience, these seem to be the two extremes in dolls. Either dolls are like Barbie and girls pretend they are sexy adults or they are babies, encouraging little girls to play mommy. Not that playing sexy adult or mommy is necessarily a bad thing for girls, but it is certainly troubling when these are presented as basically the only options for little-girl play. The doll certainly isn't disturbingly white, which seems to be another point in its favor. I remember the days when almost all dolls were white. The Just Like You concept is supposed to combat this. A little girl is supposedly able to find a doll that looks like her whether she is African American, Latino, Asian, Jewish, or anything else. Of course, the fine-tuning is not great (remember that the technician selected the same doll for me, a Jew, as the one that was supposed to have Asian features for Grace). It was actually funny when I realized that we had identical Just Like You dolls.

So, here is a doll that does not seem inappropriately sexy, is not emaciated, is marketed as athletic and professionally successful, and isn't disturbingly white. All of these are major pluses from a feminist perspective (Young 2005). And yet I found my experiences of buying and interacting with this doll not only disturbing but profoundly so. My feminist alarm bells went off like crazy every time I even got near this doll. In thinking about why I was *so* disturbed by a mere doll, I came to some striking conclusions, using various feminist analyses.

To begin with, an obvious and not-so-striking issue is the cost of the doll. Feminists in general, and ecological feminists in particular, have offered critiques of the massive consumerism that has led to various ecological crises, the most recent glaring crisis being global warming (Warren 1990, Plumwood 1993, Davion 1994). Teaching children that it is appropriate to spend obscene amounts of money on items such as dolls is to teach poor global citizenship. In fact, perhaps the most disturbing thing about the doll is that it is produced by Mattel, a company that uses sweatshops in China and other locations to produce its toys. Sweatshops used by Mattel have been cited for numerous health, safety, and economic violations. Workers are forced to work many hours of overtime, paid less than minimum wage, exposed to hazardous materials, and forced to live in factory housing under horrible conditions. Some of these factories have been cited for hiring children (China Labor Watch 2011). As adults (parents or not), it is our job to help instill worthy values in children. After all, this will have to be part of instituting social change. Interestingly, when I teach feminist philosophy, which I do on a fairly regular basis, my students often say that we need to change the way we socialize children in order to change the world. At the same time, students and others often say that it is morally problematic for people to try to work on their political agendas through children. The fear seems to be that this will somehow limit a child's ability to form her identity without coercion. It is worth noting, however, that we cannot have it entirely both ways. If shaping our children's values is to be a part of how we effect future change, then we shall indeed be working political agendas out through our children to some extent. The key seems to be to avoid the kind of fanaticism that really narrows a child's potential for various kinds of development. It is a balancing act (Ruddick 1993). This is all that I am going to say about the doll and money (although I would very much like to know where and under what conditions these dolls are produced, and by whom they are produced, information not made readily available by the manufacturer). I am not going to say more about this obvious yet very troubling issue, because much has been said about these kinds of issues and because, unfortunately, they are in no way unique to the Just Like You doll.

While cost is an obvious feminist concern, I realized that there was much more to why I was so disturbed by my doll. I said that at first glance she does not *appear* sexy, and that this seemed like a good thing in a toy aimed at very young children. In thinking more about my experiences buying and pampering the doll, however, I came to the striking conclusion that she is indeed extremely sexy in a fascinating way. To show this I begin by borrowing from Sandra Lee Bartky's well-known critique of femininity (Bartky

1993). Using a Foucauldian model, Bartky argues the "disciplinary practices of femininity" produce docile female bodies. It is a well-known idea
in radical feminism that "femininity is an artifact, an achievement" (1993,
161). In her analysis, Bartky notes three categories of practices that produce feminine bodies: (1) the production of a body of a certain size and
shape, (2) those that bring forth a specific repertoire of gestures, postures,
and movements, and (3) those that are directed toward the display of body
as ornamented surface. With respect to the first category, the doll fares well.
She is not victim to what Bartkey calls the "tyranny of slenderness." It is
hard to know what to say about the second category. The doll certainly
has a smile plastered on her face, but I am not convinced that this is a bad
thing in a seven-year-old girl's toy. The doll, however, clearly flunks when it
comes to the third category, disciplinary practices that are directed toward
the display of the body as an ornamented surface.

As I mentioned before, I wasn't really fascinated or disturbed by the
doll store until I hit the dollie hair salon. Bartky rightly points out that a
major part of the discipline of traditional femininity is good hair and skin
care and the proper application of makeup. Really good skin-care habits
require expertise in the use of a variety of aids and devices, including facial
steamers, electric massagers, back brushes, complexion brushes, loofahs,
pumice, and so on. "Skincare discipline requires a specialized knowledge:
a woman must know what to do if she has been skiing, or swimming in
chlorinated pools; or if she has been exposed to pollution, heated rooms,
cold, sun, harsh weather, the pressurized cabins of airplanes, saunas, or
steam rooms, fatigue, or stress" (1993, 165).

The same goes for hair care, which requires a similar investment in time
and a specialized knowledge and mastery of a set of techniques: "The
crown pinnacle of good hair care and skincare is, of course, the arrangement of the hair and the application of cosmetics. Here the regimen of hair
care, skincare, manicure, and pedicure is recapitulated in another mode. A
woman must learn the proper manipulation of a large number of devices—
the blow dryer, styling brush, curling iron, hot curlers, wire curlers, eye-
liner, lipliner, lipstick, eyelash curler, and mascara brush" (Bartky 1993,
165). Clearly the American Girl products can be seen as a training ground
for teaching little girls the importance of learning these disciplines, particularly the doll salon. According to their literature, aimed at adults (mostly
women), a little girl should be able to "bring her doll in for a new 'do.' Our
stylists specialize in giving dolls a fresh now look—from pretty ponytail flip
to curly braids. Your girl gets to choose her favorite hairdo, then watch as
the magic happens, or pick up her doll later. You can even add extra packages to make her doll shine" (Americal Girl). Extra packages include the
"Pampering Plus Package" and "Doll Ear Piercing":

> For that extra bit of care that every doll needs, add the Pampering Plus package
> for only $5 to your Doll Hair Salon Visit. Our stylists give each doll a thorough

facial scrub to wipe her clean and send her off with a set of nail decals to take
home....

   If all her doll needs is a little sparkle, choose this package for just $14! It
includes doll ear piercing, a pair of silver star earrings, and the classic silver
earring collection. (American Girl)

The idea that every doll needs that "extra bit of care" provided in the
"Pampering Plus Package" tells the story. If even dolls need facials, such
things must be tremendously important. That the disciplinary practices of
femininity are being taught through the salon became even more obvious
to me when I got my doll home. I spent hours trying to get tiny curlers
wrapped in white paper, wetted down, and into the doll's hair. The instruc-
tion booklet was daunting and warned that while I needed to spray water
onto the hair to get it to curl, if I somehow got it onto the doll's eyelashes
they would fall out and she would have to go to the dollie hospital (yes,
there is one at the store). So, girls are learning the disciplinary practices of
femininity at the age of seven, becoming beauty experts and mastering the
knowledge of such things as curling hair.
   Another one of Bartky's points is that although things such as makeup
and other beauty aids are marketed claiming that they encourage individuality, this isn't the case. "Making up the face is a highly stylized activity
that gives little rein to self-expression. Painting the faced is not like painting a picture; at best it is like painting the same picture over and over again
with minor variations. Little latitude is permitted in what is considered
appropriate makeup for the office and for most social occasions; indeed,
the woman who uses cosmetics in a genuinely novel and imaginative way
is liable to be seen not as an artist but as eccentric" (Bartky 1993, 165).
American Girl does not sell doll makeup, although it does push manicures
and pedicures. However, something oddly analogous to the idea that most
makeup makes us unique goes on in its marketing via the Just Like You
line. As stated, the company claims that doll-sized clothing and accessories
"reflect the wide variety of lifestyles and interests of contemporary girls
and encourage them to express their own unique style and personality."
Girl-sized matching clothing is supposed to enhance this experience. As I
shopped for matching clothing to wear with my doll, however, I found that
the Just Like You doll didn't look just like me, but I was beginning to look
(and feel?) just like her. After all, there is a very limited selection of matching girl/doll clothing, and the star hoodie outfit I bought myself to match
the doll's outfit was clearly not my style. I certainly did not feel encouraged
to express myself!
   The doll, then, is clearly feminine, and the marketing teaches young
girls the art of femininity. The subject of femininity is highly controversial among feminists. Some argue that femininity is nothing to worry about
and can even be empowering (Richards 1980, Walter 1998). Others argue
for the opposite conclusion (Butler 1990, Wolf 1991, Bartky 1993, Bordo

1993). The specifics of this debate are beyond the scope of this essay. My position is that *uncritical* displays of femininity are problematic, although I believe one can use the tools of femininity, such as makeup, in a self-consciously *critical* way to critique traditional patriarchal norms.

The problem is that the doll does not represent challenges to traditional femininity but rather is an affirmation of it. If there is nothing wrong with teaching young girls the art of being feminine, then the doll is not problematic on this front. However, feminists have good reason to be, and have been, suspicious of traditional femininity as acted out under patriarchal norms. One example of such a critique is offered by Marilyn Frye. To demonstrate what is wrong with traditional femininity, Frye begins by critiquing the ubiquitous association of feminism with lesbianism. In particular the pervasiveness of the practice of calling women who are out as feminist "man-hating lesbians" in order to intimidate them from expressing the kind of strong, angry (though not man-hating) feminism that real change demands. According to Frye, this labeling of feminists as lesbians reveals an implicit theory of sexuality in which sexuality is highly political and not a biological drive at all. It is the theory that women who comply with patriarchal feminine norms and do not signal that they wish to change patriarchal institutions are heterosexual, while those who actively rebel against them are lesbian, to at least some degree. Hence, "it must follow that those who are very feminist, *uncompromisingly* feminist, *radically* feminist must BE lesbians flat out" (Frye 1992, 128). This is not a theory of sexuality determined by the sex of whom one sleeps with. It concerns behaviors and attitudes. I believe Frye is obviously correct in suggesting that this theory is floating around in mainstream contemporary culture. Each semester I begin my feminist philosophy class in the same tongue-and-cheek way by saying, "We all know the problem with feminists, they are actually ... "—and every single student in the class, including the class I am currently teaching, chimes in, "Man-hating lesbians!" Card makes many relevant points on dealing with homophobia in "Surviving Homophobia" (2013).

Frye offers a similar picture of heterosexuality. Heterosexuality, with its centerpiece of traditional femininity, signals compliance with patriarchal norms. Just as the sex of the person with whom one is sleeping has nothing to do with who counts as a lesbian according to the implicit theory of sexuality discussed above, heterosexuality is not a natural biological drive or instinct. It is a set of social institutions and practices that is "regulated by patriarchal kinship systems, by both civil and religious law, and by strenuously enforced mores and deeply entrenched values and taboos" (Frye 1992, 132). One of Card's objections regarding the induction of women into the institution of heterosexuality regards marriage. In particular, Card believes that the institution promotes violence against women by creating "safe" places for husbands to abuse their wives and makes exit from marriage extremely difficult for wives (Card 1996b).

For Frye, the primary sights of the induction of women into the institution of heterosexuality include "courtship and marriage arrangement, romance, sexual liaisons, fucking marriage, prostitution, the normative family, incest and child sexual abuse" (1992, 130). It is through these practices in patriarchal culture that girls and women are habituated to abuse and insult, and where girls are reduced (an interesting phrase) to women. And, Frye continues, "the secondary sights of the forced female embodiment of subordination are sights of the ritual preparation of girls and women for heterosexual intercourse, relations, or attachments. I refer to training in proper deportment and attire and decoration, all of which is training in and habituation to bodily restriction and distortion. I refer to diets and exercise and beauty regimens which habituate the individual to deprivation and punishment and to fear and suspicion of her body and its wisdom" (130).

A striking feature of this analysis is the claim that training in proper deportment, attire, and decoration are *secondary* sights for the reduction of girls to women. My thinking about the doll, however, has led me to believe that this is false. The disciplinary practices of femininity encouraged by American Girl, and marketed to girls and their mothers and aimed at girls as young as seven years old, can be seen as *primary* sights of training into the institution of heterosexuality. These come first and are seen as innocent fun. This has led me to the startling insight that I was wrong to say that the American Girl doll is not sexy. She is heterosexy, in the way that Frye suggests. She is extremely feminine, although her femininity is marketed as of the wholesome rather than the slutty variety. She is the perfect feminine role model, training girls into the institution of heterosexuality.

Thus, if even a portion of both Card's and Frye's critiques of the institution of heterosexuality is right, American Girl products are not teaching young girls anything at all about empowerment or individuality. They are creating "heterosexuals," in a very disturbing way. Indeed, my doll is certainly not a lesbian on Frye's analysis of lesbianism. Frye says that women might be able to create spaces for intimate sexual relationships with men outside the institution of heterosexuality. She claims that the proper question is not "Do you have to be a lesbian to be a feminist?" but rather "Can a woman be heterosexual and be radically feminist?" She answers, "My picture is this: you do not have to be a lesbian to uncompromisingly embody enact radical feminism, but you cannot be any version of a patriarchal wife. Lesbian or not, you have to be a heretic, a deviant, an undomesticated female, an impossible being" (1992, 136). That is, such a being seems impossible at the moment, and the space for such beings has to be actively created. If this is right, the Just Like You doll is a version of the enemy, habituating little girls into the practices of femininity that create heterosexuality. Even more disturbingly, the Just Like You Doll is encouraging girls toward extreme femininity at younger and younger ages.

Thinking through my profound distress concerning this doll yielded the conclusion that the doll is disturbingly heterosexual, encouraging girls to participate in patriarchal male supremacy. This alone would have been enough to explain my distress, and to turn me off the doll altogether. I realized, however, there is more. The doll is troubling in relation to issues of race and ethnicity as well. Recall that she is not disturbingly white, just as she is not explicitly sexy, which appeared to be a plus at first glance. A major step forward in teaching the idea that whiteness is not normal, better, prettier, and so on, than other colors. So, at a superficial level, the Just Like You doll, offering a variety of race and ethnicity options, is extremely positive. As I went through the exercise of picking out a doll that matched my ethnic background, however, I began to wonder whether things hadn't tipped too far the other way, from disturbingly white to disturbingly insulated. Remember, the doll is marketed as a combination of best friend and sister. While the company seems to push the best-friend angle, the notion that girls and dolls will look exactly alike and wear the exact same outfits pushes a kind of identical-twin idea that implies biological sisterhood.

While I certainly want to encourage diversity in doll options, the idea that one's sister should look exactly like oneself is problematic, given the number of blended and mixed families there are. What about adopted sisters? Where do they fit in? I was not asked by my doll technician whether I wanted a doll that looked like me or whether I might have preferred an African American doll from the generic doll selections. When I questioned it, I was informed that the game of purchasing this kind of doll included matching the doll to myself (getting a Just Like You doll). In fact, when I pushed the point, the doll technician actually became somewhat agitated, which I found extremely odd. I worried that rather than encouraging respect for diversity and difference, this whole Just Like You campaign actually promotes the belief that similarity (in particular, racial and ethnic similarity) is the key element of friendship and family. I found the obsession concerning skin, eye, and hair color eerie, and I was particularly disturbed by it in attempting to select "the perfect doll for me."

Again I wondered why I was so upset at the game of looking for a doll that was a combination of an identical best friend and sister. I began to wonder whether I was indeed becoming some kind of fanatic feminist that couldn't even let a fairly harmless game go. Again I looked to feminist analysis, the work of Maria Lugones (1990) in particular, for insight. According to Lugones, love should not be seen as fusion or the erasure of difference and is in fact incompatible with such. Real love reveals plurality and not unity, which is tied to domination rather than love. In loving another, one recognizes differences. Failure to recognize them results in arrogant perception, seeing others as if they are identical to oneself, or just not seeing them at all (Frye 1983). Cross-cultural loving requires an ability to see oneself in others who are quite different from oneself. In order to do this, Lugones suggests something she calls world traveling. While outsiders to mainstream culture (by which she means white/Anglo culture in the United States) must learn how to world travel, those within mainstream culture can consciously do it as well.

In order to successfully engage in cross-cultural world traveling, one must leave arrogant perception behind and begin to understand how the other sees himself or herself as a subject in that world. Worlds can be defined in a variety of ways, but they should be thought of not as particular geographical locations but rather as cultural ones. "A world needs to be a construction of a whole society. It may be a tiny construction of a small portion of society. It may be inhabited by just a few people. Some worlds are bigger than others" (Lugones 1990, 395). My favorite example of two different worlds is when I am with my family and when I am at work. I am constructed by those around me in very different ways, I construct myself differently, and I am not always in control of how I am constructed. As I mentioned, cross-cultural world traveling is needed for cross-cultural loving. We must be able to enter worlds of those very different from us and see the people in them as subjects.

According to Lugones, outsiders to mainstream culture must learn to travel in order to survive, while insiders can learn without their survival depending upon it. For everyone, however, cross-cultural loving, loving that embraces plurality rather than unity, loving that is not arrogant, depends upon the ability to world travel. This requires a certain flexibility and open-ness to new surprises. Lugones suggests that in order to promote cross-cultural loving, world traveling should be done with a playful attitude. By play she does not mean competence or knowing the rules but rather means being open to new things with a positive attitude. This kind of play is the opposite of a game like baseball, where one must be competent and the object is to defeat others. Racism discourages playful world traveling because it is difficult and perhaps impossible to maintain racist attitudes when one begins to perceive as actual subjects the people about whom one has those attitudes.

One thing that discourages world traveling and encourages arrogant per-ception is being what Lugones calls "maximally at ease in a world" (1990). Things that encourage being at ease are fluency in the language, being nor-matively happy there (liking the values), being humanely bonded with peo-ple one loves, and having a shared history. The more at ease one is in a world, the less likely one is to be curious (or maybe even aware?) that there are other worlds out there. This encourages arrogant perception of those who inhabit other worlds and often leads to racism. Hence, I argue that we should be encouraging our children (and ourselves) to world traveling as much as possible as a way of fostering cross-cultural loving and discourag-ing racism.

I argue that the Just Like You doll discourages learning the skills that are required for world traveling, and that it also implies that such skills are not important. The idea that my best friend or sister should be exactly like me pushes the notion of love as unity, not plurality, and thus teaches our children the skills of arrogant perception. So, while the Just Like You concept appears to combat racism by offering dolls of all different races and ethnicities, it may actually promote racism by discouraging world traveling.

My conclusion is that the feminist alarm bells I heard when being anywhere near the doll were justified. The final question to be asked is: Would I buy my child a Just Like You doll? Of course, only those with the money to purchase such toys truly need to consider the possibility. But the conceptual point is there for everyone. I would like to answer no, of course not! However, as Sara Ruddick has so famously pointed out, mothering (whether done by women or by men) is a highly complicated practice. Our children wish to be accepted, and what I have called the "dollie craze" puts tremendous pressure on children to want these dolls so they can play with their friends who have them, and on parents to keep their children happy and accepted by peers. This is the problem of "raising an acceptable child" (Ruddick 1993), and the dollie craze offers an excellent example of the dilemma. In patriarchal white supremacist societies, the practice of mothering can often become contradictory, in that raising a so-called acceptable child results in having to compromise on many of one's own ideals (provided that one is politically opposed to such societies). The American Girl doll is a perfect example of these complexities. Thus, while I may hate my doll, she is well worth thinking about from various feminist perspectives.

References

American Girl. 2012. Accessed September 27. http://www.americangirl .com/corp/corporate.php?section=about&id=11

Bartky, Sandra L. 1993. "Foucault, Femininity, and the Modernization of Patriarchal Power." In *Women and Values*, edited by Marilyn Pearsall, 155–61. Belmont: Wadsworth.

Bordo, Susan. 1993. *Unbearable Weight: Feminism, Western Culture, and the Body*. Berkeley: University of California Press.

Butler, Judith. 1990. *Gender Trouble, Feminism and the Subversion of Identity*. London: Routledge.

Card, Claudia. 1996a. *The Unnatural Lottery: Character and Moral Luck*. Temple University Press.

———. 1996b. "Against Marriage and Motherhood." *Hypatia* 2, no. 3: 1–23. Chapter 12 in this collection.

———. 2005. *The Atrocity Paradigm: A Theory of Evil*. London: Oxford University Press.

———. 2013. "Surviving Homophobia." David Ross Boyd Lecture Series, University of Oklahoma, October 11.

———. 2014. "Surviving Poverty." In *Poverty, Agency, and Human Rights*, edited by Diana Tietjens Meyers, 21–42. London: Oxford University Press.

China Labor Watch. 2011. "Mattel's Supplier Factory Investigation." http://www.chinalaborwatch.org/proshow-69.html (accessed September 27, 2012).

Davion, Victoria. 1994. "How Feminist Is Ecological Feminism?" In *The Environmental Ethics and Policy Book*, edited by Donald Vandeveer and Christine Pierce, 288–95. Belmont: Wadsworth.

Frye, Marilyn. 1983. *The Politics of Reality*. Freedom, N.Y.: Crossing Press.

———. 1992. *Willful Virgin*. Freedom. N.Y.: Crossing Press.

Lugones, Maria. 1990. "Playfulness, World-Travelling and Loving Perception." In *Making Face, Making Soul Haciendi Caras: Creative and Critical Perspectives by Women of Color*, edited by Gloria Anzaldúa, 46–54. San Francisco: Aunt Lute Foundation.

Plumwood, V. 1993. *Feminism and the Mastery of Nature*. London: Routledge.

Richards, Janet R. 1980. *The Sceptical Feminist: A Philosophical Inquiry*. London: Routledge.

Ruddick, Sara. 1993. "Maternal Thinking." In *Women and Values*, edited by Marilyn Pearsall, 368–79. Belmont: Wadsworth.

Salkin, Allen. 2009. "American Girl's Journey to the Lower East Side." *New York Times*, May 24.

Walter, Natasha. 1998. *The New Feminism*. London: Little, Brown.

Warren, Karen. 1990. "The Power and the Promise of Ecological Feminism." *Environmental Ethics* 12, no. 2:125–46.

Wolf, Naomi. 1991. *The Beauty Myth: How Images of Beauty Are Used Against Women*. New York: HarperCollins.

Young, Iris. 2005. *On the Female Body Experience: "Throwing Like a Girl" and Other Essays*. Oxford: Oxford University Press.

INDEX

Criticism and Compassion: The Ethics and Politics of Claudia Card.
Edited by Robin S. Dillon and Armen T. Marsoobian.
Chapters and book compilation © 2018 Metaphilosophy LLC and John Wiley & Sons Ltd.